CHRONICLES

OF

BOW STREET POLICE-OFFICE.

PATTERSON SMITH REPRINT SERIES IN
CRIMINOLOGY, LAW ENFORCEMENT, AND SOCIAL PROBLEMS

A listing of publications in the SERIES *will be found at rear of volume*

SIR JOHN FIELDING, "THE BLIND MAGISTRATE."

PUBLICATION NO. 136: PATTERSON SMITH REPRINT SERIES IN
CRIMINOLOGY, LAW ENFORCEMENT, AND SOCIAL PROBLEMS

CHRONICLES

OF

BOW STREET POLICE-OFFICE

BY

PERCY FITZGERALD

REPRINTED WITH THE ADDITION OF
A NEW INTRODUCTION
BY ANTHONY BABINGTON
AND AN INDEX

TWO VOLUMES IN ONE
ILLUSTRATED

MONTCLAIR, NEW JERSEY
PATTERSON SMITH
1972

98284

First published 1888 by Chapman & Hall Ltd.

Reprinted 1972 by arrangement
by Patterson Smith Publishing Corporation
Montclair, New Jersey 07042

New material copyright © 1972 by
Patterson Smith Publishing Corporation

Library of Congress Cataloging in Publication Data

Fitzgerald, Percy Hetherington, 1834–1925.
    Chronicles of Bow Street police-office.

    (Patterson Smith reprint series in criminology,
law enforcement, and social problems. Publication
no. 136)
    Reprint of the 1888 ed. with a new introduction
and index.
    1. London—Police.   2. Crime and criminals—
London.   1. Title.

HV8198.L7F6 1972   363.2′09421   78-129313
ISBN 0-87585-136-3

This book is printed on
permanent/durable paper

INTRODUCTION TO THE
REPRINT EDITION.

THE BOW STREET OFFICE originated in 1740 at the private residence of a well-known London Justice of the Peace. During the next one hundred years the Office was destined to play an equally important part in the development of the British magistracy and the development of the British police.

At the beginning of the eighteenth century the methods of maintaining law and order in Britain had been little varied and little improved since the Middle Ages. They were designed essentially to meet the needs of a decentralized feudal society in which crime was sporadic and unsophisticated. As there was no regular police force, the cornerstone of the whole system was the Justice of the Peace, who in addition to his numerous judicial and administrative duties was responsible for investigating criminal offences and detaining and charging the culprits.

In country districts the great majority of justices
were wealthy local landowners who enjoyed a natural
power and standing in their own localities. Although
the office of justice carried no remuneration, appointment to the Commission of the Peace was considered an honour and a privilege. In the performance
of their policing function the justices were assisted
by the petty constables of the parish where an
offence had taken place. The petty constables were
only amateur, part-time parish officials with no
special training and no special skill; theoretically
every able-bodied man was supposed to serve his
term as a petty constable in rotation, although in
practice he was allowed to pay a substitute to act
in his place.

The Justice of the Peace had a substantial jurisdiction to try cases on his own without a jury. As
there were no magistrates' courts at that time he
sat judicially in the privacy of his home, observing
no set legal procedures and, in many instances,
keeping no record of his adjudications. He could
sentence his prisoner to a fine, a whipping, a spell
in the stocks or a short term of imprisonment, and
there was little opportunity for appealing against
his decisions. There can be no doubt that what took
place at these private magisterial hearings was very
often a complete mockery of justice; but to a peas-
antry steeped in feudal tradition the magisterial

power seemed neither immoderate nor unduly oppressive.

While this ancient system of law-enforcement was still operating with reasonable efficiency in rural areas, it proved to be wholly impracticable in the rapidly expanding cities and towns, where the settled stability of a village community was non-existent and where there were no local squires to join the Commission of the Peace. In the metropolis of London a suitable type of justice was almost impossible to find. "In places inhabited by the scum and dregs of the people and the most profligate class of life," said a contemporary writer, "gentlemen of any great figure and fortune will not take such drudgery upon them." As a consequence the Commission in London was filled with tradesmen and small-time professionals who were intent on making the maximum income possible from their work as magistrates. These men, known contemptuously as "trading justices," were universally feared and detested. Because they were subject to little or no supervision they had numerous opportunities for illicit profit. By an old custom a small fee* was payable by every person who appeared before a mag-

---

*The basis and purpose of these fees was obscure; but it is doubtful if any part of them was intended to be for the benefit of the magistrates. They were often used for the payment of the magistrates' clerks.

istrate on any administrative or criminal matter,
and the trading justices sought continuously to
increase this revenue by expanding the volume of
their work. It was said that one magistrate used
to authorize indiscriminate arrests solely for the
sake of the fees which he could collect when he
admitted his victims to bail. In addition, trading
justices made a practice of retaining a large proportion of the fines they imposed, exacting protection-
money from keepers of brothels and gaming-houses
as an alternative to prosecution, selling liquor licences
to the highest bidders, and resorting to the wholesale
acceptance of bribes.

In addition to the corruption of their magistrates,
Londoners were afflicted with the most inefficient
policing arrangements imaginable. The metropolis
was divided into a number of separate parishes, each
of which was entirely responsible for the protection
of its own inhabitants. There was no overall control
and no liaison between neighbouring parishes; some
parishes chose to leave their streets entirely un-
patrolled. And the duties of a constable in London
were extremely hazardous and extremely exacting—
Daniel Defoe once said that the office "takes up so
much of a man's time that his own affairs are
frequently totally neglected, too often to his ruin.
Yet there is neither profit nor pleasure therein."

Many of the London streets were patrolled at night by watchmen—known as "Charlies" from the fact that Charles I considerably extended their use. They were employed by the individual parishes and went on duty equipped with staffs, rattles and lanterns. For the most part the watchmen were completely ineffectual; they were utterly unorganized, and because of their low rate of pay the applicants for this employment were of very poor quality. Henry Fielding wrote about them in 1751 that, "being to guard our streets at night from thieves and robbers, an office which at least requires strength of body, they are chosen out of those poor, old, decrepit people who are from their want of bodily strength incapable of getting a livelihood by work. These men, armed with a pole which some of them are scarce able to lift, are to secure the persons and houses of His Majesty's subjects from the attacks of gangs of young, bold, stout, desperate, well-armed villains. If the poor fellows should run away from such enemies, no-one I think can wonder, unless it be that they were able to make their escape."

In view of the total inadequacy of these policing arrangements in urban areas the Government, in their efforts to control crime, began to rely increasingly on a system of bribes, pardons and rewards. The Tyburn Ticket was introduced in 1669. This was awarded to any person who had instigated a successful prosecution against a felon, and it afforded the recipient exemption for life from any of the compulsory parish duties, including his term of office as a petty constable. Since Tyburn Tickets could be sold, complete with the rights attaching to them, they had an appreciable financial value. From 1692 on payments, known as "blood-money," were made to the principal prosecution witnesses after every conviction for a serious crime. Furthermore, free pardons were granted to accomplices who elected to turn king's evidence against their fellow-accused; these people, incidentally, would also be eligible for blood-money if the prosecution was successful. These monetary rewards for securing convictions led inevitably to false accusations and perjury; they also led to the advent of the private thief-takers—men, often with unsavoury backgrounds themselves, who sought a living by tracking down and prosecuting criminals.

Such was the state of London when Thomas (later Sir Thomas) De Veil was appointed a Justice of the Peace for Middlesex and Westminster in 1729 and set up his first office in his house at Leicester Fields. Seven years later he moved to Thrift Street (now called Frith Street) in Soho, and in 1740 he transferred both his home and his office to a house in Bow Street.

De Veil's residence in Bow Street was on the west side of the road a few yards south of the Covent Garden Theatre (which stood on the present site of the Royal Opera House). It had almost certainly not been occupied by a justice before; indeed it formed part of a row of houses which had only been built in 1704 and whose original owner had been a prominent London surgeon. De Veil established his office in one of the principal rooms on the ground floor. He was probably the first magistrate in Britain to have his office designed as a court, with a raised bench, a gallery for spectators and a bar at which the prisoner was made to stand either for questioning or for judicial proceedings. De Veil was an excellent detective. In his biography, published by an anonymous author two years after his death, it was said, "There was no quality by which De Veil was more distinguished than his sagacity, except his diligence. If he was once furnished with a few hints, he knew how to form them into a clue . . . when once he had hold of this clue, he never parted with it till he had brought the whole discovery to the view of the public." De Veil became the terror of the London underworld not only because of his ruthless tenacity and the efficiency of his system of intelligence, but because of his skill as an interrogator. "He knew so well how to throw those he examined into confusion," according to his biographer, "and was so able to catch up on their unguarded expressions to piece together broken hints, and sometimes, by feigning to know all, put these wretches upon detecting themselves, by justifying against what he knew to be false, that he was very rarely deceived."

Although De Veil did not hold any position to distinguish him from the other justices in Westminster and Middlesex, it is apparent that he was sometimes unofficially employed by the Government for their own security work, since the records show that he received several grants from the Treasury for his services. After his death in October 1746 there was no reason why his house should have remained a magisterial office, apart perhaps from the fact that he had gone to the expense of equipping it like a court. The contemporary rating ledgers show, however, that in 1747 the house was occupied by Thomas Burdus, another Westminster justice, and that it afterwards remained empty until Henry Fielding became the tenant early in the month of December 1748.

It was a fortunate chance that brought a man of

Henry Fielding's abilities and integrity to the Bow Street Office. Although he was only forty-one years of age at the time, he had already lived a very full life and, in the opinion of most of his contemporaries, had reached the end of his public career. Fielding himself shared in this pessimistic view of his future. His vogue as a satirical playwright was over; his first novel had had a disappointing reception; he had failed as a barrister; his second marriage had been socially unacceptable; and he was broken in spirit and in health. The appointment was not considered an honourable one; in fact his cousin, the celebrated Lady Mary Wortley Montagu, wrote disgustedly about "the highest of his preferment being raking in the lowest sinks of vice and misery." Worse still so far as Fielding's pride was concerned, he was well aware that the Government had offered him what they considered an ignoble though profitable post as a reward for his political services as a writer and pamphleteer. He had revealed later that the Duke of Bedford, the Secretary of State for the Home Department, had declared to him on several occasions that he "could not indeed say that acting as a principal Justice of the Peace in Westminster was on all accounts very desirable, but all the world knew it was a very lucrative office."

Henry Fielding took up his duties as a magistrate

towards the end of 1748. His first office was in Brownlow Street, near Drury Lane. He then moved to Meard's Court in Soho, and finally to De Veil's house in Bow Street. The earliest reference to his tenure of the Bow Street Office was made in a paragraph in the *St. James's Evening Post* for December 8–10, 1748, which read:

> Yesterday John Salter was committed to the Gatehouse by Henry Fielding Esq., of Bow Street, Covent Garden, formerly Sir Thomas De Veil's, for feloniously taking out of a bureau in the house of the Rev. Mr. Dalton a quantity of money found upon him.

During his initial months at Bow Street Henry Fielding had only one person to assist him, his clerk Joshua Brogden, who had sat at the Office, he said, "for almost sixteen hours in the twenty-four in the most unwholesome, as well as nauseous air in the universe, and which in his case corrupted a good constitution without contaminating his morals." Fielding himself worked prodigious hours investigating crimes, examining suspects and trying offenders. His blind half-brother John, who was first appointed a magistrate in 1750, became his active assistant during the summer of 1753. Henry Fielding also nominated both his clerk and his close friend Saunders Welch, the High Constable of Holborn, for appointment to the Commission. Brogden never became a justice, and Saunders Welch had to wait until after Fielding's death, though he helped him continuously in an unofficial capacity.

One of the first steps taken by Henry Fielding after his arrival at Bow Street was to persuade the Government to pay him a small salary so that he would not have to rely for a living upon the fees paid by the men and women who appeared before him. He was thus the first true stipendiary magistrate in Britain. The amount of his salary is unknown, but it was certainly very meagre as he suffered from constant poverty. Being a barrister, he conducted his judicial work as though his office was a proper court and not just a room in his private house.

Henry Fielding soon appreciated that the growing crime wave would never be curbed by ill-organized and ineffectual parish peace-officers. As a beginning he attempted to achieve a unified direction by setting up a control centre in the Bow Street Office which would be manned by a messenger night and day. In February 1749 he published a "Notice and Request to the Public" in the *General Advertiser,* stating that "all persons who shall for the future suffer by robbers, burglars etc., are desired immediately to bring or send the best description they can of such robbers etc., with the time, place, and circumstances of the fact to Henry Fielding, Esq. at his house in Bow

Street, or to John Fielding, Esq. at his house in the Strand." Thereafter similar announcements appeared in the press at regular intervals. Next he formed his own little band of thief-takers, the forbears of the Bow Street Runners. At first these men were amateurs who performed their police duties in their spare time. Later they became so proficient under the tutelage of the experienced Saunders Welch that they gave up any other form of employment and made their living out of the various forms of reward-money for successful prosecutions. Although they were really little more than civil mercenaries, they were bound together, according to John Fielding, "by connections of good fellowship, friendship, and the bonds of society." Henry Fielding's scheme was simple in the extreme. A few of his thief-takers were always in readiness at the Bow Street Office and, directly they received information about a theft, a house-breaking, a highway robbery or any other serious crime, they would mount their horses and set off in pursuit of the criminals.

The importance of accurate information with regard to crimes was constantly emphasized by Henry Fielding, as was also the necessity for the victims of recent offences to try to identify the perpetrators amongst the people who were subsequently arrested. Within a week of his arrival at Bow Street he arranged for the *St. James's Evening Post* to publish an account of a case which had come before him in which a man dressed as a sailor had attacked and injured a girl with a cutlass. The report concluded, "It is hoped that all persons who have lately been robbed or attacked in the street by men in sailor's jackets . . . will give themselves the trouble of resorting to the prison in order to view him."

Henry Fielding died in October 1754. Even if his Bow Street house had had no other claim to fame it might still be remembered as the place where he completed his two great novels, *Tom Jones* and *Amelia*. However, the Bow Street Office had become so firmly established during his lifetime that it seemed only natural for John Fielding to keep it in being after his death. John Fielding and Saunders Welch, who now became his assistant, were both paid small salaries by the Government which enabled them to devote their whole time to their work as magistrates. The position of the Bow Street Office remained an anomalous one, as it had no official status to differentiate it from any other justice's office in London or elsewhere. The house in Bow Street was still a private residence, maintained by John Fielding at his own expense. (Percy Fitzgerald is mistaken in saying that the house was "burnt to the ground" during the Gordon Riots in 1780. A letter from Sir John has recently come to light in which he describes the damage done by the rioters as being easily reparable.) The Bow Street thief-takers, too, of whom there were usually about six, remained a private, unofficial force, although the Government agreed to make an annual grant to cover their basic expenses. John Fielding adopted and elaborated Henry's scheme for notification and pursuit. Six days after his half-brother's death a notice appeared in the *Public Advertiser* commencing, "Whereas many thieves and robbers daily escape justice for want of immediate pursuit, it is therefore recommended to all persons who shall henceforth be robbed on the highway or in the streets, or whose shops or houses shall be broke open, that they give immediate notice thereof, together with as accurate a description of the offender as possible, to JOHN FIELDING Esq., at his house in Bow Street, Covent Garden." The notice continued, "And if they would send a special messenger on these occasions, Mr. Fielding would not only pay that messenger for his trouble, but would immediately despatch a set of brave fellows in pursuit, who have long been engaged for such purposes, and are always ready to set out to any part of this town or kingdom at an hour's notice." In addition, it was said, Mr. Fielding would notify the details of all stolen articles to the leading pawnbrokers in order to assist in their recovery.

Sir John Fielding (he received a knighthood in 1761) remained the senior Bow Street magistrate until his death in 1780. During his tenure at the Office he sought continuously to improve the efficiency of both the policing and the judicial side of its activities. He introduced a system by which the Office would operate as a courthouse for regular hours each day, and, although not a qualified lawyer himself, he conducted his judicial business according to the set procedure of the superior courts. The Bow Street Runners became the only skilled detective force in Britain, and besides their customary duties of criminal investigation they were employed on such tasks as guarding the King and the maintenance of security in the Bank of England, the Post Office and the House of Commons. For these duties they received special fees above their modest retainer and, indeed, they were available for hire by anyone who wished to carry out a private enquiry into a crime. John Fielding established at Bow Street a register in which were recorded the details of offences throughout Britain and the particulars of all arrested or wanted criminals. This register was made available to any magistrate seeking information; and Fielding also urged the Justices of the Peace throughout Britain to keep him posted on the movements of known or suspected criminals in their localities and to cooperate with him generally in the suppression of crime.

Sir John Fielding never doubted that Bow Street was the premier magistrate's office in Britain and that he himself was the premier magistrate. Although he had only been appointed a Justice of the Peace for Westminster and for five of the counties around London, he did not accept any territorial limitations to his own jurisdiction or to that of his private police force. Long before his death it had become accepted that the senior Bow Street magistrate enjoyed a special position as unofficial adviser to the Government on matters of law and order.

A proposal had been made by Sir John Fielding that London should be divided into five or six areas, each with its own Police Office formed in the image of Bow Street and presided over by a legally qualified salaried magistrate. In 1792 the Government partially followed this suggestion when they set up in London seven so-called Public Offices, each of which was manned by three stipendiary magistrates and had its own staff of six stipendiary constables whose work was similar to the routine duties of the Bow Street Runners. Even after this the Bow Street Office remained in being as a private house, as it was not incorporated into the official scheme. In 1812 the Treasury provided funds for the Office to be enlarged by the purchase of the neighbouring house on the south side.

The stipendiary magistrates appointed immediately after 1792 were a motley collection, and it was not until 1839 that the Government reverted to John Fielding's original idea and decreed that the position in future would only be open to experienced barristers. By an Act of Parliament in 1839 the Public Offices became Magistrates' Courts; the position of the Bow Street Office was at last officially recognized and it was placed on a par with the rest;* and the senior Bow Street magistrate was, for the first time, granted an official position with the title of Chief Magistrate. The new stipendiary magistrates—Police Magistrates, as they were called—became a branch of the professional judiciary, and in the middle of the nineteenth century they were of identical status with County Court Judges—although they were not called "Judge" and were not given the designation "His Honour" like the latter. Outside London the Justices of the Peace continued to carry out their individual

---

*Fitzgerald is in error when he states that the Bow Street Office was formally constituted by an Act of Parliament in 1792; the Middlesex Justices Act of that year, to which he refers, made no mention of it.

duties from their own homes and offices until 1848,
when an Act of Parliament specified that they should
thenceforth carry out their judicial duties in properly
constituted magistrates' courts. It is therefore true
to say that the original Bow Street Office set the pattern for all the magistrates' courts in Britain as they
exist today.

For a police force, the British Governments in the
eighteenth and the early nineteenth centuries pre-
ferred to rely on the semi-autonomous Bow Street
force rather than re-organize the antiquated parish
peace-officer system. In 1790 the Bow Street Foot
Patrol was inaugurated. A few years later this body
consisted of sixty-eight men who, divided into squads
of five or six, patrolled the streets of the metropolis
every evening between dusk and midnight. They did
not wear uniform but were armed with pistols, carbines and cutlasses. In 1805 Sir Richard Ford, the
senior magistrate at the Office, set up the Bow Street
Horse Patrol, based on a scheme which had been attempted by Sir John Fielding in 1763–64. The new
Horse Patrol was a para-military force which patrolled the immediate approaches to London and
whose attentions were principally directed against
highway robbers. It was the Horse Patrol, not, as
Fitzgerald erroneously states, the Bow Street Runners, who were nicknamed "Robin Redbreasts," on

account of their scarlet waistcoats. Sir Robert Peel, then Home Secretary, authorized the formation of a small uniformed Bow Street Day Patrol in 1822 to tour the principal streets of the metropolis on foot between 9 A.M. and nightfall. When in 1829 Peel established the Metropolitan Police, the first regular British uniformed police force, he envisaged his scheme very largely as an elaboration of the existing Bow Street patrols. The Bow Street Runners continued to form the only British detective force until their disbandment in 1839.

Percy Fitzgerald published his *Chronicles of Bow Street Police-Office* in 1888, seven years after the original office's closure. He was principally concerned, as he states in his preface, with "the humours of the Police Court" and with "the eccentricities of the magistrates and their officers." (He does, however, probably exaggerate the extent of the quarrel between John Fielding and David Garrick, the celebrated actor, over Mr. Addington's play. This dispute only arose during the winter of 1775–76, and cordial relations between the two men were certainly re-established by the summer of 1776 when Garrick retired from the stage.) It was not his intention to place the Bow Street Office in what is for us its most important context—to explain its significant role in the history of British civil administration. But, notwithstanding an absence of balance in the selection of his material and a lack of cohesion in its presentation, we are indebted to Fitzgerald for collecting together a most valuable assortment of anecdotes and reports connected with this, the most famous magistrate's office in the world.

ANTHONY BABINGTON.

LONDON,
July, 1971.

CHRONICLES

OF

BOW STREET POLICE-OFFICE

WITH AN ACCOUNT OF

THE MAGISTRATES, " RUNNERS," AND POLICE ;

AND

A SELECTION OF THE MOST INTERESTING CASES.

BY

PERCY FITZGERALD, F.S.A.

IN TWO VOLUMES.

VOL. I.

WITH NUMEROUS ILLUSTRATIONS.

LONDON—CHAPMAN AND HALL,

LIMITED.

1888.

[facsimile of original title page]

TO

GENERAL THE HON. WILLIAM FEILDING.

My dear General Feilding,

You will find that your ancestors, the illustrious author of "Tom Jones," and his brother, Sir John Fielding, figure prominently in the following pages, both exhibiting a rare spectacle of fortitude, in the performance of duty, under grievous physical infirmity. There is something appropriate, therefore, in inscribing this narrative to their descendant, while I at the same moment gratify myself by associating the name of an old friend with my labours.

PERCY FITZGERALD.

ATHENÆUM CLUB,
June, 1888.

PREFACE.

~~~~~~~~~

RECENTLY, in the course of the "improvements"
round Covent Garden Market, the old Bow Street
Police Office—for almost a century the scene of many
exciting and eccentric incidents—was levelled to the
ground, to be replaced by a spacious and commodious
building. With it has gone a large portion of Inigo
Jones' Piazza, notable for its elegant proportions and
Italian air. Here were bound up many traditions and
old associations which usually disappear, or are forgotten, when the old stones have been carted away.
For nigh a century the old Court was the scene of
many dramatic and eccentric incidents—engendered
for the most part by the old school of manners and
morals, long since happily reformed. Such are
full of interest as illustrating a phase of forgotten
London manners : and in the following pages I have
attempted to furnish an account of what took place
within those narrow precincts.

During the past twenty or thirty years, there have

been many criminal cases of extraordinary dramatic interest, the incidents of which are but faintly remembered. It may be urged, indeed, that the serving-up these afresh is but pandering to an unwholesome taste. Such is indeed abundantly catered for in works like the Newgate Calendar; but it has always seemed to me that, quite apart from their tragic interest, such cases generally furnish extraordinary and even grotesque exhibitions of character : or odd and perplexing combinations of circumstances and evidence. These in themselves have extraordinary, even bizarro interest, such, for instance, as the curious and invariable tendency of criminals—when making a confession—to confess what is untrue. It is for this reason that I have dwelt at length on the remarkable case of Thurtell, which has always seemed to offer a sort of fascination from the weird, almost romantic incidents which attended it. Familiar as it is, and an oft-told tale, there will be here found much that is novel.

The " humours " of the Police Court, with the eccentricities of the magistrates and of their officers, are all duly recorded in these pages, in which, it is hoped, the " benevolent reader " will find entertainment.

CONTENTS.

~~~~~~

LIST OF ILLUSTRATIONS.

~~~~~~~~~

CHRONICLES

OF

BOW STREET POLICE-OFFICE

~~~~~~~~

CHAPTER I.

BOW STREET.

At the top of Wellington Street, and close to the more crowded portion of the busy Strand, is to be found one of the most interesting spots in London, where exciting dramas of real life and passion, as well as their mimic reproduction, are daily played. This characteristic quarter has been always the centre of criminal as well as of theatrical life. The eyes of the actor, as well as those of the rogue, often turn to it with an almost painful interest ; and there is hardly an hour of the day during which members of both communities may not be seen lounging opposite the buildings where their respective interests are concerned in some critical issue. Here, within a small area, are clustered the great theatres of Drury Lane and Covent

Garden, with the Lyceum, and the costumiers, as also the newspaper in which players put forward their wants, and often their merits. Close by are the greater journals in which the merits and defects of the players are dealt with, and the favourite houses of resort and refreshment—the taverns and wine-shops, which are never without the cluster of professionals, busy discussing their hopes and grievances. In short, the quarter offers as distinctly marked and interesting characteristics of its own, as do others which the metropolis offers in plenty—such as the French quarter in Soho, the Banking district in the City, the Jew quarter, and others. Here, we come upon the entrance to the great Flower Market, lately the luckless Floral Hall, which was tried as a concert-room with equal lack of success. It has just reverted to its original purpose, and, at midnight, when the theatres have discharged their audiences, throws open its gates and begins its performance. Then the wains and carts draw up and begin unloading their fragrant burdens —all through the night the heavily laden vehicles are heard rumbling by, and by dawn every adjoining street is blocked—an extraordinary spectacle of business and industry, literally unknown to, and perhaps unthought of, by the lazy Londoner who rises late.

But there is a large section of the community for which none of these things offer so much interest as

does an important building which has lately been
reared opposite Covent Garden Theatre. For such a
class the " Bow Street " office suggests strange and
painful associations—an interest that is extended often
to the respectable working-man's family. In such is
commonly found some misguided youth, whom bad
company or bad connections has brought to sad
acquaintance with the initial processes of the law as
established at Bow Street.

A few years ago there used to be a painful and not
undramatic scene witnessed every afternoon in the
street, which furnished a sort of excitement for the
motley and uncleanly crowd which never failed to
attend. This was the arrival of the funereal-looking
prison van in front of the straitened little office
door. Clustered round it, could be seen patiently
waiting as strange a miscellany as could be conceived.
It was then that the curious observer could study the
habitual criminal " type," and note how mysteriously
habits of crime seemed to impress revealing marks
and tokens on face, expression, bearing, manner, dress.
In older followers this evidence was not so conspicuous;
but there was in the juvenile section, in the youths and
girls—a strange and revolting air of precocity—a
hardened air that would strike even the most careless.
When at length the moment arrived, the circle narrowed,
and the draggled procession began to emerge, each item
having a separate display of his own. Then passed

by, with an assumed bearing that was almost dramatic, the reckless prisoners, each being saluted with encouraging cries from the friends who had, with a touching loyalty, come to see him "off." Some "danced out," and tripped into the van with a familiar air ; others, who had not recovered from the surprise of their sentence, passed on with a sturdy scowl. More painful was the shame of the decently-dressed first offender—victim, it might be, of circumstances, who shrank from the unclean, but really indifferent, gaze of the throng. For *them* even the shelter of the van was a relief. Almost as characteristic was the stolid *insouciant* bearing of the police in charge, who attended each prisoner forth with a carelessness that came of strength and security. The last guardian—the necessary blue papers in his hand—closed the strange defile, and locked himself in with the rest. Then came the strange cries of comfort and farewell from their "pals," those of experience uttering their words under the very floor of the van, and receiving some sort of response. And thus "Black Maria," heavily laden, and drawn by powerful steeds, reels off and sways as she moves, to discharge her load at one of the great prisons.

This strange and indecent scene had, until a few years ago, been repeated daily from the beginning of the century. It seems to have been an agreeable break in the day. Yet it was doing its part in the wholesale education in crime. It made familiar and recognized what ought to have been mysterious and unknown. Instead of. being a vulgar show to be lightened by the encouragement of friends and "pals," it would have been far more wholesome that the criminal on sentence should have sunk out of view and have been at once lost to society. Happily, with the opening of new Bow Street offices in 1881, this salutary principle was recognized, and the degrading scene is no longer witnessed.

We may contrast with this picture what the old Bow Street and its neighbourhood was some fifty years ago. It shows how completely life and manners have changed in the interval, and how the so-called Bohemian elements have been eliminated. Where now is "Kelsey's" or "Harris's;" or the boys shouting "Bills of the play!" or the "Coal-Hole;" or the "ham-sandwiches a penny"?

"It is just half-past five, and the grey dawn is struggling in the east to diffuse a few faint rays over the western portion of the horizon. There are but few wanderers in the street at this early hour. St. Paul's, Covent Garden, chimes the hour of *six*, and the rumbling of market-carts laden with flowers and vegetables, now begins to disturb the tranquillity of the street. *Seven*, and blinds begin to be drawn up. The baker's shop has already opened, and at the oilman's, on the Broad Court corner, the shutters are being likewise taken down. *Eight*, and hot rolls, comfortably enveloped in green baize, emanate from the baker's. Now a youth suddenly rushes from Harris's towards the newspaper offices, and returns home laden with a copious supply of morning papers. The head waiter of the ' Garrick's Head ' now makes a lingering appearance at the street door. *Nine*, and the shops are all opened, and people go to work in earnest. Peripatetic fruit-women begin to arrange their little stores and stalls for the day, and a crowd begins to assemble at the police-office, anxious to await the result of the morning's investigations. Those addicted to matinal moistenings now imbibe a drain of *max* at ' Kelsey's,' whilst the more prudent few indulge in the luxury of three-halfpennyworth of coffee for their morning draught. *Ten*, and the magistrates have taken their places at the bench ; seedy individuals, with dilapidated castors and eleemosynary *kicksies*, wend their way slowly into the office, and the hairdresser's shop begins to be adorned with the bust of a particularly fascinating wax figure with corkscrew ringlets and lavishly-vermilioned countenance. *Eleven*, and actors, who had a call for a ten o'clock rehearsal, begin to bustle into the theatre with evident symptoms of perturbation and anxiety ; managers look glum, and machinists nervous, whilst the prompter glances hatchets and tomahawks at those unlucky supers who have been three minutes behind time. Now do ladies,

with pink parasols and sky-blue bonnets, hasten to
Kenneth's, the dramatic agency office, for an engagement; the theatrical generally leading to a matrimonial one. *Twelve*, and Harris's shop gets thronged
with votaries of the sock and buskin. Papers are
read, notes are written, and criticisms spoken of.
During that dreary interval invariably occurring at
rehearsals, this is the spot where actors ' most do
congregate,' and this is the tribunal where disputes,
appertaining to the mimic art, are referred for decision.
One, and the steaming vapour that exhales from the
cuisine of the *Globe* begins to assail the nostrils of the
peckish passenger. Collarless coves, with long frock
coats, buttoned tight up to the throat to conceal the
want of a waistcoat, now supply the cravings of
nature by eagerly inhaling the savoury steam that
indicates the kind of preparation going on below,
thus making one sense relieve the privations of the
other. And now the business of Bow Street labours
under an interregnum of several hours' duration; a
dread *hiatus* occurs in its proceeding, and, with
the exception of Saturday, when the treasury delays
their departure, scarcely an actor can at this time
be observed in this previously Thespian-thronged
thoroughfare. The first signs of returning animation
are seen in the arrival of crowds and carriages at the
Covent Garden portico, waiting for the opening of the
doors. On every side rings the well-known cry of

'Bill of the play, gentle*men* ;' the last syllable receiving, from a habit, a double allowance of emphasis. Now comes the withdrawal of bolts; the rush of many feet and the crowd disappears, a few stragglers alone remaining undecided in the avenue. Crossing over the way to the tobacconists, we find a group of mingled amateurs and professionals chatting together at the door, or else seated upon diminutive casks, in the most theatrical and picturesque manner, imbibing the fumes of the choice cigar. Attentively perusing the play-bills that decorate one side of the wall, is a tall, thin young man, with a pale countenance and dark brown hair, falling in savage profusion over his coat collar. That is the *Hamlet* of the preceding night, a would-be aspirant to dramatic fame, and who, having *once* smelt the lamps at a minor theatre, will rest not until he has succeeded in getting an engagement at one of the theatres royal. Next to him stands one who played *Laertes* on the same night, and this very day week they play *Richard* and *Richmond* together, with the combat most awfully protracted, for that night only. But the performances have concluded, and the rumbling of carriages, hackney-coaches, and cabs is heard once more. The cry of 'Ham-sandwiches, only a penny,' blends most harmoniously with 'Coach unhired.' Some of the company wend their way to the Coal-hole, others to the Wrekin, whilst many, with visions of rump-steaks

GARRICK'S HEAD

BOW STREET.

Exactly Opposite the Grand Entrance to the

ROYAL ITALIAN OPERA

Listen, ye Nocturnal Wanderers in pursuit of joyous hours after the turmoils of industrious daylight! Come & Sup at the **Garrick's Head**

NICHOLSON

HAS COME BACK, AND SO HAS

THE GRIDIRON

THE

JUDGE & JURY SOCIETY

At Nine o'Clock, after which the Lord Chief Baron departs from judicial dignity to become the Chairman of the lively board. Give him a look in!

Such Singing by Old and New Favourites!

Will you go, Bob? Yes. So will I,
And the old Baron's Gridiron try,
A Chop or Kidney at this hour,
With Pratee like a ball of flour :
Or Steak upon his Lordship's plan,
Will renovate the inward man ;
A Sausage, Tripe, or Toasted Cheese,
Stout, Ale, or Water, which you please ;
And after that up stairs repair,
To see the Baron in the chair.
To hear the lively song and joke,
A glass of Grog, and have a Smoke.
Come from Casino's mazy thread,
To Supper at the GARRICK'S HEAD !

Mr. NICHOLSON begs to solicit attention to the fact that the Front Coffee-room of the Establishment is **a Public Supper Room**, for Ladies and Gentlemen. The most Elegant **Private Dining and Supper Apartments** Up Stairs, for Large and Small Parties visiting the Theatres.

The Lord Chief Baron NICHOLSON politely reminds his Friends and Patrons of the great accommodation offered in this splendid Establishment. Excellent Bed Chambers, 1s. 6d. ; Breakfast, with Eggs, or a Rasher of Bacon, 1s. 3d. Dinners and Nic Nacks from 1 o'Clock. A Hot Joint always at 6, the LORD CHIEF BARON presiding, charge 1s. 6d.

J. W. PEEL's Steam Machine. 74. New Cut. Lambeth.

and stout before their eyes, cross over to the Garrick. At the head of the table is Mr. Fly, the chairman, an eminent hand at the bass, often going down so low that it takes him half-an-hour to get up again. To the right is the tenor, Mr. Gorgon; at his elbow sits Mr. Tart, a very staid individual, who always seems as if he were going to laugh and *couldn't.* Listen to what emanates from the chair. 'Now, gentlemen, with your kind permission, we will attempt a glee.' Loud cries of 'Hear, hear,' and 'Bravo' resound throughout the room, and the glee is forthwith attempted. A capital glee it is, too, with plenty of ha ! ha's ! and clipping of monosyllables."

Bow Street, according to an old writer, took the name from its shape " running in the shape of a bent bow," as may be seen to this hour, on one side. The other side seems to have been somewhat straightened when the Opera House was built. It was once an exceedingly fashionable district, and, at its northern portion, was quite close to the country fields. About one hundred and twenty years ago it was almost as *recherché* as St. James's Street and the quarter about it now. Interesting, too, are the many historical associations which make the whole area " sacred ground." What a history would be that of Covent Garden Theatre alone, with its traditions of manager Rich, Peg Woffington, Garrick, Kemble, and the terrible " O.P." Riots, down to the fatal March 5,

1856, when it was burnt to the ground, under the
vulgar patronage of a " Wizard of the North." Some
amateur had a souvenir made out of the charred
remains, some four inches long by two and a half
broad, its massive sides of highly-polished oak giving
it an imposing look. Its edges are of the orthodox
dull red, its back of morocco. The title is " Theatrical Ashes," and its wooden walls were cut from a
partially burnt log of oak taken from the ruins of
Covent Garden Theatre, after an orgie snobbishly
called a *bal masqué.* There are many amateurs at this
moment busy collecting all the facts and cuttings that
bear on the history of Bow Street and the adjoining Covent Garden—on " the Hummums," lately re-
built and rejuvenated, the Bedford Head, Inigo Jones's
Church, Tom Davies' shop, and the curious and eccentric beings that " hung loose " upon the society of the
district. The old antiquarian associations have been
retailed at length in the innumerable topographical
works on London, and scarcely concern us here.
Wycherly, the dramatist, after his marriage with the
Countess of Drogheda, was, according to an oft-told
tale, so harassed at his fireside, that he often retired,
for peace' sake, to the tavern opposite, but he was
ordered to keep the windows open so that his lady
might see with what company he was engaged. The
old police-office, it is believed, stood upon the site of
Waller the poet's house. It is curious to think that

the well-known " ham-and-beef " shop at the corner, which still displays its old tiled roof, was once " Will's Coffee House," to which the most famous wits used to resort. And in Russell Street the house still stands where Boswell was introduced to Dr. Johnson. The vivacious O'Keeffe, when he first came to town, was deeply impressed by these recollections, and used to recall the speech in the " Constant Couple " where Beau ·Clincher talks of his going to the jubilee at Rome :—" Supposing the corner of a street—suppose it Russell Street here," &c. " Well, thought I," he adds in his natural way, " here am I at last, standing at the corner of Russell Street ! " William Lewis, the comedian, lived in the very house in Bow Street that belonged to Wilkes, the original Sir Harry Wildair in the " Constant Couple ;" and used the same private passage from it into Covent Garden Theatre. This Wilkes was an Irishman. Lewis also lived in another celebrated house : it was in Great Queen Street, on the right hand going to Lincoln's Inn Fields. In Queen Anne's reign it belonged to Dr. Radcliffe. Sir James Thornhill, the painter, lived in the next house, and I saw the very door the subject of Dr. Radcliffe's severe sarcasm against Thornhill. " *I don't care what he does with the door, so he does not paint it.*"

The older Bow Street office, a " squeezed " building, which had witnessed so many dramatic scenes, having lost its purpose, was allowed to linger on for some half a dozen years. It fell into the occupation of Stinchcombe, a well-known theatrical *costumier* and wig provider, who here carried on his duties till the middle of ·the year 1887. About September the Duke of Bedford was busy restoring the Floral Hall close by to its original function of a flower-market. The old-fashioned Bedford Hotel, which had once flourished under Inigo Jones' cheerful Piazzas—having been abandoned and reduced to being a warehouse for the sale of potatoes and other vegetables, was clearly on its way to demolition. There was a tract of valuable space between the hotel and the police office, for both were *dos-à-dos*. In October, as was to be expected, the *costumier* Stinchcombe had gone, hoardings had been put up, and in a few weeks not a vestige of old Bow Street office was left. Lately passing by, as three " housebreakers "—the professional name—were at their work, the old railings even attracted the eye, which were of a symbolical and impressive character ; the supporting standards representing lictors' fasces with a double axe. The building was not a hundred years old. When Sir John Fielding, " the blind magistrate," succeeded his half-brother, the novelist, he came to live here in one or other of the two houses marked " 4 " and " 4A." Here, under his extraordinary disability, he dispensed justice for forty years until the disastrous June of 1790, when the " No Popery " riots broke out, when, as was to be expected, so vigorous a chastiser of evil-doers was marked out for vengeance. His home was burnt to the ground, and the unfortunate magistrate himself died in the September following, at Brompton. On the ruins the late squalid and inconvenient buildings were erected, which served, in spite of all pressure and inconvenience, till a few years back. The history of a place such as Bow Street office would naturally be one of extraordinary interest owing to its curious not to say eccentric associations.

It has been stated that Mr. Burnaby, formerly chief clerk of Bow Street police-office, who retired from office several years ago, had kept a diary of his experiences in Bow Street. " Unfortunately, however, in the depth of his sorrow for the death of his son, he destroyed this record." [1]

April 4, 1881, was a day of mark in the Bow Street annals, for a boy named McCarthy was charged at the old office with having stolen some logs of wood, with a view to cutting them up into firewood. This was on a Saturday, and after his case was heard, the old office was closed for ever, and on the Monday, April 4, the business was removed to the new and rather ambitious offices over the way.

[1] However, this sense of irreparable loss is purely speculative, and always recalls the story of the letter which Johnson lost, and which the owner said was of enormous value when lost ; but when it was after great exertion recovered and restored to him, he carelessly said " that it was of no consequence."

"Antiquarians," says Mr. Sala, "of the type of White-locke and Howell, of Strype and Aubrey, of Pepys and Stow, and, above all, of old Peter Cunningham, will hereafter take note of a naughty little boy, named MacCarthy, who has stolen some logs. His offence is petty ; and yet Master MacCarthy is the last prisoner who has been put at the bar of the old Bow Street police-court. To-day, we may remind our readers, the old Bow Street offices are closed finally, and henceforth their business will be transacted in the new block of buildings on the opposite side of the street. Indeed the condition of the old police-court had long been a public scandal. It had changed little, if at all, since Dickens described it in 'Oliver Twist,' and dwelt upon the general air of greasiness and of dirt which hung about it, and which seemed more or less to choke and to stifle the faculties and perceptions of all who were engaged in its business, from the Chief Magistrate himself down to the door-keeper. It was, in truth, an evil old place, and it is therefore, perhaps, pleasant to know that it will soon be swept away. In the earlier editions of the 'Newgate Calendar,' a work of immense research and of some value among bibliophiles, is a 'correckt viewe' of the Court-house at Bow Street. It is a 'commodious' room with a 'bar' across its midst. Behind the bar, at a table, sits the Magistrate, attired in a Court suit of the days of Goldsmith, and girt with a sword. By his side

sits his 'clerke,' occupied in the 'reduction' of the
depositions, and clad in a gorgeous periwig. The
prisoner is guarded by a couple of Bow-street
'runners,' and the general public is represented by
some dozen or so of fashionably-attired ladies and
gentlemen, who are strolling about and exchanging
snuff and pomander boxes, and watching the proceedings with a languid interest. Such was Bow
Street in the days of the earlier editions of the
'Calendar,' when Jonathan Wild was still a hero.
The Court was small, inconvenient, ill-ventilated, and
approached by narrow and ill-arranged corridors. It
would be, perhaps, too much to say that it was as
badly laid out and badly managed as the Bail Court
at Westminster, where the Court of Queen's Bench
still sits.''

CHAPTER II.

THE Bow Street Magistrates have always presented a special type, quite distinct from the functionaries who preside at the other offices. They were of a more interesting and dramatic kind, and exhibited a distinct personality, and marked points of character. Their names being brought prominently before the public are familiar, whereas the others are forgotten. This peculiarity, it will be seen, is owing to the nature of their functions. They were the heads and directors of such police as existed at the time; and like the French " Chiefs of Police," they not only arrested, but examined, the prisoner who was brought to them by their officers; hence the common phrase, so familiar by repetition, "of being brought up at Bow Street." The list is not a long one. Though the Bow Street office was not formally constituted by Act of Parliament until the year 1792, these magistrates administered justice there for many years before. We find Henry Fielding, the novelist, there in 1753; to be succeeded by his half-brother, Sir John Fielding, in 1761. The next was Sir W. Addington, in 1780, who was thus the first regular Bow Street magistrate. Next followed Sir R. Ford in 1800; Mr. Read in 1806; Sir Nathaniel Conant in 1813; Sir R. Baker in 1820; Sir R. Birnie in 1821; Sir F. Roe in 1823; Mr. J. Hall in 1837; Sir T. Henry in 1864; and Sir J. Ingham in 1876. Nearly all these functionaries were remarkable persons in their way; notably the two Fieldings, Sir R. Birnie, and in our time, Sir Thomas Henry. They were distinguished for energy, sagacity, a good common sense and quick decision; qualities which came of long practice and experience, and contact with the singular miscellany which daily passed before them. As will be seen further on, the Bow Street police-office was a sort of theatre, where performances of the most original and *bizarre* kind were given, and the "seamy" twists and turns of human character were displayed in endless variety.

In the last century there stood in St. John's Street, Clerkenwell, facing Smithfield, a court-house, described as "a very plain brick edifice, with a portico at the entrance." This was known as Hicks' Hall, and it was used by the Middlesex justices for holding their sessions. It was called Hicks' Hall, from being built by Sir Baptist Hicks, afterwards Lord Campden, who had been a merchant in Cheapside, and who had died in 1629. This building has long since been swept away.

This seat of justice is, however, most familiar to the

world of letters, from its association with the much-ridiculed Sir John Hawkins, Knt., who presided there for many years, and who, mainly owing to Boswell's jealousy and dislike, has been considered a pompous, empty-headed, and even malignant being. The well-known distich—

> Here lies Sir John Hawkins,
> In his shoes and *stalkins*,

—was supposed to express his solemn and pedantic style of thought and utterance. Yet Sir John was a man of letters and a musician—was a friend and executor of Johnson, and wrote his life; a respectable and interesting performance, full of much curious information. Boswell, who was sensitive to a degree, and so tortured by his prejudices that he could not, even when he tried, hide them, seems to writhe as he thinks on the injury he suffered by being thus forestalled in his great work. Sir John also wrote a History of Music, which exhibits at least research; and finally, he was chairman of the magistrates at Hicks' Hall, to the duties of which he devoted himself with extraordinary enthusiasm. He was really a painstaking and successful magistrate, and intrepid when the occasion required. No doubt he was an old Tory and narrow-minded—qualities he often displayed to a ludicrous degree; but his merits seem considerable when contrasted with the qualifications of his brethren. These formed a singular miscellany." It used to be said of one of them" (says his daughter, Miss Letitia Hawkins), " whose name was David, and who had been a bricklayer at the east end of the town, where, by prescription, these *justices* were of the lowest order, that he never wrote more of his baptismal name than the first two letters, having a doubt in his mind as to one of the subsequent ones. I myself heard this personage say, that he had ' breakfasted on such a day with government, and that his daughter was going to send to government's daughter a present of a pair of turtle-doves.' He was soft in his manners; and if my father was at all less informed than was requisite to understanding him, he would patiently explain. For instance :—talking one day of 'the generals,' he saw that he was not perfectly clear ; he therefore spoke more diffusely, and said, ' There are two generals, the soliciting general and the returning general.' Sir. J. H. thanked him for the trouble he had taken; they were now on equal terms, and could get on.

" So carelessly made were the appointments, and so easily were they obtained, that on one day a magistrate might be seen sitting at Hicks' Hall, and some weeks later would be brought up to receive sentence, in the Court of King's Bench, for corruption in his office. Nor was this corruption confined to those in an inferior station. The difficulties of administering pure justice often came from those who were high in office.

A culprit with good connections could set potent forces in motion to work on the magistrate. He had tried a man for assaulting a sheriff's officer. I do not know whether the offence would not *now* be deemed *capital*, as it consisted in stabbing the man near the stomach. The man was found guilty, and sentenced to two years' imprisonment in Newgate. He petitioned the Crown, and my father had the usual letter from the Secretary of State, commanding him to report upon the case : he did so, but was very much surprised to find that, contrary to all usage, it was wished that he would reconsider his opinion ; and above all, when he had done so, and only strengthened his report by argument, to hear that the remission of the sentence was to be looked for.

"While the matter was agitating over his head, solicitation to himself was not spared. The man set every engine to work, and somehow interested in his behalf a person of the name of Hutton, then at the head of the society of Moravians. I had the perusal of a most curious epistle, in pathetic bombast, which this advocate addressed to the lady of Sir Charles Whitworth, to obtain his mediation with my father. It began thus : "Will Lady Whitworth, in some easy moment," &c., &c. Her ladyship forwarded the supplication ; and I remember Sir Charles bringing it to my father : but I fancy he saw the propriety of leaving the law to take its course.

HENRY FIELDING, ESQ.^R

"An intimation that, if thus unreasonably counter-
acted, he should immediately quit the situation he
held, was the last resource, and this succeeded: but
while the offender was wearing out his sentence,
carriages that told too much, were, by eight in the
morning, seen at the door of Newgate; and, on
inquiry, my father learnt that the Moravian trafficked
in that favourite commodity, ' small diamonds.' "

Such was this frightful abuse of the "*Trading
Justices*"—persons appointed to the Bench without
any fit qualifications, and from the meanest class, and
who indemnified themselves for their gratuitous services
by taking bribes. This name, "*Trading Justice*," now
happily without meaning, became a bye-word and a
popular term of reproach.

It must not be supposed that all the members of the
Magistrates' Bench were of the same pattern as this
corrupt class. A striking contrast was Mr. Saunders
Welch, an upright, accomplished man, who did his duty
fearlessly; and Sir John Hawkins himself, who, for all his
"stalkins," was an admirable official. Sir John had
often the privilege of delivering charges to the grand
jury of Middlesex, and these were, in general, marked
by practical sense. Thus, on the rebuilding of Newgate, when it was proposed to throw the burden on
the country at large, he disposed of the matter in a
way that shows him to have been a man of sound
judgment. The charge is, moreover, interesting, as

showing the incredible neglect and abuses that prevailed in dealing with prisoners.

But we must turn back to two most conspicuous magistrates of Bow Street, who were really the founders of the police of London. These were Henry Fielding, the novelist, and his half-brother, John, afterwards Sir John. The services of these two men were of an extraordinary kind, when we consider that the first was altogether worn out, and not far from his death, when he took up the duties of his office; and that the second was blind! Yet these brothers carried on a battle *à outrance* with the criminal classes for nearly forty years, and which ended in complete victory.

Henry Fielding, as all his countrymen know, was dramatist, satirist, journalist, a Bohemian also, as it is called. Late in life he had become a novelist, then a barrister, when he vainly sought for practice, and finally obtained a magistracy. He, however, gave but the fragment of a dissipated, almost riotous life, and a constitution shattered by gout and various maladies, to his magisterial duties. He had turned to the Bar too late to make it profitable; and, through the interest, it was said, of Lord Lyttelton, was appointed a magistrate at Bow Street; adopted, it would seem, as a sort of *pis-aller*, a sort of promotion not unknown to our own generation. In what spirit he, at first, applied himself to the duties of his office, will

be seen from a strange disorderly sketch, given by
Walpole, and furnished on good authority. "Rigby,"
he says, about a year or two after Fielding's appointment, "gave me a strong picture of nature: he
and Peter Bathurst t'other night carried a servant
of the latter's, who had attempted to shoot him, before
Fielding; who, to all his other avocations has, by
the grace of Mr. Lyttelton, added that of Middlesex
Justice. He sent them word he was at supper; that
they must come the next morning. They did not
understand that freedom, and ran up, where they found
him banqueting with a blind man, a ——, and three
Irishmen on some cold mutton and a bone of ham,
both on one dish—and the dirtiest cloth. He never
stirred or asked them to sit. Rigby, who had seen
him so often come to beg a guinea of Sir C. Williams,
and Bathurst, at whose father's he had lived, for
victuals, understood that dignity as little, and pulled
themselves chairs;—on which he civilized."[1]

The "blind man" who shared in this squalid revel
was, of course, his brother and assistant. But the
manly spirit of the novelist soon rose to the responsibility
of his situation. He took up his duties with ardour:
planned reforms; strove hard to check the disorders
of the streets; captured thieves and highwaymen,
and was indefatigable in examining malefactors at his
house in Bow Street. He suggested ideas for passing

[1] "Letters," vol. ii. 162.

wholesome Acts of Parliament; and discussed in pamphlets various notable cases which had excited public sympathy. One of these was the curious one of Pen Lez, which excited much public interest and discussion.

An extraordinary riot took place in 1749. The sailors were discontented at the time, and one night one of them rushed into the street complaining that he had been robbed in a house of doubtful character, which, strange to say, was in the Strand. As occasionally happens, a phrenzy of virtuous indignation seized on the mob: there were clamours for the destruction of the house, and of all such places where " honest mariners " were so ill-treated. The street was filled with infuriated crowds. They attacked a tavern called " The Star," where enormities were supposed to be practised, and set it on fire. An obnoxious draper's house was also attacked; his goods were carried out, and heaped up in front, to be set on fire. But the police were active, and prevented further destruction. A young man who was seen running away was seized, and some of the plundered linen was found upon him. It was attempted to bring him away to prison, but the crowd was so violent that the soldiers had to be sent for. Fielding ordered him to be taken to Newgate, but he was eventually brought to his house in Bow Street, to be examined. An enormous crowd collected in front of the house while the examination was going on ; and the magistrate, always intrepid, appeared at the window and addressed the people, charging them to disperse.

The prisoner was named Bosaven Pen Lez, or Penley, and was a respectable young man, the son of a Welsh clergyman. His story, on being arrested, was that his wife, or some woman, had made away with his domestic linen—a not very intelligible justification. He was tried, and sentenced to death. Immense efforts were made to save him, but he was eventually executed. Fielding published a pamphlet on the subject, vindicating the authorities and his own conduct in the transaction. To this task he brought all his knowledge of law, proving by Acts of Parliament, and comments thereon, the justice of the sentence. He furnishes the depositions of the witnesses, and, it must be said, makes out his case.

Another more celebrated case was that of Eliza Fenning, which still more excited the public, and was hotly debated in the newspapers and in pamphlets. One of the latter was contributed by Fielding, who once more vindicated the action of the authorities. The general opinion, however, was that the supposed criminal, who maintained her innocence on the scaffold, was innocent.

There is something touching in the circumstances which signalized the close of his labours. Always manly, straightforward, and thorough, his resolution was never more displayed than when, utterly broken in health and fortune, he unflinchingly applied the last few months of his life to the serious question of grappling with the crime which, of a sudden, had infested the streets of the metropolis. He had been appointed a magistrate in 1749, and was destined to hold the post but five years only; but they were years of activity and exertion. His name must be always associated with reform at Bow Street. Borne down with disease and suffering, he was on the eve of setting out for Lisbon in the vain hope of finding cure, or at least alleviation. The state of London, its utter insecurity and disorder, had long engaged his most anxious thoughts. His experience as a magistrate furnished him with daily proofs of these disorders, many of which are found in his striking novel of " Jonathan Wild." He injured his impaired health by his exertions. He often sat sixteen hours out of the twenty-four, for it long continued the custom for the magistrate to return about seven o'clock and sit on till midnight, so as to be on the spot to deal with offenders. Many of the magistrates contrived to largely increase their incomes by taking bribes or by a system of perquisites;—*Trading Justices* as these were called. Fielding, however, disdained these courses.

" I had vanity enough," he tells us, " to rank myself with those heroes of old times, who became voluntary sacrifices to the good of the public. But lest the reader

should be too eager to catch at the word *vanity*, I will
frankly own, that I had a stronger motive than the
love of the public to push me on : I will therefore confess to him, that my private affairs at the beginning of
the winter, my compromising the quarrels of porters
and beggars—which, I blush to say, has not been
universally practised—and my refusing to take a
shilling from a man who most undoubtedly would not
have another left, I reduced an income of about 500*l.*
a year of the *dirtiest* money on earth to little more than
three hundred, an inconsiderable portion of which
remained with my clerk. A predecessor of mine
used to boast that he made 1000*l.* a year in his office ;
but how he did it, is to me a secret. His clerk, now
mine, told me I had more business than he had ever
known there : I am sure I had as much as any man
could do. The truth is, the fees are so very low, and
so much is done for nothing, that if a single justice
of the peace had business enough to employ twenty
clerks, neither he nor they would get much by their
labour. The public will, therefore, I hope, think I
betray no secret, when I inform them that I received
from Government a yearly pension out of the public
service-money, which I believe indeed would have been
larger had my great patron been convinced of an
error "—and here he supplies a happy ironical touch—
" *that mine was a lucrative office.*"

"About the latter end of the year 1753," says the

blind magistrate, "a most notorious gang of street robbers, in number about fourteen, dividing themselves in parties, committed such daring robberies, and at the same time such barbarities, by cutting and wounding those they robbed, as spread a general alarm through the town." He then describes how the King issued his proclamation offering 100*l*. reward for the apprehension of any one of the gang. But this step "though humanely intended as a remedy for the evil," was actually to increase it, for the hope of the reward made some villains decoy many "unwary and ignorant wretches" into committing robberies, then giving them up and claiming the money. It was this state of things that led to the Duke of Newcastle's sending for Henry Fielding.

In short, the town seemed to be in complete possession of the thieves and housebreakers. These flourished in regular gangs. The community was helpless. There was no police, to speak of; and Fielding, almost in despair, was driven to devise plans for the extirpation of the evil. In August he was sent for in a pressing way by the Duke of Newcastle, and at once repaired to his house, where, after being kept waiting, he was sent away. He was, however, invited to submit a plan for dealing with the evil. He simply asked to have a sum of 600*l*. placed at his disposal, and engaged to clear the town of marauders. He tells the result in his own graphic way :—

"After some weeks the money was paid at the Treasury, and within a few days after 200*l.* of it had come into my hands the whole gang of cut-throats was entirely dispersed, seven of them were in actual custody, and the rest driven, some out of the town, and others out of the kingdom. Though my health was now reduced to the last extremity, I continued to act with the utmost vigour against these villains, on examining whom, and in taking the depositions against them, I have often spent whole days, nay sometimes whole nights. . . . Meanwhile, amidst all my fatigues and distresses, I had the satisfaction to find my endeavours had been attended with such success, that this hellish society was almost utterly extirpated, that, instead of reading of murders and street robberies in the newspapers, almost every morning, there was in the remaining part of November and in all December not only no such a thing as a murder, but not even a street robbery was committed. In the entire freedom from street robberies during the dark months, no man will, I believe, scruple to acknowledge that the winter of 1753 stands unrivalled."

Yet this intrepid magistrate was at the moment a dying man; dying, as he said, "in a deplorable condition, with no fewer or less diseases than a jaundice, a dropsy, and an asthma, all together uniting there for the destruction of his body."

Never surely was there such a spectacle of a duty so

calmly undertaken, without flourish. " I was now," he said, " in the opinion of all men, dying of a complication of disorders." But he could not resist mentioning three simple facts; one that the " proclamation offering 100*l.* for the apprehending felons for certain felonies, which I prevented from being revived, had formerly cost the Government several thousand pounds within a single year; secondly, that all such proclamations, instead of curing the evil, had certainly increased it, and multiplied the number of robberies ; thirdly, that my plan had not put the Government to more than 300*l.* expense, and had actually suppressed the evil for a time. I had plainly pointed out the means of suppressing it for ever—this I myself would have undertaken had my health permitted—at the annual expense of the above-mentioned sum."

Having performed this signal service to the State, he resigned his office, and in very touching fashion speaks of the little provision he was enabled to make for his family ; then set off on his " Voyage to Lisbon," of which he has left so graphic and interesting an account. His cheerfulness and spirit never abated, though his sufferings for want of surgical attendance were great. He died shortly after his arrival, and his grave is one of the spots of interest for all Englishmen who visit that capital.

And here it may be said that one of the special products of the nation, exemplified in his person, is the modest, hardworking, sensible magistrate, who receives, and indeed does not seek, little approbation for his service, and who day after day, from year's end to year's end, works on at his monotonous duties, in a crowded, unhealthy court—painstaking, and never flagging in his exertions. It is only when we compare him with his showy brother in France, who is ever " playing to the gallery," and takes but little heed of the prisoner's interests provided he himself can make a display, that we see his genuine merit.

It will be seen that Mr. Fielding does not tell us what his notable plan was for the destruction of the robbers, though we look for the details with considerable curiosity. The truth was, he was rather too sanguine about it, and, as his brother tells us, it was only a temporary relief, for presently " a fresh gang, as desperate though not so numerous as the former, made its appearance," which had to be taken in hand by the blind brother, who now comes on the scene with a bandage on his eyes, thus literally reproducing the familiar image of Justice. It was always a strange spectacle for the numerous thieves and forgers who were " brought up " at Bow Street to find themselves in presence of a *blind* magistrate, who we may be sure furnished a stale topic of illustration to the reporters, and other scribes, in the fact that "justice ought to be blind." Not many years ago there flourished in Ireland a certain ancient Baron of the Exchequer who went circuit, heard "motions," "charged" juries, and went through all his judicial duties with fair credit and success, though "stone blind." The recent instance of the lamented Mr. Fawcett, as postmaster-general, whose duty is the care of letters, is a more curious instance still. Mr. John Fielding's remaining senses and faculties seem, however, to have been quickened in an extraordinary degree by his loss, and he acquired a reputation as a singularly prompt, vigorous, and successful magistrate.

Dr. Somerville gives a sketch of him which supplies yet one more instance of the skill with which blind persons contrive to make up for the infirmity which itself seems to stimulate and develop other gifts. The doctor describes the arrest of a fellow-passenger in the coach, a forger, and how the blind magistrate only a few hours later, setting his emissaries to work, had discovered the lodgings of all the other passengers.

"I was so much amused and interested," he says, "with the appearance of Sir John Fielding, and the singular adroitness with which he conducted the business of his office, that I continued there for an hour after the removal of Mathewson, while Sir John was engaged in the investigation of other cases. Sir John had a bandage over his eyes, and held a little switch or rod in his hand, waving it before him as he descended from the bench. The sagacity he discovered in the questions he put to the witnesses, and a marked and

SIR JOHN FIELDING IN HIS COURT.

successful attention as I conceived, not only to the
words, but to the accents and tones of the speaker,
supplied the advantage which is usually rendered by
the eye; and his arrangement of the questions leading
to the detection of concealed facts, impressed me with
the highest respect for his singular ability as a police
magistrate."

Almost at once he put his brother's plan into operation against the revived gangs. The idea appears to
have been the philosophical and radical one of cutting
off the source of supply, and destroying the haunts or
" nests " where these criminal pests were engendered.
He would thus begin by putting down "low music
meetings and dances," where thieves met each other;
by abolishing " begging and street-walking;" and by
harrying and harassing the whole community until it
found its occupation intolerable.[2] " These reigning
gangs of desperate street robbers were attacked, and
in the space of three months no less than *nine* capital
offenders were brought to justice,—though not without
bloodshed, for one of Mr. Fielding's people was killed
and one of the robbers cut to pieces,—among whom
were the famous Birk, Gill Armstrong, and Courteney.
Nor has any considerable gang appeared since, till
lately. The next set of villains," viz. the highway-

[2] See his tract, " An Account of the Origin and Effects of a
Police set on foot by his Grace the Duke of Newcastle in 1753, upon
a plan presented to him by the late Henry Fielding, Esq. 1758."

men that robbed near town, "were by this new method brought to justice; so that scarce one has escaped from that time to this." The worthy Sir John quite gloats over his performances in this line. The lead-stealers—a distinct profession—and house-breakers were next pursued and harried, until they were totally dispersed and sent to Tyburn. These "more considerable objects being removed," the vast shoal of pickpockets, shoplifters, &c., were left at his mercy, and were every day taken up in numbers. He mentions a curious instance of four infant thieves, the eldest five years old, who were brought before him, and who were proved to be all children of different persons collected by one woman to "beg and steal, *to furnish that beast with gin.*"

One of his methods for protecting the suburbs, then almost at the mercy of the highwaymen, was the inviting of small subscriptions to defray the expense which he could not obtain from the City or Crown. This part of his scheme is thus described :—

"*Substance of Mr. Fielding's Plan for preventing Robberies, within twenty miles of London.*

"He proposes that any number of gentlemen, for instance twenty, whose country houses are situate at different distances from five to twenty miles from London, subscribe two guineas each, to be lodged in the hands of one of the subscribers. That this money be subject to the draughts of all the subscribers, and if any highway robbery be committed in the neighbourhood of any of the subscribers, let the first that hears of it obtain an exact description of the robber, his horse (if he had one), and whatever is taken from the person robbed. This let him put in writing, always adding, if possible, the name and place of abode of the party robbed; for it sometimes happens when a highwayman is apprehended, that the prosecutor not being to be found, the former escapes justice and is let loose again upon the public. Next let a man and horse be immediately hired and despatched to Mr. Fielding, in Bow Street, Covent Garden, with full authority to that gentleman to advertise it in what manner he thinks proper, and to receive of the treasurer of the subscription the expense of the advertisements. Meantime let the messenger communicate to all the bye-ale-houses, public-inns, and turnpikes, in his way to and from London, the robbery, with a verbal description of the man and horse. On the messenger's returning to the subscriber who sent him, and producing a testimony from the justice of his having delivered to him the said description, and setting forth the hour of his arrival in town, the subscriber shall give the messenger a draught upon the treasurer for such a sum of money as he shall think he deserves. Now as the acting magistrate, besides having the whole civil power within his jurisdiction at command, can every day, upon notice given of any robbery, call together a number of men, always ready to pursue and attack the most daring villain, it must be impossible for villains ever to escape justice.

"The alehouse-keepers, stable-keepers who let horses to hire, and pawnbrokers should constantly read the advertisements inserted by Mr. Fielding in the Public Advertiser. The first would then never harbour a rogue; the second would never furnish a highwayman with a horse, without knowing it time enough to detect him and save the horse; and as to the latter they have already found so many advantages from what is here recommended that nothing farther need be said."

Sir John, like his brother, had a keen sense of humour, and utilizing his experience, published some advice to the public in reference to thieves and sharpers, the very form of which has a droll turn. It was printed on a sheet. This was a " Description of London and Westminster," published in 1776; and to this he added, " *Proper Cautions* to the Merchants, Tradesmen, and Shopkeepers; Journeymen, Apprentices, Porters, Errand Boys, Book-keepers, and Innkeepers; *also very necessary* for every person going to London either on business or pleasure." They are to be wary of what he calls " *Sky Farmers,*" one of whom dresses himself extremely genteel, and takes upon himself either the character of a private gentleman or respectable tradesman. He is attended by two men in the character of country farmers, with clumsy boots, horsemen's coats, &c. The objects pitched upon for imposition are good charitable old ladies, to whom the sky farmer tells a dreadful story of losses by fire, inundation, &c., to the utter ruin of these two poor farmers and all their families; their wives are with child, their children down with the small-pox, &c. A book is then produced by the sky farmer, who undertakes this disagreeable office purely out of good nature, knowing the story to be true. In this book are the names of the nobility and gentry set down by himself, who have contributed to this charity; and by setting out with false names, they at length get real ones, which are of great service to them in carrying on their fraud; and these wretches often obtain relief for their false distresses, whilst the really miserable suffer, from their modesty, the asserted afflictions. A woman stuffed so large as if she was ready to lie in, with two or three borrowed children, and a letter giving an account of her husband's falling off a scaffold, and breaking his limbs, or being drowned at sea, &c., is an irresistible object.

"But the highest rank of cheats," he continues, "*who attack the understanding* have made use of the following stratagems :—One of the gang, who is happiest in his person, and has the best address, is pitched upon to take a house, which, by means of the

extreme good character given of him by his comrade
to the landlord, is soon accomplished.   The next consideration is to furnish it, when Mr. ——, a young
ironmonger, just set up, is pitched upon to provide the
squire's grates, who, glad of so fine an order, soon
ornaments his chimneys with those of the newest
fashion.   This being done, Mr. ——, the upholsterer,
is immediately applied to for other furniture, and is
brought to the house, in order that he may see the
grates, which he no sooner beholds than he tells his
honour that he could have furnished him likewise with
grates of the best kind at the most reasonable rates, to
which Squire Gambler replies that he intends taking
some little villa in the country, where Mr. —— shall
furnish everything he can.

" The house being now completely furnished, the
squire dresses himself in his morning gown, velvet
cap, and red morocco slippers, puts one or more of his
comrades into livery, then sends for the tailor, linendraper, silversmith, jeweller, &c., takes upon him the
character of a merchant, and by getting credit of one,
by pawning the goods the moment he has got them he
is enabled to pay ready money to others ; by which
means he extends his credit and increases his orders till
he is detected; which sometimes does not happen till he
has defrauded tradesmen to a very considerable value.

" There is a set of sharpers who have lately purchased several estates without money in the following

manner :—They make a bargain with the seller, or his agent, and promise to pay the purchase-money at such a time; they then go to the tenant and show him the articles of agreement, and tell him that he will soon have a new landlord, upon which the former begins to complain of the old one, and hopes his honour will repair this, rebuild that, and alter something else, which the landlord promises to do. Credit being thus gained with the tenant, the new landlord falls in love, perhaps, with the farmer's daughter, or with a fine horse, or else borrows money of him and gives him a draught upon his banker in town, who seldom has any cash in hand, and often is not to be found.

" The old trick of *ring-dropping* is practised by fellows who find a paper full of ' gold rings,' which they take care to pick up in the sight of a proper object, whose opinion they ask, saying that he had rather have found a good piece of bread and cheese, for he had not broken his fast for a whole day; then wishes the gentleman would give him something for the rings, that he might buy himself a pair of shoes, a coat, &c. He will immediately bite, and thinking to make a cheap purchase of an ignorant fellow, gives him 20s. for four or five brass rings washed over. Or, what is more frequent, and yet more successful, is the picking up of a shilling or a half-crown before the face of a countryman, whose opinion of it is immediately asked, whether it be silver or not, and he is invited to share the finder's good luck in a glass of wine or a pot of ale. The harmless countryman, pleased at such an invitation in a strange place, is carried to an ale-house where the sharper's friends are waiting for him, and where cutting or playing at cards is soon proposed, and the countryman most certainly tricked out of all his money, watch, and everything valuable he has about him." All which shows how well skilled was the blind magistrate in the tricks and devices of the fraternity. The style is pleasant enough, and has the ironical flavour of that of his more gifted brother.

This excellent man was knighted by the king in 1760, one of the first acts of his reign.

So vigorous was he in the prosecution of his duties, and such a terror to the evil-doer, that he incurred much odium, and received a threatening letter informing him that " the die was cast, and the knight's fate was determined." This was because he had refused bail in the case of a woman named Chandler, accused of stealing lace.

In 1771 we find Mrs. Cornelys giving her celebrated masquerades in Soho Square, a portion of her ball-room being now the Roman Catholic Chapel. She however added the attraction of a dramatic performance, which brought down the ire of the sturdy blind magistrate upon her. She was summoned to Bow Street, and convicted in a penalty of 50*l*. for this illegal performance. It was said that " the noblemen and gentlemen who patronize her puppet opera are so exasperated at a certain justice, that they have entered into very large subscriptions to answer all the penalties that may be levied on her." The speech of the magistrate was admirable, if a little eccentric, and after his own special manner. "Rank," he began by saying, "when it shall be opposed to law will never convey any idea of fear to this bench, but on the contrary, it ought and will animate the magistrates to greater exactitude and attention." After dwelling on the number of places of amusement in the metropolis, all under proper regulations, he proceeded in this rather sarcastic vein :—" In the first place there are two Theatres Royal under the management of two of the greatest geniuses that ever were in the same situation. Then at the Theatre Royal in the Haymarket you have everything elegant that music can produce, and over the way you have the great Mr. Foote, who makes us shake our sides with laughter. Then have you Ranelagh, the politest place of amusement in Europe, under the direction of the great Sir Thomas Robinson. At Sadler's Wells you have everything to entertain that tumbling and feats of activity can afford. At Marylebone you have music, wine, and plum cake. Then you have the White Conduit House and other tea-drinking houses all round the town, and what honest Englishman can say he wants amusement ? Surely it is evident that luxury has been taking such gigantic strides as

ought to make magistrates jealous of dire dangerous
progress. And before I conclude I cannot help observing that what the magistrates, the counsel, and the
witnesses said on Feb. 20th, *as well as what none of them
said*, has been published in a newspaper, and though I
again repeat that I wish all my actions, not as a magistrate only, but as a man, might be known through the
whole world, and though I am content that every one
who heard me be a short-hand writer, yet do I desire
that nothing may be published but the truth, for I fear
not truth, but misrepresentation."

Like many persons afflicted with so serious an infirmity, Sir John seems to have grown into a morbid
state of sensitiveness. This was particularly shown in
his relations with that most amiable of actors, Garrick,
to whom, like Charles Surface in the case of Sir Peter,
it is to be feared "he had given considerable uneasiness." A play of his brother's, the novelist, bearing
the same title as one of Goldsmith's, viz. "The Good-
Natured Man," had been found, and it was suggested
that it should be brought out. Garrick took up the
project with much ardour and warmth, but he found
difficulties and delays, as the piece in its existing state
was not suited to the stage. The touchy magistrate
thought he saw a desire to withdraw from the engagement, and hence arose an angry feeling which
embittered their future intercourse in a very grotesque
way.

"The beginning of my correspondence with Sir John Fielding," wrote Garrick in a MS. letter, now before me, and dated 1772, " was thus :—His brother, the late Mr. Fielding, and my particular friend, had written a comedy, which being lent to his different friends, was lost for twenty years. It luckily fell to my lot to discover it. Had I found a mine of gold upon my own land, it would not have given me more pleasure. I immediately went to his brother and told him the story of my discovery, and immediately, with all the warmth imaginable, offered my services to prepare it for the stage. He thanked me cordially, and we parted with mutual expressions of kindness."

But during the course of these proceedings, Sir John grew fretful and impatient of delay, and showed his irritation in a curious way. A French pyrotechnist had come to London with strong recommendations to Garrick, who had assisted him to obtain leave to give his exhibition. This manager was astonished to receive a letter from the magistrate reproaching him with doing what was contrary to law.

"Dear Sir," wrote the good-humoured actor, "if I were sure you would not laugh, I should be very angry with you. What can you possibly mean by telling my brother that *you are surprised at my countenancing Torrè in an illegal act?* Are you really serious, or, what I like much better, joking with me? You cannot sure be misled by newspaper intelligence. The affair

between me and Torrè stands thus," and he proceeded
to give an account of his share in the business. " This
is the plain fact; and how they can accuse me of
countenancing Torrè in an illegal act, by being merely
civil and friendly to an ingenious, worthy stranger,
recommended to me by one who had been particularly
civil and friendly to me, I shall leave to your own
judgment. I have consulted no lawyer for him, nor
applied to any magistrate, nor have I conversed with
any upon the subject but yourself; so, my good friend,
pray explain yourself to me. I wish Torrè well, for
he has great worth, spirit, and genius, in his way.
But I would not countenance my *brother* in an illegal
act. I honour the laws of my country, and no man,
I trust, less offends them than, dear sir, your most
obedient servant."

Not being able to quarrel on this topic (and it was
exceedingly difficult to quarrel with Garrick), Sir John
next took objection to the business of the play. He
" takes the liberty of communicating his opinion of his
brother's play, which he found too long, and wanting
in business. There is certainly *a very daub* of carica-
ture in young Kennel. I wish it were possible to
encourage his economy of oaths. Further, the two
expressions ' spindle-shanked beau ' and ' rampant
woman's immorality ' are *most abominable.*"

This was amusing enough. But a more serious
business presently occurred, arising out of a quarrel

behind the scenes between the manager's brother and
Mr. Addington, another Bow Street magistrate, who
had turned dramatist and had been roughly or unceremoniously treated. This gentleman having written
to assure Garrick that Sir John had said nothing
against him and had no share in the quarrel, Sir John
himself wrote with acerbity to the same effect. He
had no intention of giving offence, and " he took the
opportunity of *cautioning him against misrepresentation.*"
Garrick replied, and it is curious how their language
became gradually inflamed, that " with a proper regard
for Sir John, he shall not now mention in its proper
colours, the false accusation and unjustifiable behaviour
of one of his friends to his brother, whose warmth was
too natural to merit the severe censure it met with.
Mr. Garrick imagined that the great compliment he
paid the police by giving up his interest to their
opinion, deserved justice, at least, from any magistrate
in Westminster."

This thrust angered the blind magistrate exceedingly.
He wrote in reply :—

" Sir John Fielding has too great a value for his own
character, to give himself the least trouble in settling
the etiquette between Mr. Garrick as manager, and Mr.
Addington as an author. Nor shall he interfere otherwise than to show him what ungenerous treatment he
has met with on his account, but if Mr. Garrick
would be *manly enough* to say in what instance through

life Sir John ever gave him offence—he is persuaded he can undeceive him; for, although he hates defending and proving, he should always think it his duty to give a *satisfactory answer to the lowest and meanest of his Majesty's subjects*, for to save and serve, and oblige, has always been his principle. And it is rather extraordinary that because Sir John Fielding, being ashamed at some very severe conversations that threatened the welfare of his reputation, should communicate his apprehensions in the most delicate manner, and because on the same day he used his utmost endeavours to prevent his brother George from exposing himself, and that from an act of friendship to David Garrick, and an act of humanity to his poor infirm brother, he should not only be treated with disrespect himself, but oceans of anathema to be denounced against the innocent family of his brother to whom, if fame be of any value, Mr. Garrick has the highest obligations. . . .

" As we are not likely to meet again, permit me to say that I hope I am mistaken in declaring that you are egregiously so; I therefore most sincerely forgive you all your unkindness. I hope you will recover your health. You will be pleased to take notice that in the course of my life I have ever stood forth, and once with great danger to shelter David Garrick from the resentment of the public, and that I have twice interfered to prevent disputes between his brother and Mr. Addington

being carried to improper lengths. That I have twice
been insulted for these kind offices, that I have never
received favour from Mr. Garrick in the course of my
life."

This was becoming a serious and painful quarrel.

" Your worship grows out of humour," Garrick
replied, " and I have not, I hope, been uncivil or out of
temper." Then saying that he was just out of an
illness, " We will, if you please, not be the trumpets of
our own virtues, but take care the innocent do not
suffer by our own mistakes. Now that it is past you
are sorry you used such language. . . . ' Barbarity '
is as much a stranger to my nature as falsehood is to
yours. If you have obliged and honoured me, I thank
you ; that you never were in the way to be obliged by
me is certain, or I should have done it. Some reciprocal
acts of kindness passed between your brother and me,
too trifling to be remembered." After promising to
do all he could about the play, and for the family, he
concluded, " *What you have said kindly I will remember,
what unkindly I will forget.*" We think this a charming
and a model letter, clever as it is admirable.

In September 1773, Garrick had announced the
Beggar's Opera for performance—when Sir John came
to the Bench of Justices and announced to them
that this piece was dangerous to morals, and increased
crime. He had written, in the last year, to Mr.
Garrick begging of him not to perform it. He now

begged therefore the magistrates to join with him in remonstrating with the manager, who had announced it for the following Saturday. Sir John declared that it was never performed on the stage without creating an additional number of real thieves. The Bench immediately agreed, and " a polite card was despatched to Mr. Garrick " for that purpose. To which Mr. Garrick returned for answer that his company was so imperfect and divided (many of the performers being yet in the country) that it would be exceedingly inconvenient, if not impossible, to open with any other piece than that which he had advertised, but added that he would in future do everything in his power to oblige them.

But four years later, when Garrick was about to retire from the stage, and all the world was offering their valedictions, the worthy old magistrate felt compunction, and sent his tribute with the rest.

" Sir John Fielding presents his compliments to Mr. Garrick, and does most sincerely congratulate him on his retirement from the theatre whilst in full possession of his extraordinary talents, and whilst riches and fame, with united charms, invited his longer stay on the stage. From this manly resolution there is every reason to hope that this retirement will be adorned by elegance, hospitality, and cheerfulness, *to the great benefit of his select friends.* And though it has fallen to his lot to be the object of a very premature resent-

ment, who ought to be that of his esteem and respect,
he shall always take delight to say (as he can do it
with justice) *that the chastity of Mr. Garrick*, as a
manager of a public theatre, and his exemplary life as
a man, have been of great service to the morals of a
dissipated age; and whilst posterity shall behold him
as an inimitable actor, they will no less admire him as
a good man. These, sir, are the sentiments of your
sincere friend and obedient humble servant, J.
Fielding.

"P.S.—This, sir, is a tribute which I have already
paid to the distinguished merit of many whose retirement like yours has been the effect of wisdom and
prudence."

There is here a quaint old-fashioned term of phraseology, that is very refreshing, notably, in the passages
that are underlined. As a matter of course the retiring
manager met him in the same cordial spirit :—

"Mr. Garrick presents his best compliments to Sir
John Fielding, and is very happy in receiving so
flattering a mark of the approbation of one whom he
always esteemed and respected. No one is more
sensible of Sir John Fielding's merit, nor has more
publicly declared it." He was only jealous that an
"old family connection of love and regard was given
up to a late acquaintance. He will be more cheerful
if Sir John will come and dine occasionally."

During certain riots that took place in 1765 the

mob had attacked the Duke of Bedford's house, and his Grace was much irritated at Sir John's irresolute conduct, as he considered it, in the business. This led to a quarrel or coolness between them. A few years later the Duke gracefully made the *amende* by extending the lease of Sir John's house, which drew forth this grateful acknowledgment :—

" *March,* 1770.

" Sir John Fielding presents his compliments to his Grace the Duke of Bedford, and takes the earliest opportunity to acquaint his Grace that he was this day honoured with his generous gift of the additional ten years to the lease of his house in Bow Street, and for which he returns his warmest acknowledgment, and assures him that the satisfaction he receives on this occasion is infinitely superior to the value of the present, for he has long had the mortification to know that he has been represented in a false light to his Grace ; and a very terrible mortification it was, as he is conscious that it was impossible for any man to be more sensible of a favour conferred on his family than he was of that princely instance of generosity which his Grace showed to his late brother, Henry Fielding, or to be more attached from principles of gratitude and respect to your Grace's honour, welfare, and interest than I ever have been, notwithstanding it has been my misfortune to be misrepresented, until my behaviour was subjected to the observations of my impartial friend Mr. Palmer, to whom I shall ever esteem myself highly indebted, should he be the happy means of convincing your Grace, from his experience of my conduct, how respectfully, gratefully, and effectively I have, on all occasions, endeavoured to acquit myself towards his Grace, to whom I have a real pleasure in being obliged, and am, with unfeigned truth,*&c."

This worthy magistrate was "worthy" in a better sense than the one in which the hackneyed newspaper term is usually applied. He took on himself the care of his brother's children and brought them up. One of them, Mr. William Fielding, was trained in his office, and later became a magistrate himself. It must have been curious, so recently as 1822, to have heard him give evidence before a committee of the House of Commons, and speak of his father the author of "Tom Jones." In his evidence there is a certain prosiness, with an occasional touch of the family style. It is curious to think of three of the family thus holding the same office.

"I remember," he said, "the 'Apollo Gardens,' the 'Dog and Duck,' and the 'Temple of Flora,' and a dreadful society of vagabonds were certainly collected together in those places. In that time of day the character of highwaymen on horseback was a more frequent character than it has been of late years. I think the horse-patrole of the Office at Bow Street has been of a very considerable degree of service in putting

down that class of depredators ; the character of the
highwaymen is certainly less heard of since the putting
down of *those two infernal places of meeting,* the 'Dog
and Duck,' and the 'Temple of Flora,' which were
certainly the most dreadful places in or about the
metropolis ; they were the resorts of women, not only
of the lowest species, but even of the middle classes ;
they were the resorts, as well of apprentices as of every
sort of dissolute, profligate, and abandoned young
men."

As we have said, during the long period Sir John held
office, nothing is so conspicuous as the evidences of
his activity. He is one of the figures of his time. Is
there a highway robbery, or murder, or riot, we invariably hear of the indefatigable Sir John Fielding
being personally on the scene, despatching his
emissaries to arrest or search. Is there an arrest,
he is promptly "brought before Sir John Fielding"
and examined. There was a daring robbery at Lord
Harrington's, when jewellery, snuff-boxes, watches,
money, to the amount of nearly 3000*l.* were carried
off. "Sir John Fielding," we are told, "is all day in
the house and a good part of the night. The servants
have all been examined over and over again." Sometimes he showed himself in an amiable, patient light.

In 1769 a young shoemaker named Griffiths had
become attached to a girl in service ; they were called in
church, but the girl, who had lost her place, and had

pawned all her clothes, positively refused to be married
in her rags. In despair the shoemaker purchased a
pistol, and, accusing himself of having committed a
crime, gave himself up. Brought before Sir John, the
deception was soon discovered. But the magistrate,
finding that he bore a good character, interested himself in the case. The girl, hearing of her lover's
trouble, fell into fits. The goodnatured magistrate
appointed a day for both to come before him, when he
would see what could be done towards getting them
married, which he arranged, and a young nobleman
who was present gave five guineas to buy clothes.

Sir John figures largely in the calendar of Home
Office papers. Thus we find Lord Halifax directing
the Postmaster-General to send all letters of one
Trench and one Swift to Sir John " for his perusal."
In 1765 he received a letter from Mr. Conway, the
secretary, to wear a badge and ribbon, which we
accordingly find displayed conspicuously in all his
portraits. In these records he is shown, as usual, on
the *qui-vive* for everything, indicating his suspicions to
the court, warning, &c. It is strange to find that he
was one of the Poor Knights of Windsor in 1772.

CHAPTER III.

THE episodes of serious and dramatic interest which Sir J. Fielding took part in unravelling, comprised some of an exciting kind, and indeed were some of the most important in the last half of the century. A few of these, of which certain graphic descriptions have been left, one might be almost certain were described by his own pen. There is one account which has much of the style and pathos of his brother, and indeed is given in so competent and effective a style as to be worthy of the great writer. It is thus lifted above the ordinary " reporter's " vernacular, which so often vulgarizes some natural and touching episode. This particular one reads like some paper in the *Tatler*. There can be little doubt that the narrative is Sir John's own.

§ *The Story of Sarah Metyard and her apprentice Ann Naylor.*

" In the year 1758," he tells us, " Sarah Metyard, the mother, kept a little haberdasher's shop in Bruton

Street, Hanover Square, and her daughter, then about
nineteen years old, lived with her. Their chief
business was the making of silk nets, purses, and
mittens, and they took parish children apprentices.
They had then five : Philadelphia Dowley, about ten
years old; Sarah Henderson, about twelve ; Ann Naylor,
about thirteen; Mary her sister, about eight, and
some others." They were kept at work in a stifling
room from morning until night, and allowed out but
once a fortnight, while the dreadful Metyard, who
hated them all as parish children are hated, seemed
to grind the very life out of them. Ann Naylor had
a whitlow upon her finger so bad it was obliged to be
cut off, and being besides a weak, sickly child, became
particularly obnoxious to the inhumanity and avarice
of the petty tyrant of whom she was condemned to
be the slave.

" The unfortunate child, not able to endure this
tyranny, attempted to run away, but was brought
back. The street-door was then kept locked, and she
was kept ' short of food.' Her strength beginning
to fail, she made another attempt to escape. She took
advantage of the milkman coming to slip out and run
away ; but the daughter missing her while she was
yet in sight, called out to have her stopped, and the
milkman, as she was running with what strength she
possessed, caught her in his arms. The poor child
expostulated with the man, and pressed him with a

moving earnestness to let her go : '*Pray, milkman,*' says she, '*let me go, for I have had no victuals a long time, and if I stay here I shall be starved to death.*'

" The daughter dragged her into the house by the neck, slapped to the door, and forced her upstairs into the room where the old woman was still in bed, though she had started up and joined in the cry upon the first alarm. Here she was thrown upon the bed, and the old woman held her down by the head while her daughter beat her with the handle of a hearth-broom ; after this she was forced into a two-pair-of-stairs back room, and a string tied round her waist, she was made fast to the door, with her hands bound behind her so that she could neither lie nor sit down. In this manner was she kept standing without food or drink for three days, being untied only at night that she might go to bed, and the last night she was so feeble that she was obliged to crawl up to bed upon her hands and knees.

" The first day she said little, her strength failing her apace ; the next day she said nothing, but the pains of death coming on she groaned piteously ; on the third day, soon after she was tied up, her strength wholly failed her and she sank down, hanging double in the string which bound her by the waist. The children being frightened ran to the top of the stairs and called out, '*Miss Sally! Miss Sally! Nancy does not move.*' But she was so far from being touched with pity that she cried out, '*If she does not move, I warrant I'll make her move*; and immediately the daughter came upstairs and found her without any appearance of sense or motion, hanging by the string, her head and feet together."

How simple, natural, and pathetic is this description!

Finding, however, notwithstanding her blows, which were very hard, that the poor wretch showed no signs of sensibility, fear took to alarm, and she hastily called up her mother. When the old woman came up she sat upon the garret stairs at the door where the child was still hanging, and the string being at length cut, she laid her across her lap and sent Sally Henderson downstairs for some drops. This vile pair then hid the body upstairs, locking the door, and pretended that the child had a fit, from which she had recovered, giving out that she had made another attempt and had escaped from the garret. To support this the hall-door was left open and a sort of craftily acted scene was arranged of affected astonishment at the child's escape.

The old woman and her daughter, however, did not know how to dispose of her body, and they actually kept it in the garret for two months, until the atmosphere became intolerable. The pair then cut it up into pieces, and burnt one of the hands, "cursing the unhappy creature because her bones were so long consuming." They then carried out two bundles of the remains " to the great gullyhole in Chick Lane, where is the common sewer which flows into the Thames." They tried to

throw these pieces over the wall where the sewer is
" open," but failing, " threw them down in the mud and
water before the grate and returned home." There
they were found by a constable and were buried, it
being assumed that they were remains from a dissecting-
room.

" The mother and daughter," the narrative goes on,
"had always lived upon very bad terms, and though
the daughter was between nineteen and twenty, her
mother used frequently to beat her. The daughter,
hoping to terrify her into better behaviour, would,
when thus provoked, threaten to accuse her of the
murder, and make herself an evidence to prove it.
This rendered their animosities more bitter. Sometimes she urged her mother to let her go to service,
and sometimes declared she would drown herself.
Thus they continued to hate, to reproach, and to
torment each other until two years after the child had
been dead," when one Mr. Rooker, who had been a
dealer in tea, took a lodging in the house.

Mr. Rooker pitied the condition of the girl, and
when he removed to another residence, took her into
his service, to the fury of the demon mother, who,
with a strange infatuation, pursued her from place to
place, causing disturbances before the door. " When
orders were given to refuse her admittance she cursed
in front of the house. Once she got in and attacked
her daughter, when it is probable that she would have

been killed if assistance had not been at hand, for she was once found forced up into a corner by the mother, who, having torn off her cap and handkerchief, and greatly bruised and scratched her face, had laid hold of a pointed knife, which she was aiming at her breast. This continued until the 9th of June last, and it had been observed that in the height of their quarrels many doubtful and mysterious expressions were used that intimated that some secret of importance was between them." The mother used to call Rooker " the old Perfumer Teadog," and the daughter would reply, " *Mother, remember you are the Perfumer*," alluding to her having kept the child's body in a box till it could not be endured. At other times the daughter, when provoked, would say, " *You are the Chick Lane ghost. Remember the gully in Chick Lane!* " Suspicion being thus roused, the matter was put into Sir John's hands. He made diligent inquiry into the case, which led to the arrest of the two women, and their trial. The daughter accused the mother of the murder, though the mother did not accuse the daughter. They were found guilty and sentenced to death. " But even after this there continued so bitter an animosity between them that it was necessary to confine them apart."

" They were both overwhelmed with a sense of their condition, and about six o'clock in the evening before the execution, the mother, who had neither eaten nor drunk for some time, fell into convulsions, and continued speechless and insensible till death. The daughter, though she was present when this happened, *took no notice of it*, but continued her conversation with a friend who was come to take leave of her."

All the touches in this striking narrative show an artistic sense both of reserve and selection. There is a power in the phraseology and a dramatic instinct that is remarkable, and recalls the style of Henry Fielding himself. For this was after all but a " police case," where an old woman had ill-used her apprentice to death, but the incidents of horror are so adjusted and deepened that it rises to the dignity of tragedy.

§ *The Fate of Miss Ray, the Singer.*

One morning in April, 1779, towards five o'clock, Sir John Fielding came over to the " Shakespeare Tavern " to examine the condition of a man who had been carried there about midnight the night before, in a desperate condition, as it was thought. He had discharged a pistol at a lady as she was coming out of Covent Garden Theatre, and had unhappily killed her. He had then attempted to blow his brains out with another pistol, but not so successfully as in the case of his victim. He had been carried over to the " Shakespeare," and had been allowed to remain there on account of his state. The magistrate, finding the wounds not dangerous, sent him to Tothill Fields prison. This is the well-known extraordinary, if not

romantic, case of Hackman, who had murdered Miss
Ray, of whom he was jealous. The unfortunate lady
was a public singer, and her relations with Lord Sandwich were but too notorious. She had been to the
theatre with her friend, Madame Galli, wife of her
singing-master, and was walking under the Piazza to
her carriage, attended by a Mr. Macnamara, when a
man touched her on the shoulder. She turned round,
when he fired a pistol at her head, and she sank down a
corpse. He then fired another pistol at his own head,
but the ball grazed the part, inflicting only a slight
wound. He was seen frantically beating his skull
with the butt-end of the weapon. When he had somewhat recovered he inquired about his victim, and being
told that she was dead, desired that " her poor
remains should not be exposed to the gaze of the
curious." This absurd solicitude in a murderer is
truly singular.

Lord Sandwich was a great musical amateur, and
used to give performances at his house, generally of a
sacred cast, in which the lady took the leading part.
She particularly excelled in rendering the ballad of
" Auld Robin Grey," which she gave with much
feeling. His lordship contented himself with a modest
share in the orchestra—performing on the kettle-
drums. We are told by invited visitors of the scru-
pulousness with which the host watched that his
cantatrice should not in any way shock the delicate

instincts of the company. She kept herself retired and spoke to no one. Once, indeed, a lady indiscreetly went up to her to compliment her on her singing of a sacred melody, but Lord Sandwich called a friend of hers, Mr. Cradock, aside, begging of him to speak to the lady and warn her against such behaviour; for, as he sagaciously observed, " once this sort of thing got in, we should have to give up our pleasant musical meetings." The kettle-drum would be silent. This went on for many years.

Miss Ray's portrait has been engraved, and presents rather an ordinary " common " face. Mr. Cradock, who has written some entertaining recollections, was on friendly terms with her, and she was encouraged, shortly before the unfortunate casualty, to open herself to him on a delicate matter—her "precarious" position in reference to his lordship—hinting that he might suggest what was called " a settlement." The gentleman, however, for obvious reasons, declined to interfere.

An officer in the 68th Regiment, named Hackman, had come to the neighbourhood of Huntingdon to recruit. While there he was invited out to Hitchinbrook and entertained by Lord Sandwich. He conceived a sort of insane passion for Miss Ray, who was about double his age. He was the son of a respectable tradesman in Cheapside, while the lady had been apprenticed to a Mrs. Fores, then a fashionable milliner. He was a young man of good address, " of a very pleasing figure and most engaging behaviour." He soon proposed marriage, but the lady told him plainly "she did not wish to carry a knapsack." In despair at being thus dismissed, he left the army, and, obtaining a living in Norfolk, took orders, hoping, no doubt, thus to secure a better provision. As he was still rejected, he determined on this act of violence. The morning, which was April 7th, he spent reading "Blair's Sermons," and dined with his sisters. He then wrote letters of the usual farewell kind, and lingered in one of the coffee-houses in Covent Garden till the play was over.

That old reprobate, Lord Sandwich, was deeply shocked at the event, and, it was said, did not recover it for years. He was once induced to go to a musical party, when a lady of good voice was asked to sing, which, it was reckoned, would have a soothing effect. The singer selected a song that was then popular, and, with admirable tact and *apropos*, "struck up," "*Shepherds, I have lost my love, Have you seen my body?*" Not unnaturally, the nobleman was seen to grow uncomfortable, and presently rising took leave of his hostess.

This catastrophe made a sensation, and moreover became oddly associated with other persons and incidents. Thus it engendered a violent altercation between Johnson and one of his friends, "which, having made much noise at the time, I think it proper, in order to prevent any future misrepresentation, to give a minute account of it." Thus Mr. Boswell tells us :—

"In talking of Hackman, Johnson argued, as Judge Blackstone had done, that his being furnished with two pistols was a proof that he meant to shoot two persons. Mr. Beauclerk said, 'No; for that every wise man who intended to shoot himself, took two pistols, that he might be sure of doing it at once. Lord ——'s cook shot himself with one pistol, and lived ten days in great agony. Mr. ——, who loved buttered muffins, but durst not eat them, because they disagreed with his stomach, resolved to shoot himself; and then he eat three buttered muffins for breakfast, before shooting himself, knowing that he should not be troubled with indigestion; *he* had two charged pistols; one was found lying charged upon the table by him, after he had shot himself with the other.'— 'Well (said Johnson, with an air of triumph), you see here one pistol was sufficient.' Beauclerk replied smartly, "Because it happened to kill him." And either then, or a very little afterwards, being piqued at Johnson's triumphant remark, added, 'This is what you don't know, and I do.' There was then a cessation of the dispute; and some minutes intervened, during which dinner and the glass went on cheerfully; when Johnson suddenly and abruptly exclaimed, 'Mr. Beauclerk, how came you to talk so petulantly to me, as, "This is what you don't know, but what I know?"

One thing *I* know, which *you* don't seem to know,
that you are very uncivil.' Beauclerk: 'Because *you*
began by being uncivil (which you always are).' The
words in parentheses were, I believe, not heard by Dr.
Johnson. Here again there was a cessation of arms.
A little while after this the conversation turned on
the violence of Hackman's temper. Johnson then
said, ' It was his business to *command* his temper, as
my friend, Mr. Beauclerk, should have done some time
ago.' Beauclerk: 'I should learn of *you*, sir.'
Johnson: ' Sir, you have given *me* opportunities
enough of learning when I have been in *your* company. No man loves to be treated with contempt.'
Beauclerk (with a polite inclination towards Johnson) :
' Sir, you have known me twenty years, and however
I may have treated others, you may be sure I could
never treat you with contempt.' Johnson : ' Sir,
you have said more than was necessary.' Thus it
ended."

More curious, however, was what happened to a
friend of the eccentric artist Barry, who used often to
relate the story. On the ill-omened night in question,
he was crossing from Islington, to call upon a brother
artist in Spa Fields towards the dusk, when he saw a
young woman throw herself into the New River, near
Sadler's Wells. He immediately ran to the spot, and
plunged in, when she seized him in the struggle of
death; and it was not only with difficulty that he

saved her, but himself, from drowning. Indeed, he was so exhausted, that he was pulled out by some persons brought to his assistance by his shouting for help.

From thence he went to his friend in Paradise Row, borrowed a change of dress, and procuring a hackney coach, desired to be driven home, when, proceeding up Gray's Inn Lane, the vehicle was stopped by a gang of footpads, who robbed him of his watch and money.

" Arriving at his house about ten o'clock, he took off his borrowed attire, and re-dressing, sent for another hack, and desired to be driven to the " Shakespeare," in the Piazza, Covent Garden, where he had engaged to sup with a party who were to meet there after the play. As his coach was drawing up at the corner of Russell Street, a gentleman's carriage whipped furiously in—for the play was just over—and upset him, when he cut his hands and face with the glass. " The devil!—what next? " he exclaimed, as he paid the driver, who " hoped his honour was not seriously hurt." " No," said he, " I am only scratched ; " and making his way, his face streaming with blood, at a quick pace, towards the coffee-house, to procure surgical aid, he had only advanced a few yards, when a pistol was exploded close to his ear, and a lady fell at his feet. He stood aghast, when instantly another was fired by a young man at his own devoted head.

Scared out of his wits at such a succession of strange disasters, he flew to the house of a friend in King Street, and for some minutes was so overcome with amazement that he could not collect himself sufficiently to relate to the astonished family the tragic accidents which had driven him thither."

A strange book appeared, called "Love and Madness," written or compiled by Sir Herbert Croft, and which had a large sale. In this it is difficult to distinguish the genuine from the imaginary portion, and it was said that the author had come into possession of some of the unfortunate man's letters and papers.

A well-known figure in the last generation was Mr. Basil Montagu, who was the son of the murdered singer, and whose daughter is the accomplished and lamented poetess, Adelaide Proctor.

Hackman was tried at the next Old Bailey Sessions, and of course was found guilty. He made a studied speech, *ad misericordiam*, declaring himself to be " the most wretched of human beings;" but that he had conceived his murderous plan " only in a moment of phrenzy." At the execution the intrusive Boswell was present, actually obtaining a seat in the mourning coach, beside the prisoner, and a good place on the scaffold !

§ *A second Jonathan Wild.*

The line of villainy taken by Wild had at least the merit of originality, and was celebrated with

happy sarcasm, and an analysis of the roguish mind
and motives that is even happier. It is strange to
find that not many years after Mr. Wild's public
death, a successful copyist of his method arose, who
pursued his career unchecked for some years. This
gentleman was one James Bolland, and his system
was exactly modelled on that of Wild's, viz.,
to employ the law as an aid to his own particular
villainies. He was the son of a Whitechapel butcher,
and had opened an establishment on his own account.
But being much thrown with bailiffs, thief-takers, &c.,
their trade seemed to have a greater fascination for
him than his own, and he speedily determined to adopt
it. An awkward discovery of his practice in business
probably contributed to his change of profession. He
supplied the old St. Thomas's Hospital with meat, and
to increase his profits adopted a 56 lb. weight, which,
though in appearance like its iron fellows, was made
of *wood*, and weighed but 7 lbs. This happy and
original idea would have done credit to Mr. Wild.
" His journeyman," we are told, and again I fancy by
Sir John, from the Fielding-like touches, " observing
this and similar deceptions, thought he might re-
taliate on his master by defrauding him of his cash."
So, by a happy compensation, the profits brought
in by the wooden 7 lbs. weight were subtracted in
another shape. At this stage of our hero's career,
it is remarked incidentally that, " owing to his ill-

usage, his wife fell a victim to grief and despair."
Mr. Bolland next succeeded in becoming a sheriff's
officer, and set up "a spunging house" near St.
George's, Southwark. Here he found large and varied
opportunities for his ingenuity. He had a peculiar art,
or gift, of griping and entangling the miserable
class of debtors who fell under his control. He
squeezed them dry, as it were, and yet contrived that
it should be more or less their own act. " He had
at his nod a number of watchmen, who, being his
prisoners and out upon parole, were compelled to do
all his dirty work in negotiating bills and bailing
at command. This practice," it was quaintly added,
" soon brought many of them to a prison, where
they are now lodged, probably for life." Others
were despatched into various parts of the country, to
execute orders upon the credit of those in town.
Young fellows of a comely aspect, who fell into his
clutches, obtained a temporary liberty in order to
defraud tradesmen, and, by increasing his stock of
furniture and plate, they increased their debts to such
a pitch that they became incapable ever after to
extricate themselves.

When no more was to be got, they were instantly
despatched to the prison. With this trade he united
that of a horse-dealer, bill-discounter, and indeed any
nominal calling that would help him to plunder. At
a fair at Oxford he wished to purchase a horse from

a farmer, but would not agree as to the price. Going to the inn where the horse was stabled, he told the landlord he had bought it, and rode it up to London. The farmer followed, and applied at the police-office, on which Sir John issued his warrant, and sent the thief to Tothill Fields Prison. The crafty fellow, however, speedily invited the farmer to see him, and " over a cheerful glass " speedily came to an arrangement, and obtained his release.

A pleasant instance of his villainy was furnished by his treatment of a young Irish gentleman, who, having " run through " his property in town, found himself under Mr. Bolland's care. The latter, assuming an air of good-natured *bonhomie*, declared it was a pity and a shame to see a fine young fellow deprived of his liberty for a trifle, and suggested that if he had any friend on whom he could draw for a sum of money he would take it, and let him go. The young man accordingly " drew " on some of his friends in Ireland for 30*l*.—about double the debt—and Mr. Bolland gave his note for the difference. He then set the prisoner free, but a few days later invited him and his friend to supper, when he told him that his note had come back unpaid.

However, the glass went round cheerfully, and when the guests proposed going Mr. Bolland very amicably acquainted them that he had writs against them both, and they were compelled to remain his involuntary guests for the night. Next day the pair, seeing it was useless to contend with him, procured the money; but they reminded him that he had a note of theirs for 13*l.* "What note, sir? I never gave you one." "There it is, sir, in your own writing." "Aye! aye! let us see it." They eagerly presented it; he tore it in pieces, still persisting it was all a mistake.

More cruel was his treatment of a sea-captain's wife, whose furniture, in her absence, he seized on. She was so affected that in her agitation she set the house on fire. The captain had paid the debt. She was tried, convicted, and respited, " upon the face of the affair appearing so uncommonly aggravating." Soon after the husband came home from sea, and in order to distress him and prevent his commencing an action Mr. Bolland contrived to have him arrested for a considerable sum. "We need not be surprised," runs the chronicle, "at Mr. Bolland's perseverance in these knavish pursuits, as he did not even lay claim to any probity, for whenever his integrity was called in question by any of his employers, he would reply with great coolness, ' Look you, sir! You know I do not pretend to be honest, but try. I'll never tell you a lie!' Another sentiment of this extraordinary man should not be omitted, as it carries with it an appearance of being prophetic. Whenever he was asked for a toast in company, the first he gave always was, 'May hemp bind those whom honour won't,' which is quite in Mr.

Wild's own manner, and uncommonly like the Fielding style.

When the office of City Marshal was vacant, this worthy man offered himself as a candidate. After a spirited bidding—for it was purchaseable—he was declared the highest bidder, and gleefully deposited his deposit—a sum of 2400*l.*—scraped together by a most hideous course of villainies. But this was found rather *trop fort*, and he was told that it was impossible to appoint a person of his description. He threatened an action, but wisely forebore proceedings against the Corporation of London, and proceeded reluctantly to withdraw his deposit. But here a happy stroke of retribution overtook him. Certain creditors whom he had defrauded had got wind of the matter, and obtained an order impounding the deposit. At the same time he was overtaken by justice, and for a very trifling peccadillo—at least compared with his previous enormities—lost his life. Raising money on a bill, he put a fictitious endorsement on it at the request of the discounter, " J. Banks ;" was tried, found guilty, and hung, to the great satisfaction of the community and of his many victims.

§ *The Perreaus.*

On a Saturday evening on the 11th March, 1775, Mr. Addington, the Bow Street magistrate, was asked by a respectable man to hear his complaint against a

woman, who, he said, had given him a forged bond for
7500*l.* The woman denied this ; and the pair recrimi-
nated and upbraided one another. From which the
shrewd magistrate argued that both had a share in the
offence, if offence there was, and sent them both off to
prison to wait further inquiries. The man was an eminent
apothecary or medical practitioner living in Golden
Square, Robert Perreau by name ; the woman a notorious Mrs. Rudd. Robert's brother Daniel came to see
him in his trouble, but found himself detained in the
prison, under suspicion of being engaged in the business.
It came out that in the January previous Robert Perreau
had gone to Drummonds, the bankers, where he was
known, to borrow 1500*l.* for ten days, which he obtained
on the security of the lease of a house in Harley Street.
The ten days, however, stretched out to two months,
when he again appeared with a proposal to borrow no
less a sum than 7500*l.* on a bond of a well-known gentleman, Mr. William Adair, and out of which the Drummonds were to be repaid the original loan. When the
bond was examined, Mr. Drummond expressed some
doubts as to the signature. One of the partners coming
in, also doubted. He was directed to call next day, and
in the interval consulted friends of Adair, who assured
him that it was not his writing. An intimate friend
named Dr. Brooke had been victimized to the amount of
1500*l.*, lent on a forged bond for 3100*l.* The trial of the

two brothers which followed excited extraordinary interest. It was firmly believed they were the innocent victims of this scheming, artful demirep, Mrs. Margaret Rudd, who had contrived to make them believe that these deeds were genuine. This theory was ridiculous. Such credulousness does not affect persons in sore straits and difficulties, who from experience find how difficult it is to procure money; especially as they knew the character of their female associate.

This woman, who was good-looking, clever, and interesting, became a heroine. When Perreau came again, the banker told him he was afraid he had been imposed upon, and suggested that they should go to Mr. Adair himself and ask him, was it his signature? That gentleman at once declared it to be a forgery, on which Mr. Perreau smiled incredulously. The bond was detained, and Perreau was followed, when he was observed to join his brother and Mrs. Rudd. When it was seen that the trio were gathering all their valuables and had got into a coach, evidently to make their escape, suspicion became certainty. The party were arrested, brought before Sir John at Bow Street, where the examination took place. Other charges were then made, it being found that sums of 4000*l.* and 5000*l.* had been raised on similar forged deeds. What was more heartless, and not the least skilful of Mrs. Rudd's proceedings was the adroit fashion in which she contrived to extricate herself by taking advantage of the critical situation of the brothers. She lived with Daniel Perreau, and had three children. She now came forward and offered herself as evidence for the crown. Strange to say, by this disagreeable spectacle of treachery there was no disgust aroused : everybody crowded to see the interesting " King's evidence," who declared that " she was the daughter of a nobleman in Scotland, had married an officer, that she had a reserve of jewels and 13,000*l.*, all of which she gave to Perreau, whom she had always loved tenderly, though latterly he had grown peevish, uneasy, and much altered to her. He had cruelly constrained her to sign the bond in question by holding a knife to her throat, swearing he would murder her if she did not comply ; that, being struck with remorse, she had informed Mr. Adair of the whole." Mr. Drummond, however, described an interview with her in which she took the whole forgery on herself, and, on his doubting that she could be skilful enough, she took up a paper and wrote Mr. Adair's signature, exactly like the one which appeared on the bond. The defence was ingenious ; that the woman had always acted as intermediary and carried on her operations without allowing Perreau to see Adair. It should be mentioned that the business was further complicated by the fact of the two brothers being twins, so like as to be scarcely distinguishable. Another incident of the case was the number of persons of rank who deposed to the character of Daniel Perreau—Sir John Moore, General Rebow, Lady Lumsden, who declared " she would as soon have thought of committing a forgery herself as of supposing that Mr. Perreau was capable of such a thing." Both brothers were found guilty and sentenced to be hung. Immense exertions were made to save them. No less than seventy-eight leading bankers and merchants petitioned the king. Paragraphs filled the newspapers, all to the one tune that the brothers " were the dupes of a designing woman." Their extraordinary fraternal affection—often found in the case of twins—excited universal sympathy. Yet it is impossible to read the evidence without feeling convinced that as men of business they must have at least known that such sums could not have passed lawfully or without connivance and co-operation on their part.

While their fate was in suspense, it was determined to put Mrs. Rudd herself on trial, for it seems that at the time, the law was not settled as to the immunity granted to " approvers." Here was another entertainment for the public, who were immensely excited by the charms and demeanour of this lady. The interest was developed to a tragic degree when it was known that the unfortunate wife, Mrs. Robert Perreau was to appear and be examined, so as to do something to neutralize the woman's evidence and try and save one so dear. The responsibility of such a situation was almost awful. Mr. Angelo was present and thus reports the dramatic scene :—

" Mrs. Rudd's counsellors," he says, " were said to have managed her defence with uncommon exertion and skill. On the day of her trial, the court was crowded to excess. Being there early by favour of Mr. Reynolds, the clerk of the arraigns, I obtained a station near her, at the bar. She was in person of the middle size, with small but beautiful features, and very fair. She looked pale, and appeared much affected. Such was her address, that no one could have discovered in her manner the least consciousness of that deep-designing wickedness, which had wrought the ruin of these unhappy brothers, and destroyed the peace of a once happy and virtuous family.

" During her trial, Mrs. Perreau was placed in the evidence box, to endeavour by circumstances which she knew, to exculpate her husband, and to inculpate the wicked woman at the bar, the seductress of her husband and his brother, then tried and convicted prisoners in Newgate; but, being cross-examined by Counsellor Davy, and, as it was thought, with too little delicacy towards the feelings of a lady in her pitiable condition, she was so entirely overwhelmed that she burst into an agony of tears, and was carried out of court in a state of insensibility. As the jury returned, the prisoner fixed her fascinating eyes upon the jury-box, when the conduct of the foreman, a well-known gay

auctioneer, did not escape observation ; for by a smile,
which he significantly glanced towards her, many anticipated the verdict. She was acquitted."[1]

[1] A grotesque farcical incident is associated with these tragic
events.

"Among others," Angelo tells us, "who exerted themselves for the
doctor, was the late Thomas Tomkins, of Sermon Lane, the most
celebrated penman that this or any other country had produced.
Richard Wilson, the landscape painter, Henderson, the comedian,
with some others, constant evening cronies at the " Shakspeare," were
discussing the question of the King's prerogative some weeks before
Dr. Dodd's execution, in the coffee-room there. Tomkins was at the
moment exhibiting a large sheet of vellum, on which the head to Dr.
Dodd's petition was written, in Roman capitals, round-hand, italics,
German-text, and all the varieties of which his pen was so prolific ;
and so wrapt was the good man, with the importance of his handy-
work, that he insisted, with the addition of a tasteful allegorical
design of Cipriani's or Mortimer's, of Mercy and Justice, with their
respective attributes, placed around this superlative specimen of his
art, it could not fail to move the Sovereign. Wilson, though at this
time as gloomy, from his own misfortunes, as man could well be, was so
involuntarily and suddenly wrought upon by this extravagant self-com-
plaisance of the penman, that he roared with laughter. 'To think
of moving the King and his council by a pen and a picture !—Ha !—
ha !—ha !' In this cynical mood, he appealed to every one who
entered the tavern, all of whom caught his fit of risibility, so as to
render the scene truly of the tragic-comic character. Tomkins, however, highly offended at this insult to his self-importance, hastily
rolled up the parchment and took himself off. Tomkins, who had
never seen Dr. Dodd, on hearing of the vast exertions that were
making to obtain subscribers' names to the petition, went to Newgate
and introducing himself to the prisoner, offered to write the prologue
to the lists to be laid at the feet of the King, which lists were written
on several score yards of parchment, and joined together. This offer
was gratefully accepted by the doctor, and the penman, as is said,

Mrs. Rudd had a particular admirer in the person of Mr. James Boswell, who got introduced to her, attracted, he told his friend Johnson, by her address and irresistible powers of fascination. The Sage himself went so far as to declare that he envied his friend this privilege, and added that he also would have sought her acquaintance only for the fear of its getting into the newspapers. The sly Boswell altogether concealed from his friend the extent to which he followed up his introduction.

The first victims to the law, making forgery a capital offence, were these unhappy brothers. " Had the crime of the Perreaus been anything less than forgery, they might have escaped ; but the stern and inflexible counsels of Lord Chancellor Thurlow stopped the current of compassion in the breasts of the Privy Council ; and the Sovereign, notwithstanding the mildness of his nature, was prevailed upon to let the law take its course."

The assumed necessity for this severity was opposed to the extraordinary exertions made for the sparing of Dr. Dodd. Hence, the execution of the Perreaus was held to be so irrevocable a precedent, that there was no possibility of departing from it, Lord Thurlow having said, with his accustomed force, " If Dr. Dodd

inspired by the importance of the subject, produced, on a large sheet of vellum, the most elegant specimen of caligraphy that ever was seen."

be saved, the Perreaus have been murdered." There was also another forgery case, that of William Wynne Ryland, the celebrated engraver ; and it cannot escape observation that these memorable forgeries succeeded each other so nearly. The Perreaus suffered in 1776 ; Dr. Dodd, in 1777 ; and William Wynne Ryland in 1783.

In spite of all efforts, the brothers were ordered for execution. Angelo, before quoted, who took interest in all existing events in the town, has given a curious and interesting account of the unwholesome excitement that attended such " hanging days," and which contrasts with the complete exclusion, in our own times, of the public from such horrors.

" Generally, an execution day at Tyburn was considered by various classes as a public holiday. The malefactors, being exposed thus publicly through the main street for three miles, it was supposed, would tend to morality by deterring many who were witnesses of the agony of the miserable culprits, from the perpetration of those vices which had brought them to their pitiable fate. This, however, was at length discovered to be a mistaken policy, for these cruel spectacles drew thousands from their lawful occupations, and emptied the manufactories and workshops."

The amusing though garrulous fencing-master, goes on : " At an early hour on the morning of an execution, thousands of mechanics and others who had on the previous night agreed upon the making a ' *day of it*,' met at their proposed stations. It was common throughout the whole metropolis for master coach-makers, framemakers, tailors, shoemakers, and others who had engaged to complete orders within a given time, to bear in mind to observe to their customers, ' that will be a hanging-day, and my men will not be at work.' There were also various grades of amateurs of these sights, both high and low, whose ardour in the pursuit excited them to know and to see the whole appertaining to the scene from the first examination of the prisoner at Sir John Fielding's office in Bow Street, to his exit at ' fatal Tyburn tree.' Foote, speaking of some prominent characters of this class, designated them, ' The Hanging Committee.' Mr. George Selwyn and another wit, the famed Duke of Montague, were two distinguished members of this coterie ; and a much respected nobleman, who frequented my father's *manége*, to gratify this *penchant* was said to have attended at the Tower in the capacity of a barber to perform the operation of shaving one of the Scottish rebel lords during their confinement, a few days previous to their being beheaded on Tower Hill.

" Another nobleman, a great patron of the arts, was present, by favour, at most of the private examinations in Bow Street, in the memorable days of old Sir John Fielding, and frequently went to Newgate in disguise to see extraordinary characters whilst under sentence of death. Thomas Warton, the poet, was one of the most ardent amateurs of these spectacles. When he was absent from Trinity, and inquiries were made as for what part of the world he had suddenly departed, those who knew his propensity would refer the inquirer to the public accounts of the progress of the judges. An execution took place after the Oxford assizes, of a man for sheep-stealing, whilst the poet was absent. On his return to College, one of the Fellows told him of the event with exultation, and reminded him of the loss of so interesting a sight. ' I knew of it,' replied Warton, ' but I have been into a neighbouring county where a man was hanged for murder ! '

" Those of the lower grade who were most eager for these sights, early in the morning surrounded the felons' gate at Newgate to see the malefactors brought forth, and who received nosegays at St. Sepulchre's. Others appeared at various stations and fell into the ranks according to convenience; hence, the crowd accumulating on the cavalcade reaching St. Giles, the throng was occasionally so great as to entirely fill Oxford Street from house to house on both sides of the way when the pressure became tremendous within half a mile of Tyburn. The Old Bailey, Newgate Street, from St. Sepulchre's Church, Snow Hill, and Holborn, as high as Furnival's Inn, on some of these occasions, were filled with one dense mass of spectators.

" Nothing can be conceived more impressing than the solemn manner in which the unhappy criminals were received by the multitude. At the execution of Dr. Dodd, my station, with a late distinguished member of Parliament, and a celebrated author, was at a window of the late Mr. Langdale's, the distiller. The unfortunate malefactor was permitted to go in a mourning coach. His corpse-like appearance produced an awful picture of human woe. Tens of thousands of hats, which formed a black mass, as the coach advanced, were taken off simultaneously, and so many tragic faces, exhibited a spectacle, the effect of which is beyond the power of words to describe. Thus the procession travelled onwards, through the multitude, whose silence added to the awfulness of the scene. The two Perreaus, Dr. Dodd, and Ryland, in consequence of their previous respectability, were indulged with mourning coaches, in which they proceeded from Newgate to Tyburn. A hearse, containing the coffin, to receive the body of the malefactor, also formed part of the procession. The Reverend Mr. Hackman was also permitted to go to the same place of execution in a mourning coach.

" Ryland I knew from my boyhood ; he and Gwynn, the painter, were frequently at Carlisle House. My father, who went to offer his condolence to Mrs. Ryland, used to declare, that the scene presented by her and her children on this occasion was so pathetic that he could not sleep for several nights; until his imagination became so entirely possessed with the wretched group, that he feared to retire to his bed.

"Poor Ryland! After his condemnation he petitioned for a respite, which was not only granted for the time required, but renewed. The circumstance which urged him to this, excited universal sympathy. He made this request to enable him to finish a very fine engraving which he had begun, the last of a series, from the paintings of Angelica Kauffman, and I believe the subject was Queen Eleanor sucking the poison from the arm of her royal consort, King Edward the First. However that may be, he was indulged with the permission, as he alleged that his object was not to prolong his wretched existence, but to enable his wife, after his decease, by this addition to his stock of plates, to add to her support, and that of his fatherless children. It is said that he laboured incessantly at this his last work, and that when he received from his printer, *Haddril*, who was the first in his line, the finished proof impression, he calmly said, 'Mr. Haddril, I thank you, my task is now accomplished;' and resigning himself to his fate was executed within a week from that day.

" Ryland was a man of extraordinary self-command. I recollect, immediately after the discovery of the forgery, large placards being posted all over the town, offering a sum of five hundred pounds for his apprehension. He first secreted himself, as was believed, in the

Minories, and though he was cautioned by his friends
to remain in his hiding-place, yet, after a few days'
confinement, he could not resist his desire to take a
walk, after dusk, though he knew of the placards and
the reward offered. Thus determined, he put on a seaman's dreadnought, and otherwise disguised, set off,
and wandered about, for a considerable time, when,
returning across Little Tower Hill, a man eyed him
attentively, passed, and repassed him, and turning short
round, exclaimed, ' So, you are the very man I am seeking.' Ryland, betraying not the least emotion, stopped
short, faced him, and returned, ' Perhaps you are mistaken in your man, sir ; I do not know you.' The
stranger immediately apologised, owned his mistake,
wished the refugee good-night, and then they parted.

"Another instance of this self-command and presence
of mind occurred at the India House, when he presented his forged bond for payment, for the sum of
three or four thousand pounds, on a large sheet of
paper, one face of which was nearly covered with signatures. The cashier, on receiving the document,
examined it carefully, and referred to the ledger ; then,
comparing the date, observed, ' Here is a mistake, sir;
the bond as entered, does not become due until to-
morrow.'

" Ryland begging permission to look at the book, on
its being handed to him, observed, ' So I perceive—
there must be an error in your entry of one day ; ' and

offered to leave the bond, not betraying the least disappointment or surprise. The mistake appearing to the cashier to be obviously an error in his office, the bond was paid to Ryland, who departed with the money. The next day the true bond was presented, when the forgery was discovered, of course; and, within a few hours after, the fraud was made public, and steps were taken for the discovery of the perpetrator.

" This document, lately in the possession of a gentleman, now deceased, I have often seen. It is, perhaps, the most extraordinary piece of deceptive art, in the shape of imitation, that was ever produced. There are, speaking from recollection, thirty or more signatures, in hands of various styles, and in letters of as various dimensions; some being in a large and flourishing letter, others in a cramped, and some in a small hand, as well as inks of different degrees of blackness; the whole so wonderfully imitated, that it appeared, as well on the trial as subsequently, that not one, whose name was inserted in the bond, could have ventured to swear that it was not his own veritable signature.

" Mrs. Ryland, the widow of this unhappy artist, for some years after his decease, kept a print-shop in Oxford Street. Ryland was the first who engraved successfully in the dotted style. Those plates which he executed from the designs of Angelica Kauffman, were of a circular form, and printed in a red colour.

They were greatly admired, and are still considered among the most beautiful productions of the kind."

Thus far for the principal experiences of this magistrate. We shall now turn to his exertions, and to the fruits of those exertions which were to be displayed in quite another direction.

CHAPTER IV.

THE BOW STREET FORCES.

§ *The Patroles.*

To Sir John Fielding the public was indebted for the introduction of a useful check on highway robbery, so simple and obvious in character that it is astonishing it was not suggested before his time. Knowing the unprotected state of the roads in the environs of the city, the notorious Hounslow, Blackheath, and the unguarded commons, his energetic mind conceived the idea of an organized force, which, however small, would still furnish protection. A few men, well armed, patrolling the lonely roads, and meeting each other at fixed points, was the idea that presented itself. It took its rise in what was rather ambitiously styled THE PATROLE, which, beginning as a very small force, later developed into an important and efficient body of men. At its origin it consisted of thirteen " parties," each with a " conductor ;" that is, eight

" country parties " and five " town parties." The blind
magistrate took a particular interest in this force of
his own invention, and was always eager for its exten-
sion. This plan was found to be of extraordinary
benefit; but he received support for it in so grudging
a fashion, that we find him pleading, as if for a
personal favour to himself, for a continuation of
assistance, even for the useful horse-patrole :—

" Sir J. Fielding presents his most respectful compliments to Mr. Jenkinson, and in consequence of what
has passed with him this morning, begs he will do him
the honour to acquaint Mr. Grenville that his application for the continuance of the horse-patrole for a short
time longer, as a temporary, but necessary, step, in
order to complete that which had been so happily
begun. . . . He flatters himself that from the amazing
good effects this patrole has already had by bringing so
many old offenders to justice, that a little further
assistance of this kind may be sufficient to prevent
these outrages from arising to a great height for a
considerable time."

So successful was this plan of "a patrole" found that
it was extended, in different shapes, under other
magistrates. It is a popular delusion that until the
advent of the New Police the safety of London was
entrusted to the incapable " Charlies," or watchmen,
who were supposed to perform their duties by constantly sleeping in their watch-boxes. But, in truth,

there was an efficient body of patroles, mounted and on foot, who kept careful watch upon the roads while others looked after the streets. A more particular account of this force will be found interesting. The "Bow Street Horse-Patrole" was not established until the year 1805, by Sir Richard Ford, who was then chief magistrate. He himself undertook the direction of it. In that year highway robberies in the various country roads leading to London became very frequent, and this practical mode of checking the abuse was adopted. Their uniform was an odd one, consisting of a leathern hat, blue coat with yellow metal buttons, blue trousers and boots, with the invariable scarlet waistcoat, while they were "armed to the teeth" with cutlass, pistols, and a truncheon. They were all splendidly mounted, and were indeed awkward customers to encounter on the high and cross roads. They were retired cavalry soldiers, received 28s. a week as pay, and in the year 1828 amounted to no more than fifty-four men, with six inspectors. It is astonishing to think that this modest force should have been able to watch over the innumerable high roads that converge on London; but it is agreed they did their duty with wonderful efficiency. The whole cost did not exceed 16,000l. a year.

The duties of this force were carried out in this fashion. They came on their "beat" at five or seven in the evening, according to the season, beginning at

a distance of about five miles from London, and proceeding from five to ten miles, until after midnight,
when they went home. The officer was directed to
make himself known to all persons he met in carriages or on horseback by calling out in a loud and
clear tone, " Bow Street Patrole ! " The highwaymen were much disturbed by their operations, and we
constantly hear of captures and encounters. The
force was under the personal direction of one of the
Bow Street magistrates, to whom it reported, and
from whom it received instructions.

So efficient was this found that it was soon determined to add to it another, which was oddly named
" The Police Dismounted Horse-Patrole," whose duty
it was to protect the road lying between the beat of
the horse-patrole and the city. This body was
organized on a different system. They were divided
into parties, each with a conductor, which patrolled a
regular district of its own. Their uniform was the
same as that of the horse-patrole, and they were armed
with pistol, truncheon, and cutlass, and, of course,
displayed the invariable scarlet waistcoat.

To these motley and heterogeneous bands Mr. Peel,
in 1822, added yet another, which was called the
" Day Patrole," and which seems to have been a mere
roving body that could only hope by some rare chance
to be of any service, for the whole body consisted of
but twenty-four men and three inspectors. In 1821

it was ordered by Lord Sidmouth that, in consequence of the numerous robberies that had taken place in the public streets and squares, the services of the night patrole should be confined altogether to the city, which was accordingly divided into sixteen districts, each with a conductor. But the whole force did not exceed some eighty men. But these were merely the preventive element. The Bow Street authorities relied more directly on another kind of assistance, and which was concerned entirely in the work of detection.

§ *The Bow Street Runners.*

In fiction as well as in reality the dramatic element nearly always was supplied by the " Bow Street Runner," popularly supposed to be a miracle of detective skill; though indeed, at the beginning of the century, the establishment at Bow Street for the detection of crime, was of a character that would have made a modern policeman smile. The business of inquiry, pursuit, and arrest of criminals, was conducted by a few " officers," not more than eight in number. Each of these, however, had, from practice and training, acquired skill, and was so trained in the peculiar school or system of Jonathan Wild, that he was equivalent to a host of constables. The " Bow Street runner," as he was called, was a name of terror to the burglar and thief, and their red waistcoats were familiar everywhere. " Their ensign of office," says one writer, " was a tiny baton with a gilt crown on the top ; but malefactors knew perfectly well that their pockets held pistols as well as handcuffs, and that a ' Robin Redbreast ' of Bow Street was as bold as his volatile namesake. In the time of Sir Richard Birnie the ' Robin Redbreasts ' numbered a dozen : to wit, old Townsend and Sayer, and ten officers under these, among whom the most prominent were Ruthven, Taunton, Salmon, Leadbitter, and Gawner."

The most celebrated of these men was the well-known Townsend, who was besides a " character " in his way. He and his companions were employed in all sorts of duties, and told off for any emergency, for there appears to have been no rule or system. They attended at court, at races, and on all special occasions. They also enjoyed various perquisites and presents from those whose property they recovered. Mr. Charles Dickens, though he was an enthusiastic admirer of the modern police, has presented a rather unflattering portrait, in his " Oliver Twist," of the Bow Street runners. When Mrs. Maylie's house was broken into by Sikes, two officers were sent down.

" ' Open the door,' cried a man, ' it's the officers from Bow Street.' Brittles opened the door to its full width, and confronted a portly man in a great coat, who walked in without saying anything more, and wiped his shoes on the mat as coolly as if he lived there.

" The man who had knocked at the door was a stout personage of middle height, aged about fifty, with shiny black hair cropped pretty close, half whiskers, a round face, and sharp eyes. The other was a red-headed, bony man, in top-boots, with a rather ill-favoured countenance and a turned-up, sinister-looking nose.

" ' Tell your governor Blathers and Duff is here, will you ?' "

These visitors proved themselves, according to "Boz," a very incapable, weak-kneed pair, for they accepted the story prepared by the family as to Oliver, whose presence on the premises, shot as he had been, required accounting for. They were given to long stories, and readers will recall their account of " Conky Chickweed." [1]

---

[1] The same delightful writer has left us a sketch of the office and the magistrate. The " Mr. Fang," of whom so odious a picture is given, did not belong to Bow Street. His real name was Lang, and Dickens went specially to draw him, and it is said thus caused him to resign. When the " Dodger's " career was cut short, and he was brought up at Bow Street, one of his friends and admirers attended to see how he behaved. Here was the scene. " He found himself jostled among a crowd of people, chiefly women, who were huddled together in a dirty, frowsy room, at the upper end of which was a raised platform, railed off from the rest, with a dock for the prisoners on the left hand against the wall, a box for his witnesses in the middle, a desk for the magistrates on the right, the awful locality last named being screened off by a partition which concealed the

Much petted as was Townsend, and profound as was
the belief in his sagacity, one is inclined to suspect
that he was something of an impostor. He seems
to have impressed every one—thieves included—with
an idea of his infinite experience, a belief he was
enabled to encourage by a good memory and a useful
knack of remembering faces. He cultivated an
acquaintance with thieves and their places of resort,
and by some lucky *coups* added to his prestige. The
pleasant Angelo, before quoted, who knew " all sorts
and conditions of men," shall introduce him :—

" The last time I went to a masquerade was at the
Pantheon, which must have been nearly thirty years
ago. I went in a domino, keeping my mask on, and
after near an hour wandering about, at length I met
with one whom I had known many years, dressed in
a domino, with his mask on, and his portly figure
soon discovered him to me. This was my old and
very pleasant *slang* friend, Townsend, of Bow Street
memory. Well met, arm-in-arm, we paraded together
until the supper-rooms opened. ' Now,' said he,
' I'll show you some fun, only stop, when we soon

bench from the common gaze. The room smelt close and unwholesome, the walls were dirt-discoloured, and the ceiling
blackened. There was an old smoky bust over the mantelshelf,.
and a dirty clock above the dock, the only thing that seemed
to go on as it ought." Every one will recall the Dodger's pleasant
familiarities.

shall see the *coves* and *motts* fall to *grub;* they'll then
doff their sham phizzes. You'll see I shall soon un-
kennel them.' Having such a *protégé*, I kept close
to him; though I have enjoyed many a masquerade
adventure, this was a superior treat to me. He kept
his word; for the very first room we entered he had
something to say of the parties. At supper, between
two ladies, was an elegant-looking young man, in
regimentals and black domino; he had a handsome
cut-steel button and loop to his hat, which was surmounted by a lofty plumage. He was just touching
his glass to his two fair companions, when my intelligent *conducteur* went behind him, and tapped him on
the shoulder.

" ' Come, be off.' ' Mr. Townsend,' said the would-
be captain, ' don't take me from my bub and grub.'
Townsend, however, with great good-nature, suffered
him to remain, but as he was a notorious character
the myrmidons of the police kept an eye upon him.
In the course of the evening, to my surprise, I had
many individuals, gentlemen of the ' conveying fraternity,' pointed out to me, whom, from their genteel
appearance, I considered to be men of fashion; indeed, some of them I had spoken to, as coffee-house
acquaintance. Many years ago, at the Opera House,
when it was the fashion, between the acts, to go
behind the scenes, Townsend was always to be seen
there, and many of the sprigs of fashion used to

Drawn, Etch'd & Pub'd by Dighton, Char'g Cross, Dec'r 1, 1805

The TOWNS-END.

crowd round (for he was a general favourite), with
'How are you, Townsend? what's the go?' when
with good-humour he would indulge their fancy,
answering them in such a manner (knowing their
drift to get him into conversation) that the greater
part he said was quite unintelligible to them.

"Once, however, my witty acquaintance, Townsend,
met with his match behind the scenes in the Haymarket, as an individual was present who seemed to
know the whole slang vocabulary by heart, and the
conversation highly delighted a number of persons
who stood round to listen. The gentleman to whom I
allude, was an officer of the Guards, on duty there that
night. Though Townsend was *up to it*, the officer
certainly was *down upon him*, to the great amusement
of the listeners, and the former was scarcely able to
keep pace with him."

Townsend, from his long experience, and the
select duties in which he was employed, became a
" privileged " person, and, as it is called, " quite a
character." A chronicler, who had seen a great deal
of "life," named Richardson, has left us a not very
favourable account of him. "This man," he tells us,
"who was said to have commenced life as a coster-
monger, became by effrontery and impudence, enhanced by a certain share of low cunning and low
wit, the head of his profession. He derived a large
income from the Christmas boxes of the nobility and

of other parties at whose routs he was employed to detect, or keep away, improper characters, who, he persuaded his patrons would be present if *he* were not in attendance. As to his personal appearance, he was a very smart little man, clean as paint, to use his own phrase, and I think peculiar in his costume. He was generally encased in a light and loud suit, knee-breeches, and short gaiters, and a white hat of great breadth of brim. Once, when he was bathing near Millbank, some thieves maliciously stole his clothes, and it was said he was compelled to run home in the state he emerged from the water. At his death it was reported that he had made accumulations from the guinea a day at the bank, the nobility, the money from prosecutions, &c., to the amount of 20,000*l.* He was often seen in familiar conversation with George III., whose good-humoured face was convulsed with laughter at his stories."

Captain Gronow tells us that " He was a sort of privileged person, and could say what he liked." On one occasion the Duke of Clarence recommended Townsend to publish his memoirs, " which he thought would be very interesting." Townsend, who had become somewhat deaf, seemed rather surprised, but said he would obey H.R.H.'s commands. A few weeks afterwards Townsend was on duty at Carlton House, when the Duke asked him if he had fulfilled his promise. His answer was—

" Oh, sir, you've got me into a devil of a scrape!
I had begun to write my *amours*, as you desired,
when Mrs. Townsend caught me in the act of writing
them, and swore she'd be revenged; for you know,
your Royal Highness, 1 was obliged to divulge many
secrets about women, for which she'll never forgive
me."

When the Duke became king, on a memorable
occasion, in a fit of anger, he swore he would order a
hackney-coach to go to the House. Upon which
Townsend, to the amazement of every one, cried out
from behind a screen,—

" Well said, sir; I think your Majesty is d——d
right."

The King, much surprised and amused, called out,—
" Is that you, Townsend ? "

" *Yes, sir; I am here to see that your Majesty has
fair play !* "

At an installation of the Knights of the Garter,
the then Duchess of Northumberland was fain to
put herself under his protection, and accept his arm,
" as he conducted her *through a mob of nobles and
others,* to her place in the chapel."

From an account of him, given in a ' Trip to
Ascot,' we learn how he was led to the profession.
" Originally he was fond of hearing the trials at the
Old Bailey, and also of *noting* down in a book persons
who were acquitted, and likewise those found guilty,

with their sentences, &c., by which means he became a sort of oracle at ' the *Start*,' and obtained the title of ' Counsellor Double Head.' His superiority of information respecting the thieves and other bad characters in the metropolis, thus obtained by his assiduity and attention, gave him a certain notoriety, which soon made its way to the *listeners* of the *beaks*, and our hero accordingly was appointed to the situation of a police officer. The *slouched* castor, the open breeches at the knees, the short jacket, the *fogle* loosely twisted round his *squeeze*, the large *wedge* broach, the long-quartered shoe and silver buckles, the bit of myrtle in his *gig*, and the cut altogether of a ' *rolling kiddy* ' was banished for the more reputable appearance of a smart *Trap*.

" Townsend soon proved himself a most active officer ; and his *name* alone became a terror to the wicked and abandoned part of the community. It became a fashion with great personages to say, ' How do you do, Townsend ? ' It was not uncommon to announce some crowded rout with the advertisement— ' *Mr. Townsend will attend.*' This was pursued to a ridiculous extent, and the artful fellow, to increase his imposture, would, in particular crowds, caution noble ladies to be on their guard, and they would hand over their watches and jewellery on the spot to Mr. Townsend's kind and safe keeping. In the restoration of the articles it was equally the fashion to remunerate Mr. Townsend for his thoughtfulness and trouble. At Christmas time he grew into the habit of 'making' friendly calls upon 'the nobility and gentlemen' to offer them his compliments of the season, while congratulations were returned in a suitable way." (The italicised words belong to the " flash " style of the times.)

Amongst other anecdotes circulated respecting Townsend, the following shows his aptness: Mr. Bond, a most active, intelligent police officer, was made a magistrate at Bow Street for his services. In a dispute some time afterwards Mr. Bond rather warmly told him that " he took too much upon himself ; but he supposed Townsend thought himself a magistrate." " No, indeed I do not, your worship," replied Townsend, in a sarcastic manner, " the King said he had committed an error in making one police officer a magistrate ; but he would not repeat the mistake by elevating another."

" Two young noblemen meeting him one day near the palace, one of the above *sprigs* of nobility said to the other, ' I will introduce you to old Townsend, I know him well. Come here, Townsend!' said he with considerable hauteur, at the same time taking a pinch of snuff, and surveying the veteran officer from head to foot; 'I wish to ascertain a fact; but 'pon my honour, I do not intend to distress your feelings ; in the early part of your life were you not a coal-heaver ? '

'Yes, my lord,' answered Townsend, making a bow with the most profound respect, 'it is very true; but let me tell your lordship, if you had been reared as a coal-heaver you would have remained a coal-heaver up to the present hour.' "

Townsend, a few years after he had obtained great notoriety as a police officer, underwent a severe cross-examination, at the Old Bailey, by Counsellor Garrow (now the present venerable Judge Garrow).

Question. How do you get your living, sir?

Answer. You know me very well, Mr. Garrow.

Q. I insist upon knowing how you get your livelihood? Recollect, sir, you are upon your oath.

A. Yes, sir, I have taken a great many oaths in my time; but *I* ought to have said, *professionally !*

Q. To the question, and no equivocation?

A. Why then, sir, I get my livelihood in the same way you do!

Q. How is that, fellow?

A. I am paid for *taking up* thieves; and you are paid for "*getting them off !*" that is much about the same sort of thing.

Q. You consider yourself a *sharp shot,* don't you, Townsend?

A. No, sir,—but I like to *hit* the MARK.

Q. You may stand *down,* fellow?

A. I am glad, sir, you found me *up !*

This seems poor wit enough, but it shows us that

the pert, self-satisfied, and "spoiled " official, Grum-
mer, in " Pickwick," was of the same type, and, it is
not unlikely, was intended for Townsend. This
acquired position almost seemed to entitle him to
equal rights with the magistrates, who did not venture
to chcck, or interfere with him. As when a well-
dressed thief was brought up for robbing a gentleman
in the park, we find the old officer, when giving
evidence, offering his own opinions and professional
instincts, instead of legal evidence.

He told his story in his usual peculiar quaint way.
" I was going," he said, " that morning down the passage leading from Spring Gardens into St. James's
Park, as a party of the Foot Guards had passed before
in that direction. I found there was an obstruction,
and a gentleman said to me, ' Townsend, what is the
cause of this ; the road is choked up ? ' I said to him,
'You may depend upon it some old acquaintances of mine
have caused the obstruction to create a confusion and
to pick pockets.' I then went to the iron pillars, and
saw the prisoner and two other fellows talking in their
usual slang language ; they had surrounded an elderly
gentleman, and were *ogling* his pockets, when he
appeared to be aware of their intentions, and prevented
them from carrying them into effect. One of the
robbers said to the prisoner, who was acting in concert
with them, ' I had nearly drawn that old flat's *skin*,
but he baulked me.' I (continued Townsend) looked

the prigs full in the face, and said, ' If you had drawn his *skin*, I would have *grabbed* you—(laughter)—and they ran off as fast as they could." Mr. Hall : " What is the meaning of ' skin ' and ' grab,' Mr. Townsend ? " Townsend, " ' Skin ' means purse, and ' grab ' means to apprehend. When they ran off, I cut round into the park in another direction, and fell in with the prisoner, and gave him into the charge of a policeman." This was all amusing enough, and gratifying to the " runner." But the magistrate naturally asked, " Are you certain he was committing a robbery ? " Townsend, answered, " I never saw the prisoner before, but when I saw him *ogling* the gentleman's pocket, and being a *cover* to the other thieves, I said to myself ' Townsend, as sure as thou art in existence, that's as arrant a thief as ever drew a *wipe* from the tail of a coat.' On inquiry I found he was one of the most active robbers, &c."

The peculiarities, vanity, and garrulousness of the old officer, were yet more effectively displayed in a scene which took place in the Bow Street Office, in October, 1827, when Sir Richard Birnie humoured him to the top of his bent. An eccentric Mr. Summerfield had applied for a warrant against a baker, residing at Islington, who had sent him a challenge to fight a duel. Having shown to Sir R. Birnie the letter containing the challenge, a warrant was ordered to be issued immediately. During the investigation of this case, Townsend, the police-officer, " who has the honour of being police attendant on His Majesty," entered the office. Sir Richard Birnie said to him, " John Townsend, you are come very opportunely to execute a warrant, and prevent a duel from taking place; here is a challenge sent by a baker to the clerk of a lead-mill proprietor." John Townsend raised himself upon his toes, and looked at Sir R. Birnie, with his usual knowing expression of *physog.*, hardly conceiving whether the magistrate was in jest or in earnest, and replied,—

" Why, Sir Richard Birnie, I beg leave to tell you, that I think it would lessen me a great deal if I were to execute a warrant upon a barber (he had mistaken the word baker for barber), after forty-six years' service, during which period I have had the honour of taking Earls, Marquises, and Dukes. No, no, Sir Richard, let the barber fight if he likes it; but don't let me be degraded by executing the warrant." Sir Richard Birnie intimated to the veteran officer, that he meant nothing more than a jest in asking him to serve the warrant. Townsend said he thought so; and having adjusted his flaxen wig, he said, " Why, Sir Richard, I was employed to apprehend the late Duke of Norfolk and Sir John Honeywood, when they went out to fight a duel; and I also apprehended Colonel Macnamara and Colonel Harvey Aston, the latter of whom was afterwards shot in a duel in the East Indies. I also apprehended the late Marquis Townshend and Mr. Ponsonby, on a like occasion ;

and I remember that I received the warrant to apprehend Colonel Lennox (afterwards Duke of Richmond) and the Duke of York, and prevent their fighting a duel; but they had met, and settled their dispute before I got to the spot. God knows how many great men I have taken—why I apprehended Mr. King and Lord Paget (now Marquis of Anglesea), when they were going out to fight a duel; and I remember Lord Paget's father (the Earl of Uxbridge) told me not to prevent their meeting, for his son was good for nothing if he did not go out and fight. Besides, now it occurs to me, that I was applied to at my own house, by Mr. Pitt and Mr. Dundas, late one night, to go in quest of Earl St. Vincent and Sir John Orde. The fact was, that Earl St. Vincent, who had nothing but his country's glory in view, broke through the rules of Royal etiquette; and, instead of sending the second in command, Sir J. Orde, on an expedition to the Nile, he despatched the immortal Nelson; and after the victory was over, and the naval armament returned to England, Sir John Orde sent a challenge to Earl St. Vincent, and I took the parties and prevented their meeting."

Sir R. Birnie complimented Townsend upon his public services, and another officer was sent to serve the warrant upon the baker, at Islington. The officer who was entrusted with the warrant, stated that he had been unable to apprehend Mr. Summerfield, and he had discovered that a hoax had been played off upon Mr. M'Diarmid.

This specimen of Mr. Townsend's style in a public office shows that the old officer must have become something of a standing nuisance, with his perpetual reminiscences of the Royal family and of noblemen and gentlemen.

But with age and an increasing reputation his many peculiarities increased. He gave his opinions freely to king and princes, and there was certainly a free and easy self-sufficiency in his remarks that was highly amusing. What caused his employment about the Court was the attack by Margaret Nicholson upon the King. The palaces were afterwards frequently infested with mad people, one of whom actually got into the Queen's Palace, and found his way into the private apartments of the Princess of Homburg. Three of the porters were in consequence discharged ; and Townsend and "the late Macmanus" were appointed to attend the Court.

Soon after he commenced his attendance at the levées, a nobleman had the insignia of the Order of the Garter cut from his side. The loss was instantly discovered, and notice of the fact was given through the rooms, and down-stairs, to detect the thief, as the company passed him. At length a person passed who, he had a strong suspicion, ought not to be at Court, but the difference of Court dress changes the appearance of a person so much, that he was not certain as to the character. He therefore followed the man a few paces, looking him full in the face, and then discovered him to be an old thief, and took him into custody; and on searching him, the stolen property was found.

When the Catholic Question was under discussion in the House of Lords, Townsend met in Parliament Street, two members of the peerage, one an opponent of the Catholic claims, and the other, a much younger man, an advocate of them. In answer to some observation by Townsend on this subject, the elder peer made a strong remark, which appeared to please the veteran police-officer. The young peer then offered an opinion on the other side, but was interrupted by Townsend, who said, " Young man, young man, mind what his lordship says—treasure up every word of it." " But, Mr. Townsend," said the peer, " allow me to explain." " Explain—explain! I want no explanation, I know all about it, and his lordship understands it as well—young man, young man—it is a question of life and death, *Go home and consider it.*"

Speaking of George the Fourth, he would say, " God rest him, he *was* a king, only two or three people could get at him; but this new king (William the Fourth) why, bless you, sir, he isn't half a king; he makes himself too cheap. Anybody may get at him." Whilst speaking of the opera, alluding to the upstarts, as he

called them, he said, " Bless you, sir, I knew the opera
fifty years ago, and then it was worthy of being called
a King's Theatre, for only the nobility had boxes ; but
now you may see a duchess on one side and a wholesale cheesemonger's wife on the other. I remember
the time when there were masquerades, too, and the
king—God bless him !—(he was only Prince of Wales
then) used to have nice freaks on such occasions. Many
a time have I taken him by the skirt of the coat when
he was going in, and said to him, I would advise your
Royal Highness, if you have got any money about you, to
leave it with me for safety ; and then he would pull out
a purse with fifty or sixty guineas in it, and say, ' Well,
but Townsend, you must allow me something to spend,
you know ;' and upon that I used to hand him over
about five guineas, keeping the rest and his watch in
my own pocket, where few people would have thought
of looking for them."

Once in St. James's Park, he met the Duke of
Clarence. " Holloa, Townsend, where do you come
from ? " " I am just come from your royal brother of
York, and he gave me one of the best glasses of wine
I ever tasted." " Well, Townsend," said the Duke,
" come and see me, and I promise to give you as good
a glass of wine as my brother York can give." " Ah ! "
says Townsend, " that's not all, for when I admired
the wine, your royal brother of York calls for his
butler, and desires him to bring two bottles for Mrs.

Townsend; and here," added Townsend, "here they are," pulling one out of each pocket, and showing them to the duke.

This singular functionary continued in the service till his death, which occurred in the year 1832. It was remembered that he was much depressed during the passage of the Reform Bill; and he used to say, shrugging up his shoulders, " It's all up now ! "

About five days before his death allusion being made to the peculiar cut of his hat, the old officer said, " That hat, sir, was given to me by George IV., God rest his soul." " Well, but Townsend," said the gentleman, " I thought it had been your own cut." " God bless your soul, and so it was ; the King took his cut from mine, and many times used to say, that till that time he had never looked like a gentleman."

" On the Wednesday previous to his decease, when attending the King's levee, he enjoyed his usual health, and was full of joke and conversation in his way, particularly with the Marquis of Wellesley and the Marquis of Salisbury, who congratulated him on his good looks, and how well he carried his age, &c., &c. The Sunday following, he went to St. Peter's Church, Pimlico, where he had a pew, and regularly attended divine service. He enjoyed the company of a friend the latter part of the day. On the Monday morning he rose early and proceeded to the bank, where his indisposition increased to an alarming degree. He returned home to Pimlico in a coach, when he was taken ill and died shortly after." Such was Townsend.

Vickery, another well-known runner, had been a harness-maker, and came from the neighbourhood of Basingstoke. Becoming an officer at Worship Street, his activity and intelligence made him a great favourite with Mr. Nares, the magistrate; and when that gentleman was promoted to the chief office, Bow Street, he obtained his appointment there also. Vickery was conductor of the east-end party of the patrole. The responsible duty of escorting the dollars to be stamped at Birmingham was entrusted to him, in conjunction with the late Stephen Lavender. It was to Vickery that instructions were given to apprehend the French prisoners of war who had escaped upon their parole of honour, and in this business he was wonderfully successful.

A very ingenious plan was laid to rob the Post Office. Vickery received information of the fact, and communicated it to the authorities. They doubted the truth of this story, and a special meeting was called, at which were present the Postmasters-General, for at that time there were two, Sir Francis Freeling, and Mr. Anthony Parkin, the then solicitor to the establishment. Vickery attended, and to the astonishment of every one present, actually produced the keys that had been made for the purpose of effecting the robbery, and opened every door in succession, until he arrived at the treasure which was intended to be the prize of the thieves. It appeared from the information he had collected, that the robbers had twice or thrice visited the premises, but would not take away the booty, thinking that if they waited a little longer, it would be much increased. This was one of the happy *coups de théâtre* by which the runners knew how to impress the public.

His activity and energy were conspicuously displayed in reference to the great robbery at Rundell and Bridge's. Two Jews called at their shop on Ludgate Hill, and selected articles of jewellery to the amount of 35,000*l*. Having done so, they requested to be allowed to seal them up that no mistake might occur, and they would call on the following day and pay for them. No suspicion being entertained, they were allowed to pack up the goods, and seal them. Being provided with small parcels resembling the others, they adroitly possessed themselves of the valuable ones, leaving in exchange some rubbish, packed and sealed in the same way. Vickery was consulted, and he was not long in ascertaining that a portion of the property had gone to the Continent. He started in company with one of the firm, and traced the delinquents through France, Holland, Frankfort, and eventually succeeded in recovering 20,000*l*. worth of the stolen property. The firm made him a very liberal present.

Another of these functionaries, Donaldson, had

special care of the saloons at the theatres Covent
Garden and Drury Lane. It seems astonishing now
that under the direction of the austere John Kemble,
these disorderly places should have been tolerated.
Even now as we enter the one theatre in London
which represents the old dispensation, viz. Drury
Lane, we wonder at the spaciousness and magnificence
of the deserted saloon, with its pillars and arches, and
can scarcely realize the time when it was crammed to
overflowing with a strangely mixed crowd of the so-
called " fast " of both sexes, as, indeed, we may see in
the adventures of "Tom and Jerry," and their friend
Bob Logic.

" This man," says Mr. Richardson, " never bore a
very high reputation for virtue of any sort. He was,
however, perfectly acquainted with the haunts, proceedings, practices, and plans of thieves, pickpockets, and
rogues ; and in the state of London at the time his
services were found useful. There was plenty of
carrion in the saloons of the theatres, and plenty of
pickpockets were there also. Donaldson was accustomed from time to time to exclaim with a loud
voice,—

" ' *Take care of your pockets !* '

" Most persons considered this exclamation as a
warning to the unwary. Others, less charitably inclined, affirmed that it was a notice given to the pickpockets to be on the look-out, and take heed who the

gentlemen were who, immediately put their hands in their pockets to ascertain that the contents were safe, and thus furnished the thieves with a clue to where they could go to work with the greatest chance of success."

This officer's death was as strange as his life. He was sitting amongst the company at the Brown Bear, Bow Street, indulging in the things in which he and his associates delighted, and in that kind of discourse which expands distinctions of opinions into a mode of argumentation that neglects all distinctions whatever. After the re-establishment of order, the company resumed their seats, and everything went on well for some time. One of the party, looking round, asked,—

"What's become of Donaldson?"

"Oh," replied another, "he's ' cut.' "

The conversation was renewed, and some regret expressed at the absence of him, by whose contributions it was generally enlivened. After some time, a gentleman present observed,—

"Here's a dog fast asleep under the table; I have kicked him several times, but he won't move, and now he has rolled round against my legs."

"Turn him out," said the landlord; "I'll have no dogs here," and stooping down, he laid hold of what he thought was the dog, when, to his alarm and surprise, he perceived the body of Donaldson, who had passed from "life into death," with a suddenness, and under circumstances which startled the apathy of those assembled, though accustomed to scenes of horror.

One of the boldest and most resolute of the Bow Street officers was Macmanus. It was on his death, as we have seen, that Townsend and Sayer were appointed to fill his situation of attending the King. His successor Sayer, was often heard to express the highest admiration of the courage displayed by Macmanus upon all occasions.

"A service of danger," said he, "had no terrors upon his mind ; he went in pursuit of the most desperate characters with the utmost cheerfulness, ease, and indifference : and he performed his arduous duty like a brave but humane officer. With the *mild*, he was mild ; yet terrible amongst the *terrible ;* but when he was resisted in his situation as an officer of Justice, and compelled to fight in his own defence against those abandoned persons whose lives had become forfeited by their crimes, his existence appeared no object to him ; and," observed Sayer, " I have known Macmanus lose rivers of blood ! "

After the establishment of the " New Police " a few of the " runners " lingered on, pensioned, or following other callings. One of the most celebrated died so lately as 1844. This was George Ruthven, one of the most intrepid of men, who was concerned in some desperate arrests and conflicts. " He was the oldest and most celebrated of the few remaining Bow Street runners, among whom death has lately made such ravages, and was considered as the most efficient police-officer that existed during his long career of usefulness. He was for thirty years attached to the police force, having entered it at the age of seventeen; but in 1839 he retired with a pension of 220*l.* from the British Government, and pensions likewise from the Russian and Prussian Governments, for his services in discovering forgeries to an immense extent connected with those countries. Since 1839 he has been landlord of the "One Tun Tavern," Chandos Street, Covent Garden, and has visited most frequently the spot of his former associations. Among his many notorious captures may be reckoned those of Thistlewood, for the Cato Street conspiracy, in which daring enterprise Smithers was killed: the taking of Thurtell, the murderer of Mr. Weare, and the discovery of bank robberies and forgeries on Government to an enormous amount. He was a most eccentric character, and had written a history of his life, but would on no account allow it to meet the public eye. During the last three months no less than three of the old Bow Street officers, namely, Goodson, Salmon, and Ruthven, have paid the debt of nature." This was written in 1844.

But indeed the intrepidity of the officers was always remarkable, and the desperation and violence of the lawless characters they were sent to arrest often rendered their service one of extreme danger. Armstrong, who died in 1828, had a long record of hand-to-hand encounters with burglars and such characters. On one occasion he and a noted highwayman fought along the roofs of three houses in Chatham. The robber fired a pistol without effect, and Armstrong closing with him, the fellow endeavoured to precipitate both into the street; but the officer succeeded in bringing him down, and he was afterwards executed. The noted Jeremiah Abershaw and Armstrong had a similar *rencontre* in Bridgwater Gardens, but not with the same success, for "Jerry," after snapping his pistol, dashed himself through a lath and plaster partition, and escaped by the roof of the house. About seven years ago, Armstrong, on going through Rose Lane, Spitalfields, alone and without arms, was suddenly rushed upon by a noted highway-robber, named Barry, and four others, who beat him in an unmerciful manner. Armstrong, four years ago, petitioned to retire, and, as his salary was only 25s. per week, he naturally expected full pay; but he was allowed to retire, after fifty years' public service, upon a pension of 18s. per week."

It was Ruthven who, at the peril of his life, apprehended Thistlewood. Thurtell, a desperado of the blackest caste, was, with singular ingenuity, seized by him, and conveyed by that officer alone to Hertford gaol. He travelled after delinquents to all parts of the continent and America, and was eminently successful in his captures. Yet, after such service, when the New Police was established, these old servants were dismissed with small pensions, to the indignation of their friends and admirers, and of the public.

One of the most persevering and successful of these thief-takers was Keys, who is said to have captured the last malefactor that was executed for coining. To the detection of this branch of crime—" smashing," as it was called—he devoted himself. There was a coiner, one James Coleman, who was so shrewd and cautious as to defy all attempts made to secure him. Such was his ingenuity and tact that he evaded justice, during a hot pursuit of the police, for many months. Keys, at that time, was in the Bow Street day patrole ; he knew that Coleman was *" making the showful,"* as it was called in the slang, but could not discover where he lived. The plan pursued by the coiner was this : he never entered even the street where he lived if he observed any one about at all strange to the neighbourhood, nor did he take the produce of his labour out himself for sale, but was always followed by a little girl with a basket containing it. He supplied shillings at the rate of four shillings a score, and other spurious moneys in proportion. The little girl left the counterfeits with the *smashers*, and Coleman received the money. Limbrick, of the Hatton Garden office, who was at the time very zealous in the cause of the Mint, and had earned some fame by apprehending coiners, used every exertion to take this man, but without effect. Either Keys or Limbrick could have brought home to him the connection with the little girl and the basket, but that was not sufficient for the ends the Mint had in view ; their object was to get him taken for the capital offence, viz. in the act of coining ; and to that end Keys set his ingenuity to work. He hired a man, at an expense of three-and-sixpence per day, to pass through the street where he suspected Coleman lived, morning and afternoon, in the garb of a milkman, carrying a yoke and a pair of pails, having previously been made acquainted with the person of Coleman by Keys. After the man had done this duty for nearly two months he began to think it useless, but Keys knew that if Coleman did reside in the street, the longer the man with the pails continued his employment the better, because it would lull suspicion to him, if he entertained any, of his being a spy. At length their patience was rewarded by Coleman making his appearance. Looking out about eight o'clock one morning, and seeing no one in the street but the milkman, he ventured from his door to feed his chickens. The supposed milk-dealer hastened to inform Keys of the circumstance, and that officer, in conjunction with others of the patrole, surprised the coiners that night. " When I got to the top of the stairs," said Keys, " I could hear Jem and his woman, Rhoda Coleman, as she was called, conversing about the coin while work-ing. 'That's a rum 'un, Rhoda,' said Jem. I was about," continued Keys, " to break the door in with my foot ; in fact, I had lifted my leg up, and had placed my back against the opposite wall for that purpose, when I heard Coleman say, ' Rhoda, go and get us a quartern of gin.' I waited about two minutes, and she opened the door to go out for the gin. I and my comrades rushed in and secured Coleman with the moulds and work red-hot in his hands. He was surprised, but cool. ' Do yer want me, master ? ' said he, looking up in my face. 'Of course I do, Jem,' said I ; and having handcuffed him, I proceeded to search the place. We took away upwards of twenty pounds' worth of counterfeit coin, as well as all the implements, &c., used in the process of manufacturing it." Coleman was tried, convicted, and executed. The woman was acquitted.

" Rhoda," continued Keys, " removed the body to her lodgings, and kept it for twelve days. I had information three times that if I went I should find Rhoda coining again, and that the moulds, &c., were concealed in the coffin, under the body of poor Jem Coleman. This, I afterwards ascertained, was the fact."

CHAPTER V.

THE POLICE SYSTEM.

In 1828, Mr. Stafford, who had been connected with the police twenty years, and who was well known as the official chief clerk at Bow Street, gave a little sketch of the office and staff to the committee of the House of Commons. He said that the eight principal officers at that time attached to the office were Townsend, John Sayer, John Vickery, Daniel Bishop, Samuel Taunton, William Salmon, George Ruthven, and James John Smith. "Townsend and Sayer generally attended his Majesty when he was out of town. They are now at Brighton. Salmon and Ruthven have been upon the continent in pursuit of persons who have absconded with property belonging to their employers in the city. They are both returned. Bishop has been at a variety of places in the country—I think three or four different places— on business. Taunton has been to the assizes. A little while before that he followed some offenders to Scotland, and brought them from thence. Vickery has been employed a good deal in making inquiries

for the post-office, relative to some offences that have
been committed there. He has been also in Hampshire, where he is remaining unwell. In fact, he has
never been well since he was very ill-used some time
ago, and nearly murdered. Smith has been employed
in a variety of matters in Kent and Essex, and at
Norwich, and latterly at Baldock, in Hertfordshire.
In fact, when they are not called out of town to attend
to offences committed in the country, they devote their
time and attention to the discharge of their duty
in London." He then explained how, when an application was made for the attendance of a police officer,
and the party proposed to remunerate the police-
officer for his time and trouble, the practice was to
attend to such applications, and if an officer could be
spared, to send one to perform it. " If he cannot be
spared we generally select one of the most intelligent and best-informed men upon the police
establishment. Of course the magistrates attend to
the nature of the offence committed. We have
frequent applications with regard to matters that
perhaps are not thought to come exactly within the
scope of the police, and the parties do not get the
attendance of an officer. The remuneration, I believe,
is very little considered. If the magistrates thought
it an offence of that magnitude that required their
immediate attention and assistance, an officer would
be sent. At all events the question of remuneration

would be left to be settled afterwards." This, however, as will be seen, was quite too partial a view. The wheels of the detective car moved but sluggishly, or scarcely at all, if ungreased, as it was called. When the system was most flourishing, viz. about 1820, it will scarcely be credited that the whole force available for despatch to the country, was no more than six or eight ! These were the "runners" of the first class, such as Ruthven, Townsend, Sayer, Vickery, Bishop, and others, whose long experience and professional "scent" rendered even a single visit about as valuable as that of a first-rate physician brought down "special" for a desperate case. Each of these men was entitled to receive but 1*l.* 5*s.* a week regular salary. But any one sending for them was expected to pay a guinea a day, besides 14*s.* a day travelling expenses. It was obvious that this wretched remuneration would not suffice to stimulate the energies of the officers ; and where some great robbery, say from a bank or house of business, had been committed, handsome gratuities were looked for and received. It was noted that the men were always anxious to leave their town duties for these " country jobs." Sir Richard Birnie, who, from long service and old fashion, believed that his Bow Street officer was " the best of all possible officers," declared that though this remuneration was expected, it was never enforced, being left to the liberality of the parties ; and on such not being forthcoming, the office took care that the men did not lose by their journey. It was boasted, indeed, that at Bow Street, of all the police offices, " everything was paid for " liberally.

As might be expected from such a system, the " runners " indemnified themselves in many less legitimate modes. Indeed, it almost came to this, that every real service became a special one, and no efficient aid was likely to be rendered unless it was recognized on such special terms. Townsend and Lavender frankly expounded these methods. It was a custom that a sum of 40*l.* was usually allowed for distribution among the witnesses and officers on a conviction for a felony; the latter estimating their total receipts under this head at about 20*l.* to 30*l.* a year to each officer. It was believed, however, that much more was received. Thus, when there were Bank or City prosecutions, the officers were paid by the particular bank, and for their attendance at the trial. There was also the sale of what were called the " Tyburn Tickets," and for special duties at the Court and Brighton. But, in his own characteristic style, Townsend thus recounted these sources of profit. He explained that " his duty was to attend when any of the magistrates want my assistance within the jurisdiction of Middlesex, for I cannot go out of town on account of attending on the court-days, and particularly if there is anything wanted at Windsor. Or supposing that the Prince goes out of town to Brighton, and so on, then we attend there. When the Regent goes to Brighton, for instance, Sayer and I go. It frequently happened, in the early part of my life, that the public may want an officer, especially public bodies; for instance, the Excise office, the Custom House, the Stamp office, the Bank, they all come there ; and if they see an officer, whoever is in the way, they instantly go, because if they were to wait for matter of form, perhaps the party they wanted to apprehend would be gone. An officer from Bow Street is not constantly in attendance at the Bank. Only ten days a quarter. That Sayer and I do every quarter, and have done for many years—these five-and-twenty years, I dare say. Depredations used to be committed there dreadfully at dividend times. We have a guinea a day for it. That is paid by the Bank."

He then explained the system of giving rewards on conviction. " The usual way in distributing the 40*l*. on conviction is, that the recorder gives the prosecutor from five to fifteen and twenty pounds, according to circumstances, and the apprehender the remainder ; that comes to, perhaps, only three or four pounds apiece, though the world runs away with the ridiculous idea that the officers have 40*l*. It is a singular circumstance, but in all cases of felony there are but two cases where there is any reward at all ; those are a highway robbery and a burglary; all the others are mere bagatelles."

He then explained the nature of the Tyburn Tickets, which exempted from serving as constable and other parish offices. "These are worth 20*l.* apiece. I have sold them as low as 12*l.* In such a parish as St. George's, Hanover Square, the people are of so much consequence that they will serve themselves. The highest is in Covent Garden, where it is worth 25*l.*; for the constable of the parish must sit up, I think, one night out of three; and whoever is hit upon as a parochial constable says, 'This is a hard thing, and therefore I will buy myself off;' and a ticket in that parish, therefore, is worth more. If an officer gets a guinea a day, it is a chance whether he gets any reward; that must depend upon the liberality of those public offices who choose to pay it. *I am very sorry to say that sometimes they are rather mean upon that subject.*

"Sometimes I have myself, in the early part of my life, when I was in the habit of going to do the business for public offices, been out of town for a week or a fortnight. I went to Dunkirk in the year 1786 to fetch over four that were hanged. I went for Mr. Taylor, a Hamburg merchant. There are certain cases in which we may be employed longer. There have been officers for eight or ten days on the poaching cases. Vickery was down for a fortnight in Gloucestershire, with Colonel Berkeley. Frequently it takes a great deal of time to detect a banditti like that. In those cases where the individual, in a case similar to that you have just mentioned, sends for a Bow Street officer, the expense of his journey, and the payment of his trouble, is defrayed by the individual."

Townsend, when he was examined before the Committee, furnished quite an entertainment, so shrewd and sensible were his opinions. He gave his evidence in an amusingly familiar tone, as indeed was then expected from one so intimate with the royal and noble personages. On being asked as to the policy of rewarding police in cash for obtaining convictions, and whether it would not be better to leave it to the decision of the magistrate or judge, he said,—

"I have always thought so; from the earliest part of my time I have thought it, and for the best of all reasons; I have, with every attention that man could bestow, watched the conduct of various persons who have given evidence against their fellow-creatures for life or death, not only at the Old Bailey, but on the circuits, and I have always been perfectly convinced that would be the best mode that possibly could be adopted to pay officers, *particularly because they are dangerous creatures;* they have it frequently in their power (no question about it) to turn that scale, when the beam is level, on the other side; I mean against the poor wretched man at the bar. Why? *this thing called Nature* says profit in the scale; and, melancholy to relate, but I cannot help being perfectly satisfied, that frequently that has been the means of convicting many and many a man.

"*I told Sir Charles Bunbury my opinion* upon that subject thirty years ago, when he wanted to get rid of rewards, that it should be in the breast of the judges on the circuit, if they see the officer has done his duty towards the public, they should have a discriminating power to pay that officer according to the nature of the case. Then the officer does not stand up and look at this unfortunate creature, and swear to this or that thing, or the other thing, for what, for the lucre—*for Nature is Nature, do with us what you will;* for I have been always of opinion, that an officer is a dangerous subject to the community, if he is not so kept and so paid as to afford him the means of being honest; for in some cases, God knows, it has been frequently the case.

"I remember a case, which was proved, in the time of the trading magistrates, where there was a fellow who, a public officer belonging to Justice Hyde, was hanged, and yet he was one of the officers. Justice Welch in Litchfield Street was a great man in those days, and old Justice Hyde, and Justice Girdler, and Justice Blackborough, a *trading Justice* at Clerkenwell Green, and an old ironmonger. The plan used to be to issue out warrants and take up all the poor devils in the streets, and then there was the bailing them

2*s*. 4*d*. which the magistrates had; and taking up a hundred girls, that would make, at 2*s*. 4*d*., 11*l*. 13*s*. 4*d*. They sent none to gaol, for the bailing of them was so much better. That was so glaring that it led to the Police Bill, and it was a great blessing to the public to do away with those men, for they were nothing better than the encouragers of blackguards, vice, and plunderers; there is no doubt about it."

Being asked was it not likely that a rich criminal might have an influence over a needy officer? " No question about it," said he. " I will give the committee a case in point; supposing, for instance, when I convicted Broughton, which, I believe, is now twenty-two years ago, and who was convicted for robbing the York Mail, I convicted at the same assizes, the summer assizes, a celebrated old woman, Mrs. Usher, worth at least three thousand guineas, for she made over that property by her attorney. I was then in the habit of attending Vauxhall, for which I received half-a-guinea, and a half-pint of wine, which I relinquished, and took the fifteen pence.

" Mrs. Usher picked a lady's pocket; I was close by, and secured her. She was tried before Baron Hotham. Mr. Ives, the gaoler in Surrey, before the trial, came to me, and said, ' Townsend, you know Mother Usher very well?' ' Yes,' said I, ' these ten years.' He said, ' Cannot this be *stashed?* ' meaning put an end to.

"I said, 'No, it was impossible that it could be; because the case was very plain, and of all women upon earth she ought to be convicted: and in my opinion, if she is convicted capitally, nothing but her sex and her old age ought to save her from being executed; and I shall think it my duty when she is convicted to state to the judge, after conviction, my opinion upon her case,' which I did.

"She was convicted, and Baron Hotham ordered me my expenses, which expenses, I believe, amounted to four guineas and a half. I set off immediately in a post-chaise to give evidence against Broughton. The present Attorney-General was her counsel. Baron Hotham said to me, 'This woman you seem to be well acquainted with?'

"'Yes, my Lord,' said I, 'I am very sorry to say she is a very old offender; but her age, which your lordship has heard her give, and her sex, are the only plea that ought to save her;' for the jury found her guilty of stealing, but not privately, which took away the capital part; therefore she was sentenced to two years' imprisonment in the new gaol in the borough. I then lived in the Strand; two of her relations called upon me, trying to see what could be done, and they would have given me 200*l.* not to have appeared against that woman. She was a very rich woman, and made over all her property before she was convicted; she got the best part of it by plunder.

" I, it is true, have steered clear, but I do not owe that to any merit myself. I have been lucky enough to have situations where I have been very liberally paid; and whether it has been my own sobriety or attention it matters not; but I have had many gratuities, and from the first people in the nation, or I might have been as liable to temptation as any one in London; but I have a fellow-feeling for other officers, and I must say that I think that some officers deserve every praise, though I do not change ten words with some of them in the course of a week."

It is extraordinary to think that all the incidents familiar from romances, such as "Jack Shepherd," with the informers, spies, "flash-houses," were in full working order at the beginning of the century, and a regular part of the criminal system. Townsend is specially garrulous on the subject of "flash-houses." " The fact is," he tells us, " a thief will never sit amongst honest men, it is not his province to do it, nor would he trust himself with those people; therefore there must be bad houses, because A says to B, I will meet you at such a place to-night. I know, five-and-twenty or six-and-twenty years ago, there were houses where we could pop in, and I have taken three or four, or five and six at a time, and three or four of them have been convicted, and yet the public-house was tolerably orderly too. It has often turned out, that when the information has come to the office, as it

might be this morning, of a footpad robbery done so-
and-so, poor Jealous, and another officer, Macmanus,
who was many years in the office, and I have slipped
out and gone to some of the flash-houses, and looked
about—nobody there; and gone to another, and very
likely hit upon the party going to it or in it."

Then, as was his wont, the thief-catcher rambled
off on the subject of his own merits :—

" Certainly, the flash-houses can do the officer no
harm if he does not make harm of it ; if an officer
goes there and acts foolishly, and does anything improper, the same as for me to go to-night to all the
disreputable houses (I believe I know all of them, but
was there ever any one who would say that I went
and asked to have a glass of wine, and so on there,
and that no money should be asked), what sort of a
servant should I be ? I ought to be turned out, and
never employed in the department of the police again.
*Who has been more in confidence than I have been with the
youngest part of society of the highest rank ?* How often
have I gone to such places, there to talk over a little incident that might happen to A.'s son or B.'s son, or
my lord this or the other's son ? but the consequence
was not a morsel of liberty, or how would Townsend
act upon those functions of authority, and get what
the parties asked me to do ; no, he must go there
full of power, with great distance towards the owner.

" And as to the poor wretches, in many cases, I

have been employed to bring their daughters home
to their parents, persons of the greatest respect and
consequence; we have not found them at one place,
but at another; we have taken them home, and there
has been an end to it. The respectable young men,
however liberally educated, *are often very great fools*,
for they often subject themselves to vast incon-
veniences through their own misconduct, by committing themselves ridiculously, and absurdly getting
into scrapes, and what has been the consequence?—
the consequence is, ' Townsend, what is to be done?'
sometimes with the father, and sometimes with the
party himself. But how would this thing be executed
if I were to attempt anything like what I stated before? No, I will take upon myself to say, I never
drank a glass of wine with those sort of characters,
because it will not do; in order to execute my duty
properly I must keep them at a proper distance, and
it is only a foolish man that would attempt it."

He was then asked whether he thought that the
morals and manners of the lower people in the metropolis were better or worse than formerly:—

" I am decidedly of opinion that, with respect to
the present time, and the early part of my time,
such as 1781, 2, 3, 4, 5, 6, and 7, where there is
one person convicted now, I may say, I am positively
convinced there were five then. We never had an
execution wherein we did not grace that unfortunate

gibbet with ten, twelve, to thirteen, sixteen, and twenty, *and forty I once saw twice.* I have them all down at home. I remember, in 1783, when Serjeant Adair was Recorder, there were forty hung at two executions. I agree with George Barrington, whom I brought from Newcastle; and however great Lord Chief Baron Eyre's speech was to him, after he had answered him, it came to this climax—' Now,' says he, ' Townsend, you heard what the Chief Baron said to me; a fine flowery speech, was it not?' ' Yes.' ' But he did not answer the question I put to him.' Now how could he? Now after all that the Chief Baron said to him, after he was acquitted, giving him advice, this word was everything, says he, 'My Lord, I have paid great attention to what you have been stating to me, after my acquittal. I return my sincere thanks to the jury for their goodness; but your Lordship says, you lament very much that a man of my abilities should not turn my abilities to a better use. Now, my Lord, I have only this reply to make—I am ready to go into any service, to work for my living, if your Lordship will but find me a master.' Why, what was the reply to that? ' Gaoler, take the prisoner away.' Why, who would employ him? that was the point. It is really farcical with me sometimes, when I have heard magistrates say, ' Young man, really I am very sorry for you; you are much to be pitied; you should turn your talents to a better account; and you should really leave off this bad course of life.' Yes, that is better said than done—for where is there anybody to take these wretches ? "

He was next asked did he think any advantages arise from a man being put on a gibbet after his execution? " Yes, I was always of that opinion, and I recommended Sir William Scott to hang the *two men that are hanging down the river.* I will state my reason. We will take for granted that those men were hanged as this morning, for the murder of those revenue officers—they are by law dissected; the sentence is, that afterwards the body is to go to the surgeons for dissection, there is an end of it—it dies. But look at this : there are a couple of men now hanging near the Thames, where all the sailors must come up, and one says to the other, ' Pray, what are those two poor fellows there for ? ' ' Why,' says another, ' I will go and ask.' They ask. ' Why, those two men are hung and gibbeted for murdering his Majesty's revenue officers.' And so the thing is kept alive. If it was not for this, people would die, and nobody would know anything of it. In Abershaw's case I said to the sheriff, ' The only difficulty in hanging this fellow upon this place is its being so near Lord Spencer's house.' But we went down and pointed out a particular place; he was hung at the particular pitch of the hill where he used to do the work. If there was a person ever went to see that man hanging, I am sure there was a hundred thousand." Some of his recollections as to the pitiless severity of courts in the matter of sentences are curious and interesting; especially what he recalls about highway robberies: " I remember, in very likely a week, there should have been from ten to fifteen highway robberies. We have not had a man committed for a highway robbery lately; I speak of persons on horseback; formerly there were two, three, or four highwaymen, some on Hounslow Heath, some on Wimbledon Common, some on Finchley Common, some on the Romford Road. I have actually come to Bow Street in the morning, and while I have been leaning over the desk, had three or four people come in and say, I was robbed by two highwaymen in such a place; I was robbed by a single highwayman in such a place. People travel now safely by means of the horse-patrole that Sir Richard Ford planned. Where are there highway robberies now? *As I was observing to the Chancellor, when I was up at his house on the Corn Bill;* he said, ' Townsend, I knew you very well so many years ago.' I said, ' Yes, my Lord; I remember your coming first to the bar—first in your plain gown, and then as King's Counsel, and now Chancellor. Now your Lordship sits as Chancellor, and directs the executions on the Recorder's report; but where are the highway robberies now?' And his Lordship said, 'Yes, I am astonished.'

" There are no footpad robberies or road robberies now, but merely jostling you in the streets. They used to be ready to pop at a man as soon as he let down his glass—that was by bandittis." When asked if he remembered the case of Abershaw, "I had him tucked up where he was ; it was through me. I never left a court of justice without having discharged my own feeling as much in favour of the unhappy criminal as I did on the part of the prosecution ; and I once applied to Mr. Justice Buller to save two men out of three who were convicted ; and on my application we argued a good deal about it. I said, ' My Lord, I have no motive but my duty; the Jury have pronounced them guilty. I have heard your Lordship pronounce sentence of death, and I have now informed you of the different dispositions of the three men. If you choose to execute them all, I have nothing to say about it; but was I you, in the room of being the officer, and you were to tell me what Townsend has told you, I should think it would be for a justification for you to respite those two unhappy men, and hang that one who has been convicted three times before.' The other men never had been convicted before, and the other had been three times convicted ; and he very properly did."

But there were graver evils, really caused by the

system itself. The thief-takers, underpaid, as we
have seen, were necessarily uncontrolled in their dealings. Their operations were secret : they were in
constant communication with thieves and the companions of thieves, and there was no authority over
them save that of the Bow Street magistrate. It was
asking for impossibilities that this handful of men
should, by their own unaided efforts, discover or bring
to justice the criminals of such a metropolis as
London, and they were obliged to rely on rather
unclean agencies, the practical value of which had
been taught and bequeathed to them by Mr. Wild.
The most important of these aids was these "*Flash
Houses,*" or Thieves' Tavern ; and they were largely
employed as the means of obtaining information about
thieves or of seeing them. It can scarcely be credited
to what an extent this abuse was tolerated, even so
lately as fifty years ago. The officers who frequented
these places grew familiar with the faces and figures
of the thieves. The magistrates, however, affected to
deny the existence of such places, and Sir N. Conant
could not be got to admit that such a system was
tolerated at all. "I do not know that there are flash
houses existing ; and if I did, I would, as far as the law
enables me, immediately suppress them. If I say the
officers look to those places, it implies that those places
exist ; but I believe they do not exist upon system. I
send police officers to every licensing meeting, to give

evidence against houses that have come to my knowledge, as encouraging a resort of thieves. There is no feeling in Bow Street to nurse such places, either in the magistrates or officers. The police-officers go into them to seek for thieves whom they know are likely to associate at a particular place. A man discharged at the Old Bailey, yesterday, for a robbery, would go the same night to the place where he was last taken into custody."

This evidence was pointed at certain notorious houses which were actually within a few doors of the Bow Street office, and of which more presently.

The "runners," however, were more candid than the magistrates, and frankly owned that it was a valuable agency in their system. Thus Sayer, the officer, declared that he knew such places " perfectly well ; I very often go to those flash houses, and find many thieves in most of them."

" Whom you know to be reputed thieves ?" " There is no doubt of it."

" The flash houses collect the thieves together. In Sir John Fielding's time there was the ' Blakeney,' in Bow Street, next door to the office ; that was a house that men and women used to drink in. We would find a great deal of difficulty, when informations were brought to Bow Street, in being able to apprehend the offenders, unless there were such houses ; but when this sort of people use the house in Covent Garden or

St. Martin's Lane, we should have him at once by merely going there."

Vickery was equally outspoken :—

" I am of opinion that these flash houses tend to facilitate the detection of offenders. I am sure they do ; I am well aware they do ; but these houses are not now as they were, because they are visited by the officers from time to time, whenever they think fit, without the least molestation or inconvenience ; they may go into these houses, look round and see what company there are there, and what they are doing, without any interruption : formerly we could not go into these houses without a magistrate's warrant ; and probably if we went to make any inquiries, we should not come off without some insult or molestation ; but now it is quite otherwise. I hold myself much above this kind of gentry, and I am always treated with great civility.

" There are a number of houses of that sort frequented by particular bands of thieves. They are attended with this advantage, for they often furnish the means of detecting great offenders : they afford an opportunity to the officers of going round, and knowing the suspicious characters, or of apprehending persons described in advertisements.

" It is desirable that the officers should know there are such houses, for there is a regular correspondence carried on between the thieves of Birmingham, Liverpool, and Manchester, and other places, and the thieves of London."

This familiarity with thieves led, as might be imagined, to another gross scandal, viz. the purchase of immunity or tolerations by bribes to the underpaid officers, and, what was more discreditable, the entering into regular treaties for the compounding of great robberies, when, on restitution of a portion, prosecution was forborne. This practice became rife, being encouraged by the great banking-houses, who were eager to recover their property, or a portion of it, on any terms. Worthy Sir Richard Birnie, however, in 1828, could not bring himself to believe in such practices. But the Committee of 1828 made some extraordinary discoveries. These compromises were generally negotiated by solicitors or police officers, or by both, with the plotters of the robbery, and receivers, or, as they are commonly called, "the putters up" and "fences." These persons usually planned the robbery, found the means, purchased the information necessary, and employed the actual thieves as their agents, themselves running no material risk. These sums have been apportioned, mostly by a percentage, on the value of the property lost ; but modified by a reference to the nature of the securities or goods, as to the facility of circulating or disposing of them with profit and safety.

" A great majority of these cases have taken place

where large depredations have been committed upon country bankers. Two banks, that had severally been robbed of notes to the amount of 4000*l.*, recovered them on payment of 1000*l.* each. In another case, 2200*l.* was restored, out of 3200*l.* stolen, for 230*l.* or 240*l.* In another case, Spanish bonds, nominally worth 2000*l.*, were given back on payment of 100*l.* A sum, not quite amounting to 20,000*l.*, was in one case restored for 1000*l.* In another, where bills had been stolen of 16,000*l.* or 17,000*l.* value, but which were not easily negotiable by the thieves, restitution of 6000*l.* was offered for 300*l.* In another case, 3000*l.* seems to have been restored for 19*l.* per cent. In another case, where the robbery was to the amount of 7000*l.*, and the supposed robbers (most notorious ' putters-up ' and 'fences') had been apprehended, and remanded by the magistrate for examination, the prosecution was suddenly desisted from, and the property subsequently restored for a sum not ascertained. In the case of another bank, the sum stolen, being not less than 20,000*l.*, is stated to have been bought of the thieves by a receiver for 200*l.*; and 2800*l.* taken of the legal owners, as the price of restitution. There is proof of more than sixteen banks having sought, by these means, to indemnify themselves for their losses; and that property of various sorts, to a value above 200,000*l.*, has, within a few years, been the subject of negotiation or compromise. They have proof of nearly

12,000*l.* having been paid to them by bankers only, accompanied with a clearance from every risk, and perfect impunity to their crimes."

It is perhaps not extraordinary that bankers, who have been so repeatedly subject to heavy losses, should take measures to procure indemnity. A highly respectable banker has said before the Committee, " I have no hesitation in mentioning, that at a meeting in our trade, I have heard it said, over and over again, by different individuals, that if they experienced a loss to a serious amount, they should compound." This is by no means considered to be the universal opinion of that respectable body. Another object was, to render the information obtained in one case, available for the prosecution or examination of another, which was effected, when every case passed through the hands of the same solicitor. To him, of course, the active agency and executive proceedings of the society were committed. For the purpose of furthering their objects, means of intercourse, or at least of communication, were sought with notorious "fences," and those who are commonly called "family men." In consequence of the knowledge thus acquired of thieves and their haunts, he has been generally employed by the country bankers upon the loss of parcels, and information obtained from him as to the robbery of coaches, a species of depredation which appears not to be among the objects of prosecution by the society ; but which has been so common, that a banker's parcel is known by the cant name of " a child." It is not extraordinary, that from such intercourse a belief should have prevailed abroad, that a regular channel was thus established, through which offers might be made and terms negotiated for the restitution of the stolen property of bankers.

The same committee probed this matter to the bottom, and succeeded in obtaining such revelations that they thought it impolitic and dangerous to print the evidence. These negotiations have been frequently carried on by solicitors (few, it is said, in number) of that class whose practice lies chiefly in the defence of culprits, and commonly denominated "Thieves' Attornies."

With respect to the agency of police officers in these transactions, confined to those of the City and of Bow Street, it was notorious that the leading Bow Street officers were deeply concerned in such treaties. But it is amusing to find with what simplicity Sir R. Birnie affects to be ignorant of all such business. Sir R. Birnie admitted himself to have had suspicions formerly, as, when questioned whether in the late cases of parcels being stolen from coaches being restored, he had been able to trace any connection between the police officers and the parties who had lost their property, he replied, " Certainly not ; and I will venture to say that in one particular case, where it was roundly asserted that it was done through the medium of a police-officer, I have reason to believe that it is untrue." Mr. Halls says, 'I had my suspicions, but I had no knowledge of it ; and so far from having any knowledge of it, I had given my mind, if possible, to ascertain the means of acquiring a knowledge of it.' An inquiry was also instituted by the Home Office during the last year, into a compromise, in which an officer was rumoured to have been concerned, without any discovery being made, though every officer in the establishment was sworn and examined. This ignorance could not therefore arise from attention not having been called to the subject.

The Committee were still inclined to believe that, however readily the officers of Bow Street and the City Police have undertaken the negotiations of these compromises, they seem in some instances to have been induced to do it without a corrupt or dishonest motive; and individuals of them have been satisfied with a much less sum for effecting the compromise, than the reward offered for the apprehension of the guilty parties. Suspicion has arisen in one case, that 800*l.* more was received by the officer who negotiated than the thieves asked or received ; and in another, 50*l.* was paid to procure restitution of 500*l.*, and neither the 500*l.* nor the 50*l.* were ever restored. In no case, however, does it appear in evidence that any one of them stipulated for a reward beforehand; nor connived at the escape of a thief; nor negotiated a compromise, when he possessed any clue that might lead to the detection of the guilty. Your Committee have before adverted to the ignorance in which the magistrates appear to have been kept as to these practices by the officers. It should seem, from the evidence of Sir R. Birnie, that they only supposed a very small number of compromises to have taken place, and those through the medium of attornies. Looking, however, to the regular system and undisturbed security with which the officers acted, it would not be strange if they should have conceived that the magistrates did not disapprove; and entertaining the same opinion as Sir R. Birnie, ' that the magistrates must have means of detecting them,' should have thought them disinclined to interfere, unless some unlucky publicity forced these practices upon their notice."

Sir R. Baker, another magistrate, when asked concerning such compromises, " Would you have considered, if it had come to your knowledge, that it was a crime?" answers, " Not merely the recovery of the goods; if they connived at the escape of the parties, I should say it was a crime, not otherwise." This, it should be remarked, refers to a period previous to 1821, from which year Sir R. Birnie more particularly dates his disbelief of such transactions.

This practice was a flagrant offence against the law, and the history of the statute 4 Geo. I. c. 11, is given in the words of Mr. Justice Blackstone : " An eighth offence, is that of taking a reward under pretence of helping the owner to his stolen goods. This was a contrivance carried to a great length of villainy in the beginning of the reign of George I., the confederates of the felons thus disposing of stolen goods, at a cheap rate, to the owners themselves, and thereby stifling all further inquiry. The famous Jonathan Wild had under him a well-disciplined corps of thieves, who brought in all their spoils to him, and he kept a sort of public office for restoring them to the owners at half-price : to prevent which audacious practice, to the ruin and in defiance of public justice, it was enacted by stat. 4 Geo. I. c. 11, that ' whoever shall take a reward under the pretence of helping any one to stolen goods, shall suffer as the felon who stole them ; unless he causes such principal felon to be apprehended and brought to trial, and also gives evidence against him.' Wild, still continuing in his old practice, was upon this statute at last convicted and executed."

This statute was repealed, and its provisions re-enacted next Session, by stat. 7 and 8 Geo. IV. c. 29. s. 58 ; but which makes the offence no longer capital, and limits the highest punishment to transportation for life. One officer stated, that his brethren had agreed " to give up all transactions of the sort ; as they thought some mischief would come of it under Mr. Peel's Act." But it does not appear that this agreement took place till after the inquiry, before alluded to, had been instituted by order of the Home Office. It is extraordinary, say the Committee, in the most innocent way, that the police officers, with the severe Act of Geo. I. in existence, could have considered themselves as committing no crime; and your Committee infers some deficiency in the law, which the statute of last Session may not have completely remedied.

" The Committee was further convinced that the frequency of these seemingly blameless transactions, has led to the organization of a system which undermines the security of all valuable property, which gives police officers a direct interest that robberies to a large amount should not be prevented; and which has established a set of 'putters up' and 'fences,' with means of evading, if not defying the arm of the law; who are wealthy enough, if large rewards are offered for their detection, to double them for their impunity; and who would in one case have given 1000*l.* to get rid of a single witness. Some of these persons ostensibly carry on a trade; one, who had been tried formerly for robbing a coach, afterwards carried on business as a Smithfield drover, and died worth, it is believed, 15,000*l.* One was lately the farmer of one of the greatest Turnpike Trusts in the Metropolis. He was formerly tried for receiving the contents of a stolen letter, and as a receiver of tolls, employed by him, was also tried for stealing that very letter, being then a postman, it is not too much to infer, that the possession of these turnpikes is not unserviceable for the purposes of depredation. Another has, it is said, been a surgeon in the army. The two others of the four have no trade, but live like men of property; and one of these, who appears to be the chief of the whole set, is well known on the turf, and is stated, on good grounds, to be worth 30,000*l.* Three of these notorious depredators were let out of custody, as before stated, when there was a fair prospect of identifying and convicting them. It is alarming to have observed how long these persons have successfully carried on their plans of plunder; themselves living in affluence and apparent respectability, bribing confidential servants to betray the transactions of their employers, possessing accurate information as to the means and precautions by which valuable parcels are transmitted; then corrupting others to perpetrate the robberies planned in consequence."

Opposite the Bow Street office was ' a low tavern called the " Brown Bear," of which more later on; it was a sort of " flash house," the resort of thieves, and a valuable adjunct to Bow Street office. It was patronized by the " runners," as here they were always sure to find any delinquent that was wanted. From this *quasi* connection with the chief office, the

" Brown Bear " was often made use of as a sort of chapel of ease, owing to the want of accommodation over the way, and officers were allowed to take their prisoners there for the night, when they had arrived too late to attend the office. This was analogous to the practice of keeping debtors in the neutral confinement of the " spunging-house."

A curious picture, which illustrates this system, is furnished by Samuel Bamford, one of the smaller Radical fry in the train of Henry Hunt, during the Manchester plots of 1814 and 1815, and when the spy system was rife. The conspirators had been arrested in the country by two " king's messengers." and were taken up to town in their custody:—

" We arrived in London," says Bamford, in his natural and genuine narrative, " about twelve o'clock, and were immediately conveyed to Bow Street. We were placed in a decent room, our irons were immediately removed, and most of us wrote home to our families. A gentleman named Capper was introduced, and I thought he seemed to scrutinize us very much. Sir Nathaniel Conant, an elderly and respectable-looking gentleman, also came in, and informed us that Lord Sidmouth could not see us that day, and that we should be well provided for at a house in the neighbourhood. Soon afterwards we were conducted in couples to a room prepared at the 'Brown Bear' public-house opposite; where, after supper, the doctor amused ourselves and keepers (who were eight or ten police officers) with several recitations in his most florid style. Messrs. Williams and Dykes, the messengers, came and brought with them a friend, and they each seemed much entertained. Mr. Perry, one of the chief officers at Bow Street, afterwards entered and apologized for having to submit us to what might be a small inconvenience. It was customary, he said, to secure prisoners during the night, by a chain, and he hoped we should take it as a mere matter of form; we expressed our readiness to submit to whatever restraint might be deemed necessary. Small chains being produced, myself, Lancashire, and Healey, were fastened together, and the other five were in like manner secured, after which we continued our amusements during an hour or two, and then went to rest on beds in the same room, still secured by chains to the bed-posts, and to each other."

The scenes that followed are worth recalling, as illustrating the summary process by which sedition-mongers were dealt with in these critical days. This system of questioning and examination by the ministers seems to belong to foreign procedure, and reads strangely now.

" About four o'clock p.m. we were conveyed in four coaches to the Secretary of State's office at Whitehall. On our arrival we were divided into two parties of four and four; and each party was placed in a separate room. A gentleman now appeared, who asked severally our names and occupations, which he wrote in a book and then retired. In a short time another person came and called my name, and I rose and followed him, along a darkish passage. I must confess that this part of the proceedings gave rise to some feelings of incertitude and curiosity, and brought to my recollection some matters which I had read when a boy, about the inquisition in Spain. My conductor knocked at a door, and was told to go in, which he did; and delivered me to a gentleman, whom I recognized as Sir Nathaniel Conant. He asked my christian and surname, which were given : he then advanced to another door, and desiring me to follow him, he opened it, and bowing to a number of gentlemen seated at a long table covered with green cloth, he repeated my name, and took his place near my left hand. The room was a large one, and grandly furnished, according to my notions of such matters. Two large windows with green blinds and rich curtains, opened upon a richer curtain of nature, some trees which were in beautiful leaf. The chimney-piece was of carved marble, and on the table were many books; and several persons sat there assiduously writing, whilst others fixed attentive looks upon me. I was motioned to advance to the bottom of the table, and did so ; and the gentleman who sat at the head of the table said I was brought there by virtue of a warrant issued by him, in consequence of my being suspected of high treason—that I should not be examined at that time, but must be committed to close confinement until that day sennight, when I should again be brought up for examination. Meantime, if I had anything to say on my own behalf, or any request to make, I was at liberty to do so ; but I must observe, they did not require me to say anything.

" The person who addressed me was a tall, square, and bony figure, upwards of fifty years of age, I should suppose, and with thin and rather grey hair : his forehead was broad and prominent, and from their cavernous orbits looked mild and intelligent eyes. His manner was affable, and much more encouraging to freedom of speech than I had expected. On his left sat a gentleman whom I never made out ; and next him again was Sir Samuel Shepherd, the Attorney-General, I think, for the time, who frequently made use of an ear-trumpet. On Lord Sidmouth's right, for such was the gentleman who had been speaking to me, sat a good-looking person in a plum-coloured coat, with a gold ring on the small finger of his left hand, on which he sometimes leaned his head as he eyed me over ; this was Lord Castlereagh.

" 'My Lord,' I said, addressing the president ; ' having been brought from home without a change of linen, I wish to be informed how I shall be provided for in that respect until I can be supplied from home.' The council conferred a short time, and Lord

Sidmouth said I should be supplied with whatever was necessary.

"'You will be allowed to communicate with your family, said his lordship; 'but 1 trust you will see the necessity of confining yourselves to matters of a domestic nature. You will always write in the presence of a person who will examine your letters; you will therefore do well to be guarded in your correspondence, as nothing of an improper tendency will be suffered to pass. I speak this for your own good.'

" The other prisoners were then severally called in and informed of the cause of their arrest, in the same terms that I had been; and that they would be again examined on that day sennight. One characteristic incident was, however, said to have occurred before the privy council. On the doctor being asked how he spelled his surname, he answered in broad Lancashire : 'haitch, hay, haa, l, hay, y,' (H, e, a, l, e, y,) but the pronunciation of the e and a being different in London, there was some boggling about reducing the name to writing, and a pen and paper were handed to him. The doctor knew that his *forte* lay not in feats of penmanship any more than in spelling; and to obviate any small embarrassment on that account, he pulled out an old pocket-book, and took from it one of his prescription-labels, on which the figures of a pestle and mortar were imposed from a rudely engraved plate; and these words, ' Joseph Healey, Surgeon, Middleton.

Plase take——Table Spoonfuls of This Mixture Each ——Hours.' This he handed to Lord Sidmouth, who, as may be supposed, received it graciously, looked it carefully over, smiled, and read it again, and passed it round the council-table. Presently they were all tittering, and the doctor stood quite delighted at finding them such a set of merry gentlemen. The fact was the first blank had been originally filled with a figure of two : ' Plase take 2 Table Spoonfuls,' &c.' "

This "Brown Bear" faced the Bow Street office, and was usually the scene of such arrangements, indeed was a notorious " flash house." The facetious " Joe Munden," whose house had been robbed, came to Bow Street to make his complaint. The magistrates, having heard his story with much interest, he being a public favourite, gave him a friendly piece of advice. " Munden," they said, " you must not tell any one we gave you this advice, but to prosecute will cause you a great deal of trouble and unpleasantness, and you had better put up with the loss." One of the magistrates whispered to an officer and inquired, " Who was on the North Road last night ? " " Little Jemmy, with a party, your worship." " Have you ascertained, Munden," rejoined Sir William Parsons, " how the robbers gained an entrance ? " " By forcing up the parlour window." " Was there an impression of a very small foot on the mould beneath ? " " Yes." " Enough ! Should you like to see the leader of the

gang that robbed your house?" "I have rather a
fancy for it," said the astonished comedian. "Then
go over to the 'Brown Bear' opposite, at one o'clock
to-morrow afternoon; enter the room on the right,
and you will see Townsend, the officer, seated at the
head of a table with a large company. You may be
assured that all the rest are thieves. If he asks you
to sit down do so; and the man who sits upon your
right hand will be the person who planned and conducted the robbery of your house." With the glee
consequent upon a relish for humorous situations, the
actor promised compliance. He attended at the
appointed time; knocked at the door—was told to
enter, and a group of gaol-birds met his eye, headed
by Townsend, who was diligently engaged in carving
a round of beef. "Mr. Townsend," said the
aggrieved child of Thespis, "I wanted to have spoken
to you, but I see you are engaged." "Not at all,
Mr. Munden; I shall be at your service in a few
minutes; but perhaps you will take a snack with us.
Jemmy, make way for Mr. Munden." Jemmy, with a
wry face, did as he was bid. The actor sat down;
turned towards his uneasy neighbour, and examined
his features minutely. The company, believing that
Jemmy was undergoing the process of identification,
laughed immoderately. It happened that a round of
beef, with the remnant of a haunch of venison, had
formed the repast with which Munden's uninvited

guests had regaled themselves. The thieves, who were well aware of the burglary, and knew the person of the victim, indulged themselves in extempore and appropriate jokes. " Jemmy, your appetite is failing," said one; " have a little more. You were always fond of boiled beef." Curiosity satisfied, the actor withdrew, greatly to the relief of Mr. Jemmy, to whom he made a low bow at parting. This hero afterwards suffered the last penalty of the law for some offence of greater magnitude. These were the customs that prevailed half a century ago. The officer had the thieves under his immediate eye, and seldom gave them much trouble until they were worth 40*l.*; that is, candidates for the gibbet and the halter. If much stir was made after a *lost* gold watch, and a handsome reward offered, a hint from the man in office recovered it; and when the final period of retributive justice arrived, this functionary fearlessly entered a room crowded with malefactors, and, beckoning with his finger, was followed by his man, who well knew " he was wanted." The " Brown Bear " was as safe a place of retreat for the thief as any other. It is even said that a famous highwayman ensconced himself for some time very snugly in lodgings near it, knowing that search would be made after him in every other direction; as young Watson did in Newgate Street, when every wall was placarded with a large reward for his apprehension.

A case that made considerable noise at the time, the robbery of the Paisley Bank, when over 20,000*l*. was carried off by two expert housebreakers, who had come down specially for the purpose, was to exhibit the convenience of the " Brown Bear " in a most striking way. This, as will be related later, was the work of the notorious Jemmy Mackcoull, who, with a confederate, carried the scheme through with the most perfect success. He found that it was impossible to get rid of such a mass of notes whose numbers were known. He accordingly determined to enter into treaty with the prosecutors for the restitution of the booty It forms an edifying commentary on the maxim, " Honour among thieves," and migh tbe scenes from the Beggar's Opera.

The prospect of reward made all concerned in the detection very keen and suspicious of each other. " Huffey White," the confederate, was captured on an old charge, at once, and lodged in jail. Sayer, the police officer who was concerned in the business, relates what took place. " Mackcoull," he says, " on the arrival of the burglars in London, was entrusted with the whole of the booty, but only on condition that the following morning he was to place it in the hands of one, William Gibbons, a celebrated pugilist, who, although not a thief himself, was yet well known to the higher order of thieves, and being a man of some property, was frequently trusted with the care

of plunder; *indeed, so high did he stand in their esti-
mation, that it was believed he could be trusted to any
amount.* Mackcoull, however, never intended to let
the notes go out of his own possession, and when
White and French met him next morning, he told
them that Gibbons was out of town, and would not
return for some days. In fact, he had already cheated
his confederates out of 4000*l.*, for although the notes
taken from the bank amounted to 20,000*l.*, the memorandum he had given at Wellwyn stated only 16,000*l.*;
so that, from the very first, he never intended to
behave fairly." It will be noted that this is in the
business-like spirit of Mr. Wild, particularly the happy
bit of aphorism underlined.

Mackcoull had himself a narrow escape from being
apprehended with White. On entering Tower Street,
he caught sight of the officers, and instantly hurried
off to the residence of a friend in Swallow Street,
whence he despatched a confidential messenger to his
wife, with orders that if the officers had not then
been in search of him she was to put the whole of
the notes into a small trunk, and send them back in
a coach with the messenger. Mrs. Mackcoull sent off
the notes accordingly, and scarcely had an hour
elapsed before the officers arrived, and searched every
part of the house, but being unable to discover anything of a suspicious nature, they concluded that the
notes might be in the possession of French.

"Mackcoull, having meanwhile received the whole of the notes, counted over about 6000*l.* worth, which he concealed on his person, and then getting into a hackney-coach, hastened off with the remainder, locked up in a small trunk to Bill Gibbons. Gibbons, however, insisted on the notes being counted over, which was done; the entire sum amounting to 13,800*l.*, which having been made up into a parcel, Gibbons immediately secreted in a back parlour chimney.

" French having in the meantime heard of the apprehension of White, and knowing that nothing but giving up the money taken from the bank could save either White's life or his own, had an interview with Mrs. Mackcoull, and told her he was willing to give up his share of the plunder, begging her at the same time to go to her husband and tell him that he (French) thought it would be best, for the sake of all parties, to endeavour to open a negotiation with the bank upon the subject. This Mrs. Mackcoull promised to do, adding that she had no doubt her husband would agree to the proposal.

" Now, the house at which Gibbons used commonly to smoke his pipe of an evening was the " Brown Bear " in Bow Street, the landlord of which was, at that time, a Mr. Hazard, with whom, as may be readily supposed, Gibbons was on terms of intimacy. Of him Gibbons learnt all the news of the day, and among the rest the robbery of the Paisley Union

RUSSIAN HOTEL
LODGINGS for GENTLEMEN
MEUX'S ENTIRE

THE BROWN BEAR.

Bank, and the apprehension of Huffey White. On
hearing this Gibbons hastened to Mrs. Mackcoull, and
had just time to tell her that he had been at the
' Brown Bear,' when she, suspecting what he had
heard, interrupted him by exclaiming, ' Oh, how glad
I am to see you, my dear Mr. Gibbons; will you step
in and take tea?' and then she went on with a long
lamentation about the ' unfortunate affair,' and said
she thought that, to save Huffey's life, the notes ought
to be returned, proposing that he (Gibbons) should
enter into a negotiation, and be paid properly for
his trouble. Gibbons assented readily to the suggestion, and on leaving the lady, bent his steps to Bow
Street, to break the matter to his friend Hazard, the
publican, through whom he intended opening the
arrangement with the bank.

"Now, Gibbons, finding that Hazard had heard
every detail of the affair from two of the waiters,
who had put up at his house, and also from the
officers who had been at Scoltock's, unceremoniously
proposed to him to break the negotiation to Vickery,
the officer. Hazard agreed, and Vickery readily
undertook to see the agent for the bank. Gibbons
had scarcely reached home, when Mrs. Mackcoull
arrived, and told him that her husband was willing to
give up the notes, and that, on the following morning,
he would put down in writing what he thought ought
to be the terms of the treaty.

" Now, Sayer was an old acquaintance of Mrs. Mack-coull, and Mackcoull therefore fixed on him to conduct the negotiation in the way he wanted. The bank had offered a reward for whatever part of the money might be recovered, and as Sayer was fond of money, there was thus an inducement for him to undertake the job. Mrs. Mackcoull accordingly called upon Sayer, who undertook to make to the bank agent the following proposals :—namely, that, on the money being returned, White and French should be pardoned for escaping from the hulks ; that no prosecution should be instituted against any of the parties ; and that Mackcoull should not be troubled or molested about any old story of nine years' standing ; all which the agent for the bank, thinking he was going to get back his employers' 20,000*l*., readily agreed to, and the pardon having been obtained for White and French, a time was appointed for the money to be paid over. Accordingly, one evening at ten o'clock, Mrs. Mackcoull waited on the agent for the bank, and, in the presence of Mr. Sayer, produced a small basket, containing, as she said, all the notes that her husband possessed, but which, to the utter amazement both of Sayer and the agent, on being counted over, were found to amount only to 11,941*l*. Of course, the lady affected to know nothing about the remainder, and, of course, also a variety of lies were subsequently told to account for Mackcoull knowing nothing about the deficiency, which, I need scarcely add, never made its appearance.

"Shortly after this Mackcoull went out of town for a time, causing his friends to circulate the old report of his having gone to the *West Indies*,—a story so firmly believed by the bank and their agents that they gave up all hopes of ever seeing or hearing any more either of Mackcoull or the remainder of their money."

A police-officer who wrote his recollections of his services, relates the sequel of this strange transaction. According to his story, "Sayer was so dazzled by the splendid booty he had been dealing with, that, so soon as Mackcoull was secured—which he was a long time after—he sought out the woman, his old acquaintance, and lived with her for many years, in Lisle Street, Leicester Square. She was thrown out of a gig and killed. After which, he removed to the neighbourhood of Chelsea, where he expired, at an advanced age, about four years back, worth upwards of thirty thousand pounds. Just before he died he pointed to a closet and the fire, and made motions to convey to the relatives about him, that he wished them to destroy something. They could not comprehend his meaning, and a few minutes after he breathed his last. The old fellow had not long left this sublunary world, when the stolen Glasgow and Paisley notes again made their appearance in circulation. Inquiries were instituted,

Ruthven was employed, and the principal police-officer of Glasgow, Mr. Miller, came to town, to assist in the investigation, which ended in a man, by trade a copperplate printer, being taken into custody, who, it appeared, was a relative of Sayer's, and had innocently come into the possession of the notes, they being a portion of the property found on the premises at the decease of that officer. Extraordinary means and exertions were adopted to ascertain if any more property could be found; even the garden at Sayer's late residence was dug up for several feet, and a vast number of picklock-keys and housebreaking implements found; but, saving these things, no property of any description was discovered. The copperplate printer was, of course, discharged. The only method of accounting for Sayer's possession of the notes is, that the woman must have had them from Mackcoull, and, from the supposition that they would some time or other become available, had kept them by her; for it is not likely that Sayer had received them from the thieves, either as hush-money or as a portion of the plunder to be restored to the bank. If he had compromised his honesty and honour, by accepting a present from the cracksmen, they undoubtedly would have turned round upon him after their apprehension; and it is not likely that he would have applied them to his own use, instead of returning them, because they were to him quite valueless, and their circulation would have been his entire ruin. There is no doubt that when in his dying moments he made an effort to be understood, by pointing to the cupboard and the fire, that he wished them to be burned, for in that identical cupboard the notes were found."

With such temptations it was impossible to prevent "black sheep," as they might be called, bringing discredit on the force. In 1816, ugly rumours got abroad that some of the officers were in the habit of holding out inducements to burglars and others, to carry out their schemes, in the hope of obtaining the reward that was likely to be offered. This system was discovered by mere accident, and it was found that a well-known efficient officer, Vaughan, was concerned in a villainous plot against the lives and liberty of innocent persons. A certain "wooden-legged man," named Drake, had given one of the horse-patrole, whose name was Vaughan, information of a burglary that was about to be committed. Five men were arrested and examined before the magistrates, when it came out that they had been "put up" to the business by Vaughan. On a further examination it appeared from the evidence of the wooden-legged man, that the patrole met him and three others at Sadler's Wells, where the plan of the burglary at Hoxton was arranged for the following night; the patrole first asking whether they could not put him up to a *crack*, by getting some young fellows into the thing and informing of it. The wooden-legged man procured three brothers, another man, and a boy, to join him in the burglary on the following night. Next day, he sent a boy to the patrole for some money, who sent him 10*s*., with word to *lush* them well, and also furnished him with a *jemmy* (a crow), phosphorous bottle, matches, and some pick-lock keys. The wooden-legged man now prevailed on the three brothers to accompany him at night to commit the burglary, telling them it was an easy matter; that he knew there was a box which contained notes and some valuables, also a good *dab* (or bed), and a handsome dial worth 10*l*. When they consented, he informed the patrole, and took the woman to a public-house, to give an opportunity to the others to commit the burglary. He went frequently in and out, whilst another stopped to detain the woman. Edwards, a patrole from Bow Street, lay in wait to detect them.

The wooden-legged man and the parties he had engaged, came to the house. They found the door unlocked, and as the leader refused to go in, the unfortunate men who were intended to be the victims of the project also hesitated ; but the signal agreed on with the patrole being given, they all fled. The patrole made an impression with the crow-bar on the lintel of the door, to make it appear to have been forced. The crowbar and dark lantern were deposited in the house, and an alarm given that it was robbed. The wooden-legged man now led the patrole and his party to the house where the three brothers lodged, into the pocket of one of whom the patrole, as is stated by his associate, put a ring belonging to the woman of the house.

Another case was discovered in which the patrole had applied to the wooden-legged man to procure some person to commit a burglary, in order that he might share the conviction money. The wooden-legged man was at a loss to find a house, and the patrole recommended to try the house of a *friend* of his own, in Gray's Inn Lane, on which he said the attempt might be conveniently made. The plan being laid, the patrole went to his friend, and told him he had private information that his house would be robbed on the night of the 18th of June, and requested him to keep his dog tied up and quiet in the house, as he and his party should be on the watch and apprehend them. This was agreed to, and the leaders provided their party against night, and encouraged them by telling them the job was easily accomplished and that they would be sure of at least 100*l.* besides a great quantity of articles of value, which they could get, as if given them as a gift. They met at the watering-house at the corner of the King's Road, where they concerted the plan; they then went to the persons with whom they were engaged to commit this burglary; and the patrole, to give them a better opportunity, went to the watchman, who was nearly opposite, and told him he was a Bow Street officer, and had information that a burglary was to be committed, and that he and his party were in wait to apprehend them, and he desired the watchman to put out his candle and shut himself up in his box; the watchman refused, saying he would do his duty, but he would not either put out his light or quit his post, and that he would assist to apprehend any persons. Finding himself foiled in this plan, the patrole contrived to give charge of two girls, who were disputing, that whilst they and the watchman were gone to the watch-house the party might make the attempt. One of them came afterwards to the patrole, and said the — *jaffer* is out. He answered, I told you it was to be out of the way. In consequence of this disappointment, however, the attempt was postponed to another night. The patrole waited on the gentlemen of the watch-board, and made a complaint against the watchman, in consequence of which he was suspended.

The watchman, as far as he knew, confirmed the above evidence, he having seen the patrole several times before the door.

" Mr. Nares desired the watchman to call on him, and that he should be paid for the time he was suspended ; and the watchman produced a petition, which was signed by several respectable inhabitants of the neighbourhood, and which also deposed to his character. He has since been restored."

Once the system was discovered, a number of cases of a similar kind were revealed to the magistrates.

" On another occasion, Mackay saw Vaughan give two bad dollars and four bad shillings to a person named O'Shea, who was to procure an innocent man to buy some article from the mother-in-law of Vaughan, who keeps a chandler's shop in Gray's Inn Lane. A small quantity of good silver was also to be given to him, in order that when he was searched there might appear no excuse for passing the bad money. Mackay afterwards saw O'Shea go into a public-house and shortly return with a poor sailor, whom he directed to go into the shop before mentioned. The sailor did so; O'Shea fled, and immediately the former, having changed some bad money, came out with a loaf. He was instantly seized by Vaughan, who was in waiting, and having secured him and brought him before the magistrate, he was fully committed for trial and convicted."

There were several other cases of an equally atrocious nature mentioned by Mackay, which came within his knowledge by information from and connection with the parties concerned. " On Tuesday night, when Mackay was taken into custody in bed, there was found upon his table a letter addressed to Mr. Westwood of the Bank, disclosing all he knew of the circumstances of the present inquiry, and surrendering the names of the criminal parties. The principal actors in the scene as it relates to the coining, we understand to be Pelham, Brock, O'Shea, and Mac-Power. Jefferson and Dickons were, after the examination of Mackay on Thursday, ordered to appear before the magistrates.

" G. Browne, Mackay, and Drake are now in custody : Hubbard is also in Horsemonger Lane." These were all well-known officers. It was melancholy to find also that the trusty and resolute Ruthven was also implicated ; he was, however, released upon bail. But Vaughan, the chief delinquent, had as yet escaped arrest and was in hiding. But he was presently captured.

" Soon after (in July, 1816), a man came to the office and inquired for Bishop, the officer. The officer, being out upon business, he told the magistrate he knew where Vaughan, the late patrole, was concealed. The magistrate sent the information to Limbrick and Read, the officers belonging to Hatton Garden office, who were originally the cause of discovering this man to have been guilty, that they might have the credit of apprehending him again. Limbrick and Read went on Friday morning, and having procured the assistance of Freeman, the officer, belonging to Whitechapel Road, understanding that Vaughan was armed, they proceeded to Whitechapel Road, and entered a house kept by Vaughan's uncle, where they found him in a parlour, and two loaded pistols upon him. Having secured him, they brought him to the office, where they arrived about three o'clock, when he underwent an examination before Mr. Nares.

"Limbrick and Read produced the pistols, and a pocket-book which they found upon him. There were papers and memorandums in the book which throw considerable light, and tend to confirm a great deal respecting him, so that he who has been exercising a considerable portion of cunning to entrap others, had not cunning enough to put out of the way those documents which will tend to convict himself.

"He denied having run away from his regular residence, or that he was living in concealment at his uncle's house; but stated that the reason of his going to live there was, it was not convenient for him to sleep at home on account of his wife having lately been brought to bed. He considered himself not bound to appear till next sessions, at which time he had given bail to answer charges that might be brought against him, and in consequence of what had been said in public and private respecting his conduct, he did not consider himself safe in walking the streets. He denied what had been said against him to be true, but asserted that there was a conspiracy against him.

"Dickons, one of the patrole, who used to act with

him in the employ of the Bank of England in detecting the utterers of counterfeit tokens, was present, and much abuse passed between them. On Thursday it was ascertained that Dickons complained of having been classed with Vaughan, and it having been insinuated that he was concerned with him in his malpractices, he was told he ought to find Vaughan to clear himself, and Adkins, the officer, offered to give him a guinea if he would apprehend him; he set off, taking another patrole with him, but saying he did not like to go to take him without a warrant as he knew he was armed, although he confessed he was not afraid of him. In the course of the investigation it was ascertained that Dickons had met Vaughan since he had been wanted, and had advised him to run away to France. Dickons was ordered into custody till he produced the necessary bail.

" Vaughan was committed as an accessory before the fact in breaking open the house of Mrs. M'Donald in Hoxton, which was the circumstance that led to the discovery of these transactions."

Charges of another description were also made against the Bow Street officers. One of an odd, and perhaps of a rather unhandsome kind, was made by one of the foreign consuls against the patrole.

" Mr. Halls, the Hanoverian Consul, wrote to complain to Sir R. Birnie, a few days ago, that persons professing to belong to the Bow Street patrole had called at his house and asked for presents by the way of Christmas boxes, and wishing to know if such a practice was sanctioned by the magistrates. Sir R. Birnie stated that such a practice, so far from being sanctioned, was strictly prohibited, and any officer known to have asked such a thing would be dismissed from his situation. Sir Richard subsequently learned that Francis Holyland, the conductor of the Bedford Square division of night-patrole, was the officer who had called at Mr. Halls' and other houses to collect Christmas boxes, and on Tuesday morning he ordered that officer to come before him, and asked how it was that he had presumed to act in defiance of a known rule which was laid down, and always rigorously enforced by the magistrates? Holyland said he was extremely sorry, but he assured Sir Richard that it was done in ignorance, and that the moment he discovered he was wrong he discontinued it. Sir R. Birnie—"Sir, you called upon the Hanoverian Consul with a printed paper beginning ' We, the undersigned,' and at the head of the list appeared your name. You must have known, and I am sure did know, that such a practice was contrary to the orders of the magistrates, and you are suspended from your office."

Bond, another Bow Street officer, who was well-known from his connection with Drury Lane Theatre, often found himself distracted by the conflicting duties required of him by the managers and the public. Thus he was one day addressed by " Sir Richard," who told him that he had heard several complaints respecting

the want of due attention on the part of those officers
who should attend the different entrances to the pit
and boxes, to protect the public from the depredations
of thieves. The officers appointed to that duty at
Drury Lane, instead of rendering the public their protection and assistance, were placed as watchers over
the checktakers, a duty which it was never intended
they should perform, and which he (Sir R. Birnie) had
determined to put a stop to. A magistrate had just
informed him that he had been robbed of his watch,
chain, and seals, at the box-entrance, on Monday
evening, a circumstance which could not have occurred
if the police-officers had been at their posts.

Bond, in reply, said he would lose no time in communicating with his son on the subject. He added that
when he was at the theatre, attempts had been made
to place the officers under his directions over the door-
keepers and checktakers, and Mr. Winston, a gentleman connected with the management, had more than
once told him that the public might take care of themselves, and that the police were at the disposal of the
managers, whose interests they were bound, in the
first instance, to protect.

Some ingenious knaves even occasionally took advantage of the special dress of the officers to assume
their duties, and with some success. " For the last ten
days a new and successful mode of plunder has been
carried on in the neighbourhood of London by two or

three fellows who pretend to belong to the Bow Street patrole, and who are dressed in red waistcoats, and produce constables' staves. The plan of these villains appears to be perfectly arranged. They pretend to come in search of a suspected character, or to look for stolen and contraband goods. Easy access is found by assuming the authority of police-officers, and upon being shown through the different apartments, they never fail to carry away whatever is valuable and portable that comes within their reach. A few evenings since, about ten o'clock, they went to the "Red Lion" public-house, near Wimbledon Common. The landlord was not at home, and they proceeded to search the house for an ideal suspicious character; in doing so they contrived to carry off from the different apartments property to a considerable amount. The same night they went to a tradesman's house in the neighbourhood, and, he being from home, they searched the house under pretence of looking for stolen goods."

Many anecdotes used to be current as to the stupidity of the old watchman or Charlie; but the complaints periodically made at the office show that their ignorance exceeded the common belief. On the other hand the constant battering and ill-usage received could not be expected to improve their discrimination.

Thus we find that Courteney, a watchman of the Strand, brought a man before the magistrates for smoking a cigar in the street! The accused had been locked up nearly twelve hours for this *offence*. It is almost unnecessary to say that the man was instantly discharged, and the watchman received from the magistrates an admonition for his misconduct.

And again : On Wednesday night, Sands, a watchman of the Savoy, Strand, took Mr. Crosbie, the officiating clergyman of Sydenham, into custody for talking to a person in the street, and refusing to " move on " when *ordered* so to do. The gentleman was obliged to leave his watch and seals as a security for his appearance at this office the next day, where he accordingly came; and Sir R. Birnie, after hearing the case, ordered Sands to be suspended from acting in future.

On another occasion, two young men were brought up by one of the guardians of the night on a charge of disorderly conduct. The young men said in their defence that they were returning home through Drury Lane, when a chimney-sweep snatched the hat off one of them and ran away. They called to the watchman, but he refused to go after the offender, because it was a different parish. Sir R. Birnie severely reprimanded the watchman. The idea of making a distinction of parishes in such a case was mere nonsense. The watchmen were always ready enough to bring ridiculous charges, like the present, to the office ; but he never found one of them bringing a criminal charge. Their conduct, in this instance, was outrageous. The defendants were then dismissed.

§ *Amateur Police.*

A curious practice connected with the general police system, and which came out before the various committees, was that the constables in Westminster and in most of the outlying districts were requisitioned inhabitants, who had to perform the duties without pay, or, indeed, good will, or else by substitute, the latter being glad to undertake the office for a trifling remuneration. At Westminster there was a quaint, old-fashioned system in vogue up to the time of the establishment of the new police. The burgesses elected a court of their own, called a " Leet," which was presided over by the Dean and High Steward. This leet selected about eighty tradesmen of the district, always with the odd exception of the licensed victuallers. These persons were named to do the duties of constable in the district, and, it would appear for the most part, performed the duties—or undertook to perform them—in a sort of halting fashion, some coming on duty every fifteenth night, " unless otherwise engaged." A system of substitutes was, of course, encouraged, and some eight or ten men were ready, for a sum of from eight to twenty pounds, to undertake the duties. This number really represents the acting watch of the district. Deplorable accounts were given of the class of person thus appointed—paupers from the workhouses being often selected, and the others aged, worn-out creatures, picked up "anyhow and everyhow." This was to be expected, as in some districts the remuneration was no more than 1*s*. 6*d*. a night, or perhaps 2*s*. 6*d*. for an "odd job." It was confessed, however, that this was eked out by a practice of "compounding charges at the watch-house." Much ridicule of the "Charlies'" inefficiency might have been spared, for, with such a system and such materials, what could have been expected.

Acting with these wretched guardians of the peace, we find our old friend "THE BEADLE," flourishing all over London to an extraordinary degree. There were over fifty of these officials, among whose duties was that of "setting the watch," and, in some cases, of going round through the night and seeing that the watch were at their posts. These men had from 60*l*. to 70*l*. a year. In a few cases, however, the office was taken quite *au sérieux* by conscientious inhabitants; but they paid dearly for their sincerity. Thus, in the year 1828 an active young tradesman in the Bow Street district was appointed parish constable of St. Paul's. Struck with the disorders of Covent Garden and the helplessness of the police, he determined, instead of hiring a substitute, to perform the duties himself. It is instructive to find what was the fate of his well-meant efforts, and how he was treated, not by the rogues and disorderly characters, but by the authorities, who did not relish his intrusion.

When he took up his office he found Covent Garden at midnight a regular pandemonium, though Charles Lamb, who lived there about the same time and in the same scenes, was delighted with the racket. " There were thieves and ' night-coaches,' ' cads ' who attended the night-coaches, coffee-houses being open to a very late hour, and public-houses also, a number of the worst of characters, which scarcely deserve the name of men, that I have every reason to believe were of the most infamous description. By-night coaches I mean a number of coaches that ply upon the stand to take night-fares. I made it my duty to make particular inquiry with a view to get rid of that nuisance. I spoke first to Sir Richard Birnie upon the subject, and he said, ' Give them regular notice to leave the stand, and if, after midnight, any of those coaches should be found plying, I shall send a body of officers sufficient to take the whole to the green-yard.' This notice I served at the watering-house attached to that stand. I afterwards, fearful of committing myself, went to Mr. James Quaife, one of the principals of the hackney-coach office, and he said that Sir Richard Birnie had no such power ; that the hackney-coaches had a right to stand where they pleased, and at what time they pleased ; that they might form a line in any street

N 2

whatever. This was contrary to what I had heard before.

"My experience was strengthened by the injury that I myself, as a housekeeper, sustained by the noise and disorder. I was anxious, like other housekeepers, to make the most of my lodgings ; and whenever I had got respectable gentlemen into my house, I could not retain them, from the noises at night, occasioned by those men who were, to use a familiar term, sky-larking and repairing the coaches, taking off the wheels and hammering and clanking ; and sometimes they would have the girls in the coaches and upon the boxes, and riding up and down. These coaches were made any use of by thieves for the conveyance of stolen goods ; of it I have no doubt. I made myself as active as I could, because I started with the inten-tion to see how far the powers of a constable would go towards doing it, because I perceived, as everybody else does, a wonderful apathy in the police-officers ; and it was mortifying to see a party of officers stand-ing at one end of the street and, night after night, a throng of well-known thieves congregating at the other end of the street, and no steps taken to remove them. I am speaking of officers attached to Bow Street, and of that class of officers. Before I was constable, and since I have been constable, I have seen gentlemen, for instance, leaving the portico of the theatre with a lady having hold of each arm. His pockets have been defenceless, as it were, and I have seen the thieves follow him in the most audacious manner and dip their hands in his pockets, and take handkerchiefs and snuff-boxes, or anything else. I have seized them repeatedly."

The professional officers soon found an opportunity of " doing him a turn," as they called it.

"I had to contend with innumerable difficulties," he says. "I saw a marked spirit of envy, and a determination to do me all the injury they possibly could ; as if I were undertaking something I had no business to interfere with. I consider they acted as men conscious that every conviction I carried to Bow Street was a tacit reproach upon them for not doing their duty. I repeatedly heard of threats made behind my back, and those threats, in one instance, were carried into execution. While I was clearing the avenue in front of Drury Lane Theatre—having previously consulted Sir Richard Birnie, and having had from Sir Richard Birnie the promise of assistance and support—while I was doing that, I was seized by Bond and Nettleton, two of the deputed officers attached to Drury Lane Theatre, and I was struck and dragged through the streets like a felon. Sir Richard Birnie, either from some false impression, or from some feeling I could not well decipher, chose to dismiss the complaint without hearing the case gone into, treating it as a squabble between officers. They charged me with striking them, which was as false as God is true. To show the malice with which they treated me, they wanted to drag me to St. Martin's watch-house. They threatened the constable of the night that if he did not take charge of me they would take me to St. Martin's watch-house. Having given charge of me, of course they made their complaint. And that complaint was dismissed instantly."

CHAPTER VI.

OFFICE ECCENTRICITIES.

§ *Sir Richard Birnie*

THE court at Bow Street was always, in spite of attempts at alteration and rearrangement, a poor, straitened place, whose accommodation was miserably inadequate to the important work that was despatched there. We can see what it was from the picture that adorns the adventures of " Tom and Jerry," where it appears to be no more than a large room, though it is a place of more pretension in the plate given in Akerman's " Microcosm of London." On great days, in our time, when the " Slade Case," for instance, was going on, the shifts to find room for the witnesses, counsel, &c., were of pitiable kind, and the atmosphere of the ill-ventilated and crowded place was scarcely enjoyable. Yet here the patient Bow Street magistrate carried out his complicated functions, on a small salary and under many difficulties. At the beginning of the century, the total outlay for the maintenance of the office, its staff and detectives, and police officers, including the salaries of the magistrates, did not reach an annual sum of 8000*l.* From the

year 1792, when seven offices were established, their
united cost was no more than 18,000*l*., each of the sub-
sidiary offices was allowed but 2000*l*. a year; while
the total outlay for administration and the detection of
crime was only 26,000*l*. It was wonderful that with a
system thus " starved," such results were obtained ; and
these were mainly owing to the energy and spirit and
personal exertions of the Bow Street magistrates themselves. Thus unselfishness has always distinguished
the officers of the country, who show themselves eager
to supplement what the system fails in, by their own
labour. From his peculiar position and duties, the
magistrate at Bow Street generally developed qualities
and characteristics of a special kind and suited to his
position. He had, as we have seen, to act as " thief-
taker," direct the pursuit of criminals, as well as to deal
with them, and be in perpetual conflict and contact
with the disorderly classes. To Bow Street every kind
of case, some of the most strange kind, found its way ;
and as the proceedings were drawn out, there was
generally found something startling or dramatic to
enliven the cases. The magistrate's wits became as
it were sharpened, and his experience, as may be conceived, was of the most varied description. Hence
there were to be seen, and are to this hour seen, little
dramas of an amusing, an exciting kind, for what was
at stake was of a serious description—often life or
liberty, and on the preparatory struggle at this stage,
the criminal's safety depended.

One of the most prominent of the later magistrates, and whose name was most familiar to the public, was Mr., afterwards Sir Richard, Birnie, under whose auspices, as we shall see, many diverting scenes were furnished for the amusement of the public. The story of his rise shows that he was a remarkable character in his way, and must have possessed a singular resolution. The son of a saddler, he came to London from Banff, where he was born, a poor unfriended Scotch lad, with hardly " a saxpence " in his pocket.

On the ground where the Union Club now stands formerly stood a tavern, known as the Cannon Coffee House, which was at the end of a street known as Hedge Lane, but later as Whitcomb Street. Here he was glad to find lodging in an attic in a mean house. The floor below was occupied by a thrifty barber, who one day observed the lad following a coal-cart and picking up the lumps of coal which fell from it, which he carefully brought home to his garret. He was so delighted with this sign of a provident spirit that he determined on the spot that he should be his heir and son. By a lucky chance the boy obtained employment with the firm of Mackintosh, who supplied the Royal Family with harness, &c. ; and being once despatched to wait on the Regent, H.R.H. was so pleased with his style and manners, that he required that the same agent should for the future always wait on him. This " taking fancies " was a peculiarity of the Regent's. Birnie soon became foreman, then partner, and, it is said, married the daughter of his first patron, the barber.[1] He presently exhibited a serious fancy for parochial work, taking a deep interest in the smaller official life. Indeed, he used to boast that he had filled every office in the parish, save that of watchman and beadle. Such zeal was encouraged, and at the request of a duke he was made a magistrate; when he could indulge his taste with greater facility, and was to be seen constantly at Bow Street, following the cases. On a few occasions he took the magistrate's place. He was presently appointed to Union Hall Court, and later to Bow Street, and devoted himself to the duties of his post with a peculiar *goût*. He was an energetic and courageous magistrate, and these qualities he displayed with a signal effect on several notable occasions. It was he who planned the perilous enterprise of the arrest of Thistlewood and his gang, which was attended by loss of life. He led on the party fearlessly, " the balls," as it was described, " whistling about his head." In the riots connected with the Queen's funeral in the following year he showed similar intrepidity in confronting an excited mob, and when one of the magistrates shrank from reading the Riot Act, he undertook the duty.

On the bench, in the exercise of his duties, he displayed good sense and sagacity, exercising a wholesome severity, tempered by a certain good-humour. This, in

[1] Richardson's " Recollections."

SIR RICHARD BIRNIE.

process of time, was developed into a sort of freedom, or even buffoonery, which entertained the public; and displays of jocoseness and " scenes " began to be regularly looked for when " Sir Richard " was on the bench. Some of these were often dramatic, and formed a contrast to those grimly tragic episodes of which the office was too often the scene. Occasionally, Sir Richard's freedoms exposed him to unpleasant scenes. The familiar magistrate expects every one to receive his utterances in an obsequious spirit, and when he meets resistance becomes intemperate. A scene of this kind arose in connection with a cab-fare, the sum in dispute being one shilling. After an adjournment, Mr. Miller, a barrister, said he attended on behalf of Mr. Jay, by whom he had been instructed to resist the demand. The original summons was dismissed on account of some technical defect.

Sir Richard: I remember all that very well, sir. I could not convict on the first summons because of some clerical error. The coachman is entitled to his expenses.

Mr. Miller: I submit not: the party who obtains a dismissal on such a ground is never saddled with costs.

Sir Richard: I say the coachman is entitled to his expenses if the distance he goes for be correct; and more I say, he shall have them, too.

Mr. Miller: I must protest against this. The point

for your determination is of great public importance, and demands deliberation before it is decided.

Sir Richard: Am 1 not deliberate? I say he shall have his expenses.

Mr. Miller : You sit there to administer the law as it is, and I contend that such a decision is wholly unwarranted. Was not one shilling put into your hand, coachman?

Complainant: Yes, but I would not accept it.

Mr. Miller : That is immaterial : the tender was a legal due, and got rid of all cause of complaint.

Sir Richard : Stuff and nonsense; was ever anything so pitiful? Make out the order, Mr. Woods, for the payment of the shilling, and costs of the present summons.

Mr. Miller; As counsel, I am bound to offer every argument that suggests itself to me.

Sir Richard : Yes, I know you are paid for talking, and must earn your fee. The public business cannot stand still. Call on another case.

Mr. Miller : I must say that such conduct on your part justifies the opinion which is everywhere in circulation respecting your administration of the law.

Sir Richard : You had better restrain yourself, sir.

Mr. Miller : In addition, I have to thank you for your polite attention, and the epithets of "stuff and nonsense" applied to me.

Sir Richard: You mistake. I meant these to apply to your defence, and not to you.

Mr. Miller: I shall certainly never appear before this tribunal again until some more courteous and gentlemanlike person presides over it.

Sir Richard: With all my heart. I did not send for you now, much less want you.

Mr. Miller: This conduct of yours shall not be forgotten; I shall see if it can be used in a higher quarter; (saying which, Mr. Miller left the office, leaving the matter to be finally adjusted by his Worship, who made the order, which was refused to be complied with by the defendant).

This was not very edifying. In fact, during the later portion of his life, Sir Richard displayed a rather testy, not to say eccentric disposition, which exposed him to the free comments of a hostile press. On one occasion, in 1828, an unseemly scene took place between him and some of the parishioners of Covent Garden, in reference to the election of Overseers.

" On Tuesday last, a Petty Session was held at St. Paul's, Covent Garden, for the appointment of Overseers. Mr. Dow was called to the chair by the parishioners, who had prepared a list of eight householders. The late Select Vestry had prepared a private list of their own, without consulting the parishioners. On Sir Richard Birnie and Mr. Hall entering the room, the former demanded of Mr. Dow who he was. Mr. Dow gave his name, and expressed his readiness to resign the chair to Sir Richard. The worthy magistrate, however, seized him by the arm (*which, having been dislocated, was in a sling*), and said, "*Get out, sir, get out!*"

Mr. Dow: Gently, Sir Richard, you do not consider my arm; you give me great pain.

Sir Richard: I care nothing about your arm.

The Magistrate then called for the list of the "Select," and was proceeding to call from it, when his attention was requested to the list sanctioned by the parishioners.

Sir Richard: I know nothing about any lists.

Mr. Corder wished to explain.

Sir Richard: I'll hear no explanation.

A parishioner happening to express a wish not to detain the magistrates, as their official duties would oblige them to attend at Bow Street, Sir Richard interrupted him with "*Obliged,* sir! I am not *obliged* to attend. How dare you, sir, presume that I am *obliged?* I can stay away all day if I like."

Mr. Dow emphatically remonstrated with Sir Richard Birnie on his conduct, which he declared to be unmanly and ungentlemanly, adding, "You have treated me like a dog."

Sir Richard ordered Mr. Roche to take down Mr. Dow's words, upon which the latter repeated them. The meeting separated under strong feelings of dissatisfaction."

§ "*Dick Martin.*"

A frequent performer in this way was Mr. Richard or "Dick" Martin, M.P. for Galway, whose protection of animals, exhibited in the most eccentric and fanatical fashion, was set off by his natural readiness to take offence, and thus exhibit "cruelty to animals" in the case of his own species. "Martin's Act" was the result of his exertions, and the author was the most forward to enforce its provisions. He was accordingly constantly dragging some groom or driver before Sir R. Birnie or Mr. Minshull, who treated his oddities with good-humoured indulgence. These scenes were very entertaining, and the reporters took care to give his opinions with literal accuracy.

It was thus that in August, 1823, he summoned a waggoner in the service of Messrs. Fitch and Sons, market-gardeners, for "wantonly and cruelly" beating a horse.

"Mr. Martin proceeded *in his usual animated manner* to state that on Monday se'nnight, as he was approaching Covent Garden market in his gig, he heard the loud smacking of a whip, and he found the defendant flogging a horse with all his strength, and in the most wanton and cruel manner. The unfortunate animal was not in a team—he was not at work at all, but was tied up by the head to another waggon, and it was therefore quite improbable that the animal had given any provocation for the beating he had got; indeed, he

(Mr. Martin) was prepared to say upon his solemn oath, that he believed there was no necessity whatever for beating the horse in the manner described. There was another circumstance of this case which he was extremely sorry to be obliged to relate, and that was, that a person of the decent and respectable appearance and manners of him who now stood by the side of the waggoner (pointing to Mr. Fitch), should have sanctioned such cruelty. While he (Mr. Martin) was talking to the waggoner, Mr. Fitch came up and said that he had ordered his man to flog the horse, and that he deserved it, adding that the horse had a sore wither, and had set up kicking at a violent rate, and it was necessary to beat him well.

Mr. Fitch here requested to be heard, upon which,

Mr. Martin said, "*O, man alive, that will never do!* I accuse you as well as your man."

Mr. Minshull : I don't know that Mr. Fitch is not an admissible witness on behalf of his servant.

Mr. Martin : But I do, though. *Sure I charge them both.*

Mr. Fitch, without being sworn, stated that the horse in question had been kicking incessantly for more than half an hour before. The horse was irritated by the rubbing of the collar-chain against a sore place on his wither.

Mr. Minshull : What was your object in whipping him ?

Mr. Fitch: Why, sir, to make him stand still.

Here Mr Martin broke out in characteristic style, " Ha, ha! that's very good, and reminds me of an anecdote exactly bearing upon this case. A French financier under the *ancien régime* had, among his stud, a horse which had a knack of devouring another horse's corn as well as his own; and in order to put a stop to a practice so injurious both to the robber and the robbed, he ordered execution of death to be put in force upon the offender, and the horse (a beautiful animal by the bye) was shot. But, egad, the financier found that this execution had very little effect in the way of example, for other thievishly-inclined horses still robbed their neighbours, and his friends told him he might shoot the whole stud before he cured the evil; so he ordered no more executions." (A loud laugh followed the relation of this anecdote.)

Mr. Minshull said the words of the act were " wantonly and cruelly," and was Mr. Martin prepared to say that this defendant had acted " wantonly and cruelly " ?

Mr. Martin, with much warmth, said he had most undoubtedly. He had said before, and he now repeated it, that upon his oath the man acted wantonly and cruelly. The animal was tied up and perfectly quiet. If he was not convicted, all previous convictions under this act were unjust, and all magistrates who had decided against persons accused under this popular statute had transgressed the law.

Mr. Minshull said it was very difficult to define the degree of chastisement which this act contemplated in the term " cruelty."

Mr. Martin said this was precisely the line of argument adopted by the advocates of cruelty—the opposers of his bill—he meant Mr. Brougham among others ; and his (Mr. Martin's) answer, and the answer of Lord Londonderry and others too, was, that cruelty was to be defined according to received notions of it. Now he declared that this man acted wantonly and cruelly ; and he had been used to horses for thirty years, and he would moreover call his groom, who would declare the same opinion.

The groom was then called, and said he thought the horse cruelly and unnecessarily beaten.

Sir R. Birnie: But was this beating necessary ? I think a man must be permitted to exercise his own judgment as to the extent of chastisement he may inflict upon his horse.

Mr. Martin: Oh, by G—, if a man is to be the judge in his own case, there's an end of everything.

Sir R. Birnie: I must fine you 5s. for swearing.

Mr. Martin: I am sworn already.

Mr. Minshull: Yes, but you have just sworn an unnecessary oath.

Mr. Martin (taking out his purse) : Well, I'll pay.

Sir R. Birnie (smiling) : No, I will not enforce it this time. I was joking only.

Mr. Martin again very earnestly pressed for a conviction, and said that if a man flogged his apprentice with unnecessary severity, he must not be allowed to be the judge whether or not he had acted with cruelty. That must depend upon the cool, unbiassed judgment of others.

Mr. Minshull : Was the man out of temper?

Mr. Martin : Quite infuriated."

All this was highly amusing and entertaining to the audience. But these indulged *farceurs* are often inclined to abuse their privilege and turn on those who tolerate their antics. Thus, when the owner of the animal proceeded to urge that a horse was sagacious and understood what he was beaten for,

Mr. Martin replied : " Nonsense, man. As well might you beat a horse to-day for kicking this day week. I tell you what you should do to make a horse good and obedient! just go whisper in his ear, " You are a good horse, and I am a bad man," and I engage he will be as quiet as a lamb!

The Magistrate again expressed an opinion that a man must be allowed to exercise his own judgment, whereupon

Mr. Martin, with an energy of manner which beggars description, exclaimed, " Time has been that when the brains were out, the man would die;" and at the same time sprang from his seat upon the bench, and throwing down a bar which is placed to keep off the people, seemed about to leave the office, but paused a moment, and returned in great agitation to the bench.

Mr. Minshull: My brains may be out now, and I still live; but I shall act upon my own judgment as far as it goes, and I cannot make up my mind to convict in this case.

Mr. Martin: Then I tell you that it is high time you were relieved from the labours of your office.

Mr. Minshull: That was a very kind and gentlemanly remark certainly, Mr. Martin; but I will keep my temper, whatever you may do. I dismiss the case.

Mr. Martin, during the last two or three minutes that he remained, moved to and from the bench and the body of the office with great rapidity; and at length snatched up his hat, hurried out, observing as he went, that he would apply for pardon for all who had ever been convicted under this statute."

In 1825 we find this singular person engaged in conflict with the proprietors of *Blackwood's Magazine* and the *Morning Chronicle,* who had ridiculed not so much his philanthropic exertions, as the eccentric and tyrannous method by which he tried to enforce his views.

" Mr. Martin addressed Sir Richard Birnie, complaining of the repeated attacks made in the *Morning Chronicle* upon him, for his endeavours to put a stop to the ill-treatment of animals; more particularly for an article quoted in that paper from *Blackwood's*

Magazine, which the hon. legislator asserted aimed at his life—inasmuch as it was asked plainly and undisguisedly, " Why don't you kill him? "—" Thus," said Mr. M., "this paper not only disseminates the most barefaced libels upon the motives of my exertions in the cause of humanity, but actually solicits any one to knock me on the head, as he would a bullock." Sir Richard said, " Pray, Mr. Martin, may that not mean the ox, and not you? "—to which Mr. M. replied, he was satisfied it clearly meant himself. " Look," said he, " to the daily attacks which are made upon me. It was but a short time since, under an article of Police, they headed it, ' Mr. Martin and *another* unfortunate ass ; ' *and who could that mean but me?* "

On friday, Mr. V. Dowling attended as the representative of Mr. Clement. Mr. Adolphus was counsel for the defence.

The paragraph thus commenced :—" Blackwood and Martin. It is well for the former that a considerable interval separates him from Mr. Martin, otherwise we think his friends might be in some apprehension for him. Our hair absolutely stood on end when we read the following attack in the last number." Then follows the quotation from *Blackwood*, beginning, " That Irish Jack-ass, Martin, &c."

Mr. Adolphus, an adroit advocate, then proceeded to deal with the case, and, it will be seen, inflamed the

" animals' friend " almost to fury. He said that Martin
swore that he believed the intention of the journalist
was to incite people to murder him! He was
astonished at such swearing! If a man was to swear
so from ignorance he should pity his intellect—if from
malice, he would say, God forgive him!—and he would
say so in common charity, for such a man would have
much more to answer for than the miserable brutes for
which he affected to feel so much compassion! As to
the "angry gabble," it was known to all who read the
papers of the day that there was a person in the habit
of going about to the different police-offices, disgusting
everybody with his angry and vulgar gabble; loading
every *poor* wretch with such epithets as " savage
scoundrel," " atrocious wretch," "ruffianly miscreant,"
and others equally violent. If he stopped there,
perhaps there would be no great harm ; but when that
man could deliberately swear that he saw an animal
beaten with a bludgeon, which afterwards turned out
to be a switch—(*Mr. Martin* : A switch!)—yes, a
switch—when he could magnify a switch into a
bludgeon, and that too on his solemn oath—he (Mr.
A.) could not, he would not trust himself to express
his opinion of him ; and when such a man as that came
forward with a charge like the present, it ought to
be received with great caution indeed.—The paragraph
quoted from *Blackwood* began : " *That Irish Jack-
ass, Martin.*" Now, whether the writer called him

Dick-ass or Jack-ass, it was much the same. It was well known that in Essex, and some other counties, it was as common to say Dick-ass as Jack-ass, and therefore either would apply. He should like to know, indeed, if the ass was not the most libelled of the two. There was one ass that spoke but once, and never told a lie. Was that the case with Mr. Martin? He was afraid not. Mr. Adolphus, after continuing in the same strain for some time, returned to the subject of the affidavit. He would now call evidence to show that Mr. Martin's declaration here upon oath, and his assertions elsewhere, were totally at variance; and that so far from feeling any fear, he had gone even into the lion's den, the office of the *Chronicle*, a few hours after he had sworn the affidavit, and said, "Well, what's going on? What's doing? This is all nuts to me—itbrings me into popularity—I like all this sort of thing." And yet to-day he has the audacity to come forward and support that most improper affidavit.

Mr. Martin here threw himself across the table as far as he could reach, and exclaimed,—

"*You scoundrel, how dare you say it is an improper affidavit!*"

Mr. Minshull : Really, Mr. Martin, I am quite astonished. I must hold you to bail, sir.

Sir Richard Birnie : Mr. Martin, you have said you are a magistrate—pray pay some respect to the bench here, whatever may be the custom in Ireland.

Mr. Minshull said he had heard sufficient to authorize him to call upon Clement to give bail, himself in 200*l.*, and two sureties in 100*l.* each.

At the next hearing Mr. Martin appeared in person, and the affair ended harmoniously. With regard to *Blackwood's Magazine* he considered it to be the parent root which had sent forth the many branches of libels that appeared in the *Morning Chronicle* against him. He next proceeded to notice the long statement made there on a former day by Mr. Adolphus. "I myself," said he, "was greatly accountable for the extravagant length and the irrelevant abuse to which that individual had recourse, in fact, for no other purpose than that of repeating the vile libels which had appeared previously in the pages of the *Morning Chronicle.*"

Mr. Halls: Will you allow me to say, that no part of what you say has anything to do with any case which has appeared before me. I know nothing about it.

Mr. Martin: I wish to say, that if it was any fault, I encouraged it. There is also another subject which I think will be consolatory to the Bench. I was, on the occasion to which I now allude, guilty of an act of great intemperance, I was greatly criminal; and not being able at that time to apologise, I come now humbly and penitentially to make my apology for what I said when that man was addressing the Bench. My opinion is, that we ought not to inflict intemperate

punishment on the brute creation; and it was therefore particularly inexcusable in me to be so intemperate against that which was a brute—a brute, who
was a brute without reason, and exiled almost from
the society of human beings.

Mr. Halls: I must not hear this, as the parties
about whom you are speaking, are not present. I
must not, I cannot hear these observations. I have
such an opinion of the Magistrate who heard the case,
that I am sure he would not allow any imputation to
be cast on your character, Mr. Martin, which you
would not have an opportunity of refuting.

Mr. Martin: I bow. From Mr. Blackwood I have
received the most penitential letter it is possible for a
man to write. He acknowledges the atrocity of the
libel, and allows the impropriety of disseminating it :
that it got in without his knowledge; and, in the
subsequent number, which will appear in a few days,
there will appear an apology which will satisfy me.
But I doubt if an apology will satisfy me; but this will,
when he comes to be punished, serve to mitigate the
sentence which will be passed on him, whether I proceed against him by an indictment at the Quarter
Sessions, or obtain a criminal information in the King's
Bench. Now, sir, your Worship, I shall take my leave,
and, on a future day, make the application to which
I have alluded."

Sir Richard, who, as we have seen, had a character

for eccentricity, seemed to welcome these public performers, who were congenial to him, and enlivened the dull monotony of a police-court. A number of *soi-disant* " public men " were glad to advertise themselves and their "hobbies," and found Sir Richard always willing to give them the opportunity they desired. A field-day at Bow Street was thus often sought by Cobbett, Orator Hunt, and other demagogues who arrived with some grievance and were then truly welcome.

§ *Cobbett.*

Thus, the agitator Cobbett, having taken up the subject of turnpike overcharges, contested the matter so sturdily that he became a terror to the pike-keepers from his frequent summonses, and was actually allowed to go through the gates *free.* In 1823 he was very busy at this work, and on October 23 he appeared at the office, and laid informations against several turnpike toll-collectors for having taken too high a toll from poor men who kept one-horse carts, and who were very numerous on the roads leading out from Hyde Park Corner. Mr. Cobbett stated that, as nearly as he could calculate, the renters of the tolls in his neighbourhood had, for about eighty days last past, extorted to the amount of at least 5*l.* a day on the Kensington road alone ; and that, too, from some of the most industrious and hard-working men in the whole kingdom.

This was going on all round the metropolis, and even many miles out into the country in almost every direction. The tolls of all the roads from Hyde Park Corner westward are rented by rich Jews, against whose long purses poor men are wholly unable to contend. Mr. Cobbett, hearing of this system of oppression, about five weeks ago, went to the Kensington turnpike-gate, and told the toll-collectors that, if they did not desist from their extortion he would call them to account. Finding the extortion still going on, he resolved to make the complaint. He obtained summonses for several toll-collectors, and the like were obtained by seven one-horse cart men, who came to the office with him.

Mr. Levy, one of the lessees of the turnpike-roads, attended by a solicitor, appeared to answer to informations exhibited by Mr. William Cobbett against the collectors of tolls, for exacting from divers persons therein named, three halfpence more than by law allowed. Mr. Cobbett attended to conduct his case, and at the invitation of Sir R. Birnie took a place on the bench. Some amusing scenes followed, exhibiting the sturdy arrogance of the demagogue.

On the solicitor for the lessees requesting that it might stand over until they could have the assistance of counsel,

Mr. Cobbett : It is of vital importance to the public as well as the lessees, and more especially to the poor men, on whose behalf I appear—namely, the proprietors of one-horse carts, who have suffered shamefully by this system of extortion.

Mr. Levy : Why, you have never suffered, Mr Cobbett, and why need you be so warm in the cause?

Mr. Cobbett : No; because they know me; I have threatened to pull them up; and they are therefore glad to take threepence, instead of fourpence halfpenny.

Mr. Levy : Why they let you through for nothing sooner than be troubled with you; you know that you no sooner show your face, than they call out, " That's Cobbett ; let him go."

Mr. Cobbett to Mr. Levy : You are a Jew, I suppose.

Mr. Levy : I am a Jew, it is true ; but you are neither Jew, Christian, nor any other religion. *You are an Atheist, as everybody knows.*

Mr. Cobbett smiled, and observed, that what he had advanced in this office was strictly true. He had taken up the business only in consequence of an application from several poor men who were sufferers by the system. One poor man alone, a gardener, had paid more than 30*s.* in three-halfpences within the last few weeks.

Some other conversation followed, during which Mr. Levy said that he would undertake that between that day and the final decision of the case, the additional three-halfpence should not be taken. They only wanted time to meet the question properly.

Mr. Cobbett : Time! you have had time enough. I told one of your men I meant to pull you all up.

Mr. Levy asked what man?

Mr. Cobbett : How can I remember the face of any one of your men, when you change them every two hours?

Mr. Levy : But you could have seen his name over the door.

Mr. Cobbett : I did not look for his name, for I did not think such a step necessary; but I give you my word I told him so.

Mr. Levy : Your word! what is your word? You have been talking *for these three years about your Gridiron, but you are not broiled yet.*

Mr. Cobbett : No, nor *crucified* either ; nor do I wish to be.

Mr. Levy : Perhaps not ; but you might be without injustice.

Sir R. Birnie said, he could not help thinking the proposition of Mr. Levy a fair one, and if Mr. Cobbett had no very powerful objection to offer, the case should be postponed.

Mr. Cobbett : Oh, in God's name, let them have the benefit of *counsel ;* do not deprive the gentlemen of the benefit of *counsel.*

Ultimately, the hearing was postponed to Monday, October 13.

This is equally edifying whether we regard the

toleration of the bench or the decency of the disputants.

§ *The Hunts.*

The well-known violent agitator, "Orator" Hunt, was in 1818 compelled to attend at Bow Street, owing to an unpleasant fracas. The "Orator," who was himself unstinted and unmeasured in his abuse of all who were opposed, was, as we might expect, particularly sensitive as to criticisms passed on his own proceedings. The absurd extravagancies into which popular agitation may lead its votaries was well illustrated by his proceedings. He was at the time busy contesting an election in London. On his way from Covent Garden, he halted with his party in front of three newspaper-offices in the Strand, where, after denunciations against the conduct of these journals, he burnt a copy of each. He attributed the change which had taken place in a paper called *The Observer*, to an individual being (as he termed it) at the head of its reporters, named Dowling. "This," he said, "was no other than the well-known Spectacle—Dowling the Spy." This was repeated more than once. This having been communicated to Mr. Dowling, he, on Friday, proceeded to the hustings with a horsewhip, and on Mr. Hunt arriving with his son, his dumb brother, and other friends, Mr. Dowling struck him several blows with his whip. In a moment the confusion became general, the crowd closed upon Mr. Dowling, and Mr. West and others seized him and prevented further violence. During the fracas the dumb brother and the younger Hunt contrived to strike him some blows upon the face across the shoulders of those who surrounded him. The civil power had by this time interfered. Mr. H. Hunt said that he had been informed before he came to the hustings that he was to be horsewhipped, and was advised to bring his stick. Mr. Dowling acknowledged he went to the hustings to horsewhip Mr. Hunt. Mr. Birnie said that he had but one course to pursue, and that was to bind both parties over to the sessions. Mr. H. Hunt then produced a letter, which he said he had received about five months since, in which he was informed that Mr. Dowling had declared that he would horsewhip him wherever he met him; and that he (Mr. Hunt) was prevented from appearing at the election of Lord Mayor, in consequence of that threat. Mr. Birnie now said that he felt himself bound to call upon Mr. Dowling to find sureties to keep the peace towards Mr. H. Hunt, and Mr. W. Hunt also to find similar sureties with regard to Mr. Dowling. Mr. Hunt said he did not wish that Mr. Dowling should be held in any sureties. Mr. Birnie : " What, not for horsewhipping you, Mr. Hunt ? " Mr. Hunt : " No : it was a mere nothing ; my brother received the blows ten times harder than I did ; and

I should not now even be afraid of Mr. Dowling and a hundred such Irish bullies!" Mr. Dowling said the latter remark was not one which could properly be replied to in the presence of a magistrate, but that since Mr. Hunt was so courteous, he was inclined to be equally so and should not insist upon his (Hunt) being put to the trouble of entering into recognizances, as, if he considered it necessary, he could take other steps hereafter. Mr. Birnie thought both had acted with prudence, and complimented Mr. Hunt on his forbearance, after the manner in which he had been horsewhipped by Mr. Dowling. The parties then withdrew.

This singular toleration on the part of the magistrate, who did not perhaps appreciate the position, naturally led to further hostilities. The two gentlemen, not being bound to keep the peace, were panting to renew the fray, and Mr. Dowling was literally "spoiling for want of a bating." We are not surprised to find that within a few weeks Mr. Dowling appeared at Bow Street to complain of being assaulted by Mr. Hunt.

On Wednesday Mr. Hunt was brought to the office to answer a charge of assault on Mr. Dowling, who horsewhipped him on the hustings at the late Westminster election. Mr. Dowling said the simple accusation which he had to make against Mr. Hunt was that he had struck him on the preceding day in St.

Clement's churchyard. He had been informed that it was Mr. Hunt's intention to give him what is called a good thrashing, and had resolved, if such an attempt were made, to make no resistance, but to treat him in the manner which persons who had forfeited the character of a gentleman deserved. On Tuesday morning, having borrowed a newspaper of Mr. Clement, he called into his shop about half-past eleven to return it. Mr. Hunt and his son were there. Mr. Dowling laid the paper on the counter and was retiring, when Mr. Hunt exclaimed, " Well, Mr. Spectacle Spy, are you disposed to finish my horsewhipping now ? " Mr. Dowling replied, " Mr. Hunt, I wish to have no altercation with you," and was retiring, when Mr. Hunt applied to him the foulest epithets, and said he was a despicable government spy and informer. Mr. Dowling defied him or any man on earth to prove the assertion. Mr. Hunt then said, " You got it inserted in all the papers the account of your having horsewhipped me, and that I had not the spirit to resent it." Mr. Dowling in answer, rather for the ears of several persons who were in the shop than for Mr. Hunt's gratification, said, " Upon my honour, the charge is incorrect." Mr. Hunt then added, " If you did not, some of your myrmidon colleagues did, and I shall find an opportunity to give you a good thrashing," following up his threat with an invitation to go into the street then and fight it out. Mr. Dowling said that he might execute his threat then, but that he should feel himself degraded by resenting anything which so contemptible a fellow either said or did, at least in the way he seemed to wish, and was then quitting the shop, when Mr. Hunt followed him to the door, and repeated his invitation to a boxing-match in the street. Mr. Dowling again declined the proposed exhibition, and Mr. Hunt struck him a slight blow on the face, which knocked off his spectacles. "D—n you," continued Mr. Hunt, "will you resent that?" "Not in the way you would wish, Mr. Hunt," replied Mr. Dowling, "and even if I were disposed so far to degrade myself, the infirmity of being short-sighted would prevent me from engaging in so unequal a contest." Mr. Dowling then walked away, but returned, and asked for and obtained Mr. Hunt's address, with a view to the present proceedings.

This forbearance and restraint seems astonishing in one of Mr. Dowling's country, and rather suggests Bob Acres' "you're beneath my notice!" A Mr. Lydon, who was in Mr. Clement's shop when the affair took place, corroborated the statement of Mr. Dowling as to the abusive language of Mr. Hunt, and Mr. Dowling saying that he would not degrade himself by resenting anything which came from a person so well known. He said he saw Mr. Hunt strike Mr. Dowing one blow, and thought he attempted to strike him oftener, but he could not speak positively to this. This account Mr. Hunt pronounced grossly incorrect, inasmuch as he had never collared Mr. Dowling, nor did he strike him more than one blow, and that a slight one, rather with a view to make him resent it than otherwise; but Mr. Dowling had acted most cowardly, and had refused to fight. Mr. Dowling said he had much more reason to complain of the report than Mr. Hunt. Mr. Hunt : " This is a proof of the sort of fellows who act as reporters." Mr. Dowling said that he had heard Mr. Hunt had also turned reporter, and had written an account stating that he had knocked Mr. Dowling down, and performed other acts of heroism, with a view of having his account of the transaction inserted in the papers. Mr. Hunt did not deny this charge, and called upon for his defence, admitted that Mr. Dowling's statement was in a great measure correct, although exaggerated. Mr. Hunt added that the irritation of his mind, from what had happened at Covent Garden, had induced him to determine to give this bully an opportunity of finishing his horsewhipping if he thought fit; but he had, in a cowardly manner, refused to fight. Mr. Dowling : " You knew where I was to be found, and you also knew I was ready and anxious to meet you in the only way a gentleman ought to require." Mr. Hunt : " What ! meet a Government spy who attempted to swear away the life of

Dr. Watson!" Mr. Dowling repelled this attack, and Mr. Hunt left the office, after being bound over to the sessions, using the most abusive language towards Mr. Dowling. Such was this edifying scene.

The matter did not end here, and the turbulent Hunt family once more appeared at Bow Street.

"Mr. Thomas Hunt, a son of the celebrated orator, was, on Friday, brought to the office, charged with having attempted to *strangle a person* named Ferrar. The accused is about twenty-two years of age, and the accuser is well known at most of the gaming-houses. On Thursday night Ferrar and a companion of his named Quin, picked up a country squire, whom they introduced to the wine-house of Mr. Robottom, the 'Finish,' in James Street, Covent Garden, where they proposed to play at cards. Robottom refused to let them play in his house, and they drank wine till they fell asleep. Whilst Quin and Ferrar were sleeping some persons took off their hats, put a quantity of sawdust inside, and replaced them. When they awoke, on taking off their hats, the sawdust fell down their bosoms, and covered their clothes. They accused each other of playing the trick, and from high words proceeded to blows, when some one interfered, and said that Mr. Hunt had done it. Ferrar called Mr. Hunt by many opprobrious names, and Mr. Hunt, who denied having done it, said he was a blackleg, and cautioned the country 'squire' against forming

an acquaintance with him. This observation provoked Ferrar, and he uttered a most filthy and
unmanly insinuation against Mr. Hunt, whose indignation being raised, he seized Ferrar by the throat, and
gave him such a tremendous squeeze that he was, in
less than half a minute, nearly strangled.

" Robottom was examined, and he said that he had
prevented Ferrar and Quin from 'pigeoning' the
' squire,' and |that Mr. Hunt was not the person who
put the sawdust in the hats of Ferrar and Quin.

" Mr. Hunt said that he certainly could not deny
having committed the assault, but he contended that
any one possessing a spark of manly feeling on hearing a wretch apply such odious language to him,
though he might be a dwarf in stature, would rush
upon the slanderer and annihilate him if he could, so
he (Mr. Hunt) would have destroyed the villain
Ferrar if he could.

" Sir R. Birnie said that if any one had used such
language in reference to him, as Ferrar had applied
to Mr. Hunt, *he would have beaten his head off his
shoulders,* and he would not, therefore, call upon Mr.
Hunt to find bail. The sessions were sitting, and Mr.
Ferrar might go and indict Mr. Hunt. The case was
then dismissed.''

CHAPTER VII.

THE attraction of a police court, particularly for the lower classes, has always been extraordinary, and amounts to a positive fascination. A well-known humourist, and a very acute observer of the odd whims and turns of human character, and who has made a particular study of Bow Street office, Mr. George Grossmith, has described to me how much he has been struck with this odd passion. He had often seen in the unwashed crowd, herded at the bottom of the court, a particular face peering over the barrier, day after day, all absorbed in the humours of the scene. By and by, the attraction would operate on his movements, and actually draw him nearer : he would be recognized in a more convenient place for observation. In time he would be found under the witness-box, and finally, after an interval, would be recognized at the bar itself ! Then would come a blank, during which he might be presumed to be working out his sentence, when one day the face would be recognized in its old place beyond the barrier, to pass once more through the various stages, till it again faced the magistrate at the bar. This enjoyment is no doubt founded on the taste for anything dramatic, which is here provided *gratis.*

The same eagerness is also shown by the superior classes when any case affecting persons of the same degree is in progress. Then the narrow precincts are blocked by fine ladies and gentlemen ; the magistrate's bench is invaded, inconvenience of all kinds, a stifling, almost fetid atmosphere, endured and breathed cheerfully, and every stage of which is a tedious formal procedure is relished, in the hope of dramatic " bits " occasionally turning up. Sometimes thirty or forty reporters from all parts of the kingdom crowd in, and pay their acknowledgments at the close to " the courteous clerk, Mr. ——," who has been at his wit's end to find them accommodation. The Press has indeed helped to develop this taste; for, five-and-twenty years ago, only a couple of these auxiliaries attended, who gave a compressed historical epitome of the proceedings. Now, when there is anything sensational, the whole dialogue is furnished, and every question and answer set out, together with the demeanour of the audience, marked by what the French call " hilarity," or " *rires,*" " loud laughter," or " roars of laughter, in which the magistrate heartily joined." It must be a curious, original feeling, for a prisoner, whose liberty or life may be involved, to hear this merriment. We can fancy his aching wonder of heart,

"Sport to you, death to me." When such absorbing cases are protracted for many days, the audience gathered in old Bow Street is something amazing; all the courts and alleys give up their unclean miscellany; and, in the notorious Bolton and Park case, the very housetops were lined to see the accused depart in the black van.

On old bookstalls we sometimes light on an odd volume of " Life in London," or the "Finish," with the brilliantly coloured and spirited plates of the doings of "Tom and Jerry." This work furnishes a complete panorama of the gay gentleman's progress, which appeared to consist in defying all authority in the pursuit of pleasure. Scuffles with watchmen, seizure of hackney-coaches, "rows" at Drury Lane Theatre, general conflict,—this was carried out with a certain ruthless gallantry and profuse expenditure of cash, all which, strange to say, secured immunity, and even indulgent treatment, at Bow Street. The account of the doings of Tom and Jerry, as recorded, seemed gross exaggeration, but it was really an exact account of a curious time. The writer, Pierce Egan, seems to have been known to Richardson, who has left a curious account of these disorderly days. Mr. Egan, he says, was of respectable family. He had been a compositor, a bookseller, a sporting writer, and contributor of sporting news to the newspapers, &c. In the last-mentioned capacity he was employed by the proprietor

of the *Weekly Dispatch* to record the "doings of the
ring," in which employment his peculiar phraseology,
and his superior knowledge of his business, soon rendered him eminent beyond all rivalry and competition.
He was flattered and petted by pugilists and peers ;
his patronage and countenance were sought for by all
who considered the road to a prize-fight the road to
reputation and honour. Forty years before, his presence
was understood to confer respectability on any meeting
convened for the furtherance of bull-baiting, cock-
fighting, cudgelling, wrestling, boxing, and all that
comes within the category of " manly sports." If he
" took the chair," success was hailed as certain in the
object in question. On the occasions of his presence,
he was accompanied by a " tail." In the event of
opposition to his views and opinions, his satellites had
a mode of enforcing his authority, which had the
efficacy without the tediousness of discussion ; and
though, in personal strength, far from a match for any
sturdy opponent, he had a courage and a vivacity in
action which were very highly estimated both by his
friends and foes.

As the literature of Combe Wood and Moulsey
Hurst began to decline, he had the sense to cultivate
the literature of the theatre, and his tact in the deli-
neation of a certain side of life was exemplified in the
farces of which he was the writer. He had on several
occasions visited Oxford and Cambridge, and had

obtained the "honours of the sitting" prolonged throughout the night in many of the colleges of those venerable institutions.

But though reporting was in its infancy fifty years ago, the eccentricities of Bow Street permitted an odd and original form of recording all that occurred. The general tone of hilarity and facetiousness thus tolerated or encouraged by the magistrates, operated in rather a novel way. The public became interested and curious to know what was going on, and it felt that they often thus lost what was "as good as a play." The exhibitions of " fast life," the profuse use of slang, &c., were too good to be lost; and prompted some ingenious reporters to try their hands at giving a lively and dramatic air to what went on before them. One, Mr. Wight, who acted for the *Morning Herald*, gradually obtained a sort of celebrity for his powers in this direction. He had the knack of adopting a rollicking, " chaffing" tone in all that he described. He modelled his style after that of Mr. Pierce Egan, and added many strokes of what was then considered humour. The general tone was, however, ridicule of the unlucky beings who were treated, and who, in addition to their legitimate sufferings and inconvenience, found themselves laughed at by the town.

It is difficult to say how far the happy imagination of the reporter is accountable for the incidents and dialogue of these scenes. But, setting this question aside, the following sketches, besides being entertaining, from their dramatic spirit, have a curious interest as pictures of social life. One is struck by the general violence that was then abroad, and we wonder how the spirit of disorder could have been kept in check at all. The inspiration of "Tom and Jerry," it will be seen, was at work, and every one of the "right sort" was eager to show his "sort" by either "boxing" a watchman, driving off with a hackney-coach, or "bilking" a tavern-keeper. The following illustrates these noble aims :—

§ *Gentlemen Jehus making the most of a Jarvey.*

John Wigley Williams, Esquire, was put forward from amongst a group of nocturnals from St. Martin's watch-house. He had been given in charge by a hackney-coachman for non-payment of his fare. He was a young and altogether exquisite personage ; but his Parisian-cut toggery was sadly deteriorated by the dust and dirt of his subterraneous dormitory.

Coachee stated that "this gentleman and another gentleman," at eleven o'clock the night before called him off the stand in the Old Bailey, and before he could get down to let them into his coach they both jumped upon his box, snatched the reins and whip out of his hand, and began flogging and driving away "like mad," down Ludgate Hill and up Fleet Street.

He endeavoured to stop them repeatedly, but it was of no use; every time he opened his mouth the other gentleman said to this gentleman, " Shall I shove him off the box, Wigley ? " and every time this gentleman replied, " Go it ! " In this manner they galloped on through Temple Bar and along the Strand, cruelly flogging the horses at every step. " Don't flog my horses, gentlemen, they arn't used to it," cried coachee. " Shall I shove him off the box, Wigley ? " said one gentleman—" Go it ! " replied the other. At last they reached Charing Cross ; and there coachee made such a determined resistance that all three were in danger of tumbling off the box in a bunch, and the horses were stopped by some persons passing, when one of the " gentlemen " ran away like a " pickpocket," as coachee said, and the other refusing to pay anything for his ride, was handed over to the watchman, who carried him forthwith to the watch-house.

When the coachman had told his story, the magistrate, addressing himself to the captured Jehu, asked, " Pray what are you, sir ? "

" Me, your worship ? I am Mithter John Wigley Williamths."

" That is your name only. How do you describe yourself ? "

" I thuppose, your worthip, sthpeaking of mythelf, I thoud thay I am a gentleman."

" A gentleman, sir, is a very equivocal title now-a-days, and if the coachman thinks proper to prosecute you for the assault upon him I would then know something more of you."

The coachman said he would rather decline prosecuting for the assault, because it would be such a loss of time to him.

Mister John Wigley Williams said there was an agreement that they should drive themselves; and he would have paid the fare if the coachman would have let him gone on as far as he wished to go. He complained bitterly of the treatment he had met with in the watch-house, having been thrust down into a filthy dungeon——

" Where all other disorderly people are put," said his worship, to save him the trouble of finishing the sentence.

The watch-house keeper said a bed was offered to the gentleman, but he would not have it, and was so very impudent and noisy that it was found necessary to put him below.

The magistrate ordered him to pay the coachman his fare from the Old Bailey to Charing Cross, together with two shillings for his time in attending to make his complaint.

Mister Gentleman John Wigley Williams obeyed this order without demur; and having paid another shilling for his discharge-fee, he was suffered to go home to his parents.

§ *Gabriel Spriggins.*

Amongst a number of " disorderlies " who were brought up before the sitting magistrate (Alderman Garratt), for breaches of the peace or disorderly conduct, a person of gentlemanly appearance and manners, who called himself Gabriel Spriggins, particularly attracted the attention of the magistrate.

" A wretched old charwoman, who lives in a dirty, and at night dismal place, called Star Court, Chancery Lane, came forward and charged Gabriel with having broken open her bedroom door in the dead of the preceding night. She said she was a lone woman, who had but one son, a sailor, who lived in her room—a garret at No. 3—when he was in town; and it so happened that he was sleeping at her feet. The old woman, who it was evident had not yet recovered from the fright in which she had been put, ran on with a detail of circumstances, which the magistrate could only clearly collect from her son, a gloomy-looking sailor. From his account it appeared that, at four o'clock on the morning before, they were awakened by the barking of the old woman's dog, and heard a sort of scratching at the room door. The sailor thought it was a cat scratching to get in, and beat the dog for awakening him on so slight an occasion. The noise then ceased, and all was quiet for a time. Some time after she was awakened by a noise as if the door of the room had been burst open, and after an interval of silence she felt a cold hand wandering over her bed, when she exclaimed, thinking her son had got up, " Jack, is that your hand ? " " No, mother, I wasn't stirring," said the sailor. " Then there's some fellow in the room," replied the old woman. The sailor, at the word, sprung out of his bed, and felt about in the dark for the intruder; designing to send him, whoever he might be, by one step, from the top to the bottom of the stairs. He caught hold of him at last, and gave him a twist towards the door with the design mentioned, which threw him across the old woman as she lay in bed. The sailor flung himself upon the intruder, whom he found was rather a heavier opponent than he calculated upon, and threatened to blow his brains out if he stirred. Gabriel, who was under the sailor, threatened to murder both of them if they resisted him, and accompanied his threat by many " strange and desperate oaths." The old woman, as soon as she could disencumber herself from the load, went to the window and screamed out " murder ! " lustily, whilst the intruder and her son were grappling on the floor for ascendency, with various success. The watchman and a crowd of the miserable lodgers in the house soon rushed into the room and seized the prisoner. They were not a little amazed to find a person of gentlemanly appearance in the house, and in such a situation, and the whole had a most curious appearance, particularly from the figure of the old woman, with her hair hanging about her neck, and of her son, who was, of course, undressed. The prisoner threatened furiously, and resisted being carried to the watch-house, whither however he was taken, but could not be prevailed upon to give any account of himself, how he got to that height, or for what purpose. The house, it appeared, is let out in lodgings to numerous miserable lodgers, for whose convenience the door is left open, and they sleep in all that enviable security which is produced by having nothing worth taking to lose.

The prisoner, who had, during the recital of the story expressed the highest surprise and amusement, as if the witnesses had been relating a fiction, when called upon gravely by the magistrate to tell who and what he was, and to account for his extraordinary proceedings, replied, " My name is Ireland : I am *flauto primo*, which means, your worship, principal flute, at the King's Theatre, where I was last night. The whole of the strange story that these people have been telling you I know nothing of, and certain I am that I was in my own bed, long before and after four in the morning, therefore I conclude that these good people have been dreaming."

He was immediately recognized by a gentleman present, as the eminent flute player of the Italian Opera house, where most lovers of music must have heard, and been delighted with, his fine tones and brilliant execution. The magistrate saw at once that

the son of Apollo had been sacrificing rather freely to
Bacchus, and that he was still under the influence of
his libations, although it was not apparent at first
sight. He appeared impressed with the idea, as he
had slept in the Compter, that he had been in his bed
all night. The worthy alderman gave particular instructions to the officers to take care of him, and convey him to his friends. Poor Ireland is since dead :
' he was a fellow of infinite jest ;' universally esteemed,
and in his profession admirable."

§ *A Bold Stroke for a Dinner.*

Officers in the services did not disdain to try and
" bilk " a tavern-keeper of a dinner. But this again
was' only part of the morals of " fast life."

" There was a little personage in striped cotton
trousers and blue surtout, calling himself " Lieutenant
Seaman, of the Honourable East India Company's
Foreign Naval Service," brought before G. R.
Minshull, Esq., the other night, at the suit of Mr.
Jaggers, landlord of the Army and Navy Coffee
House, St. Martin's Lane ; on a charge of having
conspired, with two other persons unknown, to
defraud the said Mr. John Jaggers of three pounds
of rump steak, one pot of porter, two bottles of
sherry, &c., &c., &c.

Lieutenant Seaman, when brought before his worship, could not keep his perpendicular ; and every now

and then he came down with a hiccupping lee-lurch upon the magisterial table.

"Stand up, sir," said the attending gaoler. "Is that the way to conduct yourself before a magistrate?"

"*Hiccup!*" replied Lieutenant Seaman, opening his eyes as wide as he could; "and is that the way you address a British officer, I should like to know? Have I the—*hiccup*—honour of addressing Sir Richard Birnie?"

"No—my name is Minshull," replied the magistrate.

"Aye—I'm sorry for that, Mr. Minshull—I wish you had been Sir Richard Birnie, because I should have the honour of knowing you—and you would have known my family to be vastly respectable—and—*hiccup!*"

Here the lieutenant stuck fast; but if anybody else attempted to speak he interrupted them by desiring they would recollect the respect due to a British officer; and it was not till his worship had threatened to have him locked up, that he could be prevailed upon to be quiet.

It appeared, by the tavern-keeper's statement, that the gallant lieutenant and two other superb-looking gentlemen, came into his house that afternoon, and ordered "rump-steaks, and *etceteras* for *three;*" "And, d'ye hear," added the lieutenant—who seemed to be the leading man of the party—" D'ye hear—let them be done to a turn, and served up *instanter.*"

A dish of rump-steaks—full of gravy, tender as a chicken, and delicately garnished with fresh scraped horse-radish, was served up *" instanter "* accordingly, with India pickle, a foaming pot of porter, and all things usually appertaining to a dish of rump-steaks. These things demolished, capital Stilton, prime old Cheshire, and double Gloucester, with two bottles of excellent sherry, followed; and then—as soon as the sherry was out—two of the gentlemen *bolted* without saying a word about the bill. Still, the landlord thought the lieutenant would pay, but he was deceived; for in the next minute the lieutenant attempted to *bolt* also; and so he would have done, had not the landlord whipped out of his bar as quick as lightning, and caught him by the skirt of his blue surtout just as he was crossing the threshold. Thus awkwardly taken to, the lieutenant confessed he had no money; and thereupon the landlord consigned him to the care of a constable.

His worship now called upon the lieutenant for his defence; and the lieutenant replied, " It's all very true—and I'll pay on Friday." He was told that Friday would not do, that he must pay instantly, or be committed to prison. He declared he could not pay—" Come what, come may "—and he was committed accordingly. We understand his family is

Q 2

highly respectable, and very much annoyed by his eccentricities."

The adventures thus described and embellished were generally concerned with the so-called "Life" at the theatres, saloons, and flash houses. The impression left, it must be said, is something inexpressibly vulgar. The exhibition of "manners," at the theatre particularly, is extraordinary from its coarse brutality. Here are some further specimens.

§ *A Battle in the Boxes.*

"Young Mr. Dakins occupied a front seat in one of the boxes till the conclusion of the first piece. Then, having nothing else to do, he looked round the house. Suddenly he espied a party of friends, male and female, in the very next box. They occupied the front seat and part of the second; and he, perceiving that there was a vacant space on the second seat, went and took possession of it forthwith, and was highly delighted at the luckiness of the circumstance. In a few minutes in comes the little round man—"Hallo!" says he, "you've got my seat, young man." "*Your* seat, sir?" said the young man, with some surprise. "Yes, *my* seat, sir," replied the round one. "Well, sir," rejoined the young one, "you need not be so hot upon 't—there is a very nice seat, which I have just left, in the front row of the adjoining box—will you have the goodness to take that, as I wish to remain here with my friends ? " " No, sir," replied the round one, very waspishly—" no, sir, I shall not! This is my seat—I have *satten* upon it all the evening, and I'll have no other; and let me tell you, sir, that I think your conduct in taking it, sir, very ungentlemanly, sir ! " The young man's friends now interfered, but in vain ; and at length they told him to let the little fat man have his seat, and they would make room for him in the front row. So there they sat, enduring all the moist miseries of four in a row, till the end of the second piece ; when the young man, turning round his head, perceived the little round man's seat empty again ; and, after waiting a few minutes, and finding he did not return, he again took possession of it, to the great relief of the poor ladies in the front row. But he had scarcely seated himself when in pops the little round man again, and without saying more than " I see this is done on purpose to insult me ! " he seized the young man by the collar of the coat behind, lifted him from the seat, and very dexterously slid himself into it. In an instant all was uproar.—" Turn him out ! "— " Throw him over ! "—The little fat man lost his balance, fell backwards, and in that position he let fly " *an immense volley of kicks*," which the young man received on his stomach. The ladies shrieked, the gentlemen tried to hold his legs down, the house cried " Shame ! "—and at length, after kickings and cuffings, and pullings and haulings, quite distressing to detail, the little round man was delivered over to the peace-officers, and conveyed to the watch-house, panting like a porpoise, and perspiring at every pore.

The magistrate said there were faults on both sides. In the first place, the defendant should not have quitted his seat without saying to his neighbour that he intended to return; secondly, common courtesy ought to have induced the complainant to have relinquished it when demanded; and, thirdly, that the defendant should have demanded it civilly. Upon the whole, it was a very silly piece of business, and he would recommend them to retire, and make an end of it by mutual explanation, or apology.

This pacific advice, however, was rejected by both parties, and so the little round man was held to bail."

It is indeed extraordinary to compare the condition of the theatres of those days with their state at present, and it would seem that the people frequented them for every other purpose than that of seeing the play. This, it has not been noticed, was a consequence of the theatrical monopoly then enjoyed by the two patent theatres, which, from the great size and spaciousness of accommodation, offered attractions to the disorderly followers of what was called " Fast life." The proprietor, certain of his vast attendance, was not above offering inducements to this miscellany, and with this view prepared vast lobbies and a still more peculiar institution of the day, " *The saloon* "—

a magnificent and palatial chamber, still to be seen at Drury Lane Theatre, which was crowded every night with fair Cyprians and their followers, always encouraged to attend by even respectable managers. The saloon was as important a part of the entertainment as was the auditorium, and had its own "audiences." It may be well conceived that it became a difficult duty to preserve order and decorum in such assemblies, and a regular force of officers from Bow Street were engaged at the theatre, of whom the two Bonds, father and son, were the best known.

"Tom and Jerry," and "Bob Logic," their mentor and friend, used to repair to the theatre, not to see the play, but to "make a night of it." The boxes were constantly the scene of shameful "rows," drunken "gentlemen" forcing their way and attempting to thrust others from their seats, putting their legs on the seats, &c. Thus Thomas Baker Cox, Esq., of No. 1, Soho Square, accompanied by a friend, appeared before Sir R. Birnie, to prefer a complaint against Bond, the principal constable of Drury Lane Theatre, for assaulting him in the pit of that theatre. The magistrate immediately directed that Bond should be sent for.

"Mr. Cox stated that he went to Drury Lane Theatre on Wednesday night, for the purpose of seeing "An Operatic Extravaganza, called Giovanni in Ireland." He seated himself in the pit, and some of the scenes he applauded, and some of them he condemned, just as he thought they deserved, when he was suddenly seized by the collar, and dragged from the seat by Bond, who, in so doing, tore his shirt, and seemed strongly inclined to proceed to further violence, and drag him out of the house altogether; indeed, he verily believed he would have done so, had it not been for the repeated cries of "Shame! shame!" which resounded on all sides. These cries, however, induced him to relinquish his grasp, and he (Mr. Cox) demanded to know his name, but he answered only by producing a constable's staff; and it was not till after long hesitation and urgent reiteration of the demand, that he gave his name, and stated himself to belong to the Police Establishment at Bow Street. He added that he repeatedly observed Bond himself *applauding* the performances in the most vociferous manner.

"Well, sir," asked the magistrate, "do you not think one man has as much right to applaud, as another has to censure."

Mr. Cox: "Certainly, sir; but I think that it should have taught him the impropriety of interfering with others who were doing no more than himself."

Bond was now called upon for his account of the affray. He said the gentleman (Mr. C.) came into the pit in the middle of the performance, hurried to his seat, and without waiting a moment to see whether what was going on was good, bad, or indifferent, he began shouting, "Off! off! off!" with all his might;

until the audience became so much annoyed, that there was a general call throughout the house of " Turn him out ! " and then, and not till then, did he lay hold of him. He stated further, that the complainant was the only person in the house who expressed the slightest disapprobation ! In conclusion, he denied all that had been said about tearing the shirt, or the *extra* " dragging," and he affirmed that he should be able to bring " hundreds of witnesses " to disprove it.

Mr. Cox persisted in the correctness of his statement. He denied that he commenced his disapprobation at his first entering the house; on the contrary, he had been there a long time, and it was not until he saw a representation of a Court of Justice, in which singing was introduced, that he expressed any decided censure ; and he contended that he had an undoubted right to express his opinion of any theatrical performance in the customary manner. He then asked his worship whether he could imagine anything more preposterously ridiculous than singing in a Court of Justice ; and he was proceeding to descant on some other incongruities in the " *Extravaganza*," when—

Sir R. Birnie interrupted him by observing that he did not sit there to give opinions upon theatrical performances ; all he had to do was to ascertain whether an unjustifiable assault had been committed. The proprietors of the theatre employed several constables merely for the preservation of the peace, and it remained for Bond to show that the complainant was committing a breach of the peace, or doing anything to excite a breach of it; and, if he could not do this, his interference was certainly unjustifiable. Bond, however, had talked of having witnesses to produce; and in order that both parties might be more fully prepared, he should postpone the further examination of the matter.

On Friday, Bond, the officer, attended before Sir R. Birnie, with two persons, who, he said, would prove all that he had stated with respect to the conduct of Mr. Cox, to be true. These persons were, a publican in Newgate Market, and a tradesman of the same place. Mr. Cox was called, but did not answer, nor did he appear in the course of the day, and the matter therefore rests for the present undetermined."

Here is a sketch of a scene at Drury Lane Theatre, which shows what " Yahoos " were the professors of " fast life," as it was called.

§ *A Spree at the Theatre.*

" Christopher Dobson and Harding Montague, Esquires *of course*, but very coarse esquires, were charged with creating a disturbance, and assaulting the peace-officers, at Drury Lane Theatre, during the performances there.

They were brought from Covent Garden watchhouse, together with a gang of young thieves, dis-

orderly cobblers, drunken prostitutes, houseless vagabonds, and other off-scourings of society ; and a very
respectable appearance they made.

Eleven o'clock at length arrived, and the magistrates
having taken their seats, the demolished Corinthians
were ushered into their presence, and a charge, of
which the following is the substance, was exhibited
against them.

Between the third and fourth acts of *Wild Oats*, they
were swaggering about the lobbies, insulting everybody that came in their way; the "big one "—that
is to say, Mr. Kit Dobson—offering to *mill* " anybody
in the world," and repeatedly exclaiming, " Oh, that
a man of my own powers would come athwart me!"
—and the " thin one " (that's Mr. Harding Montague),
lisping responsively, " That's your sort! Go it, Kitty
my *covy.*" Nobody taking the challenge, *Kitty my
covy*, in the overflowing of his Corinthianism, seized
the *thin one*, dashed him against the wall of the lobby,
and shattered one of the lamps with his empty *know-
ledge-box*. The *thin one* took it in good part, but Mr.
Spring, the box book-keeper, who happened to witness
the feat, was not so well pleased, and sent for Bond,
the officer, to remove them. Bond prevailed upon
them to be a little more quiet; but in a quarter of an
hour after, he found them in the saloon, sparring,
bellowing, and capering, like a pair of inebriated
ourang outangs, as he said, to the great danger of the

mirrors, and the scandal even of *that* temple of depravity. He again attempted to remonstrate with them : but all he could get from them, was a challenge to fight from *Kitty my covy;* and therefore he called for the assistance of his brother officers, determined to remove them entirely from the theatre. Jones, Lewis, and Drummond, of the patrole, and Sayers, a parish constable, came to his assistance ; and now began what the Eganites call " *a prime spree* " *Kitty my covy* laying about him with all his might, and the *thin one* doing his little utmost to help him. The officers, however, got them out of the house ; but they obstreperously insisted upon re-entering ; and at last, after a long altercation, they conveyed them to the watch-house. In their way thither, *Kitty my covy* contrived to get hold of the hand of one of the officers (Jones), and gave it such a twist, that three of his fingers were dislocated, and the tendons of the wrist so much injured, that the surgeon of the establishment gave it as his opinion, that he would not be able to use his hand for several weeks to come. When they got into the watch-house, this same *Kitty* behaved more like a mad bull than anything else—refusing to *go below*, and threatening them with the displeasure of the Marquis of W——r. At length, however, they were put down ; but in the conflict, Lewis (an old and rather infirm officer) received such a savagely marked kick in the groin from Mr. Kit Dobson, that he was laid senseless on the floor for several minutes. Drummond, another officer of diminutive make, he also kicked violently on the stomach; indeed all the five officers engaged were injured in some way or other.

The magistrates now called upon these amateurs of "*Life*" for their defence; whereupon Mr. Christopher Dobson delivered himself *verbatim* as follows :—

" Why, your worships, all I have to say about it is, that I *do* belong to His Majesty's service, but haven't been in the habit of being much in town, and the fact is, I don't know what it is; but this gentleman (the thin one) is my friend—I suppose we were not in our regular senses; certainly we were not so sober as we might have been—but the fact is, that we must make good any damage that we have done."

Mr. Harding Montague said nothing, but he *gasped* pitifully, and looked altogether so droopingly *lackadaisical*, that the very officers seemed sorry for him.

Their worships ordered that they should put in bail, to answer the *five* distinct charges of assault at Quarter Sessions—Christopher Dobson, *Esquire*, in 100*l.*, and two sureties of 50*l.* each, and Harding Montague, *Esquire*, in 80*l.*, and two sureties of 40*l.* each.

The unfortunate gentlemen remained locked up the whole day among the *other* unfortunates, in the strong room, and in the evening they gave the bail required; but it was at the same time intimated, that the Grand Jury had returned *five* true bills against them, and that they would in all probability be taken upon Bench warrants on the morrow. Oh this " *Life !* " "

Even ladies were not secure against violence from the ungentlemanly blackguards who frequented the theatres. In our time persons in the pit suffer uncomplainingly or with good-humoured grumbling when some lofty bonnet completely obscures what is doing on the stage. Not so the " Tom and Jerry " blackguards in the boxes. Thus with a. Mr. Sadd, who had attended Mrs. and Miss Higginbottom to Covent Garden, the former lady, as it was admitted, being arrayed in an enormous hat or bonnet which shut off all view of the stage. This grievance, however, is much complained of in our own time, and the bonnet " pittite " who has come out for an evening's entertainment finds himself deprived of even the sight of the stage by some growth of hat directly in front of him. He, however, submits with a grumbling protest.

" When the opera commenced, the defendant Hutchinson, in a very rude and peremptory manner, ordered Mrs. Higginbottom to take off the " monstrous " bonnet which she had on her head. She was offended at the manner in which she had been addressed and treated his commands with contempt. The defendant used most offensive language, thrust his knees against Mrs. Higginbottom's back, and repeated his order. Gross remarks were made about the size of the lady's person, and also of her bonnet, and a young man

about seventeen years of age thrust himself between
the lady and witness, and he pushed him from him.
The defendant and another man, who was short, stout,
bald, and passionate, seized witness by the collar, tore
his coat [here the garment, tattered and torn, was
exhibited], and struck him repeatedly. Witness called
in an officer, and asked Mr. Hutchinson to give his
address. He refused to do so, and witness believed
that he was ashamed of his outrageous and ungentlemanly behaviour. The language of the defendant and
his friends was most gross, and *one of them said that
his mother's bonnet was the size of a hayrick.* Mr.
Hutchinson said, " Now, sir, the real fact is, that I and
a gentleman present, and a youth about sixteen years
of age, took our seats in the pit of the theatre, on a
form behind a very large female who wore a most
tremendous bonnet. Its size was monstrous, and
prevented me from having a view of the performances
or of the stage even." A gentleman who wore
spectacles, who sat near him, said that the bonnet
ought to be pulled off if she would not take it off. On
observing that there was room for one person to sit by
the side of Mr. Sadd, he placed his young friend there,
and Mr. Sadd violently forced himself against the
youth. Being indignant at such conduct, he seized
Mr. Sadd by the collar, and dragged him from the
youth to his proper seat.

Mr. Minshull: This *fracas* appears to have arisen

entirely out of the circumstance of a lady wearing a monstrous-sized bonnet. I own that the fashion of wearing such large coverings for the heads of ladies in theatres is a great nuisance to play-goers; but it was not right to talk about pulling the bonnet from a lady's head, and it might not be convenient for a lady at all times to take off her bonnet.

Mr. Lomas said, It was not true that Mr. Hutchinson addressed her in ungentlemanly language. The assault was first committed by Mr. Sadd thrusting himself violently against a youth sixteen years of age, his (Mr. Lomas's) nephew.

Mr. Minshull : It is a pity that such monstrous-sized bonnets should be worn at a theatre. The case has a different appearance since the explanation of Mr. Lomas.

Mr. Sadd : Mr. Lomas assaulted me, and I charge him with the outrage.

Mr. Minshull : Both gentlemen must find bail to answer the charge at the sessions. Bail was put in and the party discharged."

§ *How to catch a Customer.*

An extraordinary case in 1824 shows that the buffoonery of the day had extended even to tradesmen in their relations with their customers.

" A gentleman well known in the *rouge et noir* circles, presented himself before the magistrate to claim redress against a bootmaker in New Street, Covent Garden.

The unfortunate gentleman had walked, or rather *twaddled* to the office in a pair of loose slippers; and there was such a manifestation of suffering in his voice, countenance, and gesture, that everybody pitied him. He said he had been miserable enough to have some dispute with his bootmaker, in which he might perhaps have expressed himself rather more warmly than the occasion warranted. On Saturday the bootmaker sent him home a pair of boots which had been some time under repair, and on Sunday morning he put them on and walked out, intending to call upon several of his friends. But he had not walked more than two or three hundred yards when his feet began to feel "cursedly uncomfortable," and the more he walked the more uncomfortable they became. He returned home. "Bring the *bootjack*, Molly!" he exclaimed. Molly brought the bootjack, and with eager anticipation of ease he stuck his heel into the friendly fork, but, alas! he no sooner began to pull than his agonies were increased tenfold! and the bootjack was kicked away in despair. At last—for it is miserable to dwell upon such horrors—at last the gentleman, sweating at every pore, and wound up almost to madness with his pain, thrust his heel once more into the yawning jack, and pulled with such a desperate might, that his foot came forth with its poor toes completely scarified! Not only the stocking, but the skin was left behind, and even his very corns were torn up by the roots!

Suffice it to say, that the other foot was torn away in the same manner, and it came forth from the confounded boot almost as skinless as an anatomical preparation.

And now, what do our readers suppose wrought all this miserable mischief ? The bootmaker had, with "*malice prepense*," as it would appear, lined the whole interior of the toe part of each boot with *cobbler's wax !* The gentleman himself was firmly of opinion that it was done maliciously, and he urged the magistrate to grant him redress.

The magistrate observed that it was a new case ; and though it was certainly a most unpleasant one, he feared it could not be brought within his jurisdiction.

The gentleman suggested that it would probably come under the act for preventing the wanton destruction of property. His stockings had been destroyed, his boots had been spoiled, and his feet had been cruelly scarified. All this had been done wantonly and wilfully, he said; and in corroboration of the premises, he produced the pair of silk stockings which he wore on the agonizing occasion.

These stockings certainly were spoiled; and after much urging on the part of the gentleman, his worship consented that a summons should issue for the bootmaker's appearance.

However, it came to nothing; for in half an hour after the gentleman crept back to the office, and said

he and the bootmaker had come to an *éclaircissement*
that would render his worship's interference unnecessary. What was the nature of that *éclaircissement* did
not appear."

§ *The Champion and Coppersmith.*

"The Champion of England—not he who, gallantly
armed, rode proudly through ranks of assembled
chivalry, and challenged the world in defence of his
Sovereign—but the champion of England's prouder
pugilism—the belted hero of the prize-ring—the man
whose fist is fate—the—in a word, honest *Tom Cribb*,
entered the office covered with mud, and holding in
his giant grasp, a little, well-bemudded, wriggling
coppersmith, named *William Bull.* "And please your
worships," said the champion, "this here little rascal
(*shaking him*), comes into my tap-room, with two or
three dirty chaps of the same sort, and got so sweet
upon themselves with drinking *beer*, that they must
needs go into the *parlour* to drink *grog*, amongst the
gentlemen, your worships! and because I wouldn't
stand that, this here little rascal (*shaking him again*)
smashes two panes of glass to shivers, and then tried
to *bolt*, but it wouldn't do."

The champion was desired to loose his hold upon
the coppersmith, and he did so instantly; but he still
regarded him with a look of angry indignation, whilst
the saucy little coppersmith, adjusting his disordered

jacket, exclaimed, " My eyes, Mister Tommy ! let us ever catch you at *Bristol* again, and we'll *zarve* you out for this ! "

Mr. Bull—*Bill Bull* he called himself—was ordered to be quiet, on pain of being instantly locked up ; and other witnesses of the affair were examined, by whose evidence the champion's account of it was fully substantiated, with an additional circumstance or two, which he, with his usual modesty, had omitted to mention, viz., that he, with his own right arm, cleared his house of the three coxcombical coppersmiths in a minute ; and that when the fourth, Mr. Bill Bull, milled the glaze and bolted, the champion himself pursued with the fleetness of a wild elephant, caught the scampering coppersmith by the " scuff of the neck," and falling with him to the earth, they rolled over and over in the mud till the *impetus* of their fall was spent ! and this was the way in which they came to be so muddily encased.

The coppersmith had nothing to say for himself, except that he thought himself, " as good a man as Mr. Tommy, any day," and that he had as much right to drink grog in a parlour as any *other* gentleman.

The magistrate commended the champion's conduct ; told him he should be protected from insult and outrage in his business ; and ordered the potvaliant coppersmith to be locked up until he should pay for the windows he had demolished.

Rowlandson & Pugin. del. et sculp.

Hill aqua.

BOW STREET OFFICE.

CHAPTER VIII.

ECCENTRICITY.

§ *The Rival Bedouins.*

THERE was something highly farcical in a theatrical dispute which was taken to Bow Street for settlement. Mr. Braham in 1833 or 1834 had engaged what were called " The Bedouin Arabs," to perform at the once popular Colliseum in the Regent's Park; when Ducrow, who was installed at Astley's, put out advertisements announcing a similar entertainment, but performed by a much larger contingent of " Genuine Bedouin Arabs." Braham, who had gone to a large expense to secure his Arabs, took the extraordinary step of applying at Bow Street for a warrant to stop Mr. Astley's performances. Ducrow was an eccentric personage enough, and I believe was the author of the sagacious speech " Cut out the dialect and come to the 'osses!"—the pith and moment of all dramatic compositions. Indignant at the attempt to stop his performances, he issued this racy proclamation, which is really delightful for its spirit, coarse contempt, and a sort of " horse-coper's " raillery. " Extraordinary Equestrian and Gymnastic Arab Feats ! Surpasses anything of the kind ever produced. The public are respectfully informed that these are not the four black men who play without their shoes and stockings at the west end of the town, but upwards of forty British artists, that challenge all Europe for talent, variety, extraordinary feats of manly skill and activity, and who nightly receive thunders of applause from crowded audiences, and do not play to a dozen of daily loungers. The union of talent and Arab spectacles of this establishment does not confine itself to the tumbling of four great ugly blacks, who have been refused an engagement at Astley's, because there are so many superior and more extraordinary men of our own country nearly starving, and compelled to perform on an open race-course for a penny, whilst those four men can get one hundred pounds per week, because they are black, and foreigners.

" The reader no doubt has witnessed boys running alongside of a coach, doing what is termed ' cat-in-wheel,' and turning foresprings with one hand and then the other ; or throwing summersets from a sand-bank. Such is the grand performances of these Sauteurs, consisting of three or four blacks, who walk on their hands, with their naked feet in the air, like two black frying-pans (of course no lady or respectable person can sit and see this).

"These blacks, with the man who takes half their money, applied at Bow Street to ask if they could not prevent Astley's from using the word ' Arab Exercises,' for that the public went every night and filled Astley's, and never came to see them at all! Why, of course, the public are the best judges, and know the difference between seeing a spectacle in character, produced with splendour, to introduce the talents of the flying man, the equilibrists, elastic tumblers, the antipodeans, jugglers, dancers, men and horses, tableaux, the groups of trained horses, and other novelties! But come, see, and judge for yourselves; for this is only a small part of Astley's entertainments."

§ *" Mine Host and his Waiter."*

Enter Mr. OXBERRY, *in a long plaid cloak turned up with black velvet, as Landlord of the* Craven's Head Tavern, Drury Lane—WILLIAM CLUFF, *his waiter—* Attendants, Officers, &c.

Cluff: And please your worship, I am a waiter, what waits at taverns and places. T'other day Mr. Oxberry had a dinner of twenty-one at his house, the Craven's Head, your worship, hard by; and I was engaged to wait upon 'em, which I accomplished to every gentleman's satisfaction, I believe; and if I did

not, many of 'em are here present, and let 'em speak
to it. After dinner, saving your worship's presence,
a dessert was ordered for twenty-one, at sixpence a
head; and I set it out very handsomely, as I always
do. Then, your worship, I handed the plate to the
chairman for the sixpence a-head, and he very kindly
told me to bring another plate for something for the
waiter—that's *me*, your worship. When the bell rung,
I goes up, your worship; and the chairman says to
me, says he, " Here, waiter, there's sixteen shillings—
for the dessert, and the rest for yourself." " Thank
you, sir," says I. "Oh, no thanks," says he—" You've
been vastly attentive, and it's due to you." With that,
your worship, I takes my half to myself, and takes the
other half—eight shillings—your worship, to the bar;
whereby Mr. Oxberry blowed me up, and said a dessert
for twenty-one, at sixpence a-head, comes to ten and
sixpence. " Very well," says I, " Sir, I can't help it—
the gentlemen have done all what they pleased." So
then, your worship, without no more provocation than
this here, Mr. Oxberry said I should pay for three
plates and one glass, what the gentlemen broke ; and
says I to Mr. Oxberry, says I—

Magistrate : The warrant charges Mr. Oxberry with
assaulting and beating you—I do not want to hear
about your plates and dishes—come to the assault at
once.

Cluff : Well, your worship, by that means Mr.

Oxberry goes upstairs, and I heard him telling the gentlemen that I should say they were all a parcel of *scaly* fellows; whereby I told him it was a *lie;* by which means he laid hold of my collar and shook me, and hit me two or three times, your worship, while the other gentlemen held me.

Magistrate: And as far as I can judge at present, you richly deserve to be shaken.

Mr. Oxberry: Your worship; this fellow—

Magistrate: Keep your temper, Mr. Oxberry.

Mr. Oxberry: Your worship, I will endeavour. This person, who has been haunting my house this fortnight for employment, I engaged, as he says, to wait upon a little dinner I had at my house. I am a publican, sir—

Cluff: And sinner. (*aside*)

Mr. Oxberry: After dinner he came down to me, complaining him that the company had not paid him; whereupon I went upstairs and told them what he had said,—that they were a parcel of *shabby* fellows.

Magistrate: There you were wrong, Mr. Oxberry. I think the person who repeats a hasty expression, as bad almost as the first utterer of it.

Mr. Oxberry: Your worship, I admit it. But I had no sooner uttered the words, then he pops into the room, and calls me a *liar!* and I very naturally ordered him out of my house; but I never struck him. On the contrary, he struck *me.*

Betty Chambermaid : Your worship, I saw the waiter, Mr. Cluff, come into the room and call master a liar, and strike him—quite in a passion, your worship.

First Gentleman : I substantiate what Betty Chambermaid has said. Certainly the waiter struck Mr. Oxberry, and Mr. Oxberry did not strike the waiter.

Second Gentleman : That's *very* true.

Cluff : Your worship, these are all Mr. Oxberry's friends. Besides, Mr. Oxberry always serves his waiters so.

Magistrate : Then you expected he would beat you when you asked him for employment?

Cluff : Your worship, I knew I run great risk of it.

Magistrate : The warrant is dismissed. Good morning to you, Mr. Oxberry.   [*Exeunt Omnes.*

§ *Furicus Frank.*

" The close of the business at Bow Street office was enlivened, "to a degree," by the eccentricities of a person who called himself, in the first instance, "Captain Frank Brigges, of the Royal Navy, and a gentleman—*hiccup.*" It afterwards appeared, however, that he was not of the Royal Navy, but of the Bombay service ; and as to his gentility, he was certainly, for that night at least, the most ungentle gentleman we ever saw.

It seems that at half-past eight the same evening, he presented himself in the box-lobby of the second circle at Drury Lane Theatre, and demanded to be shown to " a d—l—sh good box." He was shown to a box accordingly ; but whether a " d—l—sh good one," or not, did not appear. We should rather suppose not ; for he had not been seated many minutes before he began to manifest symptoms of dissatisfaction. One moment he turned his left side to the stage ; then he turned the right side ; and, this not being to his mind, he turned his legs behind him, as an Emeralder might say, and placed his back towards the stage. This position did not please him long, and he tried to stand upright ; but the perpendicular was past his power ; and after *swaying* backwards and forwards and sideways, like a Lombardy poplar in a chopping wind, he came down with a lee-lurch, and seated himself on the blooming shoulders of a comely dame on the seat below him. All these varieties of position he accompanied with critical comments on the players, the house, the lights, and the ladies ; and when remonstrated with by the gentlemen in the surrounding boxes, he boldly retorted, " D—mme, arn't I an *Englishman !*" At length, when he seated himself on the lady's shoulders as aforesaid, the box-keepers were desired to interfere ; but they, not being able to quiet him, called in Harradine, one of the patrole, employed at the theatre as a constable. Harradine endeavoured to prevail upon him to be quiet, but he was answered with a " d—mme, arn't I an Englishman! " There was now a general cry of " Turn him out ! " and Harradine proceeded to remove him. He came out into the lobby quietly enough ; but he was no sooner here, than he " showed fight," refusing to stir an inch further, and challenging " all the world."

The uproar he caused made it necessary, for the peace of the audience, that he should be removed from the theatre, and Harradine took him into custody ; in doing which that officer not only received several blows within the house, but was twice fairly, or rather *foully,* knocked down in the street before he could get him to the door of the office. Finding himself at the door of the office, he became ten times more furious than before, and kicked and plunged with such violence, that the bringing him into the presence of the magistrate was more like bringing a mad bull to the stake than anything else we can compare it to ; and, like a mad bull, too, he commenced a *roaring* remonstrance against his detention, as soon as he perceived himself before the magistrate. The magistrate endeavoured to prevail upon him to be quiet, that he might hear the charge against him ; and with some difficulty he succeeded ; but the enraged captain had not been silent more than a minute before he let fly his fist in the face of Goodwin, an officer who had nothing at all to do with him, and who was standing quietly by the magisterial table. "Lock him up!" said his worship, in whose immediate presence this irreverent and wanton act of violence was perpetrated—"Let him be locked up instantly;" and now came the tug of war. The captain threw himself into an attitude of defiance, "his very look an oath," and his eyes flashing fire : three or four officers sprung upon him ; the captain forced himself out of their grasp ; they again seized him, and began tugging him towards the door, he catching at everything in his way, and clinging to every hold he made with astonishing tenacity ; and, what was very curious, he seemed to take hold of any projection with his feet, as firmly as he did with his hands. This scene continued nearly five tedious minutes—nothing but sheer silent tugging on one side, and screaming resistance on the other ; and when at length the captain's strength was exhausted, and he was left locked up in the dark by himself, he set up a long continuous howl, so loud and dissonant, that we can compare it to nothing but a concert of half-a-dozen donkeys, " when first the soul of *love* is sent abroad " amongst them, on some fine spring evening. For more than a quarter of an hour did he continue this asinine serenade, *sans intermission ;* and all the courts and avenues of Bow Street " rebellow'd to the roar."

Meantime, Harradine and the box-keepers gave their evidence, and then the captain was brought in again to hear it read. He appeared now with a pair of highly-polished very handsome handcuffs on his wrists; but, notwithstanding their brightness, it was evident they annoyed him sadly. Indeed he was quite an altered man—his blustering had vanished like the bursting of a bubble, and his bellowing had dwindled to a blubber. He approached the table between two officers, holding up his manacled hands to the magistrate, and whimpered out, " Only see here, sir, how they've served me ! "

The magistrate told him he was very sorry to see a *gentleman* decorated in such a manner, but he had brought it upon himself.

The captain gave a long " *Oh !* " and the clerk began to read over the evidence, but the captain was too much distressed both in mind and body to attend to it ; and he continued—sometimes in a deep *bass* voice, and sometimes in a squeaking *treble*, alternately deploring and deprecating the whole proceeding. " I pledge you my honour, sir," said he, in *bass*, " that I have done nothing worthy of this coercion." Then instantly going off into a *treble*, he exclaimed, " Oh ! my dear kind Mr. Magistrate, do intercede for an unfortunate gentleman—do, God bless you !—now do, that's a kind dear soul ! " Then *bass* again, " Upon the word of a gentleman, sir, I am not drunk.—Upon my honour, I have drunk nothing but water these ten days." Then *treble* again, "Oh! you d—d rascally officers, what have you used me in this manner for? Only look here, your worship—see here, what the rascals have put upon my poor hands! let me go home, and I'll go down on my knees to you, you kind, dear, kind, very kind gentleman!—I'll give you any money if you'll only let me go!" *Bass* again, "I have certainly been used extremely ill, without having given the slightest provocation to anybody," &c., &c.

Meanwhile "the big round tears coursed each other down his purple nose in piteous chase," mingling with other nameless matters, which the gaoler, who stood by his side, wiped away from time to time, for decency sake; and, at length, the magistrate—finding there was no chance of getting him to attend to the evidence—ordered that he should be taken to the watch-house, and be brought up again in the morning.

He was taken accordingly, without much difficulty, and, to cut short a story already far too long, when he was brought up on the following morning, he was so excessively contrite, that he was forgiven by all parties, and allowed to go home, and get "a plaister for his broken coxcomb.""

§ *Lord Mansfield's Wig.*

The following history connected with Lord Mansfield's wig is truly amusing from the dramatic display of characters on both sides.

" It appeared that a barber called Williams had obtained a summons against the defendant, who is clerk to Mr. Reeves, an attorney in Tottenham Court Road, calling upon him to attend on a given day, to show cause why he should not pay a debt of 39*s*. 11¾*d*.

Mr. Williams, who spoke with a sort of lisping squeak, garrulously addressed the commissioner: " He had," he said, " been a hair-dresser, man and boy, for sixty-eight years. He had served his time in the Temple, where he had had the honour of making wigs for some of the greatest men as ever lived—of all professions, and of all ranks—judges, barristers, and commoners—churchmen as well as laymen—illiterate men as well as literate men ; and, among the latter, he had to rank the immortal Dr. Johnson. But of all the wigs he had ever set comb to, there was none on which he so much prided himself as a full state wig which he had made for Lord Mansfield. It was one of the earliest proofs of his genius ; it had excited the warm commendation of his master, and the envy of his brother shopmates; but, above all, it had pleased, nay, even delighted, the noble and learned judge himself. Oh! gemmen," exclaimed Mr. Williams, "if you had known what joy I felt when I first saw his noble lordship on the bench with that wig on his head!" (in an under-tone, but rubbing his hands with ecstasy)

—" Upon my say so, I was fuddled for the three days after ! "

The Commissioner : What has this wig to do with the defendant's debt ?

Mr. Williams : A great deal : that's the very bone of contention.

The Commissioner : Doubtless ; but you must come to the marrow, if you can, as soon as you can.

Mr. Williams : I will. Well, as I was a saying— where did I leave off ?—Oh ! when I was fuddled.

The Commissioner : I hope you have left off that habit, now, my good man.

Mr. Williams : Upon my say so, I have, trust me ; but as I was a saying, to make a long story short, in course of time I left my master in the Temple, set up for myself, and did a great stroke of business. Ay, I could tell you such a list of customers. There was—

The Commissioner : Never mind, we don't want your list—go on.

Mr. Williams : Well, then, at last I set up in Boswell Court, Queen Square. Lawk me ! what alterations I have seen in that Square, surely, in my time. I remember when I used to go to shave old Lord—

The Commissioner : For God's sake, do come to the end of your story.

Mr. Williams : Well, I will. Where was I ? Oh ! in Boswell Court—[*Commissioner*, aside : I wish you were there now.]—Well, then, you must know when

Lord Mansfield (God rest his soul!) died, his wig—the very, very wig I made—got back to my old master's shop, and he kept it as a pattern for other judges' wigs ; and at last, who should die but my master himself. Ay, it's what we must all come to.

The Commissioner : Go on, go on, man, and come to the end of your story.

Mr. Williams : I will, I will. Well, where was I ? Oh! in my poor master's shop. Well, so when he died, my mistress gave me—for she knew, poor soul! how I loved it—this 'dentical wig ; and I carried it home with as much delight as if it had been one of my children. Ah, poor little things! they're all gone before me.

The Commissioner : Come, if you don't cut this matter short, I must, and send you after them.

Mr. Williams : Dearee me! you put me out. Well, as I was a saying, I kept this here wig as the apple of my eye; when, as ill-luck would have it, that 'ere Mr. Lawrence came to my shop, and often asked me to lend it to him to act with in a play—I think he called it Shycock, or Shylock, for he said he was to play the judge. I long refused, but he over-persuaded me, and on an unlucky day I let him have it, and have never (weeping and wiping his little eye with his white apron) seen it since.

The Commissioner : And so you have summoned him for the price of this wig ?

Mr. Williams : You have just hit the nail on the head.

The Commissioner : Well, Mr. Lawrence, what have you to say to this ?

Mr. Lawrence (with great pomposity) : Why, sir, I have a great deal to say.

The Commissioner : Well, then, sir, I desire you will say as little as you can, for there are a great many persons waiting here whose time is very precious.

Mr. Lawrence : Not more precious than mine, I presume, sir. I submit that this case is in the nature of an action of trover, to recover the possession of this wig ; and this admitted, sir, I have humbly to contend, that the plaintiff must be nonsuited ; for, sir, you will not find one word of or concerning a wig in his declaration. The plaintiff must not travel out of his record.

The Commissioner : What record ?

Mr. Lawrence : The record in Court.

The Commissioner : We have no record.

Mr. Lawrence : You have a summons, on which I attend to defend myself ; and that is, to all intents and purposes, *de faclo*, as well as *de jure*, a record similar to, and of the essence of, a record in the Court above.

The Commissioner : Sir, we are not guided by the precedents of Courts above here. Our jurisdiction and our powers are defined by particular Acts of Parliament.

Mr. Lawrence: Sir, I contend, according to the common law of these realms, that I am right.

The Commissioner: I say, according to the rules of common sense, you are wrong.

Mr. Lawrence: Sir, I have cases.

The Commissioner: Sir, I desire you will confine yourself to this case.

Mr. Lawrence: What says Kitty upon the nature of these pleadings?

The Commissioner: And pray, who is Kitty?

Mr. Lawrence: The most eminent pleader of the present day.

The Commissioner: I never heard of a woman being a special pleader.

Mr. Lawrence: He is not a woman, sir; he is a man, sir, and a great man, sir—and a man, sir—

The Commissioner: Do you mean Mr. Chitty?

Mr. Lawrence: I mean the gentleman *you* call Chitty, and most erroneously so call him; for you ought to know that the *Ch* in Italian sounds like an English K; and Mr. Kitty, by lineal descent, is an Italian. It is a vulgar error to spell his name with a y final, it ought to be i, and then it would properly sound Kitty.

The Commissioner: I should rather take Mr. Chitty's authority for this than yours.

Mr. Lawrence (in anger): Sir, do you contradict me?

The Commissioner: Sir, I will bring this case to a short issue. Did you borrow this man's wig?

Mr. Lawrence: I did.

The Commissioner: Do you choose to return it?

Mr. Lawrence: It is destroyed.

The Commissioner: How destroyed?

Mr. Lawrence: It was burnt by accident.

The Commissioner: Who burnt it?

Mr. Lawrence: I did, in performing the part of the Judge in Shakspeare's inimitable play of the *Merchant of Venice.* While too intent on the pleadings of *Portia,* the candle caught the curls, and I, with difficulty, escaped having my eyes burnt out.

The plaintiff here uttered an ejaculation of mental suffering, something between a groan and a curse.

The Commissioner: Well then, sir, I have only to tell you, you are responsible for the property thus intrusted to your care; and, without farther comment, I order and adjudge that you pay to the plaintiff the sum of 39s. 11¾d., which is the sum he is prepared to swear it is worth.

Mr. Williams: Swear! Lord love you, I'd swear it was worth a Jew's eye. Indeed, no money can compensate me for its loss.

The Commissioner: I cannot order you a Jew's eye, Mr. Williams, unless Mr. Lawrence can persuade his friend Shylock to part with one of his; but I will order you such a sum in monies numbered, as you will swear this wig is fairly and honestly worth. A long dispute followed, as to the value of the wig, when Mr. Williams ultimately agreed to take 20*s.* and costs, and the parties were dismissed, mutually grumbling at each other.

§ *A Great Man in Distress.*

There is a certain Shandean pathos in the following : A personage, who described himself as " General Sarsfield Lucan, Viscount Kilmallock in Ireland, a peer of France, and a descendant of Charlemagne," presented himself before the magistrate to solicit a few shillings to enable him to proceed on important business to Wexford.

General Sarsfield Lucan wore an old brown surtout, with the collar turned up behind to keep his neck warm, and a scrap of dirty white ribbon fastened to one of the button-holes ; a black velvet waistcoat, powdered with tarnished silver *fleurs-de-lis*, and an ancient well-worn *chapeau bras*, surmounted with a fringe of black feathers. He carried under his arm a large roll of writings, and all his pockets were stuffed with tin cases, pocket-books, and bundles of papers : his " fell of hair " was ruefully matted ; an enormous tawny whisker covered either cheek and his upper lip and chin,—which, for want of shaving, " showed like a stubble-field at harvest home,"—was all begrimed with real Scotch.

He said he was a native of Wexford in Ireland, and had spent the last seven years in Paris, where his cousin, Louis XVIII., nominated him a peer, and gave him a decoration (the bit of white ribbon above mentioned); but his instalment had been postponed by the then recent change in the ministry; his cousin (Louis XVIII.) assuring him, that as soon as his present ministers were kicked out, he should come in. In the meantime his father had died, and willed him certain lands and houses in Wexford; whereupon ho wrote to his sisters, who were resident there, to desire them to send him the proceeds of his estates forthwith; but instead of so doing, they had themselves administered to the will, and were dissipating his patrimony. Under these circumstances, his cousin, the king, advised him to set out immediately for Ireland, and seek redress in person. "Journeying with this intent," he landed at Dover a few days before, but on reaching London he found his finances exhausted, and he was now driven to the unpleasant necessity of applying to their worships for a few shillings to enable him to proceed.

Sir R. Birnie said, he wondered his royal cousin had not furnished him with the means of prosecuting his journey.

"Sir! I scorned to trouble him at all on such a

palthry subject as money," replied the general, with some warmth; and he then went on to state, that in order to satisfy his coach-hire from Dover to London he had been necessitated to give up possession of his working tools.

"Your *working tools !*" said the magistrate; "and pray may I ask what trade your lordship follows?"

"No trade in the world at all," replied the general; "I am not the person to be after following trades.— The tools I am *spaking* about are what I used in some of the greatest inventions the world ever saw. I invented a *happaratus* for extracting stone and gravel from the *blather* without any operation at all. I invented a machine for fishing up vessels foundered at sea, as *aisy* as fishing up an oyster; and I invented another machine for making *accouchement* the most *aisy* thing in existence—a mere *fla-bite* to the most tender lady imaginable! And it was partly these inventions, indeed, that brought me to this country now —because I did not choose to be giving foreigners the benefit of them."

"Pray, sir," said Mr. Minshull, "will you give me leave to ask whether you were ever confined?"

The General: Confined! for what would I be confined?

Mr. Minshull : If you do not understand the nature of my question I am sorry I put it; but it certainly appeared to me possible that——

The General: Sir, you appear to me to be after *taalking* in a very queer kind of a way to a *jontleman!* You ought to know what is due to a respectable and *graat* man, even though he is in distress.

Mr. Minshull: Well, sir, I will speak as plainly to you as you do to me. It is my opinion, and the opinion, I believe, of every person present, that you are out of your mind; and that if you have never been confined it is high time you were so.

The General angrily declared he was altogether *mens sana in corpore sano;* and professed himself astonished that anybody should entertain a contrary opinion; then taking from his side-pocket a round tin case, nearly as large as a demi-culverin, he offered to produce from it documents to show that he was really the important personage he professed himself to be.

The magistrates, however, had no faith in the matter; they told him it might be all very true, but they had no funds to assist him with; and, as he appeared very incredulous on this subject, they at length ordered him to withdraw upon pain of being committed to prison under the Vagrant Act.

This was an awful alternative, which the gallant "General" did not think proper to risk; so gathering up his patents and papers, he put his feather-fringed *chapeau* upon his head, and taking an ample pinch of snuff—so ample, indeed, that it rushed through his olfactory labyrinth with the noise of a mighty cataract

—he stalked majestically out of the office, muttering anathemas as he went.

§ *A Hideous Plot.*

Simple and unpretending in its details as the following story may be considered, it is doubtful if any more revolting picture of villainy can be found in the Newgate Calendar.

"In October, 1838, a merchant of the City, whom we shall call Mr. Goldsmith, had two clerks in his counting-house who were the sons of early friends, who left them destitute orphans much about the same time. Mr. Goldsmith had treated them as his own children. One was named Henry Wilkinson, and the other John Simpson Betts. Mr. Goldsmith had an only daughter, Emily, to whom he had intended one of his clerks should be married; a circumstance, in fact, which he had for some years past communicated to the boys themselves, telling them at the same time, that his daughter would be left to her unrestricted choice, and that it would depend upon themselves which would be the happy man. Her choice fell upon the younger, Betts. This decision, it appears, wounded the other's feelings so much that he was resolved upon revenge; and never did the devil suggest to the human heart a plan of revenge more diabolical than the one which Wilkinson conceived and put into execution. For the furtherance of his scheme, Wilkinson became

deeply connected with a nest of blacklegs at one of the
hells in the Quadrant, by whose assistance he was
enabled to carry his operations into effect. The charge
of Goldsmith's books was divided between the two
clerks, Wilkinson keeping the journal and ledger, and
Betts the cash and day books. It was also the duty of
Betts to keep the bankers' book, and to draw the
checks which were signed by Goldsmith, a private
mark being placed upon a particular part of the check
in order to guard against forgery. With this private
mark Wilkinson was well acquainted, and early in the
beginning of last August he *forged* a check in Mr.
Goldsmith's name upon the bankers for fifty pounds,
which he received in one note, the number and date of
which he carefully noted down. It appeared that it
was Goldsmith's custom to send for his bankers' book
at the end of every month in order to agree and
balance it with his own cash book ; so that Wilkinson
knew that nearly a month would have to elapse before
the forgery would be discovered, which gave him ample
time to secure his object. As soon as he had got the
fifty pound note he went with it to his companions at
the hell, by whom in the course of a few days he was
furnished with a forged counterpart, corresponding in
every respect with the genuine note, and bearing
exactly the same date and number. The object of this
will be seen presently.

The 1st of September was the day fixed upon

for the marriage of Miss Goldsmith to Betts, and the 28th of August had already arrived, when Wilkinson, who had been the whole preceding part of the month endeavouring to persuade Betts to make a visit to the gambling-table in question, at length succeeded in getting him there on the evening of that day under a special promise that he was not to be asked to play. Champagne, however, did its work, and Betts was drawn into the snare. He played and *won* fifty pounds. The forged note for that amount was paid him by the loser, whose services in losing the money with the assistance of his confederates, had been remunerated with the genuine note. Wilkinson whispered into his ear that *now* was the lucky time to leave off. The note was to be a handsome present to Emily on her wedding day. Betts took his advice, and they left the hell together—Betts, to make preparations for his departure next morning for the country house at Windsor, and Wilkinson to complete his revenge.

The happy party at Windsor were already in the church, and the clergyman was about to commence the ceremony, when Wilkinson rushed in, apparently breathless, and desired a moment's conference with Mr. Goldsmith. He then produced a letter from that gentleman's bankers, which stated that a check for fifty pounds had been forged in his name, and that they had reason to suspect one of his clerks of the act, because the private mark was upon the check. Thunderstruck by this intelligence, the old man inquired of Betts if he knew anything about it; but while he was making denial, Miss Goldsmith, who did not like the appearance of things, joined the trio, and very quickly settled the matter by the production of the note which Betts had given her, and which, of course, corresponded exactly with the description furnished by the bankers. All doubt was now at an end; the ceremony was abruptly interrupted and the parties retired; Emily, Wilkinson, and Mr. Goldsmith to the house of the latter, and Betts to the station-house under the charge of a policeman.

The case was investigated by Sir R. Birnie, who displayed more than his usual acuteness. With the assistance of Mr. Goldsmith he established a well-conducted inquiry. The plan he adopted was this. He persuaded Mr. Goldsmith to offer privately a reward of one hundred pounds to any one who was present at the gaming-table on the night when the money was lost. A needy swindler came forward and divulged the whole. Wilkinson was now called upon for an explanation, but was missing. It is supposed that he got on board a steamboat—for France or for Amsterdam. The proceedings in this matter have been kept so secret that no notice has been nor will be taken of them in the papers. One great good, however, has come of them—a regular manufactory of forged notes

has been discovered, the particulars of which will in
due time come before the public."

§ *Mysterious Visitors.*

Sometimes extraordinary personages came to the
magistrates : they were always received with respect
and due allowance. As on a Wednesday morning in
March, 1821, when a lady alighted from a travelling-
chariot at the door, and requested to be shown in
immediately. The carriage had an imperial on the
top, and was covered with dust. The lady herself was
apparently of middle age, and a slight genteel figure ;
but she bore in her countenance strong marks of a
fixed melancholy. She wore a blue riding-habit, with
a black beaver riding-hat ; and her whole person was
nearly covered with a large black lace veil. One of
the clerks immediately conducted her to the magistrate,
who politely requested her to take a seat ; but she
declined it with a melancholy ejaculation of the simple
monosyllable " No ; " at the same time motioning him,
with a graceful wafture of her hand, to proceed with
what he was about. The magistrate, somewhat alarmed
at her manner, requested her, since she would not sit
down, to walk round to the other side of the table.
She did so ; and the other business before the magistrate being almost immediately disposed of, he said,
" Now, madam, I will hear what you have to say."

She replied nearly as follows :—"I have only to place in your hands these pamphlets, containing matter of deep interest, such as fraud, felony, and presumptive murder; and to request you will make them public, preparatory to a public and great event.

These words were delivered in a tone of the most profound melancholy, and at the same time with the firmness of one accustomed to dictate and to be obeyed. She then handed to the magistrate two quarto pamphlets, one of which appeared, by the title-page, to be an investigation into the conduct of a certain reverend gentleman; and both of them seemed to have their margins nearly covered with writing. The magistrate, taking the books, observed that he had not time to peruse them at that moment; he would look into them at the first convenient opportunity.—" *Do so!* " instantly rejoined the lady in an authoritative manner; " *Do so!* but give them publicity—promise? " The magistrate, " I assure you, madam, I will look into them; and I will do what is right." To this the lady, dropping her voice to its former melancholy tone, replied, "I believe you, from what I have observed; I believe you. Farewell! " And having so said, she returned to her carriage, and drove off at a rapid pace; no one at the office knowing who she was, whence she came, where she went to, nor scarcely what she wanted.

In 1827 another " mysterious case " occupied the

attention of the court for a short time. In those days there were many cases which, as it were, flitted past and were heard of no more. The magistrates seem to have been accessible enough and were willing to give advice, or perhaps wished to distract the monotony of their duties. Thus one day a young man of highly interesting appearance, applied at this office to solicit the magistrate's advice, under the following novel and very mysterious circumstances :—

He stated that he had never been blessed with parental solicitude and tenderness, having from his infancy, until very lately, lived with a laundress in the Temple, named Elm, who received a liberal allowance for his maintenance down to the period of her death, an event that took place about six months ago, when the allowance ceased, and he was thrown destitute on the world. His lamented protectress had frequently stated that his friends were of elevated rank, and that he ought to have the enjoyment of an ample fortune, out of which he was kept, she said, by the turpitude of some individuals. She died without having furnished the applicant with any clue by which he could discover his parents. All he knew concerning his birth was, that he was born in the house of a surgeon, named Bradford, who, at that time, resided contiguous to the Kent Road. During Mr. Bradford's lifetime, the money allowed to Mrs. Elm for the applicant's support, came through his hands; and after his death, Mrs. Bradford paid it. She declined giving him any further assistance. But he had been told by his protectress, Mrs. Elm, that Mrs. Bradford was the only one living who could afford him any knowledge of his parents; and he hinted that her reasons for declining to do so were pecuniary.

An officer was then directed to wait upon Mrs. Bradford, and to prevail upon her, if possible, to appear at the office. Accordingly the lady presented herself. She was far advanced in years, and appeared a good deal agitated.

Mr. Minshull said, that if she knew anything of the young man's friends, in common justice she ought to disclose it. Mrs. Bradford denied that she knew anything of them.

Applicant: Surely, ma'am, you cannot deny having paid me money; and why will you not explain from whom that money came?

Mrs. Bradford: That I'll never explain to you, nor to any one else.

Applicant: Do you not know who my parents are?

Mrs. Bradford (in some confusion): Yes, I know something about them, but I don't choose to tell.

Mr. Minshull: I tell you what, ma'am, you are acting most unnaturally and cruelly, and can be *forced* to give the information required of you, by a Bill in Equity; and I hope this young person will find some solicitor to take up his case.

Applicant: For God's sake, Mrs. Bradford, tell me who my parents are?

Mrs. Bradford (with increased confusion) *:* Yes, I know something about them, but I cannot tell it.

A gentleman named White, who was sitting on the bench, here interposed : he handed the applicant his card, and bid him call at his house, saying that, from what he had heard and seen, he would do all in his power to unravel the mystery ; and if any additional information could be obtained, that he would engage to have a bill filed. Mrs. Bradford was anxious to depose that she had no property belonging to the applicant, and expressed her wish to retire.

Applicant: Mrs. Bradford, before you go, now tell me, have you not told me, on applying to you for money, that you must first speak to my friends? Mrs. Bradford denied that she said so, or that she ever knew his friends.

Mrs. Bradford: Am I at liberty to go?

Mr. Minshull: Certainly, I cannot detain you ; but before you depart, I wish you would give this young man the information he seeks.

Mrs. Bradford gave no reply, but hurried out of the office as quickly as she could. Here the matter ends for the present.

Some weeks later further information was obtained. The publication of the particulars of what had occurred at Bow Street created a pretty general public feeling in Elm's favour, and throughout the early part of the week crowds of persons assembled round the door of Mrs. Bradford, who now lived in Tottenham Court Road. By the kind interference of a Mr. White, that lady was induced to make a statement in writing of all the facts which she knew of relative to young Elm. On Thursday the whole of the parties appeared at the office, when the young man, having read the document, expressed himself satisfied with the statements it contained, and the case was dismissed.

In 1803, it seems, Mrs. —— lived not very far from Portland Place, and carried on an extensive business. She was a handsome widow, and a person of distinction one day passing by the shop, being struck with her beauty, called in and gave an order. He repeated his visits, and an intimacy commenced, which was carried on for a short time. She urged her *bon ami* to marry her, and was surprised to learn that it was out of his power to make her his wife ; but he consented to make her a handsome bonus provided she immediately married some one else. In a few weeks afterwards she was married to Mr. T., the son of a rich tradesman at Oxford, and in five months after the union she gave birth to a boy, which Mrs. Elm received from the mother at Dr. Bradford's house, in Hereford Street, Fitzroy Square, and brought up as her own. She (the mother) died very suddenly a little more than a year ago. Young Elm had learned that she was his reputed mother, and he called upon her at the house of her husband, Mr. T., and said to her, " I am the boy you put to nurse with Mrs. Elm, and I am told you are my mother." She was so affected by the unexpected communication, and the sight of the young man, who is stated to resemble her very strongly, that she fell on the floor in a fit, and never recovered the effect of the shock—she was a corpse in a fortnight afterwards, and young Elm, *incog.*, followed her to the grave. It is stated that old Mr. T., of Oxford, the grandfather of Elm, bequeathed a considerable property to his grandson ; but the query is, would Elm be able to take under that will ?

§ *A Sensitive Singer.*

A celebrated female vocalist appeared to prefer a charge against the proprietor and editor of the *Morning Chronicle*, for a libellous paragraph in that journal, tending to a breach of the peace, and instigating to murder. The paragraph was to the following effect :—

" For our parts, being moderate men, averse from any violent measures, and lovers in all things of gentle counsels, *we should incline to adopt Handel's method of making performers sensible of their faults*, thus described by a writer in the *London*. In the days of Handel if a singer gave offence, *he used to take her by the waist and throw her out of the window. This was a laudable practice, and Greatorex should revive it.* It was indeed a laudable practice—throwing singers out of window! This was letting them down a peg to some purpose; aye, in those days a man had some chance of hearing tolerable music, when such judicious means were taken to perfect the performers. If they gave themselves airs, away they went into the street; if they were out of time or tune one moment, they were out of the window the next. This was the true concert pitch. We conceive that sore throats, coughs, and colds, and hoarsenesses were very scarce in those exceeding good old times; those airings from windows must have hardened the constitutions, and braced the nerves finely—we would fain see something of the kind revived. The idea of throwing them out of window seems just the thing. Until some plan of this sort is adopted, we shall have nothing but apologies and disappointments. One decent tumble would cure all the sickness and sulkiness even of the opera company."

Mr. Minshull: Have you, Miss ——, such an opinion on the subject as to enable you to make an affidavit?"

The lady answered that she had.

Mr. Minshull: A professional man will advise you best as to the affidavit you ought to produce.

Miss —— : I have one prepared, sir. Here it is.
It was then put in and read.

"MIDDLESEX to wit. Kitty ——, of ——, in the city of ——, spinster, maketh oath and saith, that William Innel Clement, being a person of an evil and malicious mind and disposition, and unlawfully and maliciously contriving to vilify, disgrace, and injure this deponent, and to provoke her to a breach of the peace, and as this deponent verily believes, to incite the professors, amateurs of music, and others, the subjects of our Lord the King, to commit an outrage upon, and murder this deponent, on the 4th day of October instant, with force and arms, within the said city of Westminster, in the county of Middlesex and elsewhere, did unlawfully print and publish in a certain public newspaper, called the *Morning Chronicle*, a wicked, scandalous, and mischievous libel, of and concerning singers, and the deponent as a singer, that is to say, ' I hope to see those people properly appreciated. In the days of Handel, if a singer gave offence, he used to take her by the waist and throw her out of the window. This was a laudable practice, and Greatorex should revive it. It was indeed a laudable practice. This was the true concert pitch. We would fain see something of the kind revived. Let them down a story by all means,' to the evil example

of all others, and against the peace of our Lord
the King, his crown and dignity.

      (Signed)   " KITTY ——.

" Sworn before me, Oct. 5, 1825."

Sir Richard Birnie: Really, my dear madam, I
think you have no reason whatever for apprehension;
ladies are naturally timid, and we know how to make
allowance for their fears ; but these words which have
so dreadfully alarmed you, are those exaggerated expressions which signify nothing, because they say so
much, they are as unmeaning as compliments.

Miss —— then went on in the most vehement
manner : I—do—on—my—oath—really—and truly
—believe—that—the *Morning Chronicle*--had in view
—the destruction of me—and I positively swear—
that—I—think—my—life—is—in—danger.

Sir Richard Birnie : From whom ?

Miss —— (in confusion, and evidently taken by
surprise) : From the publisher. (Laughter.)

Sir Richard Birnie : What! you think, my dear
young lady, Mr. Clement put this libel of the *London*
into his paper to incite his publisher to murder you ?
(Laughter.)

Miss —— : No, I mean the proprietor. (Another
laugh.)

Sir Richard Birnie : How ?

Miss —— : I only say, and I mean to say that they

meant in this libel to incite the professors and amateurs of music to do me some grievous bodily harm; I actually, really, and positively do fear for my life.

The gentleman who attended on behalf of the *Morning Chronicle* now said that he was ready to bring forward bail for Mr. Clement if required, but he trusted that Mr. Minshull would exercise his discretion, and dismiss so frivolous and ridiculous a complaint.

The newspapers of 1825 were certainly free and outspoken in their criticisms, but nowadays it would seem to be going a little too far were Mr. Sutherland Edwards or Mr. Davison to suggest such drastic a process for a singer as was done in the *London* and *Morning Chronicle.*

Miss —— : In deciding Mr. Martin's case, which is exactly like mine in every particular, Mr. Minshull had no discretion at all; I believe that is the general impression.

Mr. Minshull: No, I have no discretion at all in cases of this kind; I know my authority, and must require Mr. Clement to put in bail, to keep the peace towards all his Majesty's subjects, and to answer any complaint that Miss —— may prefer against him at the sessions.

Miss ——, on retiring, gave notice that at an early day she should appear to require Messrs. Hunt and Clarke, of Tavistock Street, the publishers of the

London Magazine, to be held to bail for the atrocious libel and instigation to murder in that journal, as, observed she, " It shall not be said that I make fish of one and flesh of another."

§ *" Boardmen " Fifty Years ago.*

Sir Richard once expressed his detestation of the now familiar "harmless, necessary" boardmen, with whom, it will be seen, he was inclined to deal summarily. This was brought out in an amusing dialogue with one of those foolish persons—not wholly unknown in our day—who, under pretence of philanthropy, put aside the laws. Mr. Howard, a respectable Cheapside shopkeeper, had rescued a mendicant from the mendicity officers.

Elisha Pickle, one of the officers referred to, deposed, that having apprehended a notorious impostor begging in St. Martin's Court, he was conducting him to prison, when he made considerable resistance. A mob was in consequence collected, and witness and his brother officer were much abused. Mr. Howard was one of the most active ringleaders of this mob. He collared witness several times, notwithstanding he had produced his authority. Several other persons were almost equally violent, and the impostor, taking advantage of the row, made his escape from their custody. The other officer substantiated this account.

Mr. Howard being called upon for his defence, retorted the charge of violence upon the officers. They were, he said, dragging the poor fellow along in a most unmerciful manner, he crying out the while, "What is my crime? I am only guilty of being poor, and have only asked for labour." "Moved to pity by these cries, and the wretched appearance of the man," continued Mr. Howard, "I remonstrated with these men on their violent conduct. I told them they had no right to take the man to a prison, for I would that moment take him into my own service. Several respectable persons joined me in these remonstrances, but the officers treated us with contempt, and eventually, I believe, I did lay my hand on the shoulder of the fat officer."

The Magistrate : You say, Mr. Howard, that you would have taken him into your own service. Pray what are you, and what employ would you have given him ?

Mr. Howard : I am a boot and shoe maker, residing in Cheapside, but being about to remove from that street, it was my intention to employ him in carrying a board announcing that removal.

The Magistrate : Those board-carriers are some of the greatest nuisances with which the metropolis is infested; and had the officers brought some of yours here they would have been dealt with accordingly.

Mr. Howard replied that nevertheless it was a common practice, and had its advantages. As to the charge in question, he repeatedly assured the magistrate that he had only interfered from motives of humanity.

After some further conversation the magistrate proposed Mr. Howard should accompany the officers before the committee of the society, but one of the society's clerks who was present said such a step would be useless, as the society had determined to prosecute, in the present instance, by way of example, their officers having met with frequent interruption. In consequence of this notification, the magistrate called upon Mr. Howard to find bail to answer the charge elsewhere, and he having no bail ready was locked up.

The streets, indeed, if not so garish with advertisements, hoarding, &c., had special shows of a very painful kind, which have long since passed away. So late as 1830 the shocking spectacle of flogging persons at the cart's tail through the streets of London was often presented. Here was one of these scenes :—

" Shortly after the court had passed sentence, the gates of the Old Bailey yard were unfolded, and the hundreds who had long impeded both the foot and carriage-way, rushed in to be gratified with the sight of a public flogging. The unhappy culprits were Wm. Eames, aged forty-four, and Samuel Hunt, aged thirty-five, who were convicted of stealing a bushel of oats. It appeared to astonish the medical gentlemen in attendance that the culprits bore ninety-one lashes with such apparent fortitude. Our astonishment and indignation were aroused when we saw at the back chamber of a house, a matron of seventy, and four damsels in their non-age, laughing at the writhings of their guilty fellow-creatures."

In the previous year a more horrible spectacle still was witnessed. " A poor boy, aged about *thirteen years*, was flogged at the cart's tail, a distance of nearly 150 yards, for stealing a pair of shoes, and his screams after the second lash were heart-rending. He continued to shriek and cry " Oh, Lord! oh, Lord!" during the whole distance, and on being placed in the cart at the conclusion of this *English*, this *Christian* torture, the wretched child seemed too weak to support himself—his back was dreadfully lacerated. A considerable crowd was collected, who, of course (for the frequency of these revolting scenes has not yet totally obliterated the common feelings of humanity) expressed the strongest indignation at the horrid sight. The punishment was inflicted at ten o'clock on Friday morning."

It will be hardly credited what brutal cruelty distinguished some of the pastimes of the lower classes. So recently as the year 1770 it was found necessary to issue the following notice from Bow Street :—

Public Office, Bow Street, Feb. 19, 1770.

A CAUTION.

Next Tuesday, commonly called Shrove Tuesday, being that day on which the humanity of Englishmen has been usually disgraced by that no less barbarous than shameful practice of throwing at cocks : Notice is hereby given, that the high constable with the peace-officers in and near this Metropolis, will, according to custom, on that day, by the direction of the magistrates, search throughout their respective jurisdictions, in order to suppress this evil; though one would imagine that a moment's reflection on this diversion, would for ever put an end to it; for what can be more cowardly or dastardly than that of tying so inoffensive, so useful, and so brave an animal to a stake, as a poor cock, till *by large sticks this animal is either totally destroyed, or his limbs so broke that he cannot stand;* nay, *frequently the cruelty does not end here, for when they have no longer a leg to stand on to face their relentless enemies,* they are placed in a hat or pot, till they are totally destroyed. Nay, what is still worse, *pigeons, the emblem of love and tenderness, are on this day wantonly fastened to brick-bats, to share the same fate.* But 'tis to be hoped, that masters of families will carefully represent the heinousness of this offence to their servants and apprentices ; and if they should not take the benefit of their advice and this caution, 'tis to be hoped they will be apprehended by the constables, and brought to condign punishment. As, besides the above cruelty, it frequently happens that passengers passing and repassing receive great injuries from the sticks thrown on these occasions.

The curiously pathetic style of this, so foreign to the cold official strain, should be noted. Again, in April, 1812, Mr. Birnie and Mr. Nares had before them what was reasonably described as " an extraordinary case."

It appeared that as Croker, belonging to the office, was passing along the Hampstead Road, he observed at a short distance before him, two men on a wall, and directly after, he observed the tallest of them, a stout man about six feet high, hanging by his neck from a lamp-post attached to the wall, being that instant tied up and turned off deliberately by the short man. This very unexpected and extraordinary sight astonished and alarmed the officer. He made up to the spot with all possible speed, and just after he arrived there, the tall man fell to the ground with the handkerchief by which he had been suspended. Croker produced his staff, said he was an officer, and demanded to know of the other man the cause of such extraordinary conduct ; in the meantime, the man who had been hanged recovered from the effects of his suspension, got up, and, on finding Croker interfering, gave him a violent blow on his nose, which nearly knocked him backwards. The short man was then endeavouring to make off; however, the officer procured assistance, and both the men were secured and brought to the above office, when the account the fellows gave of themselves was, that they worked together on canals. They had been in company together on the Wednesday afternoon ; had

tossed up with halfpence for money, and afterwards
for their clothes; the tall man, who was hanged, won
the other's jacket, trousers, and shoes. They then in
the most wanton and brutal manner tossed up who
should hang the other; the short one won that toss,
and they got upon the wall, the one to submit, and
the other to carry their savage purpose into execution
on the lamp-iron.

They both agreed in this statement: the tall one,
who had been hanged, said, if he had won the toss he
would have hanged the other. He said he then felt
the effects of the experiment on his neck, in consequence of the time he was hanging, and that his eyes
were so much swelled that he saw double. Mr. Nares
and Mr. Birnie, the magistrates, both expressed their
horror and disgust at such conduct and language, and
ordered the man who had been hanged to find bail for
the violent and unjustifiable assault on the officer, and
the short one for hanging the other. Neither of them
being provided with bail, they were committed to
Bridewell for trial.

In 1833 the magistrates had an opportunity to
relieve their *ennui* by having a little comic performance
in their court.

At Bow Street, on March 27, 1833, Thos. M'Kean, a
respectably attired man, having a strong Scottish accent, was brought before Mr. Halls, the sitting magistrate, charged with an assault.

Mr. Burnaby, the clerk, intimated to Mr. Halls that

the defendant was the father of an extraordinary Scotch boy, who was said to be gifted with second sight, and also with the power of describing objects in a room which he could not by any possibility see in a direct way.

Mr. Halls said he should like much to see the young Gordon M'Kean, of whom he had heard and read much.

Mr. M'Kean called his son, a fine-looking lad, about eleven years of age, forward, and placing him with his back to the bench, put a handkerchief over his face, and requested the worthy magistrate to consent to an exhibition of his powers for a few minutes, to which Mr. Halls consented.

Mr. Burnaby, the boy being placed as before described, took his watch from his pocket, and said, " What have I got in my hand?" "A watch," was the reply. " What is it made of?" " Gold." "What chain is attached to it?" " None at all," said the boy, " there is a riband to it."

Mr Halls : Can you tell at what hour the hands stand ?

Boy : Yes ; at twelve.

Mr. Burnaby : More or less ?

Boy : Neither more nor less, but precisely twelve.

Mr. Burnaby showed his watch, and the hands were at twelve precisely.

Mr. Burnaby then produced his purse from his pocket, and asked the boy the colour of it, and what it contained ; and his answers were, without having the least opportunity of turning round towards the bench, that one end of the purse was brown and the other yellow, and that the brown end contained sovereigns and the yellow end silver. Mr. Burnaby admitted the correctness of the description, and taking some silver from his pocket, asked the boy to describe the different pieces. " What is this ? " said Mr. Burnaby, taking a sixpence. " Sixpence," said the boy, " and of the date of 1819." " What is the next," said Mr. Burnaby. " A shilling, and dated 1815," was the reply. And when the clerk brought forth another coin, and asked a similar question, the boy said, " That is a sixpence, and of the date of 1817 ;" and all of these guesses proved to be correct.

It would seem an extraordinary thing now were we to hear of a magistrate entertaining himself and his court with such puerilities.

CHAPTER IX.

DUELS AND GAMING-HOUSE RAIDS.

§ *A Tragic Encounter.*

ONE of the saddest instances of the duelling mania came to Bow Street in 1818, when Mr. Theodore O'Callaghan, of Gerrard Street, with Lieut. Newbolt, R.N., his second, and Mr. Thomas Phealan, were brought up for being concerned in a duel with Lieut. Bailey of the 58th Regiment.

The quarrel, it will be seen, had a thoroughly Irish character, and arose "in the most natural way in the wurrold." The two principals, having met to arrange a duel with two "friends," had fallen out in course of the arrangements. The meeting took place at Chalk Farm, and Lieut. Bailey was killed.

Mr. Adams, who occupied a house overlooking the ground, stated that about nine o'clock that morning he was in his bedroom, in the act of dressing himself, when he heard the discharge of two pistols, which induced him to look out of his window : he saw four gentlemen in two fields off his house, near Chalk Farm, whom he considered to be in the act of fighting a duel. He finished dressing himself with all possible speed, and hurried off to the spot, to endeavour to prevent the shots being repeated. Just as he arrived at the gate, and was in the act of getting over it, two pistols went off : he observed one of the gentlemen turn round. The three other gentlemen went up to him instantly; two of them supported him on each side; to prevent him from falling each of them held his arms. On his getting, up to them *one of them said to " him they were all friends."* He saw blood running down the trousers of the deceased profusely. The parties inquired of him if there was a house near, to conduct the deceased to it. They supported him to witness's house, which was about 400 or 500 yards off. The deceased appeared to be in a dangerous state. A surgeon was sent for with all possible speed. The deceased was laid on a sofa in his parlour, and while he was lying there he desired Mr. Theodore O'Callaghan to come to him, held out his hand to shake hands with him, and said he had behaved most honourably. The deceased observed that he was sensible he was dying. After this he called the other two prisoners to him, shook hands with them, made similar observations to them, and said he forgave them all. Mr. O'Callaghan, after this, went off to Hampstead to get a coach to convey him from his house ; in the meantime Mr. Rodd, a surgeon of Hampstead, arrived, who, after examining the wound, said it was impossible to remove him from where he was. The shot had entered on his right side, passed through his intestines, and had all but passed through on the left side, it only being kept from obtruding out by the skin. The shot had carried with it a piece of the cloth of his coat and other garments. The deceased observed to him that the quarrel which had been the cause of the duel was not originally a quarrel of their own, *but it had sprung out of a quarrel of two of their mutual friends, who were to have fought a duel on Sunday, and they were to have been their seconds* (*!*) The deceased lived about two hours, or two hours and a quarter. All the prisoners paid every possible attention to the deceased during the time he lived. He conversed with them all, particularly with Mr. Phealan, who, the deceased told him, had been his second, or his friend, he could not recollect which. Witness heard him request Mr. Phealan to write to his father the full particulars of the whole affair, who, he understood, lived at Limerick. Mr. Phealan then went off to London to procure more surgical assistance. On his return the deceased had expired. *Mr. Newbolt went in the meantime to inquire for lodgings in the neighbourhood.* Mr. O'Callaghan went to Hampstead to procure a coach. They all appeared anxious to do everything for the deceased, and were not inclined to abscond, but very readily surrendered.

The prisoners were not called upon for any defence.

The magistrate informed them that the law did not make any distinction in cases of murder, all being considered principals; they must all therefore be detained. Mr. Birnie added it was in evidence before him that one of the King's subjects had been deprived of life, and upon *primâ facie* evidence it was murder; he had therefore made up his mind that the prisoners must all be committed to Newgate, to take their trial for the murder of Lieut. Bailey.

The prisoners were accordingly conveyed to Newgate.

§ " *Tommy* " *Moore and Jeffrey.*

We may contrast with this the rather farcical issue of Tom Moore's quarrel with Jeffrey, and which the poet recounts with a due sense of the comical turn which the incident took. As is well known, the poet had been incensed by a severely contemptuous article in the *Edinburgh Review*, which he said " had roused his Irish blood;" though at first he did not think of noticing the affront. It is not improbable that the *éclat* of an encounter with so celebrated a person suggested itself. Moore was then a gay adventurer in town, much patronized by the great and fashionable, and a duel would be likely to increase his *prestige*. This view is supported by the fact that he admits feeling no sense of injury. He, however, naively says that the expense of a journey to Edinburgh to fight the reviewer was almost beyond his resources.

" In this mood of mind," he says, " I returned to London " (this was in the year 1806), "and there, whether by *good* or *ill* luck, but in my own opinion the *former*, there was the identical Jeffrey himself, just arrived on a short visit to his London friends. From Rogers, who had met Jeffrey the day before at dinner at Lord Fincastle's, I learned that the conversation, in the course of the day, having happened to fall upon me, Lord F. was good enough to describe me as possessing ' great amenity of manners;' on which Jeffrey said laughingly, ' I am afraid he would not show much amenity to *me*.'

" The first step I took towards my hostile proceeding was to write to Woolriche, a kind and cool-headed friend of mine, begging of him to join me in town as soon as possible; and intimating in a few words the nature of the services on which I wanted him.

" As Woolriche's answer implied delay and deliberation, it did not suit, of course, my notions of the urgency of the occasion; and I accordingly applied to my old friend Hume, who, without hesitation, agreed to be the bearer of my message. Having now secured my second, I lost no time in drawing up the challenge which he was to deliver; and as actual combat, not parley, was my object, I took care to put it out of the power of my antagonist to explain or retract, even if he was so disposed. After adverting to some assertion contained in the article accusing me, if I recollect right, of a deliberate intention to corrupt the minds of

my readers, I thus proceeded : ' To this I beg leave
to answer, you are a liar ; yes, sir, a liar ; and I choose
to adopt this harsh and vulgar mode of defiance, in
order to prevent at once all equivocation between us,
and to compel you to adopt for your own satisfaction,
that alternative which you might otherwise have
hesitated in affording to mine.'

" There was of course but one kind of answer to be
given to such a cartel. Hume had been referred by
Jeffrey to his friend Mr. Horner, and the meeting was
fixed for the following morning at Chalk Farm. Our
great difficulty now was where to procure a case of
pistols ; for Hume, though he had been once, I think,
engaged in mortal affray, was possessed of no such
implements ; and as for *me*, I had once nearly blown
off my thumb by discharging an over-loaded pistol,
and that was the whole, I believe, of my previous
acquaintance with fire-arms. William Spencer being
the only one of all my friends whom I thought likely
to furnish me with these *sine-qua-non*, I hastened to
confide to him my wants, and request his assistance
on this point. He told me if I would come to him in
the evening, he would have the pistols ready for me.

" I forget where I dined, but I know it was not in
company, as Hume had left to me the task of providing
powder and bullets, which I bought in the course of
the evening at some shop in Bond Street, and in such
large quantities, I remember, as would have done for

a score of duels. I then hastened to Spencer, who, in praising the pistols as he gave them to me, said, ' They are but too good.' I then joined Hume who was waiting for me in a hackney-coach, and proceeded to my lodgings. We had agreed that for every reason, both of convenience and avoidance of suspicion, it would be most prudent for me not to sleep at home ; and as Hume was not the man, either then or at any other part of his life, to be able to furnish a friend with an extra pair of clean sheets, I quietly (having let myself in by my key, it being then between twelve and one at night) took the sheets off my own bed, and huddling them up as well as I could, took them away with us in the coach to Hume's.

" I must have slept pretty well ; for Hume, I remember, had to wake me in the morning, and the chaise being in readiness, we set off for Chalk Farm. Hume had also taken the precaution of providing a surgeon to be within call. On reaching the ground we found Jeffrey and his party already arrived. I say his ' party,' for although Horner only was with him, there were, as we afterwards found, two or three of his attached friends (and no man, I believe, could ever boast of a greater number) who, in their anxiety for his safety, had accompanied him, and were hovering about the spot. And then was it that, for the first time, my excellent friend Jeffrey and I met face to face. He was standing with the bag, which contained the pistols, in his hand, while Horner was looking anxiously around.

" It was agreed that the spot where we found them, which was screened on one side by large trees, would be as good for our purpose as any we could select ; and Horner, after expressing some anxiety respecting some men whom he had seen suspiciously hovering about, but who now appeared to have departed, retired with Hume behind the trees, for the purpose of loading the pistols, leaving Jeffrey and myself together.

" All this had occupied but a very few minutes. We, of course, had bowed to each other on meeting ; but the first words I recollect to have passed between us was Jeffrey's saying, on our being left together, ' What a beautiful morning it is ! ' ' Yes,' I answered with a slight smile, ' a morning made for better purposes ;' to which his only response was a sort of assenting sigh. As our assistants were not, any more than ourselves, very expert at warlike matters, they were rather slow in their proceedings ; and as Jeffrey and I walked up and down together, we came once in sight of their operations : upon which I related to him, as rather *à propos* to the purpose, what Billy Egan, the Irish barrister, once said, when, as he was sauntering about in like manner while the pistols were loading, his antagonist, a fiery little fellow, called out to him angrily to keep his ground. ' Don't make yourself unaisy, my dear fellow,' said Egan ; ' sure, isn't it bad enough to take the dose, without being by at the mixing up?'

" Jeffrey had scarcely time to smile at this story, when our two friends, issuing from behind the trees, placed us at our respective posts (the distance, I suppose, having been previously measured by them), and put the pistols into our hands. They then retired to a little distance; the pistols were on both sides raised; and we waited but the signal to fire, when some police-officers, whose approach none of us had noticed, and who were within a second of being too late, rushed out from a hedge behind Jeffrey; and one of them, striking at Jeffrey's pistol with his staff, knocked it to some distance into the field, while another running over to me, took possession also of mine. We were then replaced in our respective carriages, and conveyed, crestfallen, to Bow Street.

" On our way thither Hume told me, that from Horner not knowing anything about the loading of pistols, he had been obliged to help him in the operation, and in fact to take upon himself chiefly the task of loading both pistols. When we arrived at Bow Street, the first step of both parties was to despatch messengers to procure some friends to bail us; and as William Spencer was already acquainted with the transaction, to him I applied on my part, and requested that he would lose no time in coming to me. In the meanwhile we were all shown into a sitting-room, the people

in attendance having first inquired whether it was our
wish to be separated, but neither party having expressed any desire to that effect, we were all put
together in the same room. Here conversation upon
some literary subject, I forget what, soon ensued, in
which I myself took only the brief and occasional share,
beyond which, at that time of my life, I seldom ventured in general society. But I have been told of his
saying, soon after our *rencontre*, that he had taken a
fancy to me from the first moment of our meeting
together in the field; and I can truly say that my
liking for him is of the same early date. After all the
usual ceremony of binding over, &c., had been gone
through, it was signified to us that we were free to
depart, and that our pistols should be restored to us.
I was obliged myself to return to Bow Street, in the
course of a few hours, for the purpose of getting them.
To my surprise, however, the officer refused to deliver
them up to me, saying in a manner not very civil, that
it appeared to the magistrate there was something
unfair intended; as, on examining the pistol taken
from me, there was found in it a bullet, while there
had been no bullet found in that of Mr. Jeffrey.

" Nothing remained for me (particlarly as Hume had
taken his departure) but to go at once to Horner's
lodgings and lay all the circumstances before him. I
was lucky enough to find him at his chambers; and
even at this distance of time, I recollect freshly the

immediate relief which it afforded me when I heard Horner exclaim, in his honest and manly manner, ' Don't mind what these fellows say. I myself saw your friend put the bullet into Jeffrey's pistol, and shall go with you instantly to the office to set the matter right.' We both then proceeded together to Bow Street, and Horner's statement having removed the magistrate's suspicions, the officers returned to me the pistols, together with the bullet which had been found in one of them."

" William Spencer," Moore wrote in his vexation to Miss Godfrey, " is the cause of this very ill-judged interruption, though he had pledged his honour to keep the matter as secret as the grave. I never can forgive him ; for at this moment I would rather have lost a limb than that such a circumstance had happened. And so there is all my fine sentimental letters which I wrote yesterday for posthumous delivery to your sister, you, &c. &c., all gone for nothing, and I made to feel very like a ninny indeed."

It seems that Mr. Spencer dined alone with the Fincastles, and, after dinner, told all the circumstances of the challenge, the loan of the pistols, &c., to Lord Fincastle, who (without, as it appears, communicating his purpose to Spencer) sent information that night of the intended duel to Bow Street.

" The manner," adds Moore, " in which the whole affair was misrepresented in the newspapers of the

day, is too well known to need any repetition here;
but I have been told, and I think it not improbable,
that to a countryman of my own (named Q——),
who was editor of one of the evening papers,
I owed the remarkable concurrence in falsehood
which pervaded all the statements on the subject.
The report from Bow Street was taken first (as I have
heard the story) to the office of the paper in question, and
contained a statement of the matter, correctly, thus :—
' In the pistol of one of the parties a bullet was found,
and nothing at all in the pistol of the other.' Thinking
it a good joke, doubtless, upon literary belligerents, my
countryman changed without much difficulty, the word
' bullet ' into ' pellet ;' and in this altered state the
report passed from him to the offices of all the other
evening papers."

This incident in these days of nice punctilio was
excessively awkward; and had the parties actually
exchanged shots and Jeffrey been wounded or killed,
Moore's reputation would have been for ever lost. The
affair, however, almost led to a second encounter, for
many years later, Lord Byron, in his " English Bards,"
alluded to the incident with the sneer :—

> " When Little's *leadless* pistol met his eye,
> And Bow Street myrmidons stood laughing by."

On which Moore sent him a half-reproachful, half-
threatening letter, which, had it not been met in a

gracious spirit, might have led to recriminations and perhaps to a "meeting". Instead, however, they became fast friends.[1]

§ *A Farcical Duel.*

The lengths to which "affairs of honour" were carried was even better illustrated by the following :—

Mr. Villiers, a fashionably-dressed young gentleman, stated that he and Mr. Thompson, who were both lay students, lived in the same house, and had an equal right to the use of the kitchen, but that some difference arose between them relative to the coal-hole, which could only be settled by a reference to the landlord, as it involved a point of law, and not of honour. He accordingly wrote a letter to Mr. Thompson, to which he received an answer, which, with permission of the magistrate, he would beg leave to read. It was as follows :—

"Monday, 18th July, 1828.

"Sir,—I am truly happy to find that the fears entertained for your life are groundless. I thank you for

---

[1] The witty lines of that incorrigible jester, Theodore Hook, on this adventure, are not generally known.

"When Anacreon would fight, as the poets have said,
A reverse he displayed in his vapour,
For while all his poems are loaded with *lead*,
His pistols were loaded with *paper*.
For excuses, Anacreon old custom may thank,
The indulgence don't let him abuse,
For the cartridge 'tis known is always made blank,
That is fired away at *Reviews*."

your note, as I am extremely desirous that our respective rights may be quietly adjusted. Indeed, it has been far from my wish to be under any obligation to you. As you have purchased the furniture of the kitchen, no doubt you have authority to remove them; but still I think it right to mention, that as my landlord granted me my lease with the use of these fixtures, I shall insist on the right which I have so acquired, while they remain; and if you have purchased them under a bad title, that is not my fault. As to the coals, I have instructed my laundress, for whatever purpose she may require a fire, to light ono with my coals—and if she should find a fire lighted, then to put on coals out of my cellar, and keep the fire up only on these occasions that will be required for my convenience. I do not feel myself called upon to bring an action against you; but, at the same time, I shall be most happy indeed to defend one. Should you think fit to establish your right to the kitchen and fixtures, by expelling my laundress, as you have threatened to do, I take leave to tell you, that I will hold you responsible in case you shall have recourse to force.

"I remain, sir, your very obedient servant,
"HENRY AUGUSTUS THOMPSON.
"To Fredk. Villiers, Esq., 21, Lincoln's Inn Fields."

This letter created a considerable degree of laughter, in which Mr. Minshull and Sir Richard Birnie heartily joined, especially when the writer stated "that he could not *keep up a brisk fire* in consequence of the interruption of Mr. Villiers' servant."

Mr. Thompson here stepped forward, and said he begged to be permitted to explain the transaction. In consequence of the irregularity of Mr. Villiers' servant, I never (said Mr. T.) could get my dinner cooked at a proper hour, and I accordingly remonstrated with Mr. Villiers, but to no purpose, and at length I was driven to the necessity of threatening to horsewhip him on the previous Saturday.

Mr. Minshull : Threatened to horsewhip him ! Why, I think that a more serious charge than any the letter contains.

What now escaped from Mr. Villiers, in a quiet tone, as if the thing were a matter of course—is highly amusing.

Mr. Villiers : Oh ! your worship, I challenged and fought him for that.

Sir R. Birnie : Fought about what ? A coal-hole ! Upon my word, there was nothing *slack* about you, I perceive.

Mr. Thompson : Oh yes, Sir Richard—we met at five o'clock on Monday morning, when, after an exchange of *four* shots, I *succeeded* in wounding my antagonist on the breast, and I then felt that my wounded honour was healed, especially when Mr. Villiers made the necessary apology.

Mr. Minshull: Fought and exchanged four shots, and all about cooking a dinner! From your own confession you have been guilty of a breach of the peace, and I shall hold you to bail.

He accordingly ordered them to find bail, themselves in 500*l.*, and two sureties in 250*l.* each, to keep the peace towards each other for two years.

We find noblemen and gentlemen resorting to taverns around Covent Garden, in lieu of clubs, and engaging in quarrels which led to "affairs of honour." There was a place called "Offley's" in Henrietta Street, which was often the scene of such incidents. Thus in 1821 we find the Right Honourable Lord Clanmorris exhibiting articles of the peace against an officer.

Captain William Wallace, of the army, appeared before the sitting magistrates. Lord Clanmorris stated that he was at Offley's the other night, between twelve and one o'clock, when Captain Wallace entered the room, and advancing towards him said, "You are a coward and a scoundrel; I have published you as such to the world, and am glad to meet you once more that I may tell you so to your face." To this witness replied, "It is quite impossible that anything coming from so infamous a character as you can be noticed by a gentleman." Captain Wallace then said, "You scoundrel, you deserve caning, and I will cane you." He laid his cane over the shoulders of witness, whereupon he took up a candlestick and threw it at Captain Wallace ; a contest ensued, which was terminated by the interference of the waiters. Captain Wallace said that Lord Clanmorris and he had once been on a footing of intimacy, but his lordship had chosen, some time ago, to brand him with the epithets of " scoundrel," " man of infamous character," &c., behind his back, and afterwards refused to give him any satisfaction. He saw his lordship, on the night in question, and again demanded an explanation ; upon its being re-used, he certainly did apply the terms that had been mentioned, and told his lordship that he might consider himself caned, but he did not strike him. Lord Clanmorris threw a candlestick, which broke the back of his hand, so that he was obliged to wear it in a sling ; and indeed his friends told him he ought to have taken out a warrant against Lord C. He said Lord Clanmorris was particularly scrupulous in his choice of gentlemen to fight with. Mr. Minshull said he should call both upon the complainant and defendant to find sureties for their appearance at the Sessions, and for their good behaviour in the interim.

§ *A Gaming-House Raid.*

Mr. Graham, the magistrate, was concerned in a curious and not undramatic enterprise which seems to have brought him into some discredit.

The system of rewarding or stimulating the Bow Street officials according to results, led, as was to be expected, to jealousies, on the part of the other officers. It was known that while rewards, &c., were scarcely ever given at their offices, at Bow Street "everything was done liberally and handsomely." There was often shown an eagerness to anticipate or frustrate the Bow Street men when a chance offered. This was illustrated in the course of a "raid" made on a gaming-house in St. James's, and which exhibits the worst and most corrupt features of the Bow Street system. Mr. Nares, one of the magistrates, complained in an amusing way of how his own staff had been tricked and deprived of the fruits of "the job."

"It was reported to me," he said, "that two people got 400*l.* which they ran off with." Asked to recount this incident he said "It was a warrant of Mr. Graham's, and they were brought afterwards before me. *The warrant, I am sorry to say, was put into the hands of a foreigner belonging to the Alien Office,* but our officers went with him. *That man, with two more men, rushed in before the officers, and plundered the table at first.* Then our officers came, and found but very little; and then this person, *who had no authority whatever,* searched all the gentlemen who remained in the room, and took the money out of their pockets, and kept a list of that money; and I never could get that man, he was off. I do not know

where he went to ; he never came to account for the
money. Adkins was the officer who went with the
warrant.

" The warrant was of course served by our constables.
These men said they had orders to act upon it, that is,
this foreigner and Mr. Capper, belonging to the Alien
Office, who went in a uniform, and with a drawn sword.
I never heard of such a thing in my life. It was not
legal. I never was so angry about anything in my
life, and I went to complain to Mr. Beckett about it.
This foreigner that took down the list, which was very
correct, no doubt, never brought the money forward.
I did tell Mr. Beckett that if he did not come, I should
not scruple to send a warrant after him. I did not
scruple to say that if he had come, and the gentlemen
swore to this, I should commit him for a robbery.
I sent Adkins repeatedly after this man ; I could not
find him; what did he do but leave a twenty-pound
note for Adkins, and I told Adkins to keep that money
till it was called for. Supposed to be left by the
foreigner. I think the amount of the money was an
hundred and odd pounds. But I can perfectly recollect what Mr. Beckett said. When I was extremely
angry about it, he said, ' *There ! we have got into a
gaming-house, and you are jealous that we have found it
out.*' The final result was, that the gentlemen were
held to bail that were gambling, and I never could get
at this foreigner in any way. Mr. Capper told me he

tried to get at him, and could not, or the money. This was three or four years ago. I do not know the least in the world what became of him. I said to Mr. Alley, who was counsel for the gentlemen, ' Do you find him out, and I will grant a warrant.' The money was seized by Mr. Capper and by this foreigner. We never search the pockets of people for their money, but they were made to pull all their money out of their pockets, and then there was a list taken of the money each party gave up, and this list was sent to me in the morning; and as far as I recollect, Mr. Graham said this person would come with the money, but I never could get him. He spent the money, I suppose, except this twenty pounds which Adkins is to account for. Adkins has the twenty pounds now. I went to Mr. Beckett when I discovered all this, to say I thought this a very simple transaction as could possibly be, and I said that it was a disgrace to the office, and that I was sure neither Mr. Reid nor myself would have granted such a warrant upon the evidence of such a man as that. But I fancy they did not know that Mr. Capper was to go in this uniform; he belonged to some corps. The officer very properly came, and gave the account of it to me directly."

The comments made on this singular affair, which seemed to be illegal in any point of view, were certainly just. " A more extraordinary transaction than that which this upright and honourable magistrate has here disclosed never before occurred. An information is lodged against a gaming-house, not in the usual way, before a magistrate, at his residence, or at his office, but, as it appears, at the Secretary of State's office ; and the magistrate, Mr. Graham, instead of pursuing the usual mode, by giving the warrant to one of his constables to execute, allows it to be put into the hands of a person who has no right whatever to execute it, and that person a *foreigner*, and to add to the strangeness of the transaction, a foreigner *belonging to the Alien Office*!!! How, be it asked, came Mr. Graham to be selected for this office? Mr. Graham was a favourite at Whitehall : he had *three thousand pounds* lately voted him by parliament, on the motion of Mr. Hiley Addington, Under-Secretary of State, to the utter astonishment of the public. Mr. Graham, it is known, also, was suffered to hold his situation at Bow Street years after he was incapacitated by infirmity from discharging its duties, or even from personal attendance at the office. Another magistrate of the county was employed to attend in his place, on a clear understanding between Mr. Graham and Mr. Beckett, that he should succeed to the first vacancy in the police establishment, and should even be appointed, over the heads of all his seniors, to Bow Street, on Mr. Graham's resignation.

" A Bow Street officer or two were ordered to attend, that there might be an *appearance* at least of some attention to legal authority; but it was *only* for the appearance, as the foreigner, Mr. Capper, of the Alien Office, and another individual "*rushed in before the officers, and plundered the table at first.*" Here, be it observed, that, if the parties who were playing had resisted this unauthorized, this illegal violence, and death had ensued, it would have been *justifiable homicide*, whereas, if any one of the persons at play had been killed, it would have been *murder*. "*Then* our officers came, and *found but very little*. And then, this person, *who had no authority whatever, searched all the gentlemen* who remained in the *room, and took the money out of their pockets*. A more audacious outrage was never committed. Now, be it further remarked, that Mr. Capper, a clerk in the Alien Office, and not *then* under the authority of Mr. Beckett, went to his house in a uniform, and with a drawn sword! So that the gentlemen evidently complied with the demand to deliver their money under an impression of fear!

"No less a sum than *four hundred pounds* was got possession of by these unauthorized persons, which appears to be independent of one hundred and odd pounds ordered to be delivered out of the gentlemen's pockets!"

This, in fact, appears to have been nothing more nor less than a robbery of the persons who were engaged in play.

§ *The Smugglers.*

There is always something romantic in the accounts of these daring smuggling expeditions. To this day at Folkestone are shown cellars and caves on the steep cliff side, where the houses and cottages are built for the convenience of hiding contraband wares, while old boatmen tell of the six-oared boats which of a fine night could be rowed across to the French coast. Mr. Richardson, in his recollections, describes how gangs of forty or fifty smugglers might be seen on the Dover and Brighton roads, well mounted on strong hardy horses, with half-ankers of brandy and Hollands slung across their saddle-bows, well armed, and prepared to resist force with force, making their way to London, and crossing Westminster Bridge.

" When a boy I lived in a house my father had in a wild part of Surrey, Combe, on the left of Croydon. The house was almost isolated ; it had originally been a farmhouse, and was surrounded with barns, stables, and outhouses. We were frequently disturbed in the night by the most unaccountable noises; the trampling of many horses, accompanied with the hum of voices, &c.

" It was not long before we discovered the cause of all this. About twenty or thirty men and horses were in the habit of quartering themselves, as their occasions required, in our barn. They were a mixed congregation of ' Kentish Knockers,' or smugglers from the Kentish Knock, gipsies, and assistant contraban-

dists from London. Here they arranged in what
manner to ' run ' their goods to the metropolis, and,
having done so, retired, and left the barn to its proper
owners. They never committed the slightest injury to
the place, nor did we ever suffer in any way from their
depredations. We certainly received a hint not to be
too curious in prying into their proceedings, which we
took in good part, and as they left us alone we did not
meddle with their affairs. The New Forest and the
Hampshire coast were the scenes of similar transactions. The smugglers and their confederates were too
strong for the ordinary force of the Custom House,
and when extraordinary force was brought against
them, many sanguinary encounters were the result.

" A man who has long retired from this kind of
business is still living, and after having weathered,
both metaphorically and actually, many a storm, and
been in many a fearful encounter with parties of the
Custom House officers, coast-guards, and revenue-
cutters, is in possession of a good estate in Oxfordshire, respected by his neighbours, and beloved by the
poor of his neighbourhood, to whom he has been a
very active benefactor.

" On one occasion a considerable quantity of brandy,
gin, &c., being arrived off the coast of Christ Church,
Hants, and the weather being exceedingly rough, all
the boats employed in landing contraband cargoes
were staved by the tremendous surf on the beach.

Without delay he and upwards of a hundred of his followers marched up, about an hour after midnight, to the house of this gentleman.

"P—— knocked loudly at the door, and the gentleman, aroused from his sleep, put his head out of window, and demanded what was the occasion of the visit at that hour. 'Oh, Mr. B——,' answered P——, 'we want your father's boat, all our own are rendered useless, and lie staved on the beach.'

"'Why, P——,' replied Mr. B——, 'I cannot lend you the boat; you know that would not do. I say I cannot lend it, but at the same time I cannot prevent you from breaking into the barn in which it is locked up, and taking it away with you.'

"'Ay, ay, sir! many thanks, and good night.'

"In the course of a very few minutes the padlock on the barn doors was broken, the doors opened, and the boat hoisted on the shoulders of a dozen or fourteen sturdy operatives, transported to the beach, and launched. The whole cargo was landed in safety, the boat safely returned, and a new padlock replaced that which had been broken."

The Bow Street officers were often despatched down to the Kentish coast when a seizure was in prospect. In October, 1827, application was made to Sir Richard Birnie for the assistance of one of his principal officers to apprehend some of a most desperate gang of smugglers, who had assailed and wounded several of the persons engaged in the Preventive Service on the coast of Dorchester. Captain Jackson, inspector on that station, and Lieutenant Sparks, who acts under him, had received instructions to seize upon the smugglers, and Sir Richard Birnie directed Bishop to join on this hazardous occasion. " The smugglers had, on the day the conflict took place, landed 120 tubs of spirits on the beach, when they heard the report of a pistol (the signal from the watch of the Preventive Service) amongst the cliffs. The smugglers were armed with swords, pistols, and instruments called ' swingles,' which are made like flails, and with which they can knock people's brains out. Those instruments are a new invention as weapons of attack, and there is no possibility of guarding against them, on account of their capacity of flying round the body. The place where the spirits were landed is called Kingbourn, and is in the vicinity of St. Alban's Head, and a troop of the Preventive Service speedily attended to the summons, and attacked the gang. There were between seventy and eighty of the smugglers, and no more than ten of the Preventive Service, so that the latter were, of course, overpowered. Several were wounded upon both sides, and it is believed that two of the smugglers were killed upon the spot. The swingles were found, upon this occasion, to do great execution—heads and arms were broken with them, and we understand that all

round the coast they are now in use. Some of the
Preventive Service had taken particular notice of the
ringleaders of the gang, and warrants were issued for
their apprehension. The captain of the gang keeps a
public-house called the ' Ship,' near Woolbridge, on
the Weymouth Road, his name is Lucas. Captain
Jackson, his assistant, and Bishop, went well armed,
at two o'clock in the morning, to Thomas Lucas's
house. Bishop knocked at the door gently, and the
smuggler asked, in a gruff tone, ' Who is there ? '
' It's only I, Mr. Lucas,' replied Bishop, ' Mrs. Smith's
little girl—I want a little drop of brandy for mother,
for she is bad in her bowels.' ' Very well, my dear,'
cried Lucas, and opening the door, found himself in
the formidable grasp of the police-officer."

A more exciting conflict took place shortly after :—

" Considerable interest was excited at this office on
Friday morning, in consequence of the news having
been circulated that a desperate gang of smugglers
had been apprehended in the county of Kent, and
would be brought up for examination.

" About half-past twelve o'clock George Ransley,
Samuel Bailey, Richard Bailey, Richard Wire, William
Wire, Thomas Gilliam, Charles Giles, and Thomas
Donard, all men of fierce aspect, were brought to the
office, and charged with the wilful murder of William
Morgan, a Quartermaster of his Majesty's ship
Ramillies, on the beach at Dover. The prisoners

were all dressed in smock-frocks, with the exception
of Ransley, the captain of the gang, who is a very
fine-looking man, apparently possessing great muscular
strength.

William Pickett deposed that, on the 29th of July
last he was stationed near the bathing-machines at
Dover; between one and two o'clock in the morning a
party of smugglers, fifty or sixty in number, attempted
to land some goods from a boat. Witness endeavoured
to discharge his pistol as an alarm, but it did not go
off. Deceased then came up, fired his pistol behind
him, with the same object, and was immediately shot
by the smugglers. Witness was engaged with several
of the smugglers, and wounded some of them with his
cutlass—he captured thirty-three tubs. Morgan died
a few minutes afterwards."

One of the smugglers then turned " King's evidence."
This was Michael Horn, a good-looking young man,
who made the following statement :—

" I met Ransley about ten o'clock at night ; none
of the prisoners were then present. We went to a
place called the Palm Trees, about two miles from
Dover, and were there joined by all the prisoners except Giles, and several others, to the number of sixty.
We were mustered in the presence of Ransley.
Twelve or sixteen of the party were armed with
muskets ; all the prisoners were armed except Giles
and Ransley, the leader of the party. We went to the

bathing machines at Dover, about twelve or one o'clock. Soon after a boat was run ashore. At this moment Ransley said, Hallo, come on, and placed an armed party at each side of the boat. We landed several tubs of brandy and gin, and carried off about seventy. I heard several shots fired, and I afterwards heard that a man named Morgan was killed ; we were interrupted by one of the Coast Blockade party. Ransley paid me 23s. for my night's work."

The counsel said it would be necessary to confine the prisoners in a place of more security than any afforded on the sea coast of the county of Kent, as it was a notorious fact that the smugglers had broken open or pulled down every prison in that part of the county.

Sir R. Birnie said, about five years ago, they broke open the Gaol of Dover at noonday, in the presence of several magistrates, and rescued fifteen of their gang. One of the officers of the Blockade Service now present complained that he found some difficulty in inducing the magistrates of the Cinque Ports to back warrants against smugglers, as it was said they were engaged in smuggling themselves.

This view of persons of superior station favouring the proceedings of the smugglers is confirmed by Sir R. Birnie's directions to some Bow Street officers whom he was sending down to Kent to deal with their malpractices. He said,—

" Ruthven, on your arrival in Kent it will be your duty to apply to some magistrate to back the warrants, and be sure you do not apply to one of the magistrates of the Cinque Ports, lest the object you have in view be thwarted by the party giving information to the persons accused, as was the case in a very recent instance; but go before some of the magistrates of the county who are, I believe, most of them honourable men. Very recently, when Bond, the officer, went into Kent with a warrant to apprehend a smuggler, on going before the Mayor of ——, to get the warrant signed, he was detained for some time, and the Mayor, in the interim, gave information to the wife of the smuggler, who immediately absconded." Sir Richard said he had affidavits in his possession to support what he had stated.

§ *Informers.*

A curious feature in this routine of magisterial jurisdiction was the recognition of the services of informers, who drove a brisk and profitable trade in bringing publicans before the courts for selling without licence. Thus, in 1828, one Jackson had been fined 10*l.* on the information of one of these men, and had appealed. These gentry were not, however, regarded with favour by the Bench, as will be seen from the reception accorded to this person when he reappeared a few days later with a fresh charge against the same publican. The papers took care to report the case in rather a minute and dramatic fashion, with the dialogues that took place on such occasions, particularly when Sir R. Birnie—their favourite performer —took a prominent part. The clerk expressed his surprise, and on handing the information to Sir Richard Birnie, said " it was rather hard upon the defendant to appear twice in the same week on a similar charge. I think, for my part, that it would be no more than modest in a common informer to abstain from all fresh proceedings while an appeal is pending."

" Modesty and a common informer," exclaimed Colonel Clitheroe, the magistrate of Brentford, who entered the office just as Mr. Woods gave utterance to the words ; " what an anomaly! Why, who the deuce was ever absurd enough to imagine that modesty and a common informer ever travelled together ? If you want an instance of the purity of common informers, I can furnish you with a famous one. Some time ago one of these fellows, Johnson, summoned the driver of the Letham coach for an alleged offence, and then wrung out of the hands of the poor devil three guineas for compromising the affair."

" *Sir Richard* (smiling) : Colonel, here is Mr. Johnson, he can answer for himself.

Colonel Clitheroe (making a low bow) : Oh, Mr. Johnson, I did not know you were present ; I had not the pleasure of knowing you before. You have heard what I have said, and I now tell you that I used every means to make you out; and I can assure you, that if I had established a charge against you, I should have dealt with your modestyship without either delicacy or ceremony.

Johnson: I feel convinced the magistrates must admit that I have always done my business fairly and properly. He denied what was stated by Colonel Clitheroe.

Colonel Clitheroe: I have not the smallest doubt on my mind, but that you are the same. However, it is well for you that I cannot prove the fact. I know you all well enough ; you are a d—d set of fellows, who go about laying informations, and then levy large contributions from the poor devils, under the pretext of making the matter up.

Sir Richard Birnie: It is an infamous system, and it is high time that a stop should be put to it.

Colonel Clitheroe: It is indeed, Sir Richard. But for my own part, I have come to the resolution of never receiving an information from any one of these fellows again. Mind, Johnson, I now tell you never to dare to show your nose near my house, for I will never receive any information of you or any of the tribe. When you next come down my way, you had better go at once to the Magpie and Stump.

Johnson: I never was doing business in Brentford in all my life.

Sir Richard Birnie: Oh, come, that story is long enough. I am really sorry, Johnson, to see you harassing a useful and well-regulated house in this way. This house is very different from Grub's and other houses. As Mr. Jackson has appealed, you must excuse me, I cannot take this information.

Johnson received back the information, making a most reverential stoop, in indication of his submission."

Later we are told of "several shrewd fellows who have made themselves very busy lately in laying informations against pawnbrokers, for taking more interest upon their pledges than they are allowed by law. For this purpose some trifling article is pledged, and when it has remained long enough for the legal interest to amount to three farthings, it is redeemed, when the pawnbroker, in some cases—doubtless inadvertently, demands a penny, and thereby renders himself liable to the information. One of these farthing informations came on to be heard before Sir Richard Birnie. The informer gave his name and address James Betts, watchmaker, Gee Street, Clerkenwell. Mr. Adolphus addressed the bench, and submitted that the witness was entirely unworthy of credit. Among the multitude of other arguments he insinuated that these 'fellows,' the witness, informer, &c., were in the habit of throwing down the penny, and running out of the shop without the farthing in exchange."

§ *A Gaming-House "Grab."*

The "worthy" magistrate, in serious cases, was expected to put himself at the head of his force, and lead them on, in what was often a service of danger. We thus hear of them bursting in upon assembled conspirators, or making " raids," as they were called, upon coiners and gamesters. It would be difficult to conceive of Mr. Flowers, or Mr. Vaughan, or Sir James Ingham, in this militant aspect. Such incidents were full of excitement.

Here is an account of one such spirited attempt which took place in 1822, and was described as " A gaming-house *grab*."

" Yesterday the police-office at Bow Street was crowded to excess, in consequence of a general capture made the preceding night of a large party of roulette-players at a house, No. 16, Bury Street, St. James's. It appeared that in consequence of information given by a young man, to Thomas Halls, Esq., the magistrate, a plan was laid for the informer to go into the play-room ten minutes before the officers, and by the time he had taken his station and observed who were at play, the magistrate and his party were to enter by stratagem or force and apprehend the gamesters. In pursuance of this arrangement, Mr. Halls, Mr. Richmond, Vickery, Ruthven, and eight patrole, went to the place of rendezvous, and the informer having obtained admission very readily, the police secured themselves in a long passage leading to the first barrier or entrance door, when Mr. Richmond rang the bell for admission. A porter opened the little wicket, and asked Mr. Richmond his business ; he, Mr. Richmond, said, ' I understand you play at roulette ? ' the porter answered, ' Yes, but I don't know you.' Mr. Richmond said it was all right, and handed him a card ; the door was then partially opened, but it is presumed the porter caught a sight of the officers, and instantly closed it. A formal demand being then made in the name of Mr. Halls, the magistrate, for admission, and it not being complied with, the patrole began battering with the mall that was left in the house of Marrs, by the murderer of him and his family, and also with the crow-bar left at the house of Williamson, who was also shortly afterwards murdered by, no doubt, the same hand ; but before the breach was made, one of the officers was put over the wall, and, by opening the outer door, let in the magistrate and the whole party ; when Ruthven, having burst a pannel of the inner door by one blow of the mall, Mr. Richmond sprang through it, and, followed by Drummond, one of the patrole, ascended the stairs, and found the gaming-room in great confusion, but no person in it ; they ran up another flight, and in a chimney they found seven men piled on each other, whom they were obliged to pull down by the legs. The other parts of the

house were then searched, and thirteen other persons
were found, some concealed in a coal-cellar, and others
in a closet. They were all assembled in one room,
and Mr. Halls directed their names to be taken, and
they were then conveyed to different watch-houses
until yesterday, when they were brought before Mr.
Halls and Mr. Marshall. Ruthven proved that he
found the following memorandum :—Mr. Gill is to
put into the bank, 311 ; Mr. Odell, 291 ; silver, 211 ;
sovereigns, 81. In addition to this, William Phillips,
the informer, proved that he was in the gaming-room
when the magistrate demanded admittance ; that
roulette was then playing. That on the first alarm,
Odell seized the bank and ran out of the room with
it, and the roulette wheel was separated from the
table, and the players ran and secreted themselves in
various parts of the house. The magistrate convicted
all the six persons, who were proved to be in the
room at play, and sentenced Page and Paton to one
month, and the other four to three months' imprisonment and hard labour in the House of Correction,
and all the others were ordered to enter into recognizances not to haunt any gaming-house for twelve
months."

APPENDIX.

It will be interesting to supply a few notes concerning the magistrates of later generations, who sat upon the Bow Street bench. Mr. Hall, or Halls, might be considered the last of the old school of magistrates; and when he retired, in 1864, one of the Marlborough Street magistrates was summoned to take his place. This was a genial Irishman, of much sound sense, knowledge of the world, and good-humour, the well-known Sir Thomas Henry, who was duly knighted, an honour already declined by only two of his predecessors, Messrs. Hall and Read. He administered his duties for many years to the satisfaction of all concerned. He had that liking or toleration for social enjoyment—theatrical and of other kinds—which is found to be a merit in the judicious functionary, who is thus likely to understand better, and tolerate the various transactions brought before him, and which a more rigid judge would probably misconceive. He died in June of the year 1876.[1]

[1] " By-the-bye," writes Mr. George Grossmith, who knew him well, "when I was speaking to you of his coolness and aplomb on the

The present staff of Bow Street magistrates are well known to be painstaking, conscientious men, furnished with a store of good common sense, and not without distinct points of character. There are the veteran Sir James Ingham—the *doyen* of all the magistrates of the metropolis, Mr. Vaughan, and Mr. Flowers. Mr. Grossmith, who, to his other gifts of increasing the gaiety of the community, adds that of touching gaily, and with a light and pleasant pen, the humours of the hour, a few years ago contributed to *Punch* some lively sketches of characters and manners at Bow Street. In them will be found the idiosyncrasies and perhaps oddities of the different magistrates, touched, however, in goodhumoured style. The series is entitled, "Very Trying," and will be recalled by many. The illustrations were by Mr. Harry Furniss. Here is one of the little comedies or farces, in which the solemn impressiveness of Mr. Vaughan is con-

bench, I intended to give you a forcible instance of it. He had just sentenced a woman to imprisonment for some violent assault, when she suddenly stooped down, took off her boot (no lady's drawing-room shoe, I can assure you), and flung it at his head. It flew to within an inch of his ear, and smashed the glass of the book-case behind him. I think every man in court immediately ducked his head, except Sir Thomas, who never moved, and did not even raise his eyes from the book in which he was taking notes. He was a sound lawyer, and a trifle vain of the *coup-de-grâce* which he knew how to inflict on some noisy barrister or solicitor, after which he would slyly glance round at his audience, especially to the reporters, as much as to say, 'I had him there.' "

trasted with the bewilderment of some young offender
who is before him :—

*Mr. Warn (Vaughan), the learned magistrate, address-
ing the prisoner :* Prisoner at the bar, presuming that
you are unrepresented either by counsel or an attorney,
do you intend to interrogate the officer?

The Prisoner : What?

*Gaoler (colloquially interpreting the learned Magis-
trate) :* Got any questions to ask?

The Prisoner : I don't know.

Mr. Warn : That is a statement. However, if you
desire to address the Court upon this charge, you
shall offer your defence now, as I understand there is
no further evidence to be adduced either *pro* or *con.*

The Prisoner What?

Gaoler (again interpreting the learned Magistrate) :
Got anything to say?

The Prisoner : Yus, sir. I didn't know I was doin'
any wrong.

*Mr. Warn (proceeding to sum up in the simple and
explicit manner characteristic of this particular learned
magistrate) :* Prisoner, you have been brought before me
on the sworn testimony of a Metropolitan constable for
begging within the precincts of the monument erected
in memoriam to NELSON. It is, as you must be aware,
a charge under the Vagrant Act, and I am bound to
admit, it appears to me there is a *primâ-facie* case
against you. You have made no attempt to rebut the

evidence of the officer, and I can only, as an *ultimatum*, give credence to his evidence, which admits of little doubt in my mind. The defence (if a defence it can be designated at all) that you have chosen to set up, is to my mind unworthy of the invention you have thought necessary to bestow upon it. You may not have perused the sections of the Act of Parliament bearing upon this particular charge, but every child must be aware, from maternal or paternal information, that the act of begging in any form is *contra leges*. Your defence is, therefore, totally unworthy of consideration. Now, I warn you, if *in future* you will persist in pursuing this nefarious method of existence, I shall have to sentence you to a term of incarceration without the option of a pecuniary penalty. Pray do not treat this caution with indifference. Upon this occasion, however, your liberty will be afforded you.

The Prisoner (*bursting into tears*): Oh! how long have I got? Oh! what have I got?

We are then introduced to Mr. Bowers, who is supposed to lighten the proceedings with occasional merry jests.

Mr. Bowers: Who is Alf Watson?

Complainant: He is a packer at the Stores, you know.

Mr. Bowers: Well, I didn't know, but I'm always pleased to receive information. I hope he'll stick to his packing-cases, and keep out of assault cases.

(*Laughter.*) However, we had better not interrupt the evidence.

Complainant: Let's see—where was I?—oh, I know. Well, your worship, the man in front, who I thought was Alf Watson, turned out to be defendant.

Mr. Bowers: What made you think it was Alf Watson.

Complainant: The back of his head looked like Alf's.

Mr. Bowers: Oh, I see—a phrenological similarity.

Complainant: May be, your worship. All I know is, some people's backs of their head is more recognizable than the fronts of their face. Look at the back of my head. (*The witness here turned his back to the learned magistrate, and displayed a triangular bald patch, which created considerable amusement in court.*)

Mr. Bowers: It would be as well, I think, to let the evidence now proceed without interruption.

Complainant: Well, your worship, I calls out, " Hulloh, Alf Watson!" and I leant over, and touched him gently on the back of his head with my stick—just so. (*The complainant lightly tapped with his stick the ledge of the witness-box.*)

Mr. Bowers: A rather *striking* illustration.

Defendant (interrupting) : Not a bit like it, your worship. He tapped me like this. (*The defendant here struck with his stick a tremendous blow on the ledge of the prisoner's dock.*)

Mr. Bowers: I cannot help thinking that that is a violent assault upon the court. (*Loud laughter, in which the chief usher joined.*) Now I think we must let the case proceed without interruption.

Complainant: At all events, your worship, I didn't hurt him.

Defendant Oh, didn't you? Perhaps your worship would like to look at my head. (*The defendant turned his back to the magistrate, and displayed a large contusion.*)

Mr. Bowers: Of course it's impossible to judge at this distance, but it appears to me to resemble an extra development of the bump of Philoprogenitiveness. However, I will hear your defence at the proper time, defendant; so please don't let us interrupt the witness.

END OF VOL. I.

CHRONICLES

OF

BOW STREET POLICE-OFFICE

WITH AN ACCOUNT OF

THE MAGISTRATES, " RUNNERS," AND POLICE ;

AND

A SELECTION OF THE MOST INTERESTING CASES.

BY

PERCY FITZGERALD, F.S.A.

IN TWO VOLUMES.

VOL. II.

WITH NUMEROUS ILLUSTRATIONS.

LONDON—CHAPMAN AND HALL,

LIMITED.

1888.

[facsimile of original title page]

CONTENTS.

LIST OF ILLUSTRATIONS.

CHRONICLES

OF

BOW STREET POLICE-OFFICE.

~~~~~~~~~

CHAPTER I.

A STRANGE EPISODE.

§ *The Love of Science Illustrated.*

NOTHING in our time could approach the grotesque
horror of the following. In September, 1839, Sir
Richard Birnie had before him a singular case illustrating the ardour of medical enthusiasm, and which went
so far as to sacrifice the decencies of natural affection
and relationship, as in the instance of Mrs. Gamp,
" for the benefit of science." The Vicar of Hendon,
Mr. Williams, attended to complain of an outrage in the
churchyard that was under his charge. Mr. Holm, he
said, was the father of one of the defendants, and came
to his house, and, after inquiring what tithes witness
would require from a botanical garden which his son
was about to establish at Hendon, he proceeded to
state that his son (the defendant) was quite an

enthusiast in the science of phrenology. They were parting in a friendly manner, when Mr. Holm observed, that he had a daughter, who had died within a day or two, and he wished her to be buried on the Saturday following. Mr. Holm said that he was a relation of Mrs. Haley, and the body was to be interred in the family vault. On the Thursday afternoon, witness walked to the churchyard, and the clerk informed him that Mr. Holm had requested to have the vault opened on the Friday, the day before the funeral was to take place. He told the clerk that he would not consent to the vault being opened before the day of interment, without a faculty was obtained by the parties from Doctors' Commons for the purpose. On the Friday afternoon, when he (witness) returned from London to Hendon, he was met by Mr. Holm, sen., and his son, the defendant, and the former introduced the latter to him as his son. Mr. Holm, sen., said he was sorry that he (witness) would not allow him to open the vault in the morning, and assured him, on the honour of a gentleman, that his sole object in wishing the vault to be opened the day before the interment of his daughter, was to enable them to collect some scattered bones of their relatives deceased, and to put them into a decent form; and he (witness) told him, that if their object was merely so to do, he would give orders to the clerk to have the vault opened two hours before the time appointed for the interment of his daughter, and he would have quite sufficient time and opportunity to do what he wished. He gave orders to the clerk to have the vault opened early on the Saturday morning, but he expressly enjoined him that he must not, on any account, permit any of the coffins to be touched; and if it should be attempted, to come and inform him instantly. About two o'clock on the Saturday he received information from one of his servants that the heads of two or more bodies in the vault had been cut off. He went instantly to the churchyard, and saw the defendant Wood, the bricklayer, standing by the gate near the churchyard. He asked Wood how he dared to touch any coffin in the churchyard, and to assist in the removal of two or three heads from the coffins? Wood replied that it was not he who had done it, but Mr. Henry Holm, for he (Wood) had only opened the vault as a bricklayer. " I have nothing further to state," said the witness, " excepting that, on my return to Hendon, I saw the defendant Charsley in the churchyard, and I asked him how he could possibly have been so wicked as to assist in such a shameful outrage. He replied that he had been incautiously led into it by Mr. Wood, and that he (Wood) had taken a hatchet and clove open the leaden coffin ; that he (Charsley) then got a chisel, and with it forced open the other two coffins."

Mrs. Holm, whose body had been disinterred, and whose head had been cut off, was mother to Mr. Henry Holm now present.

Sir R. Birnie: " What ! did he cut off the head of his own mother ? " The witness replied in the affirmative, and Mr. Harmer admitted the fact.

Another witness deposed that he saw Mr. Holm open one of the coffins and raise up the corpse, which he supported with an iron brick-cleaver, which he held in his hand. Witness then saw the defendant, as if he was feeling about in the coffin, or it might be cutting something. The defendant then took a head from the coffin, and put it into a bag. He then walked away, taking the bag with him.

Mr. Holm, sen., here stated to the magistrate, that the vault was his own property. The Rev. Mr. Williams said it was not a faculty vault, and the Haley family had an equal claim to the vault.

Mr. Holm, sen.: " I know it; my late wife was a Haley, and the vault was built at our expense."

A hair-dresser named Connolly, said he was passing through Hendon Churchyard between seven and eight o'clock, when he saw the defendant Holm remove a shroud from a body, and raise the body up, and support it with something which he held in his hand. Witness saw the defendant Holm hold a knife in his right hand, and cut the head off the dead body. The defendant then removed the skull to the further end of the coffin, and put it into a blue bag. The defendant then came out of the vault and went away, taking the bag with him. In some time after defendant returned to the vault, and witness saw him take another skull from a coffin, and wipe it with a white handkerchief or napkin which he held in his hand. The defence offered for this scandal was as extraordinary as the outrage itself. It was argued that the person who had cut his mother's head off was a surgeon possessing great scientific knowledge, an enthusiast in his profession, and ever ardent in the pursuit of scientific acquirements. It was true that he had actually taken the head of his deceased mother (who died in 1809) from her coffin, but when the reason of his having done so was explained, he felt convinced that all the world would acquit him of any criminal act; and, in fact, of anything like a crime. The family of Mr. Holm had, unfortunately, been habitually subjected to a disorder in the head. It was well known to many of the friends of Mr. Holm, that such a disorder was inherent in the family, and the object Mr. Holm had in view in getting possession of the head of the deceased was to enable him to ascertain the cause of the family malady, which he believed he should not only be able to do, by the application of his knowledge of phrenological science, but that he should be able to find some remedy for the disease, and eradicate it from the system of his surviving relations. He could not mean anything like disrespect to the dead, but it was to serve the living, and to extend the benefits of science to mankind, that he had violated, though only in appearance, the sanctity of the tomb.

A solicitor, who appeared on behalf of the parish of Hendon, hoped that the magistrate would require heavy bail, as the offence was one of a most heinous nature. Strange to say, bail was accepted. Great indignation and disgust was felt in the neighbourhood, and the solicitor who appeared for the parish, said it was the intention of the churchwardens and the other parish officers to prosecute the parties at their own expense. No conception could be formed of the state of excitement into which the parish had been thrown. The parties then retired, and Mr. Holm (the father) and Mr. Harmer became securities for the offenders. The same sureties were then offered for the other defendants, and accepted by the magistrates.

CHAPTER II.

§ *The Tailors.*

THERE was a sort of bond between the Bow Street magistrates and the stage; not merely from their having often to deal with disorders in theatres, but from their own actual connection with the "boards." Henry Fielding, as the reader need not be reminded, was a dramatist of importance. Mr. Addington was fond of going behind the scenes. Mr. Const belonged to a jovial club, formed of dramatists and actors, and being unable to attend one of the meetings, reluctantly sent an excuse owing to the sensational case of *Old Patch* then being "on":—

"My dear Sir," he wrote to the cheerful Thomas Dibdin, "in hopes of meeting you yesterday, I have deferred acknowledging the receipt of your kind remembrancer (although as a remembrance it was unnecessary) of Monday next. I hoped I should be able, as usual, to avail myself of your kind invitation; but this villainous *Patch* cannot be removed to any

other day.   If I cannot say, with Othello, 'Murder is
out of *tune*,' I can swear it is out of *time* on this
occasion, which to so musical an ear as mine is just as
harsh.   *I always thought business a d—d ungentleman-
like sort of employment;* but never regretted so much
being obliged to attend to it.   Should any accident
put off the trial, I shall, without ceremony, join you ;
if not, I can only regret the disappointment.

"FR. CONST."

Another of these "theatrical" magistrates was Sir
Richard Ford, son of the Dr. Ford who was co-manager
of Drury Lane Theatre with Sheridan and Linley.
He is better known for his connection with Mrs.
Jordan.

Mr. Graham was another of the Bow Street magistrates who was partial to the stage.   In August,
1805, he was hastily summoned to quell a sort of
grotesque riot that broke out in the Haymarket
Theatre.   Dowton had chosen for his benefit *The
Tailors; or, a Tragedy for Warm Weather*, which had
many years before been brought forward by Foote.
So soon as it was announced, Dowton was assailed by
anonymous letters, of which the following is a specimen :—

"August 12th, 1805.

SIR,—We Understand you have Chosen a Afterpiece
to Scandelize the Trade, and If you persist in It, It is
likely to be Attended with Bad Consequences, there-

fore I would Advise you to Withdraw It, and Subtetote Some Other, and you may depend on a Full House.

"Your humble Servant,
"A Taylor and Citizen.

"To Mr. Dowton, No. 7, Charing Cross."

Dowton, with a proper spirit, disregarded this insolent menace, and determined to proceed.

"Early in the afternoon, an immense crowd, chiefly consisting of tailors, assembled in the vicinity of the theatre, and when the doors were opened rushed into the galleries and pit, where they began shouting and knocking the floor with their sticks in the most turbulent manner. When the curtain rose Mr. Dowton came forward, but could not obtain a hearing ; a pair of scissors, or shears, was thrown from the gallery, and fell very near the actor, who offered twenty guineas reward for the discovery of the person who threw them. Papers were then handed up to the gallery, with an assurance that the piece should be withdrawn, and the *Village Lawyer* substituted in its stead ; but nothing would satisfy the 'Knights of the Thimble,' who continued more vociferous than ever. At length the managers sent a message to Mr. Graham, the magistrate at Bow Street, who speedily arrived with some officers, and having sworn in several extra constables, proceeded to the galleries, and, instantly seizing the rioters, took ten or twelve of the principal ringleaders into custody. They were next day held to bail. The performance of *The Tailors*, however, took place, in despite of the sensitiveness of the professors of that useful art. When the curtain drew up, and discovered on the stage *three tailors seated on a board*, the rage of the malcontents broke forth again, until the Bow Street officers made their appearance a second time, and dragged some of the offenders out; order was then restored. In the meanwhile a mob assembled outside the theatre, but a detachment of the horse guards, which had been despatched in aid, kept the street quiet, whilst constables, stationed in different parts of the house, checked any fresh disposition to riot. Had this spirited example been followed at the commencement of the O. P. row, the managers of Covent Garden Theatre would have been spared much expense and annoyance, the respectable portion of the audience the interruption of their rational amusement, and the public the shame and scandal of such proceedings.

§ *Strange Adventures of Bradbury the Clown.*

When the genial, and always hopeful Charles Matthews the elder was on one of his " tours " in 1811, he found himself the unwilling assistant at an extraordinary incident, in which a member of his profession was concerned. By another curious chance,

Mr. Graham, the Bow Street magistrate, happened to be in Portsmouth at the moment, and was thus enabled to take an important share in investigating the rather mysterious occurrence about to be described.

Matthews wrote from Portsmouth, on October 23rd, 1811, to his wife this account of the affair :—

" I should have written yesterday to you, but a great deal of my time, and more of my attention, was taken up by a most melancholy circumstance :—A young man of family, the Hon. Mr. ——, staying at an inn in Portsmouth, previously to sailing for India, where he was going out as an aide-de-camp to General ——, with a party of friends, also officers, joined company at supper one evening with Mr. Bradbury, the clown of Covent Garden Theatre, a person of very gentlemanlike exterior and manners, and ambitious of the society of gentlemen. He was in the habit of using a very magnificent and curious snuff-box, and on this occasion it was much admired by the party, and handed round for inspection from one to the other.

" Mr. Bradbury soon after left the inn, and retired to his lodging, when he missed his box, and immediately returned to inquire for it. The gentlemen with whom he had spent the evening had all retired to bed ; but he left word with the porter to mention to the officers early the next day that he had left the box, and to request them to restore it to him when found. The next morning Mr. Bradbury again hastened to the inn, anxious to recover his property, and met on his way the Hon. Mr. ——, and communicated his loss to him ; when he was informed by that gentleman that a similar circumstance had occurred to himself, his bedroom having been robbed the night before of his gold watch, chain, and seals, &c., and that he was on his way to a Jew in the town to apprise him of the robbery, in order that if such articles should be offered for sale, he might stop them, and detain the person who presented them. This was very extraordinary! Mr. Bradbury then met the other gentlemen of the party, and was told by them that their rooms had also been robbed—one of bank-notes to a great amount ; another of a gold watch, &c. ; and a third of a silver watch, gold chains, rings, &c. All the rooms slept in by the party were upon the same floor, which circumstance doubtless gave great facility to the thief. These discoveries, as may be imagined, created great consternation in the house, and soon became the topic of the town. All was confusion. Bills were printed and issued—rewards offered for the recovery of the property and detection of the thief or thieves. The Hon. Mr. —— was violently infuriated by his loss ; and as he was bound to sail from Portsmouth when the ship was ready, he naturally dreaded being compelled to depart without his property. He hinted, too, that he had certain suspicions of certain people, and even whispered them to some of the

persons interested; but as they were of a vague
character, they could not, of course, be acted upon.
Great excitement continued ; and the master of the
inn, reasonably alarmed for the credit of his house,
upon finding that Mr. Graham, the Bow Street magistrate, was in Portsmouth, waited upon him, and
described the situation in which he was, and the
circumstances which had led to his embarrassment.

"Mr. Graham wrote up to London for one of his most
intelligent officers—a man of the name of Rivett.
This man came down promptly, to the great satisfaction of the Hon. Mr. ——, who was most desirous of
investigating the mystery, and of detecting the thief,
his time becoming short, and his anxiety to recover his
property previously to sailing, rendering him more
impatient than the rest of the party. Mr. Bradbury
and all the officers gave their several accounts of their
losses, and Rivett was put in full possession of every
particular relating to the business. He then proposed
that he should search the house generally, and all the
trunks. This was highly approved of, and cordially
agreed to by every inmate ; and as the Hon. Mr. ——
was evidently the most eager of the party to arrive at
the truth, it was proposed that his trunks, &c., might
be the first to be examined, to which he assented, and
immediately delivered his keys, and accompanied the
officer and gentlemen, with Mr. Bradbury and others,
to his room. The ceremony of search having been

scrupulously gone through (of course, without anything being discovered), the next and the next room
was entered by the spectators, and all with similar
results. Nothing was to be found, and the affair was
inexplicable to all. The losers were in despair, and
the unfortunate aide-de-camp was much pitied on
account of his approaching voyage, which would
necessarily preclude any chance of his regaining his
valuables by his own exertions. There was a general
pause. At length Rivett addressed the gentlemen,
observing that there was yet a duty unperformed, and
which was a painful one to him—he must search the
persons of all present, and as the Hon. Mr.——'s trunks
had been the first to be inspected, perhaps he would
allow him to examine him at once. To this he agreed,
but the next moment he was observed to look very ill.
Rivett was proceeding to search him, as a matter of
course, when he requested that everybody would leave
the room, except the officer and Mr. Bradbury, which
request was immediately complied with. He then fell
upon his knees, entreated for mercy, and placed Mr.
Bradbury's box in his hand, begging him to forgive him
and spare his life ! Rivett upon this proceeded to
search him, but he resisted ; the object was effected by
force, and the greater part of the property found that
had been stolen in the house. The officer, conceiving
that he had not got the whole of the bank-notes, inquired of Mr. —— where the remainder was ; when

he pointed to a pocket-book which was under the foot
of the bed; and while Rivett relaxed his hold of him,
and was in the act of stooping to pick up the book,
Mr. —— caught up a razor and cut his throat. Rivett
and Mr. Bradbury seized an arm each, and forced the
razor from him; but he was so determined on self-
destruction that he twisted his head about violently
in different ways, in order to make the wound larger
and more fatal. To prevent him from continuing this,
he was braced up with linen round his neck so tightly
that he could not move it. A surgeon of the town,
with two assistants, came, and, after seeing the wound,
gave it as their opinion that it was possible for him to
recover, and by the assistance of some powerful
soldiers holding him, they dressed the wound. His
clothes were then cut off, and he was carried down
stairs into another room. During this operation he
coughed violently, but whether naturally or by design,
to make his wound worse, was not ascertained. It
had, however, the effect of setting his wound bleeding
again, and the dressing was obliged to be repeated.
Two men sat up with him all night. On the next
morning the depositions of the witnesses were taken
before the Mayor, and Mr. —— was committed.

"Poor Mr. Bradbury was standing close to the unfortunate young man when he committed the sudden
attempt upon his own life. The horror of the act, and
the shocking appearance of his lacerated throat, the

blood from which flowed out upon Mr. Bradbury—in short, this heartrending result of the previous agitation and discovery, acted upon the sensibility of Mr. Bradbury to such an extent as to deprive him of reason. This fact was noticeable two days after the above scene, by his entering a church, and after the service was ended going into the vestry, and requesting the clergyman to pray for him, as he intended *to cut his throat!* This distemper of mind was not too great at first to admit of partial control; but it daily increased, and ultimately caused him to be placed under restraint.

"The skill and attention of the surgeons" who were called in, had placed the unfortunate Mr. —— in a state of recovery, and he waited to take his trial at the next sessions; when, I believe, no evidence appearing against him, he escaped the consequences of his dishonourable act.

" Poor Bradbury, the clown," goes on the husband, " I heard was confined here in the gaol, as they have no mad-house. From liking to see everything, and secondly from an idea of being of service to him, as he was entirely surrounded by strangers, I went to see him. I found him strapped down to a miserable bed, in a strait-waistcoat. Strange to say, though I have a very slight acquaintance with him, he recognized me, called me by name, and became instantly calm from a raving fit. He immediately began to complain of the treatment he had received, and declared that he was completely at a loss to account for it. He then related to me all the circumstances of his journey from London to Ireland, in so coherent a manner, that I began to imagine he was perfectly sane ; but suddenly his eye changed, and he began to wander, saying that from Ireland he had been dragged all through Portugal ; and that the mayor here, who was in the room, had been offended because he had at church, during the sacrament, handed Buonaparte some wine and cake before him, and for that he had tied his arms, and employed men to dress themselves in various shapes, and to dance constantly round the room to annoy him, and so on. I now very soon calmed him again, by declaring that I would undertake to get him away that night to London (the mayor having told me that it was their intention to send him to Hoxton, near London, in a chaise that night, as they have no madhouse here). This immediately took possession of his mind. I left him with the promise of returning for him in the evening. The mayor begged I would attend, and I was most happy that I happened to be in the way, for without me to a certainty they would not have got him off. I went at five o'clock, and found that he had been raving again ; but he became instantly calm when he saw me. I told him to be quiet, and they would put on his clothes. They then took off the waistcoat, and he suffered himself to be dressed, and assisted himself. But when the strait waistcoat was offered to him again, he began to show his spirit.   The men were alarmed, as he had one day before beaten six of them, and made his escape completely to the street door, which fortunately was too strong for him.   He now declared that no man living should put it on him again.   To show how completely he depended on me, the instant I whispered to him that he ought to submit, he helped himself into it ; and winked at me with the greatest delight.   By this means we got him quietly into the chaise.   I wrote to Elliston to find out his friends, if he has any.   I assure you it was a most affecting scene, and I hope will sufficiently excuse my not writing before."

But there was yet another remarkable person mixed up in the transaction, viz. the famous clown Grimaldi, whom some admirers attempted to set up as his rival. He was much shocked to learn of his affliction, and, hearing that he was confined in a madhouse at Hoxton, went to see the sufferer.   Being shown to the cell, and seeing the usual accompaniments of restraint, shaved head, &c., he drew back in some alarm, but to his astonishment was addressed in reassuring terms by his brother clown, who wished to persuade him that he was not mad at all, and that he had merely assumed madness for a particular purpose.   This apparently rational tone had of course only the effect of making the other keep on, but at last the explanation offered began to

have its effect. His story was—and Grimaldi as well
as Matthews used to tell the tale—that great offers had
been made him by the culprit to withdraw from the
prosecution, but these he resisted until an offer rose to
the shape of a handsome annuity. To this he yielded.
The difficulty then arose of arranging the matter so as
to avoid the charge of ' compounding a felony.' It was
with this view that the madness was simulated. The
case came on for trial, when it being represented that
the prosecutor was *non compos*, and therefore unable
to come forward, the officer was discharged. As soon
as Bradbury learned the news, he gave over affecting
insanity and was discharged from confinement. Such
was the story, or perhaps legend, as reported by
Grimaldi." It will be seen that there are certain
improbabilities, as it is scarcely likely that a prosecutor,
especially one certain of earning a fair professional
income, would have submitted to such serious trials
to secure an annuity. Neither could his simulation
have been so perfect as to deceive police officers and
professional experts, whereas Matthews' account is
highly circumstantial, and describes a case of what
seems to be genuine madness. But Grimaldi reports
the final episode, which really appears to invalidate his
own story. As soon as he was released, he reappeared
on the stage, and in response to some familiarity on the
part of the audience, made some offensive and indecent
gesture for which he was hooted from the stage, and,

it is said, never reappeared. This looks as if, with the excitement, the insanity had broken out afresh. The whole forms a curious adventure, belonging as it does to the history of the stage as well as to that of Bow Street.

§ *The O. P. Riots.*

The vicinity of the great theatres to the office was, of course, another reason for their connection ; and, as the two patent theatres engrossed the chief entertainment of the town, and were conducted on so vast a scale, it may be conceived that this control was a very serious difficulty for the police. The entertainment at these places was, unluckily, not confined to what was dramatic ; and there were large portions of the houses, such as the saloons, where diversion of a less intellectual kind was sought. Theatrical riots, arising out of the discontent of the audience, either real or assumed, were ordinary incidents, and are evidences of the extraordinary social licence that then obtained. The general distribution of theatres over the town has helped to put an end to such disorders. Such sensitiveness on the ground of a theatrical oppression may be taken to show, on the other hand, a less keen interest in the concerns of the drama.

The annals of the English have often been marked by theatrical riots, during which the public, in a very brutal and savage fashion, have shown the managers how much they are dependent on the humour, ill or

good, of their patrons. Theatres have often been
sacked, the benches torn up, the stage invaded, the
chandeliers smashed. Performers who have incurred
the ill-will of the mob have been driven from the
boards. But few *émeutes* have been so disastrous and
so regularly organized as those known as the " O. P.
Riots " of 1809.

The hardship of the case was extraordinary. A fine
national theatre had been burnt down. Money was
raised, a new and more magnificent structure reared
within a short period; the savings of eminent performers were invested, when, owing to the dissatisfaction of an unruly mob, encouraged by persons of education, these ruinous disorders broke out on the very
night of the opening, and were continued for weeks,
destroying the whole prestige and prosperity of the
house, which were so much needed under such a
crushing weight of liabilities.

The management had found it necessary to re-
arrange their new house with a view to make it more
profitable, to meet the debt and other expenses, and
had introduced a row of private boxes on one of the
tiers. They had also made a slight increase of sixpence to the pit price, and of a shilling to the dress-
boxes. No one could have imagined that these
changes could have entailed the frightful disorders
and riots that were to follow. They opened their
theatre under a keen sense of security, full of hope, of

success, and profit; and no one was more secure or hopeful than the stately Kemble.

Yet there were menacing rumours abroad. It was amusing to find that the public was then afflicted with one of those recurring fits of morality, on which Lord Macaulay was so happily satirical long after, and which are difficult to account for except on the saving theory suggested by Hudibras. Loud cries were raised against the obnoxious private-boxes, the offensive arrangement of a small saloon attached to each shocking every one of decency. The decorations were sumptuous, and much admiration was excited by the chandeliers, which, it was announced, displayed no less than 25,000 glittering cut-glass drops! More legitimate cause of admiration were the statues and bas-reliefs, still to be seen in Bow Street, with the old columns, and which were chiefly the work of Flaxman.

The opening night was September 18th, 1809, and the entertainment consisted of *Macbeth* and *The Quaker*. Catalani was announced, as a great attraction, to appear later on. The house was crammed, and, it was noticed, with a number of ill-looking fellows, who had brought bludgeons. All was quiet at first, but they were waiting for Kemble. When he made his appearance to speak the Prologue the storm burst. Never was there such a scene of confusion. The bludgeon-men in the pit rose, stood on the

benches, roared, shrieked, and raised a din or combination of noises that was incredible and unendur-
able. Not a word could be heard. The play began
and continued in dumb-show. Mrs. Siddons came on,
but her appearance made no difference. The hideous
noises were sustained through the whole course of
the tragedy, the actors not taking the trouble to
repeat their speeches. At last the magistrates from
Bow Street arrived, and two appeared on the stage,
one armed with the Riot Act; but they were driven
off. Soldiers and police were brought in, and stormed
the galleries, but the leaders escaped into the boxes,
climbing down by the newly-painted and gilt pillars.
At last the house was cleared.

All who know anything of the history of mob-
violence can well fancy that such an opening was
seized on eagerly as an encouragement to repeat
this disorderly entertainment. Nothing is so exciting
or dramatic as confusion of this kind; it is "better
than any play." Even a street-row has its attractions.
Some enjoy beyond measure taking part in such
conflicts, while the more decorous feel an irresistible
attraction in looking on. Accordingly all the disorderly
spirits of the town crowded to the theatre on the succeeding nights, while leaders were found to regularly
organize their forces. A kind of animosity was worked
up against Kemble, whose cold and haughty bearing
was almost a challenge. He aggravated this ill-feeling

when, on the third night, he came forward, and, with an assumed simplicity, asked to know " *what it was they wanted?* " There were roars of anger and disgust, with cries of " What ridiculous affectation ! " And the great man had to retire. It was wonderful how he could have withstood the abuse, the ridicule of his peculiarities which was showered on him. Epigrams, offensive verses of all kinds, caricatures, assailed him every day, such as :

> Old Kemble
> Begins to tremble.

Or " Mr. Kemble's head *aitches*," or, as in a parody of " Roley Poley, Gammon and Spinach,"—

> John Kemble would a acting go,
> Heigh ho, says Kemble.
> He raised the price which he thought too low,
> Whether the public would let him or no,
> With his roley-poley, &c.

It will hardly be credited that these scenes of shocking riot went on for some sixty nights—every night the " row " seeming to increase. The mob came provided with drums, bugles, cat-calls, and every instrument that could make hideous noise ; and at intervals " the O. P. dance " was called for, when the whole pit leaped on its feet and performed a mad series of jumpings and stampings. A regular part of

the nightly performance was the making of speeches
from the boxes and pit, and the display of placards
with insulting or encouraging inscriptions. Unfortunately there were persons of education and intelligence
who saw here an opportunity of making themselves
conspicuous by leading the rioters, among whom was
a Roman Catholic barrister, the well-known Clifford,
who became the recognized spokesman of the mob.
This man lent his knowledge of law and talent to the
rioters, and he used to attend the theatre and be
saluted uproariously as the champion of the cause.
The managers, driven to desperation by the sense of
impending ruin and the loss of their gains, determined
to meet violence with violence. They accordingly
took counsel at Bow Street office with the magistrates,
and secured the services of our old friend Townshend,
with his band of followers, supported by Mendoza and
other pugilists, and also by amateurs like Lord Yarmouth. These combined forces made an attack on the
crowd. But this would not do. The mob met them
courageously; tremendous conflicts ensued without
advantage to either side. But the managers incurred
great odium, on the score of the pugilists—a step that
only consolidated the opposition. " Clifford for ever ! "
was the cry heard through the din ; for the counsellor
declared loudly that this beating of his Majesty's subjects by hired bruisers was against law, which it possibly was. Infuriated by this new sort of opposition,

the managers had him arrested outside by police officers and dragged off from the theatre to Bow Street, where the magistrates were ready sitting. But they discharged him. On which the counsellor brought an action against Brandon, the box-keeper, who had ordered his arrest, and obtained a verdict, with five pounds damages.

Meantime the rioters nightly increased in organization and violence. A new feature were the "rushes" made from one side of the house to the other. Vulgar fellows made speeches alluding to "that there gemmen in that there 'at." At last the managers saw they must come to terms. They proposed a committee, who should examine the books. A dinner was given to Clifford at a tavern, at which Kemble presented himself, and offered to reduce the boxes to the old price, and to abolish the obnoxious private boxes. The mob, however, refused to ratify the treaty unless a fresh article was added—the dismissal of Brandon, the box-keeper, who was odious to them. This, in spite of many piteous appeals—"an old servant," humble apologies from the delinquent,&c.,—was insisted upon; and at last the management surrendered the point. Then a placard was hoisted with the words, "We are satisfied;" and the "O. P." riots were over.

Many reflections will be suggested by these scenes, and it may be fancied that more exertion on the part of the police authorities would have quelled the disorders. It might seem, too, that in our day such a display would be impossible. This may be doubted. Were the mob of London seriously to take up a quarrel like this, under a sense of injury, the difficulties of dealing with it would be enormous, and perhaps insuperable. The power of expressing disapprobation, claimed as a right, could be developed easily, so as to make an interruption to the performance feasible. In a large theatre, such as Drury Lane, and with the audience of one mind, the police might be powerless. It would, of course, be more easy to deal with the evil .by way of prosecution and penalties.

The nightly incidents of this extraordinary episode— which, paradoxical as it may seem, could only have been tolerated in a free people—have the most varied cast, and would indeed fill a volume.[1] Every sort of whim and humour and shape of tumult seem to have been displayed. But such sport was death to the management, and the theatre never recovered from these disasters. People in squalid garb, and even in rags, were seen sitting in the boxes; so much had all order and control disappeared. One of the liveliest sallies called forth by the tumult was the following :—

[1] They will be found described at length in the *Dramatic Censor* of the year.

Here lies the body
of
NEW PRICE,
An ugly child and base born,
who died of the
WHOOPING COUGH,
on
23rd September, 1809,
aged
SIX DAYS.

CHAPTER III.

§ *The Paisley Bank.*

IT has often been noticed how much the changes in improvement in communication have affected social life, entirely abolishing original types of character, and fashion, of life and manners. Nothing shows this more curiously than the ever-welcome Pickwick, where even the inns and coaches seemed to have engendered a special tone of thought and eccentricity, and were the cause of many adventures. The swindler and chevalier of industry had a fine field for his operations, and, from the slowness of communication, could count on a start of days before lame-footed Justice could hear of his deeds, and overtake him.

One of the most remarkable, and at the same time successful exploits which engaged the Bow Street police, was the great robbery of the Paisley Bank, in 1810. This was long preserved among the traditions of the Runners, and Sayer, who was the one so fortunately concerned in the business, must have made his comrades' mouths water, as he dwelt on the profitable incidents of the case.

One James Mackcoull was a skilful and notorious housebreaker, of whom it was recorded, that when a child, he had shown his early skill by dexterously cutting away a bag which contained the whole hoard of a poor " cat's-meat man." He and a friend, known as " Huffey White," had planned to rob the Chester Bank; but, having entrusted a box of house-breaking implements to be conveyed by the coach, a skeleton key, sticking out, betrayed them. They were arrested, and Mackcoull imprisoned for six months, his associate being sentenced to transportation. Mackcoull, however, greatly daring, had planned a grand *coup*, and actually contrived to get his partner released for the express purpose of securing his aid in the business.

They set off together for Glasgow, and for weeks made the most minute and careful preparations before attempting this *coup*. The bank was surveyed in every direction, new and perfect tools were ordered from London ; and close relations were entered into with the employés.

A Bow Street officer has described minutely, in his " Recollections," the elaborate preparations made by these men. He tells us that, "When all was ready, they first tried their keys, which being found not to answer, Mackcoull himself took a journey to London, with a

wooden model of what they all conceived to be the
construction of the bank locks, in order that the
mistakes in the skeleton keys might be rectified. He
was absent on this errand about a fortnight, and
during that time French and White never ventured
out of doors after eight or nine at night, but no sooner
had Mackcoull returned, than they went out every
night at ten, and did not return till twelve, Huffey
White, on one occasion, remaining out all night, so much
difficulty was there, even to the very last, in getting
the keys to work. It may seem strange, perhaps,
that the burglary was delayed for fourteen days after
the depredators had made every preparation to commit it, but experienced thieves, like skilful generals,
often show the greatest skill in securing their retreat.
The policy of Mackcoull and his confederates in de-
laying the execution of their plot will be seen immediately, when it is known that the fair week was
fast approaching, and that then Glasgow, as they well
knew, would be overrun with thieves and blackguards
of all descriptions, some of whom, it was most likely,
would be suspected of the burglary, rather than three
persons who were known to have lived in respectability
at Glasgow for weeks previously. So judicious, indeed, were they, and so evidently anxious to fix suspicion on the thieves visiting the fair, that they
further delayed the robbery until the very last day of
the fair, when all who had attended it would be

leaving Glasgow, and when, therefore, a depredation
of so serious a nature would be most likely to be committed by one or more of those who had visited the
fair—but to my narrative.

"It was about one o'clock on the Sunday morning,
when Mackcoull and his companions rose from the
supper-table, where they had been regaling, in the
private room of a certain flash house in the very heart
of Glasgow, and where they had met that evening by
an appointment made on parting at the coach-office.
They took separate roads to avoid being remarked,
and met again at their final destination. Now the
premises of the Paisley Union Bank were situated at
the corner of the street, on the ground floor, the bank
itself consisting only of two rooms, in the inner of
which was an arched closet or vault, with an iron
door, where the money was always deposited every
day, when the time for closing the office arrived. The
burglars found themselves at the street door of the
banking-house; not a creature was visible near them,
nor was there any fear of the watch passing for the
next hour, having timed their visit so as to be secure
from his interruption ; besides, the outer door key
went so easy, after the repeated trials that had been
made of it, that the door, they knew, could be opened
and shut in a few seconds. Mackcoull and French
stood on the look-out before the entrance to the bank,
screening White while he opened the door. On enter-

£100
Reward!

ABSCONDED from the *Duties* of his Employment, a Man who has the audacity to call himself an *Actor*. He is about Fifty Years of Age, Five Feet Ten Inches High, of a very dark Complexion, and is well-known by the *nick name of*

BLACK JACK,

His *features* as well as his *principles* savor those of *A JEW*, and his *Temper* and *Manners*, come very close to an *Imperious BASHAW*. He had on, when he was last seen in his *Employment*, a Superb Dress of Green Velvet and Gold, which is said to have cost the *amazing Sum of*

Five Hundred Guineas,

It is supposed, that the *extraordinary* Degree of *Pride*, and the wonderful *stinginess* and unwillingness this Man has lately shewn to listen to the *voice of his* Employers, have been the *principal Causes* of his thus absenting himself; aithe' he is considered by *many* to be *touched about the Upper Tiers*, as he has been observed, when it has been his Business to face the

O. P.

side of the House, to —*start* and *stare*— and, in a most *tedious and incoherent* manner to rave out " *What do you want!!! What do you want!!!*"

Whoever will give such information of him, as may lead to his Apprehension, so that he may meet the punishment he merits, shall, upon application to the Office of the O. P.'s, at the Sign of the *Rattle and Horn, Pitt-street*, receive the above Reward.

ing—having carefully closed the street-door—Mackcoull pulled from out of his pocket a lighted lantern,
nor was there much difficulty in finding out the safe
in which the money was deposited, it being so conspicuous as necessarily to attract the notice of any
stranger. With a little trouble the burglars at last
got one of their keys to open the iron door, and then
they might almost be said to be in possession of their
booty. In fact, two of the drawers in the safe, each
full of notes, had incautiously been left open; two
other drawers were locked, and these the burglars
forced with chisels. In the drawers they found notes,
gold, and silver to an enormous amount. There was
a box, too, marked 'Edinburgh,' which Mackcoull
pounced upon the moment he saw it, and so great was
his eagerness to ascertain the contents, which he
fancied to be much more valuable than they were, that
finding some difficulty in forcing the lock, he broke
the lid of the box in two. It contained some bundles
of notes, which Mackcoull ran hastily over, and found,
to his great disappointment, that they did not amount
to more than 4000*l.*—about a fourth of the whole
plunder, as will be seen hereafter. Finding nothing
more of value in the safe, excepting acceptances and
other unavailable property, they hastened to pack up
the booty; the gold and silver he put into his pocket.
And now the burglars prepared to quit the premises,
calculating that there was yet time to do so before the

hour elapsed when the watchman would again pass the street-door. But they were wrong, and their mistake had nearly ruined all, inasmuch as a moment's more delay in quitting the bank would have caused them to run up against the very man whom they were so desirous to avoid. His voice, calling the hour, was heard behind them before they had proceeded many yards along Ingram Street—the sound was enough—they rushed down the first turning they came to, and avoiding all the highways, hastened on to the rendezvous where they had supped together about an hour previously."

It proved that the booty which they carried away, amounted to no less than 20,000*l.* in notes and gold! They had contrived the business so skilfully that nothing was disturbed so as to excite suspicion. They hurried up to London in a post-chaise—changing a 20*l.* note at every stage—and arrived at the metropolis in safety.

All that follows, as related by the Bow Street officer,—notably Sayer—is interesting, as exhibiting the impunity enjoyed by thieves at this time.

The sensation caused by this daring and successful scheme placed Mackcoull in the first rank. Not less remarkable was the skill he showed in dealing with the spoil he had secured, which was in the embarrassing shape of notes. Indeed, all through his course he showed a remarkable power and command of resource, which enabled him to control and almost dictate to those who were pursuing him. The bank, who were sorely pressed by this loss, despatched an agent to town to try and recover the property; and the robber, seeing their eagerness, contrived to enter into negotiations with them. This part of the transaction has been already narrated.[1] The successful depredator remained in possession of the most substantial portion of his spoil.

After a long interval of some years, he returned to London, when he was recognized and arrested on a comparatively trivial charge. He was kept in custody until a warrant had arrived from Scotland, and this having been endorsed by the magistrates at Bow Street, the prisoner was sent off to Scotland, decorated with a pair of "darbies," weighing upwards of forty-two pounds, said to be those worn by the famous highwayman, Rann, better known as *Sixteen-String Jack*. In addition to his leg-irons, he was also securely handcuffed, and being placed on the top of one of the coaches, departed on his journey to the north. Two days after his arrival at Glasgow he was examined by one of the baillies, to whom he told the most barefaced lies, and behaved in the most impudent manner, peremptorily refusing to answer a great number of the interrogations put to him, and finally himself ending the examination by plumply telling the baillie

[1] *Ante*, Vol. I. p. 158.

that " he had been plagued quite enough, and should not answer any more questions whatever."

" He was committed for trial to Glasgow gaol, and when there did not attempt seriously to deny the crime with which he was charged, but offered to put the bank in possession of 1000*l.* of their money, and, to show his sincerity, gave up to the agent of the branch bank of Glasgow a promissory note for 400*l.* at six months' date, granted by himself to Ann Wheeler, his sister, and bearing her endorsement. Mr. Harmer, the noted Old Bailey lawyer, managed the whole of the affair relative to the 1000*l.*, which was paid by him to the bank's agent in London, *all in Scotch bank paper*, no doubt (as Harmer himself must have well known) some of the notes of which they had been robbed, and which Harmer received from Mackcoull's mother. On the money being paid *Mackcoull was set at liberty !* and the first thing he did, on returning to London, was to sue Harmer for 1000*l.*, alleging that he had no authority whatever from him to pay it away. The lawyer, wily as he was, not being able to disprove this assertion, pleaded counter-claims as a set-off, and Mackcoull actually recovered between two and three hundred pounds."

All this seems incredible. But many such treaties were arranged at the " Brown Bear."

This extraordinary person seems to have been quite familiar with all the minutiæ of the law bearing

JAMES MACKCOULL.

on the holders of bills—valuable consideration, &c., for the bank having got possession of a draft or promissory note, which he had purchased with some of the stolen notes, he had the impudence to bring an action "for the restitution of his bills which had been most illegally taken from his person. The evidence that came out in this action was sufficient to establish his guilt in the robbery. His confederates then rounded on him, and he was at last convicted." Still his extraordinarily good fortune attended him.

"Now it was that, finding his fate inevitable, his fortitude and resolution forsook him. He was overwhelmed with despair, and repeatedly declared 'that had the eye of God not been upon him, such a connected chain of evidence never could have been brought forward.' His mental faculties became at times impaired—at one time he was in a wild fit of vivacity, and the next in the most pitiable despondency, being evidently all the while utterly unconscious of either what he said or did. By the exertions of his wife (whom he acknowledged to have treated most shamefully) a respite of his sentence was obtained, first for one month, and afterwards during his Majesty's pleasure. For a short time after this his health and spirits improved, but gradually relapsed, and at last his health became so bad as permanently to affect his mental faculties and make him completely silly and childish. In his sleep he was haunted by frightful dreams and visions, and frequently awoke with dreadful cries, starting up suddenly and uttering such horrible imprecations as to terrify all who were confined in the same cell, to such a degree that none of them would remain with him. His hair which, previous to his trial, had been of a jet-black, was now changed to the whiteness of snow. His body became frightfully emaciated, and his eyes, the expression of which was never very prepossessing, now assumed a glaring wildness that was almost demoniacal. He crawled about his cell grinding his teeth, foaming at the mouth, and uttering, sometimes, all manner of blasphemies, while at others he appeared to be suffering from extreme terror at the punishment which he believed eventually awaited him, not only in this world but the next. In short, he went through many deaths, and this horrible state of mental agony becoming at last too great for human strength and nature to endure, at last put a period to his sufferings. He died raving mad, and in the most pitiable state of terror, yet dreadfully enraged if spoken to on the subject of religion. His death occurred on the 22nd of September, 1820, in the county jail of Edinburgh."

§ *A Coach Robbery.*

Another department for the ingenuity of thieves was the robbery of mail coaches. Such operations required much daring, and were not without their dramatic elements. Here we must also admire the ingenuity and versatility of men like Vickery, who, considering the distance of places and the difficulties of communication, set off to hunt out the traces of the robber, and generally succeeded in their object. These qualities were particularly displayed in his pursuit of one Cooke, who, in 1815, had robbed the Hertford coach.

There was an agreement between Messrs. Christie and Co., the Hertford bankers, and the proprietors of the Hertford coach, which runs from the Hertford to the " Bull Inn," Holborn, a hostelry still surviving, to have a strong place in the coach for the carrying of valuable parcels, containing remittances to Messrs. Ramsbottom and Co., in London, who were their agents. On Saturday evening, the 14th of May, a parcel of notes and bills was made up and locked in an iron box; a duplicate to the key was kept by Messrs. Ramsbottom and Co., the bankers, in London. A clerk took the box to the coach before eight o'clock; the coach was then in the street, opposite the " Bell Inn," the horses not being put to. He put the box into the secure place made for it at the back part of the coach, and screwed it in safe with two iron screws.

A shoemaker who resided opposite the " Bell Inn " in Hertford, recollected seeing the prisoner on the morning of the 16th of May, particularly his having new clothes on. He was close to his windows, watching the coach before the horses were put to. He talked with a man under the market-place. This man did not go by the coach. While the prisoner was standing within a short distance of the coach, he saw the clerk put the bank parcel into it. After Mr. Henshall got out the prisoner went in, and remained about five minutes, during which time the attitude and motion of his body was the same as the bank clerk's when he was fastening the parcel in. The coach, all the while, remained in the street, and the horses were not put to.

Owen Williams, the clerk of Messrs. Ramsbottom, the bankers in London, said that on the 16th of May he attended at the "Bull Inn," Holborn, to meet the coach, unlocked the place, but found no parcel; there being no violence used, he had no suspicion of its having been stolen, but concluded that it had been neglected to be sent.

John Vickery, the officer, deposed that he had known the prisoner for between three and four years, and during that time he had been in the habit of seeing him every few days, but had not seen him since the robbery of the Hertford coach, till Sunday se'nnight, when he discovered him coming to town by the Yarmouth Telegraph coach, and apprehended him at the Whalebone turnpike, on the Rumford road. He was suspected to have robbed the Hertford coach, and bills offering a reward of 100*l.* for his apprehension were issued, and he, in consequence, called several times at a house in Lazenby Court, Long Acre, where he lived with a woman as his wife. She said he was at Brighton or Bridport, but there is no doubt but that he had been to Dieppe. He left a bill, offering a reward for his apprehension, with her.

Once on the track Vickery ascertained that about two or three months since the prisoner called upon a woman of the name of Sarah Porter; she then understood him to be the guard of the Monmouth mail coach. He left a parcel with her, and called again in about half an hour, her husband being from home, when he asked permission to go into a room which he could have to himself for a short time; she showed him into one, and after a time he called Mrs. Porter into the room and delivered to her a small paper parcel, desiring her to take care of it, as it contained bank notes to the amount of 200*l.* While she was in the room with him she observed him to have a great number of other notes; a great many of them appeared to be torn. He told her he had taken the notes in the course of his trade. The next day he called again and gave a 5*l.* note to get changed, telling her what she bought she was to have for her trouble, only to give him the change, which was done. The prisoner called upon her again in a short time after, when she got another note changed for him at the same shop, and after that she got another 5*l*. note changed for him at a linendraper's shop, but he never called for the change of that note.

Not less daring was the robbery in the same year of the Swansea mail by its guard, appropriately named William Weller. The large sum of 2300*l*. was stolen. This matter also was placed in the hands of Vickery, one of the " runners."

" It appeared that in the month of October, 1813, a parcel containing notes and bills, from the house of Foreman, Fothergill, and Monkhouse, bankers, of Newport, in Monmouthshire, was sent by the mail, directed to Messrs. Downe, Thornton, and Free, bankers, in Bartholomew Lane, London, in a box, and to guard against any suspicion of the value of its contents, the box was put into a coarse canvas bag, and directed to Mr. Richard Fothergill, a relation of one of the partners in the bank of Messrs. Shee, merchants.

" The box and canvas bag arrived as directed, but without the valuable contents. On the discovery being made an express was sent off to Newport, and every possible exertion was made by the agents in London to recover the property and detect the robber. Vickery, the Bow Street officer, was employed on the business. He met with the prisoner at Bristol, when he admitted that he was guard to the mail on the 3rd of October, 1813, being the day after it was booked to go to London, and he admitted seeing the parcel, and that he saw it conveyed from the 'King's Head' Inn, at Newport, to Bristol, on its way to London. The prisoner after this absconded, there not being sufficient evidence then to detain him in custody. Vickery pursued his inquiries, and learnt that some bank notes had been concealed in Bristol during the week after the robbery of the mail by a woman.

" The prisoner was a short time since discovered by Adkins, the officer, at the house of Jacobs, a Jew, in Duke's Place, where he went by the name of Green, but admitted to the officer, on his apprehending him, that his name was Weller. After he had undergone a private examination, he was committed to the House of Correction, in Coldbath Fields.

" The beginning of last month Adkins, the officer, and Mr. Fothergill, one of the partners in the bank, visited the House of Correction, when the prisoner voluntarily confessed to them that he stole the parcel containing the bank notes or bills, took them out of the parcel, having taken them out of the box between Newport and Bristol, and that he fastened the box again and covered it with the canvas bag, so that it should appear in the same state as before he opened it, to prevent discovery till it reached London by the mail.

" A Mrs. Hickman was then discovered, who confessed that about fourteen or fifteen months since the
prisoner came to her house and had some conversation with her daughter, who communicated to her
what had passed between them, and after that she
agreed to go to Bristol to get some notes changed
for the prisoner. He gave her two parcels of them,
each containing notes to the amount of 200*l.* When
she got to Bristol the banks were shut. The prisoner
then told her he had no time to stop, as he must go
with the mail, which was going immediately. He
then gave her a parcel containing notes to the amount
of 700*l.*, and took from his pocket other notes to the
amount of 55*l.*, which he said she might pass in Bristol, but it must be done in the course of that day, as
the robbery would be found out on the Monday following in London. She after that passed a variety
of the notes at a number of shops in Bristol. On
her return home at night she and her daughter dug
a hole in the garden, and buried the notes that she
had not an opportunity of getting changed. Handbills being published soon after, describing her person
as having passed the stolen notes from the mail, she
went to Bath and lived concealed.

" The notes which he had entrusted her with were
buried in a deep hole by one of her daughters in the
garden attached to her house, and the notes remained
buried till the month of July following. They were

then dug up and found to be in a very damaged
state, in consequence of having lain so long under
ground. But he made up his mind to bring them to
London, to make the most of them. He agreed with
Mrs. Hickman to follow him to London to assist
him, which she accordingly did. They went to a
woman who resided in Merlin's Cave, having been recommended to her by a relation of Mrs. Hickman, as
a person who could dispose of the notes, and they
gave her notes to the amount of 300*l.* for that purpose. She passed some of them, and said she had
uttered them at a linendraper's shop in Old Street
Road, and at one in Sun Street, in the purchase of
some linendrapery goods."

§ *Mail-coach Robberies.*

Mr. Edmund Yates, before he established his successful journal, and "increased the public stock of harmless pleasure," held an important position in the Post
Office, and in one of his agreeable papers contributed to
the old *Household Words* tells us, that once at a sea-
side place he found at a butterman's some old " Briefs
for the Prosecution " used as wrapping-papers, and
which he took home and perused. One case had for him
a special interest, as being connected with a robbery
in his own department, when in January, 1781, the
mail-cart from Maidenhead was, stopped and rifled.
I abridge his pleasant account of the prosecution.

" Between two and three o'clock on the morning of
Monday, the 29th of January, 1781, the mail-cart bringing what was called the Bristol mail, and which it should
eventually have deposited at the London General Post
Office, then in Lombard Street, was jogging easily
along towards Cranford Bridge, between the eleventh
and twelfth milestone, when the postboy was wakened
by the sudden stopping of his horses. He found himself confronted by a single highwayman, who presented
a pistol at his head, and bade him get down from the
cart. The boy obeyed, slipped down, and glared
vacantly about him. The robber touched his forehead
with the barrel of the pistol, then ordered him to return back towards Cranford Bridge, and not to look
round if he valued his life. He implicitly obeyed the
robber's directions, and never turned his head until he
reached the post-office at Hounslow, where he gave
the alarm. The Hounslowians turned out and were
speedily scouring the country in different directions.
They tracked the wheels of the cart on the road to the
Uxbridge Road, a short distance along that road towards London, and then along a branch road to the
left leading to Ealing Common, about a mile from
which, in a field at a distance of eight or ten miles from
where the boy was robbed, lay the mail-cart, thrown on
its side. The bags from Bath and Bristol for London
had been rifled, many of the letters had been broken
open, the contents taken away, and the outside covers

were blowing about the field. About twenty-eight letter-bags had been carried off bodily; some distance down the field was found the Reading letter-bag, rifled of its contents. Expresses were at once sent off to head-quarters ; and advertisements, giving an account of the robbery, and offering a reward, were immediately printed and distributed throughout the kingdom.

"About nine o'clock on Tuesday morning, the 30th of January (before any account of the robbery could have arrived at Nottingham), a post-chaise rattled into the yard of the 'Black Moor's Head ' in that town, and a gentleman in a naval uniform alighted and requested to be shown to a room. He despatched the waiter to the bank of Messrs. Smith, to obtain cash for several Bristol bills which he handed to him. Messrs. Smith declining these bills without some further statement, the gentleman himself called at the counting-house of Messrs. Wright, old-established bankers in Nottingham, where he requested cash for a bank post-bill, No. 11,062, dated 10th of January, 1781, payable to Matthew Humphrys, Esq., and duly endorsed by Matthew Humphrys, but by no one else. Mr. Wright, the senior partner, asked if he were Mr. Humphrys ? As the gentleman replied in the negative, Mr. Wright requested him to endorse the bill, which the other did, writing ' James Jackson ' in a rather illiterate scrawl, but receiving cash for his bill. Immediately on his return to the hotel, he ordered a post-chaise and left Nottingham for Mansfield, Chesterfield, Sheffield, Leeds, Wakefield, Tadcaster, York, Northallerton, Darlington, Durham, Newcastle, and Carlisle ; every one of which places he had to go to the bankers, and obtain cash for bills which he presented. Leaving Carlisle he departed by the direct road for London, and was not heard of for some days.

"So soon as the advertisement arrived in Nottingham, Mr. Wright concluded that the naval gentleman and the robber of the mail-cart were one and the same person. He caused descriptive handbills to be circulated, and sent persons in pursuit. Amongst other places, a number of handbills were sent to Newark by stage-coach on Thursday, the 1st of February, addressed to Mr. Clarke, the postmaster, who also kept the 'Saracen's Head' Inn. Unfortunately this parcel was not opened until about noon on Friday, the 2nd of February ; but the moment Mr. Clarke read one of the notices, he recollected that a gentleman in naval uniform had, about four hours before, arrived from Tuxford at his house in a chaise and four, had got change from him for a banknote of 25*l.*, and had immediately started in another chaise and four for Grantham.

"Now was a chance to catch the naval gentleman before he reached London, and an instant pursuit was commenced ; but he reached town about three hours before his pursuers. At Enfield Highway, a chaise and four carried him to town, and set him down in

Bishopsgate Street between ten and eleven on Friday
night. The postboys saw him get into a hackney-
coach, taking his pistols and portmanteau with him ;
but they could not tell the number of the coach, nor
where he directed the coachman to drive.

"Having thus traced the highwayman to London, of
course no one could then dream of taking any further
steps towards his apprehension without consulting
' the public office, Bow Street,' in the matter; and
at the public office, Bow Street, the affair was
placed in the hands of one Mr. John Clark, who enjoyed great reputation as a clever ' runner.' Mr.
Clark's first act was to issue a reward for the appearance of the hackney-coachman ; which was so effectual
that, on Monday morning, there presented himself at
Bow Street an individual named James Perry, who
said that he was the coachman in question, and deposed
that the person whom he had conveyed in his coach
the Friday night preceding was one George Weston,
whom he well knew, having been a fellow-lodger of his
at the sign of the ' Coventry Arms' in Potter's Fields,
Tooley Street, about four months ago. He also said
that Weston ordered him to drive to the first court on
the left hand in Newgate Street, where he set him
down; Weston walking through the court with his
portmanteau and pistols under his arm. On Tuesday,
the 6th of February, a coat and waistcoat, similar to
those worn by the naval gentleman, were found in

'Pimlico river, near Chelsea Waterworks,' by one John Sharp; and finally, Mr. Clark, of the public office, Bow Street, in despair at his want of success, advertised George Weston by name. But, although a large number of notes and bills were 'put off' or passed between that time and the month of November, not the least trace could be had of him.

"In the middle of the month of October, a well-dressed gentleman entered the shop of Messrs. Elliott and Davis, upholsterers, in New Bond Street, accompanied by a friend, whom he addressed as Mr. Samuel Watson. The gentleman's own name was William Johnson; he had, as he informed the upholsterers, recently taken a house and some land near Winchelsea, and he wished them to undertake the furnishing of his house. The upholsterers requested 'a reference,' which Mr. Johnson at once gave them in Mr. Hanson, a tradesman residing also in New Bond Street. Mr. Hanson, on being applied to, said that Mr. Johnson had bought goods of him to the amount of 70*l.*, and had paid ready money. Messrs. Elliott and Davis were perfectly satisfied, and professed their readiness to execute Mr. Johnson's orders. Mr. Johnson's orders to the upholsterers were to 'let him have everything suitable for a man of 500*l.* a year, an amount which he possessed in estates in Yorkshire, independent of the allowance made to him by his father, who had been an eminent attorney in Birmingham, but

had retired upon a fortune of 2000*l.* a year.' Elliott and
Davis took Mr. Johnson at his word, and completed
the order in style ; then, about the middle of January,
the junior partner started for Winchelsea, and took the
bill with him. Like a prudent man he put up at the
inn, and made inquiries about his debtor. Nothing
could be more satisfactory. Mr. Johnson lived with the
best people of the county; Mr. Johnson went everywhere, and was a most affable, liberal, pleasant gentleman. So when Mr. Davis saw Mr. Johnson, and that
affable gentleman begged him, as a personal favour, to
defer the presentation of his little account until March,
he at once concurred, and returned to London to give
Elliott a glowing account of his reception. March
came, but Johnson's money came not ; instead thereof
a letter from Johnson, stating that his rents would be
due on the 25th of that month, that he did not like to
hurry his tenants, but that he would be in town
the first or second week in April, and discharge the
bill.

"While the partners were in this state, in the second
week of April, no money having in the meantime been
forthcoming, enter to them a neighbour, Mr. Timothy
Lucas, jeweller, who gives them good-day, and then
wants to know their opinion of one Mr. Johnson, of
Winchelsea. 'Why?' asked the upholsterers. Simply
because he had given their firm as reference to the
jeweller, who had already sold him, on credit, goods to

E 2

the amount of 130*l*., and had just executed an order
for 800*l.* worth of jewellery, which was then packed
and ready to be sent to Winchelsea. Now consternation reigned in New Bond Street. Johnson's debts to
Elliott and Davis were above 370*l.* ; to Lucas above
130*l.* Immediate steps must be adopted ; so writs
were at once taken out, and the London tradesmen,
accompanied by a sheriff's officer, set out to Winchelsea
to meet their defrauder.

"Early on Monday morning, the 15th of April, as they
were passing through Rye, on their way, they observed
Mr. Johnson and his intimate friend Mr. Samuel Watson
coming towards them on horseback, escorting a chariot,
within which were two ladies, and behind which was a
groom on horseback. Davis pointed out Johnson to
the sheriff's officer, who immediately rode up to arrest
him, and was as immediately knocked down by Johnson with the butt-end of his riding-whip. The tradesmen rushed to their officer's assistance, but Johnson
and Watson beat them off ; and Watson, drawing a
pistol, swore he would blow their brains out. This so
checked them that Johnson and Watson managed to
escape, returned in great haste to Winchelsea, where
they packed their plate and valuables, and made off at
full speed across country, leaving directions for the
ladies to follow them to London in the chariot.

" Clearly the London tradesmen were nonplused ;
clearly the thing for them to do was, to consult with
the mayor and principal tradesmen of the town ;

clearly the place for the consultation was the coffee-room of the ' Nag's Head.' In a corner of this coffee-room lay a ne'er-do-weel, a pot-house loiterer, a tap-room frequenter. The tradesmen gave a description of the person of Mr. William Johnson, when Jack went away to the den which he called home, and, returning, requested to hear Mr. Johnson's appearance again described. Jack gave a yell of delight, and, producing from under his ragged coat the handbill issued from the public office, Bow Street, speedily showed that Mr. Johnson of Winchelsea, and George Weston, the mail-robber, were one and the same person.

" No sooner proved than action taken. Off goes an express to the post-office. Mr. John Clark despatches trusty satellites, with the result that Mr. Johnson, with his intimate friend Mr. Watson, are traced from various places to an hotel in Noel Street, near Wardour Street, Soho, where they slept on Tuesday night. Early on Wednesday morning, Mr. John Clark, duly apprised, is at the door of the Noel Street hotel, relates to the landlord his errand, and requests the landlord's assistance, which the landlord refuses. Clark sends a bystander off to Bow Street for assistance, and the landlord proceeds to caution his guests, who immediately take alarm, and come slouching downstairs with their hands in their pockets. Clark, who is standing at the door, does not like their attitude, thinks it safest to let them pass, but as soon as they are fairly in the street, gives the alarm, 'Stop thief! Stop mail-robbers!' Out rushes a crowd in hot pursuit—pursuit which is temporarily checked by Messrs. Johnson and Watson each producing a brace of pistols, and firing three shots at their followers; but at last they are both captured.

" So far my yellow-leaved, fly-blown, faded brief-sheets, which tell me, moreover, that George Weston and Joseph Weston are the Johnson and Watson of the Winchelsea drama; that they will be proved to be brothers; that George Weston will be proved to be the highwayman, and Joseph the receiver; and that there is a perfect cloud of witnesses ready to prove every indictment. I suppose they did prove it; for, turning back to the first outside folio, I find, in a different handwriting and a later ink, 'Guilty'—to be hanged at Tyburn—May 3; and later still I see an ink cross, which, from official experience, I know to be a record that the last memorandum had been carried out, and that the paper might be put by."

Mr. Yates came upon another case that was more directly connected with his department. It is more interesting, as showing how nearly sixty years ago, when neither telegraphs nor railways were at work, there was a very sound and satisfactory system of supervision, with mail agents and all the rest.

" At six o'clock on Monday morning, the 29th of

January, 1827, the Dover mail-coach, mud-bespattered
and travel-stained, pulled up before the General Post
Office in Lombard Street, and the official porters in
attendance dragged from it the receptacle for letters
(then containing correspondence from France, from
foreign countries transmitting through France, and
from Dover itself), which, in official language, was
known as the mail-portmanteau. The coachman had
jerked the horses' heads into the air preparatory to
walking them round to the stable, when a pale-faced
clerk with a pen behind his ear came rushing out of
the little side-door, tumbling over the guard, and
exclaiming, 'Hold hard, for God's sake! The mail
has been robbed!'

"When the two official porters carried the mail-portmanteau into the foreign office of the General Post
Office, they placed it before the clerk waiting to receive
it. There was little time to count and sort and
despatch the letters; the clerk in a minute had
unbuckled the straps of the square portmanteau and
thrown them back, preparatory to opening the two
compartments, when in each of the compartments he
saw a long cut, as with a knife, large enough to admit
of the enclosed bags being drawn out. Rather staggered at this, the clerk hastily turned all the bags out
on to the floor, noticing as he did so that several of
them were cut and frayed. Then he looked for the
Paris letter-bill, which he found in due course, and

read as follows :—' No. 203. Direction Générale des Postes de France. Départ de Paris pour Londres, ce Vendredi, 26 Janvier, année 1827. Le contenu de votre dernière dépêche du 24me a été exactement distribué, et ultérieurement expédié pour sa destination : l'administration vous demande le même soin pour le contenu de la présente du reçu, de laquelle vous voudrez bien lui donner avis.' Then followed a list of the bags and their weights, from France, Italy, Spain and Portugal, Switzerland, Germany, and Turkey. The clerk carefully compared the bill in his hand with the bags lying before him, and instantly found that the Italian bag, the heaviest, and probably therefore the most valuable, was missing.

" That night, when the return Dover mail left the ' Elephant and Castle,' it had for one of its inside passengers the solicitor to the General Post Office ; a man of clear head and prompt action, to whom the investigation of delicate matters connected with the postal service was confided. To him, comfortably installed at the ' Ship ' Hotel, came the postmaster of Calais and the captain of the *Henri Quatre*, the French packet by which the mail had been brought over. After a little consultation, these gentlemen were clearly of opinion that the mail arrived intact at Calais, was sent thence, and arrived intact at Dover, was sent thence intact, and was violated on the road to London. Tending to the proof of this was a special circumstance.

When the mail arrived at Dover, it was so unusually heavy as to induce a Custom-house officer, who saw it landed, to regard it with suspicion; so he accompanied the men who bore it, from the French vessel to the packet-agent's office, that he might see it opened, and be satisfied that it contained nothing prohibited. The portmanteau was unbuckled, and its compartments were thrown open in the presence of this officer, of Sir Thomas Coates, the packet-agent, and of three other persons, all of whom were certain that the compartments of the bags were in a perfect state, and that the bags were then uncut.

"So far so good. The solicitor to the Post Office, journeying back to London, and taking up the threads of his case on the way, stopped at Canterbury, made a few casual inquiries, opened a regular official investigation, and received what he believed to be very important information. For it appeared that on the Sunday night of the robbery, four inside and three outside passengers left Dover by the mail-coach for London. The four insides were booked for London; one of the outsides was booked for Chatham, another for Canterbury, or as much further towards London as he pleased, the third outside intimated that he should only go as far as Canterbury. When the mail reached the 'Fountain' Inn, Canterbury, the outside passenger who was booked as far towards London as he pleased, got down and paid his fare, stating that he should go no further; the passenger who was booked for Canterbury alighted at the same time; and the two walked away from the coach together.

" One of the mail-coach proprietors, who resided at Canterbury, happened to be looking at the mail while it was standing at the door on the evening in question, and observed two men, dressed as if they had just left the coach, crossing the street. They stood consulting together for a few minutes, and, after walking about fifty yards, stopped again, when a third man joined them. They all conversed for about a minute, and then separated; two of them went down the street on the road to London, the mail passed them, and almost immediately afterwards they returned up the street in the direction of the 'Rose' Hotel. The third man went into the coach-office, booked himself as an outside passenger for London, and went on by the mail. Shortly after the mail passed through Canterbury that night, two strangers coming from the direction in which the mail had gone, entered the ' Rose ' Hotel, and ordered a chaise to London. On being asked whether they would change horses at Ospringe or Sittingbourn, they said it was immaterial so long as they got on quickly. The waiter who showed them into the sitting-room noticed that they had a small bag with them. They ordered some brandy-and-water, and shut themselves in—in the room, not the bag. After the lapse of a quarter of an hour the waiter, suddenly opening the door to say that the chaise was ready, perceived various letters (at least twenty or thirty), and several small paper packets, lying on the table ; the men were feeling the letters, holding them up to the candles, and otherwise examining their contents. They appeared much confused when the waiter entered the room, crammed the letters into their pockets, paid their bill, got into the chaise, and at once set off for town.

" The thieves were traced through different stages, until it was ascertained that they had been set down between six and seven o'clock on Monday morning near a watch-box in the Kent Road, and that, having paid the postboy, they then walked off towards Surrey Square.

So much notice was taken of the men at the ' Rose ' Hotel, and at the places where they stopped to change horses and take refreshment on the road to town, that a description of their persons was procured, and the police communicated with. On hearing the description, the police at once considered that it implicated one Tom Partridge, and one of his associates, who had been concerned in most of the coach-robberies which had recently been committed; and private information having been obtained that these were really the men who had violated the mail, warrants were obtained, and Tom Partridge was ' wanted.' After a search of many weeks Tom Partridge was apprehended, and on the examination which he under-

went at Bow Street, was distinctly identified as one of
the persons who booked an outside place at Dover by
the mail of the evening in question, and as one of the
men who were seen on the same evening at the ' Rose '
Hotel examining letters and packets which lay open
before them. On this evidence Mr. Tom Partridge was
fully committed for trial.

" From March till August Partridge lay in prison:
immediately on his committal, he had strongly denied
his guilt, and had made application to be admitted to
bail; but his request was refused. On the 21st of
August, 1827, the assizes for the Home Circuit being
then held in Maidstone, there was more than usual
excitement round the old court-house of that town.
Very many witnesses were to be examined on the part
of the Crown, among them some French gentlemen,
clerks in the Paris Post Office, and officers of the packet,
who had been staying at the principal hotel of Maidstone for some days, and at the expense of the prosecution. And above all else productive of interest was
the prevalent belief that the whole case was one of
extraordinary circumstantial evidence; that it would
turn upon the nicest question of personal identity; and
that the prisoner intended bringing forward undeniable
proofs of his innocence.

" The prisoner himself in the dock fronting the judge,
a middle-sized stoutly-built man, with a queer humorous
face, lighted by a twinkling arch blue eye. Not a bit

daunted, but apparently rather pleased by the universal gaze, he stood leaning over the front of the dock,
playing with the bits of herbs which custom still
retained there, keenly observant of all that transpired,
but apparently fully trusting in his own resources.

" The prosecuting serjeant told the story briefly,
pretty much as it has been here stated, and proceeded
to call his witnesses. First came the French gentlemen. M. Etienne Bonheur, comptroller at the foreign
office of the General Post Office, Paris, proved that he
made up the mail for London on the evening of
Friday, the 26th of January, that there was an Italian
bag, that he handed them to M. Avier to despatch. M.
Avier, M. Gustave d'Ortell, postmaster of Calais, Captain Margot of the *Henri Quatre* steamer, John Nash,
the Custom House officer at Dover, and Sir T. Coates,
the packet-agent, all deposed to the despatch and
receipt of the mail in due course.

" The case for the prosecution was concluded, and the
prisoner, called upon for his defence, humbly prayed
that a written paper which he had prepared might be
read aloud. The court assenting, the paper was
handed to an officer, and was read aloud, to the following effect. In the first place, the prisoner denied any
participation in the crime of which he was accused,
and stated that in the month of January last he was
travelling with a person of the name of Trotter, on
business, in the counties of Somerset and Devon. That

on Monday, the 22nd of January, he and Trotter arrived at the ' George ' Inn, Glastonbury, kept by Mr. Booth. That they left the ' George ' the same day, and went to Mr. Baker's, who keeps an inn at Somerton, and thence in Mr. Baker's gig to Yeovil. That the prisoner, taking a fancy to the horse in this gig, sent word back to Mr. Baker that if he had a mind to sell it, he (prisoner) would meet him at the 'George' Inn, Glastonbury, on the ball-night, the Thursday following. That on this Thursday night the prisoner and Trotter duly arrived at the ' George,' bought Baker's horse for twelve guineas twelve shillings, borrowing the silver money from Booth, tried it on the Friday morning, and left it with Booth to get it into better condition. That he (prisoner) and Trotter left Glastonbury at half-past eleven on Saturday morning, the 27th, by the Exeter coach, which they quitted on the road about five miles from Tiverton, and walked on to that town. That at Tiverton they put up at the ' Three Tuns ' Hotel, and being cold, they called for and had some hot egg-beer on their arrival ; and that while at this hotel, having a wish to procure some clotted cream, they inquired of the waiter how they should carry it, when the waiter recommended them to have two tin cans for the purpose, which cans were procured and filled accordingly. That they stayed at the ' Three Tuns ' during Saturday the 27th, and Sunday the 28th ; and left on Monday the 29th, by the Bristol coach to Bridgewater.

" This statement of the prisoner's having been read aloud, he was called upon to corroborate it by evidence. Thereupon he summoned and produced in the witness-box, one after the other, Booth, the landlord of the ' George' at Glastonbury ; Baker, of whom he bought the horse; Ellis, the waiter at the ' Three Tuns ' at Tiverton, who produced the book containing the entries of the refreshment had by the prisoner—among them the hot egg-beer, the clotted cream, and the tins for carrying it ; and the chambermaid at the same inn. All of these persons exactly corroborated the prisoner's statement, and all of them swore positively to his identity. After the evidence of the last witness the judge interposed and asked the Crown counsel whether he desired to press his case? The serjeant turned to the Post Office solicitor, when several of the jury expressed themselves satisfied that the witnesses for the prosecution were mistaken, and that the prisoner was not one of the persons who had committed the robbery. Whereupon a verdict of acquittal was recorded; and with a smiling face and a bow to the court, Mr. Tom Partridge walked out of the dock a free man.

" Some two years after this trial, which gave rise to a vast amount of wonder as to how the Government could have been so mistaken as to prosecute an innocent man, the Post Office solicitor, wending his way quietly along Bishopsgate Street to catch the Norwood coach at the ' Flower-Pot ' Inn, was brushed against by a man going into a public-house, and looking up, saw that the man was Tom Partridge. Now, in the solicitor's leisure moments, which were few enough, he had often thought of Tom Partridge, and had puzzled his brain ineffectually for a solution of Tom Partridge's mystery. So now, having a few minutes to spare, he first satisfied himself that the man who had brushed against him was the veritable Tom, and then crossed the street and took a careful survey of the public-house into which Tom had vanished. As he stood looking up at the house Tom came out of the street-door, looked up, and called ' Hi ! ' whereupon, from an upper window of the house, appeared the head and shoulders of another Tom, an exact reproduction of the original Tom, middle-sized, stoutly built, with a queer humorous face lighted by a twinkling arch blue eye. The solicitor rubbed his eyes ; but when he looked again, there were the two Tom Partridges, exactly alike, one on the pavement in the street, the other looking out of the third-floor window. Then both disappeared into the house, whence presently emerging both by the street-door, one pointed to some distant object, and the other started off up the street, the first returning into the public-house ; each so exactly like the other that, when they separated, they looked like halves of one body.

" Next morning the solicitor was closeted for half an hour with one of the heads of the Post-Office department who had the official conduct of criminal cases ; and shortly afterwards a confidential messenger was despatched with a letter to William Barker, otherwise known as Conkey Barker, otherwise as Bill the Nobbler, otherwise as sundry and divers flash personages.

" That evening Mr. La Trappe, of the General Post-Office, sat in the study of his private house in Brunswick Square. As the clock struck eight the servant entered and announced ' a man.' The man being admitted proved very velveteeny, slightly stably, and very bashful.

" ' Sit down, Barker,' said Mr. La Trappe, pointing to a chair. ' I want a little information from you ; it can't hurt anybody as the affair is bygone. Do you recollect the robbery of the Dover mail ? '

" ' I should think so,' said Barker, grinning.

" ' Ah ! ' said Mr. La Trappe. ' We tried a man named Tom Partridge for it, and he was acquitted on an alibi. He did it, of course ? '

" ' Of course,' said Barker.

" ' Ah ! ' said Mr. La Trappe again, with perfect calmness ; ' he has a double, who went into Somerset and Devon at the same time, and worked the oracle for him ? '

" ' Well ! How *did* you find that out ? '

" ' Never mind, Barker, how I found it out. What I want to know is—who is the double ? '

" ' Tom Partridge's brother—old Sam, one year older nor Tom, and as like him as two peas. It was the best rig o' the sort as ever was rigged. Old Sam had been out in Ameriky all his life, and when he first came back every one was talking about his likeness to Tom ; you couldn't know 'em apart. Fiddy, the fence, thought something might be made of this, and he planned the whole job—the egg-hot, and the cream, the tins, and the horse what he bought. Tom's got that horse now, to drive in his shay-cart on Sundays.'

" ' One more question, Barker,' said the solicitor. ' How was the robbery effected ? The interior of the portmanteau could not have been cut unless it had been unbuckled and the compartments thrown open, and they could not possibly have done all that on the top of the coach. Besides, the guard stated he had fastened it in a very peculiar manner at Dover, and that the fastenings were in exactly the same state when he opened it in London.'

" ' Ah ! That was the best game of the lot,' said Mr. Barker. ' The job was done while the portmanteau was in the agent's office at Dover, and where it lay from three o'clock on Sunday afternoon till between seven and eight in the evening. Tom Partridge and his pal, they opened the street-door with a skeleton key. There was no one there, and they had plenty of time to work it.'

" ' And Tom Partridge's pal was— ? '

" ' Ah, that I can't say,' said Mr. Barker, looking straight into the air. ' I never heard tell o' *his* name.'

" About a twelvemonth afterwards that respectable mechanic, Mr. William Barker, was hanged for horse-stealing. Just before his execution he sent for Mr. La Trappe, and confessed that *he* had been Tom Partridge's accomplice in the robbery of the Dover mail. Mr. La Trappe thanked him for the information, but bore it like a man who could bear a surprise."

CHAPTER IV.

ACCOMPLISHED SWINDLERS.

§ *Major Semple alias Lisle.*

THE career of this singular swindler, begging and borrowing impostor, was of so adventurous and remarkable a kind, as to excite wonder that a person of such gifts should have condescended to the petty shifts which had nearly led him to the gallows.

This man—who was also known as Lisle—entered the army and served in America. He was wounded, taken prisoner, and soon after released, retiring on a pension. He next took service with Frederick the Great, but did not remain with him long, returning to England in 1779, when he married a lady of good connections whom he met by chance at Harwich. We next find him in France, busy with the affairs of the notorious Duchess of Kingston, and whom he accompanied on her journey to St. Petersburg, when a new career opened for him. He entered the Russian army, was appointed captain by Prince Potemkin, and appears to have served with distinction, receiving

many honours from the Czar. However, he grew
discontented, and in 1784 resigned his office.

But the next scene in his motley career offers a
curious contrast. Of a sudden, and without any notice
or graduated descent from his respectable position,
we find him, in 1785, indicted for stealing a post-
chaise! He contended, after the usual form in such
cases, that he had merely *hired* it, and that it was
only a civil contract, but, unluckily, he had sold the
vehicle ; so he was convicted and sentenced to seven
years' transportation. Some favourable influences
were brought to bear, and after being sent to the
Woolwich hulks, on his way to a penal settlement, he
received a pardon, on condition of his at once leaving
the country.

We next find him in France as the friend of Pétion,
Roland, and others of the Revolutionary party. He
was present at Louis XVIth's trial, but soon after became obnoxious and was denounced as a spy to the
Committee of Public Safety. He escaped with difficulty from the country and joined the allied armies,
where he appears to have fought with distinction in
various battles.

With his usual ill-fortune service seems to have
brought him no particular advantage, and he was
arrested at Augsburg, probably for some malpractices,
but escaped to England. Here we find this soldier of
fortune, by another turn, in custody at Bow Street,

charged with the contemptible offence of obtaining a shirt and two or three yards of calico and muslin on false pretences. Again the point was raised of its being merely a contract, but he was found guilty of obtaining the shirt by fraud, and he was again sentenced to seven years' transportation. Again was interest employed in his favour, among others Mr. Boswell and Edmund Burke exerted themselves but without avail, and he was despatched to New South Wales. On the way his adventures began afresh. A mutiny broke out in the vessel, of which he was one of the ring-leaders, which was quelled; but he and his brother delinquents, twenty-eight in number, were treated in summary fashion, placed in an open boat and sent adrift. After many perils they reached the Brazils, where, giving themselves out to be shipwrecked mariners, they were treated by the Spaniards with much kindness and hospitality. Semple was introduced as a Dutch officer of rank. But the mutineers having quarreled among themselves, betrayed the real state of the case. We now lose sight of him only to find him, in 1798, at Lisbon, where he was arrested by order of the English minister and sent off to Gibraltar. There he was suspected of being engaged in some conspiracy, when he was again seized and sent to Tangier. In 1799 he was brought back to England and despatched to Botany Bay.

Eleven years elapsed, and we find him once more

returned to England, where he took up the miserable *rôle* of begging for shillings, " doing," as it is called, small tradesmen. Thus, having ordered a small quantity of bacon to be sent to a particular house, he contrived to meet the messenger at the door, and sent him back for sixpen'orth of eggs—taking the other goods from him. It was then found that he did not live in the house. For this petty and contemptible trick he was, for the third time, sentenced and transported for seven years.

This finally disposed of him. But his whole story furnishes a curious contribution to the history of crime. There is a curious sketch of him in Angelo's Memoirs, exhibiting him in one of his begging rounds.

The fencing-master, who had generally contrived to see something of the seamy side of London and of London adventurers, was well acquainted with this unhappy creature, who might have sat for Jeremy Diddler. He introduced himself on the excuse of taking lessons in fencing, and having established this connection Angelo and his family found it almost impossible to shelve him off. The fencing-master gives his lively account of his tricks and devices :—

" In respect to borrowing money, however, he failed, though he tried the experiment. Pleasure being the order of the day, we had not enough to follow it up. Semple, who always stuck close to us, took care to follow us home to our door, and walking in, stopped till dinner was placed on the table, when I said, ' Captain ' (no assumed major then), ' will you take your dinner with us ? ' and though he always pretended to have an engagement, he *obligingly* put it off, and did us the *honour* to stop. In the evening, if we were going to Vauxhall, or elsewhere, he was sure to make one, and would have made our house his lodging, if I had not told him that all our beds were engaged, except my father's, and that room was always kept locked in his absence. Our spunging companion continued these intrusions for about three months, when suddenly he disappeared, without paying for his instructions, or anything else. To write of his various swindling cheats, so well-known, would be needless.

" The next time I spoke to him, which must have been twelve years after, was on board of the hulks at Woolwich. I was that day on a dinner party at Blackwall, with Lord Barrymore, his brother Cripplegate, and Lord Falkland. It was a Sunday evening, and I proposed, in order to pass away the time, to have a boat, and go on board one of the hulks ; as an old *acquaintance* of mine was among the convicts, perhaps I could procure admittance without many inquiries. My proposal was speedily accepted, and we were soon alongside the hulk. As it was Sunday, they would not permit us to go on board for some time ; on sending up my card to the lieutenant, who knew my name, we were at length admitted. (Lord Barrymore and the others desired not to be known.) I then inquired for Captain Semple. The convicts were all below, it being just previous to their supper time. On each side of the deck there were a number of wooden bowls, filled with boiled peas (such as I have used when a boy for my pea-shooter), and if I had seen them in any other place, I should have imagined they were intended for the hogs.

"After waiting some time, Semple (who had probably seen me in the boat alongside, and had been dressing himself) came on deck, and looked tolerably clean. As soon as he saw me, he spoke to me in the most unceremonious manner, *sans façon*. It was, 'How do you do?' (calling my name aloud) 'How are all your family?' to the not small amusement of our party. Having satisfied our curiosity, and given a guinea to Semple, by Lord Barrymore's desire, we took leave of the lieutenant, who politely offered us some grog. The whole party were much pleased at the strange interview with my old acquaintance, and when I approached them, they jokingly said, 'Take care of your pockets;' and threw out various hints about my connection with a convict. Two days afterwards, I received a fulsome letter from Semple, containing an eulogium on fencing, and many professions of the regard he had for my father. At the same time he requested me to send him some foils, etc.

" Many years afterwards, when I was standing at the door of Old Slaughter's coffee-house, Semple passed by, and, just at the time, a friend of mine, who was in the coffee-room, came to the door. When Semple was about to turn round the corner of Newport Street, he looked back, and saw us, as he imagined, watching him. The next day I received the following letter :—

" ' SIR,—I have from my very early days been accustomed to feel attachment to every branch of your family,—in fact, I owe so much to your father, and *you* have also been kind to me, in my hour of adversity. If I have either acquired address in arms, or the exterior of a gentleman, it is to the lessons of your excellent father. Having said so much, I need not add, that it gives me excessive pain to address you in any other language but that of friendship. You cannot have forgot that Thursday, as I came up Saint Martin's Lane, you were at the door of Old Slaughter's coffee-house ; you perceived me, you entered the door, and, after I had passed, pointed me out to a person whom you brought with you from the coffee-room into the middle of the pavement. This is a sort of conduct I did not expect from a man bred in the first societies, and to which, however innocent you may think it, I cannot, must not submit. Had almost any man but the son of Angelo done it, I should have expressed my displeasure in the instant. I think you will do me the justice to believe, that the passiveness of my conduct on this occasion, was the effect of no other motive than what I describe, and that it cannot be repeated. Do not, I request you, again expose yourself; and permit me to assure you that I still am, very much, sir,

"'Your obedient servant,

"'I. G. LISLE.

"'August 28th, 1802.'

"By his signature of Lisle (degraded as his name, Semple, was) it appeared he had changed his appellation since his visit to the hulks. Of course I took no notice of this letter, but whenever we met, we gave each other a mutual look of *effronterie*. Nine years afterwards, I received another letter, which was the last :—

"'SIR,—Having, in a recent letter, explained to you my situation, though you were at that moment absent, understanding that you are now in town, and my miseries continuing in full force, let me now pray you to accord me the very little assistance then solicited, a few shillings. The sad urgency of my situation cannot be described; I am at this hour without a fire, and without a shirt. I will only add, that whatever is committed under a *sealed* envelope to the bearer, will safely reach me, and that I am, with respect,

"'Your obedient servant,

"'I. G. S. LISLE.

"'4th February, 1811.'

"I enclosed a crown to the poor devil in answer to his letter,—most probably falsehoods to create sympathy. He took care never to appear *himself*, but had boys in different parts of the town to deliver his begging letters ; and, judging from the numerous letters he could send in one day, if they made any sort of impression, I should think he never could have been in want of a fire, or a shirt, at all events, though perhaps he was obliged to forego his former luxurious way of living."

This was the age of adventures, of disguises, of ingenious counterfeits and devices ; when there were great openings for gentlemen of versatility and talent in their profession. This will be seen from the career of another chevalier of industry whose course we shall next follow.

§ " Old Patch."

In the year 1784, there was issued from the Bow Street office, by direction of Sir Sampson Wright, the blind magistrate's successor, the following proclamation :—

" Public Office, Bow Street.

" A FELONY.

" Whereas a woman answering the following description stands charged with felony; whoever will apprehend her, and bring her before Sir Sampson Wright, at the above office, shall receive 200*l.* reward upon her commitment.

" The said woman lately lived in a house, No. 3, on

the Terrace, Tottenham Court Road, by the name of
Ann Polton. She then was dressed in a black silk
gown, black cloak, and a black bonnet; she appears,
or affects to be, very old and decrepid, though there is
strong reason to believe that it is fictitious. She is
rather above the middle size, thin face; and when she
hired the above house, and until Monday last, usually
wore clothes as above described, but on that day was
dressed in a dark blue striped linen or cotton gown,
black bonnet and cloak, a black handkerchief tied round
her neck, a black patch on her chin, and another on
her right cheek, and had a bundle tied in a white
handkerchief, light-coloured hair in loose curls, without
powder. She has lately been seen as affecting a de-
sponding situation, in the fields in the above neighbourhood. *She is connected with a man who has appeared
very aged and infirm, but, notwithstanding, hath been
observed to walk very well when he supposed he was
unnoticed.*

" The man appears to be aged, about five feet seven or
eight inches high, generally wearing a morning gown,
with a cap over his face, and a large hat flapped ; walks
decrepid, with a stick, as if infirm, and wears spectacles ;
has several times walked down to the stables adjacent
to the Terrace, and is the same person frequently before
advertised, under different descriptions.

" It is earnestly requested that all housekeepers in the
several streets, &c., between the Middlesex Hospital

and the out-buildings towards Marylebone will give particular attention to this advertisement."

From this it would appear that the person " wanted " was the woman, but this is testimony to the skill of the principal operator, who had thus contrived to make himself appear as merely an agent. He was perhaps the most versatile and successful of the many professors of swindling that have appeared. He was possessed of boundless resources, and for years baffled the Bank of England, with all the forces of Bow Street at their back. His system was a dramatic one, consisting of a series of disguises and rapid changes of residence. His name was Charles Price, but he became known as " Old Patch " from his favourite disguise. When a child he would dress himself in his brother's clothes and steal articles of his father's, then selling them to Jews, thus causing his brother to be punished as the delinquent. This trait would have been worthy of Fielding's notice. When he was placed with a hosier in London, he one day presented himself at the shop dressed as a fine gentleman, and giving his name as the " Hon. Mr. Bolingbroke," ordered a large quantity of goods. These he was desired to deliver in his capacity of apprentice, and promptly pawned, bringing back word that " Mr. Bolingbroke " was out. He next visited Holland, where he got a place in a Dutch merchant's house, owing to a forged introduction, and fled from thence, carrying off his master's daughter.

His next victim was no less a person than the shrewd
Samuel Foote, who would assuredly have ridiculed on
the stage any one as gullible as he was now to show
himself.   Mr. Foote was caught by this advertisement,
which appeared in 1775.

" WANTED, a partner of character, probity, and extensive acquaintance, upon a plan permanent and productive.   Fifty per cent. without risk may be obtained.   It
is not necessary that he should have a knowledge of the
business, but must possess a capital of between 500*l.*
and 1000*l.*   P.S.—None but principals, and *those of
liberal ideas*, will be treated with."   This was a scheme
for a brewery, and Foote actually gave his money.
We are enabled to know what tempted Foote by a
curious circumstance.   It was the opening for profit
furnished by the " extensive acquaintance," for Foote
seems to have " pushed " the beer among his friends.
It was of execrable quality, and at one house the servants " struck " and refused to drink it.   But a black
was so delighted with Foote—who was entertaining
the guests with his sallies—that he came down to his
fellows and declared " that he *would* drink Mr. Foote's
beer, he was so comical."   Notwithstanding, all the
capital vanished and Foote withdrew.   His partner
had now the impudence to suggest his joining him in
a bakery.   Foote replied, " As you brewed so you may
bake, but I'm cursed if you can't bake as you have
brewed."   This good jest, however, was dear at 500*l.*

Price next appeared as a Methodist preacher, as a marriage agent, swindling as he went along. He then tried other breweries, went to Germany, where he made 300*l.* by a smuggling expedition. But it was not until the year 1780 that he started on his grand and elaborate scheme of forgery. In this year the authorities were perfectly bewildered by the repeated complaints that poured in from all sides. In every quarter an old decrepit gentleman with the muffled throat and a patch over his eye, appeared and disappeared, carrying off a quantity of plunder. Such was the cleverness with which he contrived these Protean changes.

The late Walter Thornbury, in his favourite graphic style, has related the story of this strange being. From his " Old Stories Re-told " I take the concluding portion of old Patch's career, pruning away all the florid, and perhaps imaginative details which the writer added by way of seasoning.

" Mr. Levy, a Portuguese Jew diamond-merchant of Lincoln's Inn Fields, had advertised a parcel of very valuable diamonds for sale, and received a letter from a Mr. Schutz. This person, who wrote a crabbed, shaky, and crippled hand, begged the Portuguese merchant would bring them to his lodgings.

" The Portuguese merchant wrote that Mr. Schutz might call upon him and see the diamonds if he liked, but that it was not his habit to wait on purchasers.

At the hour fixed, a hackney-coach, containing Mr. Schutz, duly stopped at the jewel-merchant's house. He apologized for not getting out of the coach on account of his lameness; so the diamonds were brought out to him in their cases.

"Mr. Schutz seemed a poor, sickly, paralytic old man, and was bundled up in a large black camlet surtout, the broad cape fastened up over his chin. He wore the long curling wig and large cocked-hat of a country clergyman. His face jaundiced by age. For support he leaned on a large round ivory-topped cane. He bought the diamonds at about five thousand pounds. Next day, between twelve and one, he would call for the diamonds and pay for them in bank-notes.

"For those jewels Mr. Schutz never came. At the hour appointed, Sir Sampson Wright (the magistrate) and several other gentlemen waited on the expectant diamond-merchant in Lincoln's Inn Fields, told him that Mr. Schutz was a swindler, and that two Bow Street officers were then waiting for him at the shoe-shop in Oxford Street.

"At that very time, Mr. Pearson, a king's messenger, was sent with despatches to Lord North, who was then at Dover. On arriving at Dartford, Mr. Pearson, much to his vexation, found the only pair of horses had just been ordered out by an old gentleman who seemed in a great hurry. Pearson displayed his badge—the silver greyhound—and offered the old gentleman a seat in his chaise as far as Sitting-bourne. The offer was accepted. He had a large green tea-canister secured by a padlock. The road was, however, rough, and the chaise jolted so violently that down went the green tea-canister, and out tumbled —not tea, but a flood of golden guineas, at which the king's messenger secretly wondered, but said nothing.

" On his return to town, Mr. Pearson found handbills in circulation offering rewards from the Bank of England for the apprehension of an old forger named Schutz. No doubt that Schutz and the old gentle-man with the green tea canister full of guineas were one and the same ; he at once informed the Secretary of State, who told Sir Sampson Wright. The solicitor of the Bank of England, with witnesses and officers, were at once sent to follow Schutz, the forger, to Calais, carrying credentials from the Secretary of State to the Minister of France, requesting the surrender of the delinquent. At Calais, a Mr. Price, who had been formerly a partner in a brewery with Samuel Foote, the actor, generously offered his services to the officers to watch Schutz till the lieutenant of police could hear from Paris.

"Soon after this occurrence, a man of business stopped a London merchant one day on 'Change, and presented him with a letter from an Amsterdam correspondent of the house, mentioning that he had been recently defrauded of one thousand pounds by a rascal named Trevor, who frequented the London 'Change, and requesting his aid to recover part or the whole. The friend volunteered his advice as to how the trap was to be best laid and baited for Trevors.

" ' To-morrow, sir,' he said, ' he will most likely be upon 'Change, in the Dutch walk. He dresses in a red surtout and a white wig. He wears square-toed shoes with small buckles, and the rest of his dress is as plain as a Quaker's. Your best way will be to accost him, and get into conversation about the commerce of Amsterdam. Pretend he can be of service to you, and ask him home to dinner. When the cloth is gone, break the business, show him the Dutch letter I brought over, and inform him that, unless he instantly refunds the whole or part of the money, you will on the morrow expose the matter to the principal City merchants.'

"Mr. E. took the advice of his shrewd friend, met the man described in the place expected, and led him home to dinner. The cloth removed, Mr. E. made the agreed signal to his wife and the ladies ; they at once rose and retired. Then Mr. E. began to threaten a ruinous exposure.

" The swindler seemed overwhelmed with fear. He begged not to be exposed on 'Change, he offered five hundred pounds down if Mr. E. would cease all further proceedings. Mr. E. readily consented. Mr. Trevor at once produced a thousand-pound note, for which he requested change. Not having sufficient cash in the house, Mr. Trevor proposed a cheque on Mr. E.'s banker, and having received that, left the house in a state of the utmost penitence and mortification.

"Mr. E. the next morning discovered the thousand-pound note to be a forgery. He rushed to the Bank to stop payment, but found that a porter, followed by a tall thin woman, had obtained notes for the draft full four hours before.

"A short time before, Mr. Spillsbury, a chemist, of Soho Square, found a card in the hall with the name of Wilmot on it. The next evening Mr. Spillsbury received a note requesting him to call on Mr. Wilmot at half-past five o'clock that evening, as he wished to give an order for drops. Mr. Spillsbury went, and being shown in by a smart lad in livery, found Mr. Wilmot to be a decrepid old man wrapped in a large camlet great-coat. He had a slouched hat on, the big brim of which was bent downwards on each side of his head; he wore green spectacles, a green silk shade (hanging from his hat), and a large bush wig. A piece of red flannel rose from his chin. To complete this remarkable dress, the old man's legs were swathed in flannel. Mr. Wilmot instantly began to explain that, having had a tooth clumsily drawn, he wore the flannel to prevent cold. He then praised the drops of Spillsbury, and alluded to the innumerable cures men-

CHA. PRICE in his usual Dress.　　　　　　　CHA. PRICE in Disguise.

as described in the Public Papers. vide Page 13 of these Memoirs.

Published as the act directs by G Kearsley in Fleet Street LONDON, Feb.y 10.th 1786.

tioned in the advertisements, &c. The druggist left
with the promise of a large order. A week after, Mr.
Wilmot's boy called at Spillsbury's, requesting two
guineas' worth of drops, and change for a ten-pound
note. A few days after, Mr. Spillsbury heard from
Sir Sampson Wright that Mr. Wilmot's bank-note was
a forgery, and that the forger had decamped. Soon
after this, the chemist met, at a coffee-house which he
frequented, a Mr. Price, formerly a brewer and keeper
of a lottery-office : the same busy man of the world, in
fact, who had met the solicitor of the Bank of England at Calais, and did his best to aid him in apprehending the diamond thief, Schutz. Over their choco-
late, the two discussed the forgery. The chemist
expressed a little surprise at the extreme neatness of
the handwriting. Mr. Price, a simple creature, stared
through his spectacles, and kept constantly ejaculating,—

" 'Lack-a-day, good Gad ! who could believe such
knavery could exist ? What, and did the Bank actually
refuse payment, sir ? '

"Some considerable time before Mr. Spillsbury's loss,
a lad employed by a musical instrument maker in the
Strand, wanting another place, answered an advertisement dated from the Marlborough Street Coffee-house,
Carnaby Market. One day, just as it was dusk, a man
came and called him to his coach, as the old gentleman who had advertised desired to speak with him.

On getting into the coach, he found a very tall thin man, nearly seventy years of age, dressed in a camlet surtout, buttoned close up over his chin; he was apparently gouty, for his legs were huge bundles of flannel, and his feet were hidden in clumpy square-toed shoes. A broad-brimmed hat was drawn down low over his forehead, and a large black patch covered his left eye, so that the old gentleman's prominent nose, deep sunken right eye, and a small part of his right cheek, were alone visible. He had an incessant faint hectic cough which greatly distressed and fatigued him. Finding the lad honest and frank, he told him that he was guardian to a whimsical young nobleman down in Bedfordshire. On the lad's (Samuel's) master coming to the coach door and giving him a good character, Mr. Brank (the advertiser), of No. 59, Titchfield Street, Oxford Street, engaged him at eighteen shillings a week. On going to that address, Samuel saw Mr. Brank, and he still kept the patched side of his face turned towards the lad; such being the old man's constant peculiarity. He told him that his young master was a prodigal, and unfortunately a great dabbler in those deceitful and alluring bubbles, lottery-tickets. The lad was to buy, at his own expense, a drab livery, turned up with red, and to call on a certain day and hour. On keeping his appointment, old Mr. Brank told him that the thoughtless young lord had just sent letters again

requesting the purchase of lottery-tickets. He then
gave Samuel a twenty-pound and a forty-pound note,
and sent him with the twenty pounds to purchase an
eight-guinea chance at an office in the Haymarket, and
with the forty pounds to purchase the same class of
chance at an office at the corner of Bridge Street,
Westminster. Samuel had canvas bags given him so
as to keep the different shares and change distinct.
On his way to meet his master at the Parliament
Street Coffee-house, Mr. Brank hailed him from the
other side of the road, commending him for his speed
and diligence. He was then sent to Charing Cross,
and King Street and York Street, Covent Garden, to
purchase more chances and change more notes in the
same careful manner. In York Street, by a mere
coincidence, his master again met him, was pleased to
meet him, and taking him into the coach, drove him to
Cheapside to change four hundred pounds' worth
more of notes in the lottery-offices round the Exchange. For many days this went on, Samuel always
observing that whenever he entered an office a lady
stepped out from a coach behind Mr. Brank's, and
followed him in. This lady remained as long as
Samuel remained, and then walked out, purchasing
nothing.

" Four days after, Samuel, being arrested, was employed by Mr. Bond, the clerk at Bow Street, to help
to apprehend the old fox, his master. On receiving a

message to meet his master at Will's Coffee-house at a particular hour, it was agreed that Samuel should go as usual, followed at a distance by Moses Morant, an officer, dressed as a porter, carrying a knot on his shoulder, and by Mr. Bond, dressed as a lady.

"The plan succeeded at first. A porter had just called to know if Samuel had been there. Samuel instantly went back and told the lady. Mr. Brank, watching this from a hackney-coach, at once scented mischief, and drove safely off.

"His last trick had been played on a retired grocer, named Roberts, at Knightsbridge, whose friendship he had gained, and to whom he had represented himself as a stockbroker. Roberts, without consciousness of the fact, had been used by Price to change his forged notes. He had represented to Roberts that an old friend of his, a Mr. Bond—a retired broker, who had made an enormous fortune in the alley—wished himself and a trusty friend to become his executors, having no relations living except an old maiden sister. With management, Price said, all the immense property of the old man—who lived in that singularly retired part of the world, Union Court, Leather Lane, Holborn—would fall into the hands of his executors.

"On an appointed day and hour, Roberts was to meet Price at Mr. Bond's. On arriving there, he found Price had had a business appointment at the City Coffee-house; but the lady of the house showed

PRICE the SWINDLER.

him up stairs to Mr. Bond : a decrepid failing old man, buried in a great chair, with his legs on another, a nightcap on his head, and his chin and mouth covered with flannel. Mr. Bond, with many feeble coughs, lamented Price's absence, and praised that gentleman's honour, honesty, and integrity ; above all, his choice of a brother executor. After two or three visits to Mr. Bond, but never with Price, the old gentleman made his will, and put down Roberts, the executor, for such a large amount, that, on the strength of it, Price obtained nearly one thousand pounds in cash from Roberts, and bonds for two hundred pounds more.

" Price had also, disguised as an old man, succeeded in getting change for six forged fifty-pound notes from Roberts's brother, a grocer in Oxford Street, with whom he had scraped an acquaintance. On the notes being stopped, Roberts brought an action against the bankers, and actually paid Price for his zeal in obtaining witnesses for the defence and during the trial, at which he (Price) himself had the unblushing audacity to attend.

" For some weeks before these forgeries, a corpulent man, of about fifty, named Powel, had repeatedly called and pledged articles of value at the shop of Mr. Aldus, a pawnbroker, in Berwick Street. On the last occasion he had passed a forged note with many altered indorsements. One indorsement, by accident left entire, enabled the Bank to trace the note to Mr. Aldus, who had already had suspicion of the gentleman. The Pawnbrokers' Act being then in agitation, Mr. Aldus entertained a suspicion that Mr. Powel was an informer, who was going to inform against him, and bring *qui tam* actions against him for taking usurious interest. He had, therefore, employed a spy to track him home; but the spy had always lost him in the neighbourhood of Portland Street, or near a mews in Tottenham Street. The runners were for instantly searching the two suspicious places near the rogue's burrow ; for they were now sure that Price and Powel were the same man.

" On the 14th January, 1786, the keen-eyed man in the tie-wig, ruffle shirt, and buckle shoes entered a bin in Aldus's shop, and tapped the counter gently with his tasselled cane. Mr. Aldus at once gave the fatal signal. *Click !* the gin closed ; through the swinging door strode Thomas Ting, Bow Street officer, and said he wanted speak to Mr. Powel a moment, in Mr. Aldus's parlour.

" Mr. Powel was angry and surprised. Who was Ting ? What was Ting's business ? Ting was ready to tell him in Mr. Aldus's parlour. Mr. Powel grew violent, and swore. He declared Ting wanted to rob him.

" At this moment Mr. Clark entered, and instantly said,—

" ' How do you do, Mr. Price ? '

" At this, Mr. Powel turned white. He requested leave to go himself and break the news to his wife, who lodged at Mr. Bailey's, a pastrycook's, in Portland Street.

" He even offered Ting the 115*l*. (chiefly in notes) as a security for his immediate return. Ting refused the bribe, and led Mr. Price to Sir Sampson Wright's, still pressed to take the 115*l*. At Bow Street, Price was indignant and violent. He accused Mr. Bond, the clerk, of dislike to him on account of some old affair about a disputed lottery-ticket, and he even accused Abraham Newland, the venerated old cashier of the Bank, of antipathy towards him. As for Sir Sampson, he told him that it was needless to run through his history. They knew well enough who he was, and if, although he was innocent, he had to submit to a trial, he would reserve his defence till then. Upon this, Mr. Charles Jealous and trusty Ting bundled Price into a hackney coach, and, proud of their snared fox, drove him off to the Tothill Fields Bridewell.

" Determined to run through the whole gamut of fraud, this versatile rascal began a system of matrimonial advertisements ; of which the following is a specimen, from a paper of 1757 :—

" ' To gentlemen of character, fortune, and honour, who wish to engage for life with a lady who possesses the above qualities in a very eminent degree. Her person, in point of elegance, gives precedence to none.

Her mind and manners are highly cultivated, her temper serene, mild, and affable, and her age does not exceed twenty-two.   Any gentleman who answers the above address may direct a letter to A. Z., at the Bedford Head, Southampton Street, Strand; and if their *morals* and situation in life are approved, they will then be waited on by a person who will procure the parties an interview.'

"His assistant in these schemes was a Mrs. Poultney, alias Hickeringill, his wife's aunt, who had become his mistress.   Their house was in Red Lion Street, Clerkenwell; but they had also rooms in Charles Street, St. James's Square, where the accomplished lady exhibited as an Irish giantess.   Their first dupe was a rich young fool, named Wigmore, just fresh from college, full of Latin and void of common sense.   The gull, having paid fifty guineas, was allowed to see the old clergyman, the lady's uncle and guardian—Price himself in disguise—and was promised an interview, which never took place.

"In 1778, he started a fraudulent lottery-office in King Street, Covent Garden.   A Mr. Titmus, who kept a cane-shop in Pimlico, having bought a ticket of Price which came up the eighth of a 2000*l.* prize, was refused payment, although he proved his right by the entry in the Whitehall books.   Clark, an officer of Bow Street, instantly had a handbill printed exposing the fraud, and, going to Mr. Price, told him that 10,000

of those were then being worked off, to be distributed
on 'Change and in every part of London, but chiefly
daily at Price's own door. Price paid the money under
protest, and then wrote to Sir John Fielding, the
magistrate, declaring Mr. Titmus had threatened to
murder him and set fire to his house. He then decamped with the 2000*l.* prize, and the mob the same
night surrounded the house and broke every pane of
glass in the place. The following year he started a
second sham lottery-office in Butcher Row, Temple
Bar, and rivalled Mr. Christie, the then pre-eminent
auctioneer, in the grandiloquence of his advertisements.

" It was about the year 1780 that he began his vast
scheme of forgery. He took the most extraordinary
precautions to prevent discovery. He made his own
paper with the special water-mark; he engraved his
own plates; he made his own ink. He generally had
three lodgings—the first for his wife, the second for
his mistress, and the third for the negotiation of his
notes; his wife and mistress being kept ignorant of
each other's existence. He never returned home in
disguise; he never negotiated notes except in disguise.
The people he used as his instruments never saw him
but in disguise, and were never lost sight of by his
mistress, who always followed him in a hackney-coach
to receive his disguise when done with. In one fact
all, however, agreed—that all the forged notes could
be traced to *one man,* always disguised.

"In 1780, the Bank offered 200*l.* for Old Patch's apprehension. The bill described him and his mistress in the following way:—

" ' He appears about fifty years of age, about five feet six inches high, stout made, very sallow complexion, dark eyes and eyebrows, speaks in general very deliberately, with a foreign accent ; has worn a black patch over his left eye, tied with a string round his head ; sometimes wears a white wig, his hat flapped before, and nearly so at the sides, a brown camlet great coat, buttons of the same, with a large cape, which he always wears so as to cover the lower part of his face ; appears to have very thick legs, which hang over his shoes as if swelled ; his shoes are very broad at the toes, and little narrow old-fashioned silver buckles, black-stocking breeches, walks with a short crutch-stick with an ivory head, stoops, or affects to stoop, very much, and walks slow, as if infirm ; he has lately hired many hackney coaches in different parts of the town, and been frequently set down in or near Portland Place, in which neighbourhood it is supposed he lodges.

" ' He is connected with a woman who answers the following description : She is rather tall and genteel, thin face and person, about thirty years of age, light hair, rather a yellow cast in her face, and pitted with the small-pox, a downcast look, speaks very slow, sometimes wears a coloured linen jacket and petticoat, and sometimes a white one, a small black bonnet and

PATCH PRICE.

a black cloak, and assumes the character of a lady's-maid.'

"This Price was Old Patch himself, Wigmore, Schutz—all. He, and he alone, had planned and worked these endless forgeries.

"On his second examination, Patch laughed at all accusations, and expressed his hope that 'the old hypocrite would be taken.' Assured that none of his dupes could recognize him, he even sent for many of them to prove his innocence. One sharp waiter from a city coffee-house, however, swore boldly to him. Price asked, unthinkingly, how he knew him. The man replied, 'I will swear to your eyes, nose, mouth, and chin;' and the next day the mother of one of his servant-boys swore also to his mouth and chin. From that moment Price lost hope, and said he was betrayed; but he engaged an attorney, and arranged his defence, his plea being that the alteration of the teller's ticket was only a fraud. One night, when he sat over his wine with Mr. Fenwick, the governor of Tothill Fields, he pulled a ten-pound note out of his fob, and, ridiculing the carelessness of the searchers, left the note wrapped round the stopper of the decanter, as if in assertion of his powers of trickery.

"On the Sunday before the day fixed for his committal Price borrowed a Bible of the governor, and prayed with his weeping wife for five hours. On the day before, he had told his son to bring him two gimlets to fasten up the door, as the people of the prison came into his room earlier than he wished, and while he was writing private letters.

"At seven next morning, an old female servant, going into the prisoner's room, saw Old Patch in his flannel waistcoat standing by the door. She said, 'How do you do, sir?' Patch made no answer. At that moment his body swung round gently in the draught. He had hung himself from two hat-screws (strengthened by gimlets) behind the door.

" Under the old forger's waistcoat were found three papers. The first was a series of meditations from the Book of Job, some of them terribly indicative :

" ' Let the day perish wherein I was born, and the night in which it was said, There is a man-child conceived.'

" ' His mischief shall return upon his own head, and his violent dealing shall come down upon his own pate. He made a pit and digged it : he is fallen into the ditch which he made.'

" The second paper was a petition to the king, praying protection for his wife and eight innocent children, on the plea of the Danish pamphlet and his *own innocence.* The third paper was a letter to the governor of the prison and his wife, thanking them for their humanity and for their many and great civilities, and complaining of the legal tyranny that had destroyed his own reason and ruined his family."

A razor was found in his coat pocket.

Price was buried as a suicide in the cross-road near the prison soon after his death ; but a few days later, the empty shell was found beside the grave. The widow had removed the body.

Only one secret of Price's labyrinthine career remains inscrutable, and that is how the immense sum he stole (2000*l.*) was spent, as he always lived in obscure lodgings, and neither drank nor gambled.

§ *A Successful Ruse.*

Here may be mentioned one of those dramatic cases which so rarely occur, and which took place in 1774. In August of this year, one of the usual executions was about to take place at Tyburn, and two malefactors, Waine and Barnet, were actually on the cart, about to be "turned off," as it was called—a phrase often jocularly used in reference to marriages, though few think that it originally described the fatal push from the cart given by the executioner. At this critical moment, a man was seen eagerly making his way to the gallows through the crowd, insisting that he had something of the utmost importance to communicate to the sheriff. Addressing the under-sheriff Reynolds, he said his name was Amos Merritt, and that he knew that the culprit Madan was innocent. He was then called on to look at the man, and to repeat aloud what he had said. He persisted in his statement, but did

H

not accuse himself. So earnest was he that the execution of this criminal was suspended until the return of a messenger, despatched to inform the Home Secretary of the occurrence, who at once sent back a reprieve. The fortunate criminal was taken back to the jail amid the acclamations of the crowd, who were delighted at such an escape. Merritt was then arrested and brought to Bow Street office, where he was examined by Mr. Addington, the magistrate, to whom he confessed that he was the person who had committed the robbery of which Madan was convicted. Madan was accordingly pardoned and released. Strange to say, no proof could be obtained beyond this confession, and they were obliged to let him go.

Not three months later there was brought up before the justice this very Madan, who was accused of being concerned in a most daring burglary at Highgate. With a band of armed accomplices he had attacked a house, and forced his way in, using threats of murder. As so often happens in cases of crime, the narrow escape he had acted only as encouragement instead of warning. He was tried in due course, and executed.

CHAPTER V.

§ *The Murder of Mr. Blight.*

In 1805 a murder was committed, which, without having any distinguishing features, like so many others, excited prodigious interest and sympathy. Mr. Blight was a respectable ship-breaker down at Rotherhithe—a business which he had carried on with much success. In 1803 a man from Devonshire, named Richard Patch, presented himself for employment, which he obtained readily, as two of his family were already in the ship-breaker's service. Patch's father had been a smuggler; his son had been a butcher—a trade that has furnished a good many subjects to the gallows. Mr. Blight found Patch useful in his business, and agreed with him for 40*l.* a year, and board and lodging. Afterwards the salary was increased to 100*l.* a year, and he was to board himself. Patch being a very frugal man, and steady, suffered his salary to accumulate in his master's hands till it amounted to 250*l.* Mr. Blight having a very high

H 2

opinion of Patch, offered him a third of the business
for 1200*l.* the previous summer, which he agreed to,
saying he could procure 1000*l.* from the sale of an
estate he possessed near Exeter. He then enjoyed
a third share of the business from the 31st of
August, and gave Mr. Blight a note or check for
1000*l.* upon a respectable tradesman in Bermondsey,
which, not being regularly paid, brought Mr. Blight
from Margate; and it is supposed he intended to insist
upon the payment of it on the night he was shot, or
the following day. It turned out that all Patch could
muster was a sum of 250*l.* On February 22nd, after
this return from Margate, he was having tea with Mr.
Blight, when one of the servants heard her master get
up to go into the counting-house. She heard him
shut the door of that place after him; and almost immediately after she saw the flash, and heard the report
of a gun or pistol. Mr. Blight came out of the back
parlour saying he had been shot, and leaned on the
kitchen table. Patch then returned, and offered every
assistance in his power to the deceased. Medical aid
was sent for, but he died next day. Patch's account
was that, on the evening of the day when Mr. Blight
had gone to Margate, he, with the maid, remained in his
house ; and while she went to get some oysters for his
supper, a shot was fired through the shutters into the
parlour where he sat, which shattered a part of the sash,
and dashed a splinter of a venetian blind at his neck. He

RICHARD PATCH.

mentioned the circumstance to Mr. Blight on his return, and advised him to employ a man to watch the house and yard, but Mr. Blight would not do it. As Patch told the maid, he had gone out across the yard, when he heard the report of a pistol, and, running to the house, found that Mr. Blight had been shot. Notwithstanding this plausible story, some Bow Street officers went down to Greenland Dock, to the residence of the late Mr. Blight, and took Richard Patch, with Hester Kitchenor, his servant, into custody. They underwent a private and separate examination before Mr. Justice Graham at Bow Street, in order to find out whether they were concerned in the murder of Mr. Blight. The account which Patch has given of his pecuniary transactions with Mr. Blight were found to be contradictory and evasive.

The ingenious rascal had prepared carefully for the sad event. It was proved that when Mr. Blight was at Margate, Patch had sent the servant out for oysters, and as she returned she heard the report of a gun. He greeted her with " O Hester, I have been shot at." " The Lord forbid," said the woman. They then looked for the ball, but it could not be found. After the murder, one of his suggestions was that the murderer had concealed himself in an old vessel which was lying off the wharf. The men went to examine, and found that the old vessel was moored far off in the pool, and was inaccessible owing to the mud.

Such excitement was caused at the trial that crowds gathered round the court at five in the morning, and so invaded the court that it was with difficulty the counsel and others could find seats. Such great personages as the Russian Ambassador, the Duke of Orleans, the Duchesses of Sussex and Cumberland, with a large number of the nobility, were present. A special box even was fitted up for the Royal Family!

Patch was found duly guilty, and sentenced, his body, according to a common custom, directed to be consigned to the surgeons for dissection. To the last moment he repelled all attempts to get him to confess. When the cap was actually drawn over his face, and as he was still being pressed, he drew himself back with much impatience, the spectators fancying that he wished to break his neck, and thus anticipate the hangman. The sheriff, however, with professional *nonchalance*, hastily approached him. " My good friend," he cried," " *what are you about ?* " " They then conversed for about a minute and a half, during which time he no doubt set himself right in the official's mind."

§ *Robbery of Lady Downshire's Jewels.*

In 1813 the papers were filled with an account of the sensational " Robbery of the Marchioness of Downshire's Jewels," which, however, were recovered. The house was entered owing to the unintentional assist-

MRS. BLIGHT.

ance of the lamplighter, who was in the habit of
leaving his ladder against the wall of her ladyship's
house, secured by a chain. The thief had made use of
this convenient aid. At Bow Street there was much
excitement when it was known that the noble lady
was to appear and give her evidence, and she was
attended to the court by an escort. This was to
be a brilliant day for the Office. About twelve
o'clock the noble marchioness arrived, accompanied by
the Duke of Sussex. The latter took his seat on the
left of Mr. Read, the examining magistrate. The
Duke of Gloucester entered about a quarter before
one. There were also present the Marchioness of
Salisbury, Lady M. Cecil, Earl of Sandwich, Earl
Harcourt, Lord Whitworth, the Duke of Dorset, Lord
Crewe, Earl Talbot, &c. The noble marchioness gave
evidence as to the fact of her house being broken open
and robbed, described the property stolen, and identified
the different articles that had been recovered by the
exertions of Mr. Adkins, the Governor of the House of
Correction, and his brother the officer.

The robber, it seems, was a man of extraordinary
gifts in his profession, and was named Joseph Richardson. His extraordinary resemblance to another great
depredator, Napoleon Bonaparte, was remarked by
every one. His career was truly astonishing.

Some time before he committed a great burglary
in Lancashire, for which he was lodged in the New

Bailey prison in Manchester, and was confined in a cell which was secured by cast iron bars. He contrived to have a tailor's goose brought in to him ; his object was to break the iron bars with it, but he was afraid to use it, on account of the noise it would make; but at length he hit upon the stratagem of striking the bars with the goose exactly at the time a very large clock there was striking the hour ; and, after encountering a variety of other difficulties, he at length effected his escape, and was not heard any more of till he was taken into custody for breaking open and robbing the houses of the Earl of Besborough and Lord Crewe, for which he was committed to the House of Correction, Coldbath Fields, where he was confined in a cell, in the upper part of the prison ; but being a stone-mason by trade, he contrived to take up a stone of the floor and worked his way through into the hemp-room, from thence into the yard and garden, when he fastened some stones to some ropes which he procured in the oakum room and platted together ; he then contrived to throw them to the top of the wall of the prison, where there is a *chevaux de frise ;* the stones hung to the iron spikes sufficiently long to enable him to raise himself three times several yards ; but falling each time, he found himself much injured, and spit blood. He was about to return to his cell in despair, when he discovered a ladder locked and chained, both of which he broke, and ascended to the top of the wall, and

effected his escape, about two months ago, between five
and six o'clock in the morning, after an exertion of upwards of five hours ; since which time he is supposed to
have committed six burglaries. Soon after his escape
from this prison Mr. Adkins, the governor, received
information that he frequently went to a shoemaker's
in the neighbourhood of the Seven Dials. He accordingly directed Becket, one of the turnkeys, to watch
the shoemaker's house ; and on the 6th inst., about ten
at night, he saw Richardson approaching him, near the
corner of Tower Street, disguised in two great coats.
He turned down Tower Street ; and after walking a
few yards he looked behind him, and observing Becket
following him, he threw off his coats and set off running ; but Becket gaining ground on him, he threw
his hat at him, supposed to be for the purpose of
striking him in the eyes ; but Becket still pursued him
till he got into Little Red Lion Street, when a man
coming out of a public-house, ran against him and by
accident knocked him down. Becket then seized him,
and Richardson was so extremely agitated at the
instant, that he actually did not know Becket, and
asked what he wanted with him ; Becket secured him
and took him into a public-house, where, upon searching, he found on him notes to the amount of 523*l.*,
which he offered to give to Becket if he would let him
go. Becket, however, refused to accept the bribe, and
conveyed him to the House of Correction. On his

arrival there, the keeper said, " Well, Richardson, I am glad to see you back, I fear you have been doing a deal of mischief since you have been out; from the way in which the Marchioness of Downshire's robbery was committed, I suspect you were in that." Richardson replied, " Master, you have behaved so well to me, I will not tell you an untruth ; I acknowledge I was in that robbery, and I will tell you all about it." The governor then asked him, if any, or the whole of the property could be recovered ? He replied it could, if the keeper would accompany him to a Mr. Joseph's, as he could neither tell the name of the street nor the number of the house where he lived. The keeper agreed, and went without delay in a coach with him, accompanied by Becket, and another of the turnkeys. They proceeded as directed by Richardson, to Chandler Street, Grosvenor Square, and gave the private signal at the door of the house occupied by Joseph, a Jew; the door was opened by Joseph. A light being procured, Mrs. Joseph was asked for two diamond rings which Richardson said she had, and they were part of the property stolen from the Marchioness of Downshire's house. She positively denied having them ; the house was searched, but the rings were not found. The Josephs, however, were admitted as evidence against Richardson and the prisoners who were concerned in the burglary.

The Governor of the House of Correction,

Adkins, had a brother, who was at Bow Street, and who, himself, became governor of one of the prisons—the Warwickshire County Jail—which post he held for thirty years. He died so recently as 1860. A solicitor who has left some pleasant recollections of the Midland Circuit, describes his person, and knew him intimately. "Adkins was a small, compact, clean-made man, extremely active, and known as 'The Little Ferret,' from his activity in his profession. As I often dined at his hospitable table, he would relate different adventures he had gone through. Had his talent been that way, he might have made a very amusing volume of his hairbreadth escapes. He was usually in attendance in the lobby of the House of Commons during the sitting of Parliament, and was close at hand when Spencer Percival was shot by Bellingham. He also arrested Walsh, a member of Parliament, who had committed robberies of trust-moneys, of which he was the custodian, to a very great amount, particularly as regarded Sir Thomas Plomer, formerly Master of the Rolls. Walsh had fears he was suspected; and in order to deceive his enemies he attended the House of Commons, and having made a long speech from his place in Parliament, quitted the House, and disguised himself in the clerical garb, posted down to Falmouth, intending to leave the country. But Adkins was speedily on his track, and with a carriage and four reached Sellis' hotel in the town, just in time to find the bird he had sprung had retired to its rest. Unwilling to disturb him that night he placed an officer outside, opposite the bedroom window of the fugitive, himself taking his place in the hall. When Walsh came down in the morning, his eye falling upon the 'Little Ferret,' whom he knew perfectly well, he put his hand to his head and exclaimed 'Foolish man, foolish man.' He was conveyed back to London, and being tried and found guilty, was transported; but ultimately returning to England, he was living, not many years ago, in a county bordering on Warwickshire.

" Adkins used to relate one of his captures with much unction. A murder had been committed in Staffordshire under circumstances of peculiar atrocity. A large reward being offered for the apprehension and conviction of the person guilty of the deed, Adkins put himself in motion, and soon got scent of his prey down ' Whitechapel way.' Finding the person whom he suspected lived with a female in a house in one of the lowest streets in that locality, he dressed himself up as a country labourer, and thus gained admission. It was a long while ere the female would tell anything; at last she stated he had not been there since the murder, but would doubtless come; the signal of his presence being a slight tap on the window-shutter. After a week's patient waiting on the part of the officer, the much-longed-for tap was at last heard.

Adkins touched his breast, as a reminder to his hostess that pistols were there in case she broke faith with him. The man came in, and started at first on seeing a stranger present, but on being assured by the female it was a pal of hers, the two soon became social, and smoked ' the pipe of peace.' Watching his opportunity, Adkins threw himself upon his victim, and (tell it not in Gath) with the assistance of the woman, the handcuffs soon encircled his wrists. The capture made, the prisoner was tried, and being convicted, was hung.

" Another time he was on the look-out on a similar errand Haymarket way. He was aware of a house, at the back of which some of the worst characters of the day used to meet to refresh themselves. The room set apart for these worthies was ventilated by a sort of skylight from above that was thrown open. Adkins gained admission to the top, and looking down from his eyrie could observe the company below. After a weary watching for many nights, his reward came, for he saw his victim enter the room. When he perceived he had become seated, Adkins suddenly dropped himself on the table, and coming down on his feet like a cat, called out, pistol in hand, ' I want Tom Jones ; I'll shoot the first man who stirs.' Tom *only* being wanted, the rest remained passive ; and he said, using his own words, ' I took him as quiet as a lamb.'

" I had been informed that, during the time he was

governor of the gaol, some alteration had to be made in the drop, it being suggested there should be room for five. On its being put up for examination, Adkins observed it was hardly so large as he intended, at the same time expressing his doubts whether it could conveniently accommodate so many as five. Upon this the worthy carpenter, looking up at the machine and surveying it with a business eye, exclaimed, ' Lor, sir, it's all right, you may take my word for it, five could hang there werry comfortable.'

" He was a very worthy man, a first-rate officer, and held the position of governor of the county gaol for Warwickshire for thirty years and upwards, having during the whole of that lengthened period performed his duties with credit to himself and benefit to the county. He died when nearly eighty years old."

§ *Lord Cochrane.*

In 1814 the town was thrown into excitement by the well known stock-jobbing fraud of De Berenger, in which the gallant Lord Cochrane was unhappily implicated, and which ruined this splendid, daring seaman. Justice was done the unfortunate nobleman some twenty years later, and the universal opinion appears to be that he had been treated with the cruellest injustice. There were many dramatic elements in his case. This De Berenger, an adventurer, whom he had befriended, was the cause of his destruction.

About midnight on the 20th of February, 1814, he presented himself at the Ship Hotel at Dover, calling himself Colonel De Bourg, and aide-de-camp to Lord Cathcart, representing that he was the bearer of intelligence from Paris, to the effect that Buonaparte had been killed by the Cossacks—that the allied armies were in full march for Paris—and that immediate peace was certain! After this announcement he forwarded similar intelligence by letter to the Port-Admiral at Deal, with a view—as was supposed—of its being forwarded to London by telegraph; thus making the Port-Admiral the medium of communication with the Government.

He then posted up to London, dressed as an officer, but when near Lambeth, discharged his chaise, and taking a hackney coach, drove to Lord Cochrane's, where he asked leave to change his clothes. The plot succeeded, and the conspirators sold some hundred thousand pounds' worth of stock on "time bargains," before the trick was discovered. It was unlucky that Lord Cochrane's agent should have disposed of his principal's stock at the same time, though Lord Cochrane explained after that he had given a standing order to sell whenever a rise took place.

There was certainly a desperate combination of circumstances against Lord Cochrane—and which raised the most serious suspicion. He was at that moment on the point of quitting the kingdom on a cruise. Nor was it easy to explain his acquaintance with a " shady" adventurer such as De Berenger was. Lord Cochrane returned to town from his ship to meet the charges—and swore an affidavit before Mr. Graham at Bow street, in which he explained every step of his proceedings on that momentous day. The chief points in this document were as follows.

" At this time I had joined the *Tonnant* at Chatham, and was preparing to sail for the North American station, but on learning the injurious report above mentioned, I determined to denounce him, in order that if he were really the guilty person, his name should be made public at the earliest possible moment, so that no time might be lost in bringing the matter home to him. I obtained leave of absence from the ship. On my return to town, I found that although the authorities were ignorant of the name of the person who came to my house on the 21st of February, public rumour did not hesitate to impute to me complicity in his transactions, simply from the fact of the suspected person, whoever he might be, having been there. An affidavit was prepared and submitted to an eminent barrister, Mr. Gurney, to whom I disclosed every particular relative to the visit of De Berenger, as well as to my own previous, though very unimportant transactions in the public funds. I was advised by him and my own solicitors to confine myself simply to supplying the authorities with the name of De Berenger as the person seen in uniform at my house on the 21st ultimo.

"The main facts, as relating to the visit of De Berenger, are these. That early on the morning in question, I had gone to a lamp manufactory in the city, for the purpose of superintending the progress of some lamps patented by me, and ordered for the use of the convoy of which I was about to take charge on their voyage to North America. Whilst thus engaged, my servant came to me with a note, which had been given to him by a military officer, who was waiting at my house to see me. Not being able to make out the name, from the scrawling style in which the note was written, and supposing it to have come from a messenger from my brother, who was then dangerously ill with the army of the Peninsula, and of whose death we were in daily expectation of hearing, I threw down the note, and replied, that I would come as soon as possible; and, having completed my arrangements at the lamp manufactory, arrived at home about two hours afterwards, when, to my surprise, I found De Berenger in place of the expected messenger from my brother.

"A poor but talented man—a prisoner within the rules of the King's Bench—he had come to me in the hope that I would extricate him from his difficulties by taking him to America. After my renewed refusal, on professional grounds, De Berenger represented that he could not return to the Rules in his uniform without exciting suspicion of his absence. The room happened at the time to be strewed with clothes, in process of examination, for the purpose of being sent on board the *Tonnant,* those rejected being thrown aside; and at his urgent request I lent, or rather gave him a civilian's hat and coat to enable him to return to his lodgings in ordinary costume. This simple act constituted my offence, and was construed by the court into complicity in his fraudulent conduct! though under ordinary circumstances, and I was aware of no other, it was simply an act of compassionate good-nature.

" A very remarkable circumstance, afterwards proved on the trial, was this—that on De Berenger's arrival in town from Dover, he neither went to the Stock Exchange, nor to his employers, whoever they might be, nor did he take any steps on his arrival in town to *spread the false intelligence which he had originated.* He was proved on his trial to have dismissed his post-chaise at Lambeth—to have taken a hackney-coach— and to have proceeded straight to my house. The inference is plain, that the man was frightened at the nature of the mission he had undertaken, and declined to go through with it.

" Had I been his confederate, it is not within the bounds of credibility that he would have come in the first instance to my house, and waited two hours for my return home, in place of carrying out the plot he had undertaken, or that I should have been occupied in perfecting my lamp invention for the use of the convoy of which I was in a few days to take charge, instead of being on *the only spot* where any advantage to be derived from the Stock Exchange hoax could be realized, had I been a participator in it. Such advantage must have been immediate, before the truth came out, and to have reaped it, had I been guilty, it was necessary that I should not lose a moment. It is still more improbable, that being aware of the hoax, I should not have speculated largely for the special risk of that day."

Lord Cochrane, as is well known, was restored to all his honours by King William IV. and her present Majesty. At the same time it is impossible to blame the jury for acting on such a singularly suspicious circumstance as the accused furnishing him with a change of clothes. His account of the transaction, too, is so distorted by his violent prejudices and belief that his political opponents were in conspiracy to ruin him, that he absolutely weakened the force of his case.[1]

---

[1] He even accuses the prosecution of bribing the witnesses, and Mr. Croker of pretending to have lost a letter which was favourable to his case.

CHAPTER VI.

THE GREENWICH TRAGEDY.

In February, 1818, a shocking but highly dramatic tragedy engrossed all the energies of Bow Street—whence was despatched to every quarter of the kingdom, in search of the murderer, no less than twenty officers. A retired tallow-chandler, named Bird, who was past eighty, resided at Greenwich, close to the "Mitre Tavern." He was known to have made money and lived almost alone, with his housekeeper. On a Sunday morning, the 8th, it was remarked by the Greenwich folk that he was not in his seat as usual, and then several people in church remembered to have observed, as they came along, that the shutters of the old gentleman's house remained unopened. Thinking these circumstances to be portentous of evil, several of his acquaintance, on quitting church after service, proceeded to Mr. Bird's house, and accompanied by his brother, endeavoured to gain admission, but to no purpose. They then broke open a door between the house and Mr. Thomas's, and thus effected an entrance. Proceeding through the passage, they raised up the sash of the kitchen window and broke open the shutters. Mr. Thomas then entered the kitchen through the window, and made his way to the hall. On opening the back door, they beheld the body of Mrs. Simmons, the housekeeper, lying in the passage. He stepped over the body and opened the hall window, when he discovered the corpse of Mr. Bird extended on the floor in the parlour, the door between the hall and the parlour being wide open. Upon examining further, he found a quantity of blood on the hall floor near where Mrs. Simmons was lying. It was a track of blood that had evidently been caused by dragging the body to the spot where it then was. The head was dreadfully cut, and one of the ears was slit or torn in two ; some of the rails of the bannisters were broken, apparently as if done in a struggle. Close to the body of Mr. Bird, whose skull had been literally beaten in, was a candle and candlestick and a pair of broken spectacles. There was a little table upset behind the door. The whole house had been ransacked by the murderer, who had carried off much property and left as much behind him.

Mr. Bird, it was well known, was in the habit of supping at nine o'clock and going to bed at ten, when the cloth was removed, from which circumstances and the fact of the knives and table-cloth being found laid out ready for use, and the slippers placed to air near the fender before the kitchen fire, it was inferred that the murder had been committed about nine o'clock at night, but who the murderer or murderers were no one could form the least conjecture.

Intelligence of the discovery of this fearful deed having been immediately sent to Mr. Bird's son, he hastened to the house, where the agony he evinced on beholding the mangled corpse of his revered parent was so heart-rending as never to be forgotten by those who witnessed it. The following morning a coroner's inquest was held. A brick wall nearly eleven feet high divided the garden of the house from another at the end, called Powis's garden, in which the marks of footsteps were distinctly visible. A tile, newly broken by some person in climbing over the wall, lay on the ground and appeared to have fallen from the roof of the summer-house. Two empty bottles and tobacco pipes were on the table in one of the parlours, and were stained with marks of blood, the murderers having evidently sat down to regale themselves when their dreadful work was over.

All Greenwich was thrown into excitement by this outrage, and the town liberally offered the large reward of 500*l*. for the apprehension of the murderers. The pursuit and detection, it will be seen, was of the most exciting kind.

Several weeks, however, were to go by without result, when, all of a sudden, suspicion began to rest on a man called Hussey, who had lodged opposite. This fellow, a Greenwich pensioner, not more than one and twenty, had been observed, on the Sunday night when the occurrence took place, prowling about on the opposite side of the street, in front of Mr. Bird's house. In consequence he had, after the inquest, been detained for a short time and interrogated by one of the Greenwich constables; but the account he then gave of himself, and the explanation of his suspicious conduct were so extremely plausible and satisfactory that he was immediately set at liberty. Mrs. Walmsley, the landlady of the "Tiger's Head," stated that he had been her lodger ever since three weeks before the preceding Christmas; that she knew he was in the tap-room at half-past ten on the night of the murder, and that he belonged to a club of Odd Fellows, who met regularly at her house; so, of course, there could be no ground for detaining him on suspicion. But, a few days after the murder, Hussey absconded, and other suspicious circumstances having come to light, all possible means were resorted to for effecting his apprehension. Active and experienced officers were despatched in every direction, and advertisements repeating the offer of reward for the arrest of the murderer were inserted in all the principal newspapers; but no intelligence was received of him till the 3rd of April, when a letter arrived at Bow Street from the agent of a Mr. Field, an attorney at Deddington, containing highly important news.

It seems that about four or five o'clock in the afternoon of the Sunday when the murder was discovered, Hussey had called upon his brother, at Peckham, with whom he had promised to dine on that day. When he arrived, he apologized for not having been able to come to dinner, stating that he had not been well, and that during the earlier part of the day it had been impossible for any one to get either in or out of Greenwich, in consequence of the crowds of people collected in the town by the discovery of the murder of an old gentleman and his housekeeper, who lived immediately opposite to the " Tiger's Head," where he (Hussey) was then lodging. The next day, he and his brother went together to London, where they parted, and on Hussey's returning to his brother's house at Peckham that night, his clothes were wet and dirty, he having been drinking somewhat too freely and fallen, as he said, into a ditch. That night, he sold to his brother several pieces of silver (apparently parts of a broken buckle), at the price of 5s. an ounce. On the Wednesday following, three days afterwards, Hussey received a legacy of 60l., and immediately made preparations for absconding into the country. He removed his box from the house of a Mr. Litton, a cooper, called upon his sister, Elizabeth Goodwyn, at Peckham, and gained access to a box she had lately received, containing the clothes of her deceased mother. He then went out of town for three weeks, called upon his sister again, and again had access to the box—for what purpose will be seen hereafter. Away he went once more out of town, and wandered about the country, living very freely on the road, and, in fact, having little or no regard to his expenditure. This lasted about a month, when mere accident put a stop to his career, and consigned him to the hands of justice. Arriving one Saturday night at the village of Wolvercot, situate within a short distance of Oxford, he entered a public-house, and asked the landlady if he could have a bed, but she not being able to accommodate him, a butcher, who happened to be present, thinking, from the respectability of Hussey's appearance that he was one of the collegians from Oxford, offered him a night's lodging at his house, and he accordingly slept there. On the following morning he returned to the public-house to breakfast, and, it being Sunday, remained there all that day, in the course of which the landlord observed him take out of his pocket a gold ring, on which was engraved, " To the memory of six children;" a circumstance which, in London, where people have quite enough to do in minding their own affairs, would have passed unnoticed; but the landlords of village public-houses are remarkably prying when any stranger comes in, especially if his appearance is at all respectable; and so Boniface, being exceedingly perplexed about this ring and its possessor, determined, by watching very narrowly his guest's conduct and conversation, to find out, if possible, who he was, and how a gentleman who appeared to be scarcely more than one-and-twenty could be the owner of a ring inscribed to the memory of six children. Hussey's behaviour during the day was excessively mysterious, and led the landlord to surmise, that instead of having in his house one of the Oxford collegians, he was harbouring some swindler or runaway thief; so in the evening, when Hussey presented him a one-pound note in payment for that day's eating and drinking, he positively refused to take it, shrewdly suspecting that it had been either forged or stolen. In this dilemma, Hussey proposed to leave with his host a pair of ear-rings as security for the bill, saying that he should be passing through the village on his road to Oxford the following Wednesday, when he would call and redeem the property, to which the landlord assented. Hussey gave him the ear-rings accordingly, and departed, leaving Boniface wrought up to such a pitch of restless perplexity, that he immediately went to a neighbour, showed him the earrings, and had a long conversation with him as to who and what his mysterious visitor could possibly be. They both agreed, rightly enough, that he was a person of suspicious character, and at last they remembered having recently read in a newspaper an advertisement describing the person of Hussey, and offering a reward for his apprehension. The paper was immediately referred to, and the description given in the advertisement convinced them that the individual who had excited so much curiosity was no other than the murderer of Mr. Bird.

The landlord having procured a companion, immediately set off in pursuit of Hussey, and slept that night at the house of a Mr. Poulton, a publican, in Deddington, starting off again the next morning at six o'clock, after telling the landlord there the business they were on, and giving him a full description of the dress and personal appearance of the man they were in search of. It so happened that Mr. Poulton, to whom they had told all this, was himself a constable, and feeling highly interested in what he had heard, he immediately went out and read the Oxford paper, where he found the description of Hussey to correspond so exactly with the man his visitors were gone in search of, that he determined himself to join in the pursuit. But he was saved the trouble, for, not long after, he saw Hussey pass the window, and being struck by his likeness to the description given, he went out and followed him. He saw him go into the shop of a Mr. Ryman, a neighbour, and on going there after he had left, was told that he had sold a waistcoat for two shillings. Mr. Poulton now got a neighbour named Churchill to accompany him, and, continuing the pursuit, found that Hussey had stopped at the "King's Arms" inn to procure some refreshment. On his coming out of this house, they followed, and speedily afterwards took him into custody, Mr. Poulton telling him that he suspected his name was Charles Hussey, and that he was the person mentioned in the advertisement. The prisoner, after some little hesitation, confessed that Mr. Poulton was correct as to his name, and allowed himself to be searched without offering the least resistance. On his person was found a watch, and a pocket-book with a ring in it, subsequently identified as part of the property stolen from the house of Mr. Bird on the night of the murder. But the ring with the inscription was not to be found about him; and on being asked for it, Hussey said he had thrown it away at the " King's Arms " inn, where accordingly it was soon after found wrapped up in a piece of rag. On being questioned by Mr. Poulton, the prisoner denied all knowledge of the murder or robbery, but admitted being in possession of the stolen property. The watch found on him bore the maker's inscription, " Miles Patrick, Greenwich." The duplicate of a ring was also found in Hussey's possession, bearing date only a few days after the murder and robbery.

Information of the prisoner's arrest was immediately sent to London, and on the same day, the 3rd of April, about seven o'clock in the evening, a hackney coach drove up to the door of the police-office, Bow Street, containing Hussey and certain persons who had him in custody.

What had happened in the interval had been this.

The last account that was heard of him in London was on Sunday se'nnight, at the "Lamb" public-house, near Fitzroy Market, where, having drank some peppermint with a relation, who was understood to be his brother, he took leave of him, and said he was going into the country. Adkins traced him from thence to Basingstoke, and there all direct knowledge of him was lost. The officer went to Burton, in Dorsetshire, where his wife was living with her relations, and had lately been confined in child-bed. She and her family were extremely shocked on learning the crimes with which he was charged; he had not been there, nor had they heard anything of him. Most of the officers had been after him in various directions, where there had been any suspicion of finding him, but they did not succeed. On Thursday morning, however, the acceptable intelligence was brought to the office of his being taken at Deddington, in Oxfordshire, a small town six miles from Banbury, eighteen from Oxford, and twelve from Woodstock. The information was brought to the office by the law agent, in London, to Mr. Field, the attorney of Deddington, who stated that he had received a letter from Mr. Field, informing him that Hussey was taken in that town, and that he would be brought to London by the constable, accompanied by a man who was to assist in keeping Hussey secure, and also by Mr. Field himself. The letter also stated that they should travel in the Woodstock coach till within the last stage of London, and then should come from thence in a post-chaise, to avoid the bustle and confusion which their arrival in London might otherwise occasion. This communication excited a considerable degree of interest at the office in the course of the day.

After undergoing two examinations, one at Bow Street and the other at Greenwich, he was committed for trial; and at the following Kent assizes, held at Maidstone on the 31st of July, was found guilty of the murder, and ordered for execution on the following morning.

CHAPTER VII.

THE MURDER OF WEARE.

THE story of the murder of Mr. William Weare by
Thurtell and his associates, is so extraordinary in its
melodramatic incidents, so lurid in its details, that it
holds the reader with a sort of fascination, akin to the
attraction of some repulsive but absorbing melodrama.
The characters are marked and striking, the events
fall into a sort of dramatic sequence, and the hideous
mystery of the whole lifts it out of the category of the
vulgar murders which crowd the "Newgate Calendar."
Even the district round Watford seems to this day
pervaded with the horror of the tradition ; there are
the lonely roads, the ponds, the dark copses ; in the
shops you can purchase the whole story of the murder
and trial. Even now there are amateurs who collect
the literature of the trial, with illustrations, to make
the thing more graphic. Sir Walter Scott used to
praise for its unintentional dignity and pathos the flow
of the well-known doggrel lines:—

> They cut his throat from ear to ear,
> His brains they battered in ;
> His name was Mr. William Weare,
> And he lived in Lyon's Inn.

The gig which was to take down the two gentlemen by night to the cosy shooting cottage at Elstree, the ladies who entertained them there, the pond, the sound of the pistol-shot in the lonely country lane, these were all exciting elements. It moreover furnishes a good illustration of the sort of philosophy that is furnished fresh by nearly every striking case. As will be seen later, Mr. Carlyle extracted from it his " gigmanship; " but nearly every case will be found to supply some grim and cynical illustration of the kind. This, as I have before stated, seems to form the ground of that peculiar attraction which criminals and criminal cases so often furnish.

Once more the " Brown Bear " seems to have been the place where the whole business was engendered. There had met, with prize-fighters and others of " the fancy," Messrs. Thurtell, Weare, and Hunt. Thurtell was more respectable than any of the usual class of murderers, being the son of a Mayor of Norwich. He had served in the German Legion, and took part in the storming of St. Sebastian. In 1828, he became a " bombazine manufacturer," but being pressed by his creditors met them with the story that he had collected 400*l.* to settle with them, and had been set upon and robbed of the money by some footpads. To this story no credit was given. He next removed to London, and started in business with his brother, where, by another suspicious accident, their premises were burnt down.

This Thurtell used to frequent the " Brown Bear " regularly, where there was a room at the back devoted to private play, i.e., to the process of plundering "flats." In this den Thurtell, almost on his introduction, lost a sum of 300*l*. at " blind hookey." Infuriated at being thus pillaged, he was at first inclined to withdraw from the place, but thought it might be wiser to turn his dearly-bought experience to profit, and proposed to recoup himself at the expense of some other "flat." The fraternity at the " Bear " soon found this out, and, discovering that he had still something left to lose, determined " to pluck him to the last feather." They resolved to flatter his opinion of his own cleverness, and with this view introduced to him another frequenter of the "Brown Bear," one Mr. Wearo, a genuine sporting character, who was well up in " flash " and " cant," and who was pointed out to Thurtell as a green hand, and well worthy of his talent. The result was that the *soi-disant* " rook " was himself cleared of all he had left. He was now so infuriated at the way in which he had been fleeced that he determined to be revenged on all who had been concerned. The others, seeing this temper, thought it necessary to restore his good humour by *putting him on a cross*, as they called it, and letting him know of a prize-fight, the issue of which had been arranged beforehand. In this way he won 600*l.* But he still had a grudge to the more successful Weare, who was presumed to be so knowing a personage. This gentleman gambled and betted, and was further supposed to be in the habit of carrying a "private bank," i.e., a deep pocket in an under waistcoat, whence he drew any supplies that he was in need of.

Thurtell had other low friends belonging to this unsavoury class. One was named Probert, who had a cottage down at Elstree, where he kept his family, his ostensible business being that of a spirit dealer. Another was a mere useful agent, or under-trapper, named Hunt, who was a public singer, gifted with a fine, cultivated voice, with which he used to recreate his friends at convivial moments. Thurtell's father was an alderman, who in the very year of the murder, was mayor of his town. Weare lived at No. 2, Lyon's Inn, which has long since been swept away.

On Friday, the 28th of October, 1823, the magistrates were holding their usual meeting at the "Essex Arms," in Watford, when they were informed that a farmer, named Smith, had on the Saturday night, at about eight o'clock, been driving near the high road, and had heard the sound of a pistol-shot coming from a lane close by, with deep groans, which continued for a minute or two and then died away. He stopped his chaise to listen. but was persuaded by his wife that it was merely some frolic or spree. The sound of a gig in the lane was also heard. There were other ugly rumours in the district. Some labourers who were early at work near the lane that led from Gill Street Hill, met two gentlemen who were searching the hedges, and who told how they had been upset the night before and had lost some articles. After their departure the labourers searched for themselves, and found a pistol covered with blood and hair.

The magistrates immediately despatched two of the local constables to Bow Street to ask that an active officer be sent down. It was reported in the district that some strange men had within the last few days been staying at Mr. Probert's residence on Gill Street Hill, a rural-looking cottage with a garden and pond Constables were sent there and found the owner on the eve of departure, a van loading before the door. They took him into custody. At two o'clock in the morning arrived from Bow Street that well-known, active, and intelligent officer Ruthven, with whom we are well acquainted, to whom the magistrates gave warrants for the apprehension of Thurtell and his friend Hunt the singer. Ruthven set off for town and returned the following day with the two prisoners. There also arrived Mr. Noel, a solicitor, who said a client of his, named Weare, had disappeared, and was probably the murdered person.

A kind of morbid interest was already aroused in the

tale. It was felt that a terrible mystery was about to be unfolded, of which the pretty solitary cottage, standing apart in the lonely district, with its significant pond, was to be the centre. The story of the strangers with their gig, the "bald-faced horse with the four white legs," which many had noted, these things were being whispered about. That admirable artist, J. D. Harding, employed his pencil in making sketches of the cottage and other places adjoining, which are good specimens of his skill. The magistrates, when they met again, were surprised to find that there was a sort of competition between two of the prisoners, Probert and Hunt, both offering to confess the whole story of what had happened. Hunt was first in order of time, and related the hideous work of the fatal night.

Thurtell was a most extraordinary character. He was only thirty years old, but full of a sort of desperate recklessness. He was often heard to talk of " doing for " various persons who were odious to him. But it is clear that his feeling to Weare was that of simple hatred to a man who had pillaged him, as he fancied—with a longing for revenge. He was, however, at the end of all his resources, and was at the moment in hiding at a low sort of saloon or tavern. He was on cordial terms with Weare, and had invited him to Probert's cottage for a few days' shooting, offering to drive him down himself. On the next day, which was October 24, the unfortunate man, who seemed to look forward to the party with pleasure, got ready his gun-case, also a backgammon board, with other things, to add to the enjoyment of the party. Thurtell procured a gig and the horse " with the white face and legs," and, taking up his friend, they set off on their fatal night drive to Edgware.

About nine o'clock that night he drove up in the gig to Probert's cottage, along with Probert himself and Hunt, the latter having come in another gig. The ladies—that is, Mrs. Probert and her sister, Miss Noyes—and the children were unprepared for the arrival of the gentlemen, and formal introductions followed. *Some pork chops*, which Hunt had brought specially from town, were then cooked for supper; the murdered Weare then lying in the hedge! Thurtell had bought a pair of second-hand pistols at a pawnbroker's, with which he had done the deed; and he recounted how, to Hunt, whom he had met on the road.

We might imagine that long journey to Edgware— the gig rattling along the high roads and lanes, halting at lonely roadside public-houses. Probert driving his gig, and having set down Hunt, came on Thurtell waiting in that dark and lonely lane. His first question was, "Where was Hunt?" The business had been done without him. Hunt arrived, and, being abused by Thurtell for his failure, said : " Why, you had the tools?" "They were no better than pop-guns," said the other. "I fired at his cheek

and it glanced off." When he fired, Weare jumped
out of the gig, begged for mercy, offered to give up his
money. But the other pursued him up the lane, and,
finding the pistols useless, knocked him down. They
then struggled, Thurtell striving to cut his throat with
a penknife, and finally the wretch killed his victim by
—horror of horrors!—driving the barrel of the pistol
into his skull, and then turning it round and round in
his brains!

During this time there were persons on the road
who had heard the report of the pistol in the dark
lane; then voices and groans; but they seemed to
grow fainter, and finally died away.

After their pork chops, these wretches had gone out
to strip the victim and hide the body. When they
returned to the cottage, Thurtell displayed a gold
watch, with a curb chain, which he gaily and gallantly
declared was " more suited for a lady than a gentleman," and made Mrs. Probert accept it. Hunt then
sang some songs (!), and the evening was spent in
much cheerfulness. It was then proposed that Miss
Noyes, the governess, should give up her room to the
gentlemen; but Mr. Thurtell and his friend would not
hear of it, and would prefer to sit up. But the lady of
the house thought there was something strange, if not
mysterious in the whole business, and when they
retired for the night, she went to her window to watch.
Presently she saw the three men go out to the garden,

dragging with them something like a sack. The sack
seemed to be too heavy for them to manage, so the
horse was got out of the stable, and it was placed
across his back. These proceedings confirmed her
horrified suspicions, and when they returned she stole
down and listened at the parlour door. They were
dividing the money—six pounds to each—this was all
the wretched produce of the deed!—burning papers,
pocket-book, &c., at which work they remained up
very late. Before six the next morning Thurtell and
Hunt were again out in the fatal lane, and, unluckily
for themselves, were noticed by some passing labourers
as they searched the hedges. Thurtell said "it was a
bad road, and he had been upset there last night."
But the labourers, thinking to find some property for
themselves, began looking under the hedges, and discovered the blood-stained pistol, which Thurtell was no
doubt looking for. There was also blood plentifully
scattered on the ground and leaves.

The party now took their leave of the cottage, got
out the gig, and returned to town. But they felt some
uneasiness as to the way they had disposed of the
body, and having bought a spade, once more drove
down. They had hidden the body in a pond, from
which they now drew it, and placing it in the fatal
gig, drove away to a yet more distant pond, where it
was once more sunk by heavy stones attached to it.

In due course the trio were brought up to Bow

Street, and examined before Sir R. Birnie, the magistrate. Though every search was made for the murdered man, it was not until Hunt led the officers to the pond, that he was found.

In every portion of this case we find something strange and weird-like. After this early investigation, the remains of the unhappy Weare were interred towards midnight, and by torch-light, in Elstree churchyard, where they now rest in a nameless grave, and not far from the grave of Hackman's victim, Miss Ray. The mourners were the coroner's jury, who walked to the grave.

It would be impossible to give an idea of the horror and interest which spread over the whole kingdom at the news of this tragedy. The incidents of the fatal night seemed to take possession of the public mind; the agitated wife, gradually led to suspect; the men going out at midnight; the festivity in the drawing-room; the playing at whist, when Thurtell declared the cards were "cross;" and "the pork chops," which seemed to have a sort of monstrous propriety as the food of murderers. Here was a scene from the events of the night: "I did not go to bed immediately," says the hostess. "I went to the stairs to listen, and leaned over the bannisters. What I heard was all in a whisper. First, I heard one of them say: 'I think that will fit you very well.' There was the noise of rustling papers, and as of papers thrown upon

the fire. I afterwards went up to my own room. I
looked from my window, and saw two gentlemen go
from the parlour to the stable with a light. They led
a horse out of the stable, and opened the gate, and led
the horse out. Some time after I heard something in
the garden—something dragged, as it seemed, very
heavily along the dark walk. I had a view of it when
they dragged it out of the dark ; it seemed very large
and heavy, and like a sack. After this I heard a
noise like a heap of stones thrown into a pit." She
heard scraps of the talk when they were dividing the
booty. " Let us take a five-pound note each." " We
must be off at five in the morning," Thurtell was heard
to say. " Holding shall be next." It was asked, " Had
he any money ? " and the other replied, " It is not
money I want, but revenge. It is Holding who has
ruined my friend here, and destroyed his peace of
mind."

Other incidents of that dreadful restless night were
described. " There was singing," she said. " Hunt
sang two songs. John Thurtell asked him to sing
once, and I pressed him to sing the second time." A
picture of the sofa on which Hunt slept was in some
of the papers.

The party were at the cottage on the Sunday, and
one of them seemed to have suggested that the spectacle of cards on the Sunday was not good for the
morals of the children. On that day Hunt appeared

dressed up in some of the murdered man's clothes, and his friend asked the ladies pleasantly, if Hunt did not look "quite smart in his finery"? It would be impossible to give an idea of all the strange things that occurred in this case, and which quite lifts it out of the vulgar and revolting type of such events. The most singular part was the transformation of the chief actor from the moment of his arrest. From being a reckless, desperate ruffian, he became of a sudden calm, decorous, and even dignified; and this attitude was maintained even to the moment of his final exit. His speech at the trial was delivered with much force and eloquence, and characterized by singular ingenuity. He imported into it appeals to religious sentiment, which must have revolted many, but which was supported by a fervour that almost seemed genuine. "I look forward," he said at the close, "with a sweet complacency of mind, arising from a conscience void of guilt. Assisted by the Divine power, I feel supported by the consciousness of having ever acted on humane, just, and honourable principles. I trust there is not a spectator in court who does not believe these emotions to be the genuine inmates of my breast. If there be any, I would address them in the language of the Apostle, 'would to God ye were altogether such as I am, *save these bonds.*' . . . . I stand before you," he continued, "as before my God, overwhelmed with misfortunes, but

unconscious of crime; and while you decide on my
future destiny, I earnestly entreat you to remember
my last solemn declaration : *I am innocent,* so help me
God ! "

This extraordinary harangue was delivered with
much energy, feeling, and dramatic effect; at these last
words he raised his hands to heaven, and then closed
them on his breast. At passages, he was deeply
affected. In passing sentence, the admirable judge,
Park, who tried the case, was also deeply moved. " I
understand," he said at the close, " that the clergyman
of this jail is a most respectable man. He will show
you the way of salvation, he will show you that grace
that can be given to a contrite heart. Seek, O ! seek
it earnestly, I beseech you : knock earnestly at the gate
which is never shut to a repentant sinner. Pour
yourself out at the feet of your Redeemer in humble-
ness and truth, and to His grace and mercy I commit
you; and while you are seeking for it you shall have
my devout and earnest prayers that your supplications
may be heard." Sentence of death was then passed
on him and Hunt on the Friday—less than forty-
eight hours. The behaviour of the condemned was
extraordinary for its propriety. It was believed
that Hunt would be reprieved and so it proved, and
Thurtell wished him good-bye with much warmth,
" God bless you," he said, " I hope your life will be
spared, and that you will live long, and go abroad,

and be a happy man.[1] Pray remember what Mr.
Franklyn (the chaplain) has taught you." On the
morning of his execution he was sleeping profoundly,
and remarked " I have had some very curious dreams.
I have often dreamt since my confinement, and what
is very extraordinary I have never dreamt of anything
connected with this affair." In the chapel after the
sacrament was administered, a curious scene followed.
The governor addressed him solemnly and respectfully.
" Mr. Thurtell," he said, " I feel it my duty to call
your attention to a subject which requires your most
serious consideration. We are now alone, with no
other eye but that of Almighty God to witness what
passes between us. I do not ask you to make any
confession, but if you have any declaration to make of
your feeling with regard to the sentence under which
you are about to suffer, this is the most fit and proper
time to make it." After a short pause, he then placed
his hands on the governor's shoulder, and with much
agitation, made this curious and skilful reply, " I am
quite satisfied. I forgive everybody. I die in peace
with all mankind. That is all I wish should go forth
to the world. I beg you will not ask me any more
questions on this subject."

---

[1] The wretched Hunt in due course was released, but this
awful warning and narrow escape was thrown away. Strange
to relate, this creature was later tried for stealing a horse,
sentenced, and executed !

All connected with the execution was carried out in
the same calm and even friendly way, which contrasts
with the stern cold severity of our time, on such
occasions. The execution did not take place till the
comfortable hour of noon, when the convict on the
scaffold seized the chaplain's hands and thanked him
effusively for his services. To others he said firmly,
" God Almighty bless you." After the event, persons
came and took away his body—strange to say in a
sack, and in *a gig* of the same pattern which he had
himself used on the fatal night—to St. Bartholomew's,
where it was dissected and anatomized. Thus at the
end as at the beginning the mysterious vehicle took
its part.

For the public of the day, all the incidents of this
strange case had a sort of hideous fascination, which
even now, on a perusal of the case, it is difficult to
resist. There was the long night drive of twelve
miles down to Elstree, which is near Watford, where
the district seems even now of a lonely, unbuilt-on kind,
Thurtell taking down his victim to the rural-looking
cottage which stood alone and solitary on Gill's Hill,
in whose garden was a truly significant pond. But
through the lurid light which played upon the tragedy,
the public eye seemed to settle, as if fascinated, on one
object—the mysterious gig, in which the victim and
his murderer had driven down. Whether it was that

the use of such a vehicle in such a tragedy was without
precedent, or that its homely, sociable character added
a new horror to the murder, or that there was something
piquant or *bizarre* in the idea, there could be no doubt
that *the gig*, jogging along its course, appeared all
through the tragedy in almost a spectral way. Numbers had seen and noted it, as well as its " bald-faced
horse with the white feet," ostlers, innkeepers, farm-
labourers. Nay those who had not seen, recalled hearing the sound of its wheels. Drivers of carts and
coaches met it, generally on the wrong side, flying by.
A patrole heard it approaching at a furious gallop,
challenged it in the regular form. But it flew past
him with a riotous greeting from the driver, " Good
night, patrole ! " It was like the night *malle-poste*
which lends such an element of romance to the
" Courier of Lyons." It was of the kind known as a
" yellow Stanhope," and was hired in the yard of the
present " Golden Cross," at Charing Cross, to which
the horse quaintly described as " having a blaze in his
face," was brought back after his midnight ride nearly
smothered in dirt and very much distressed, while blood
was noticed by the ostler at the bottom of the gig. The
"bald-faced horse" also unconsciously took his share in
the villainies of the night. The woman who had been
watching from her window noticed the figures with a
lantern moving in the garden, and presently saw the
horse led from his stable. The animal was taken to

the lonely lane and the body thrown across his back.
He carried his burden to the garden pond, into which
it was flung.

Another of the accused, Probert, also was the
owner of a gig, a brown one, with an iron-grey horse,
which on the fatal night also made the journey down
to Elstree. It was to have met Thurtell on the
way but missed him. This particular equipage is
memorable, as having supplied a new and expressive
word to the language. Mr. Carlyle, in a note to his
article on Boswell, quotes, with enjoyment, an answer
in a dialogue which occurred, as he believed, during
the trial, in reference to this gig. A witness being
asked why he described Mr. Probert as a " respectable
man," gave the memorable answer, " *because he kept a
gig.*" This delighted our sage, whose theory of
clothes it exactly fitted, and he proceeded to coin that
singular word " gigmanity " or " gigman " and " gigmanship," which we often find used with relish in his
writings. It is strange, however, that no sign whatever of the dialogue can be found in the reports of the
trial. No one speaks of Probert's position, who was
indeed not on trial. In the report, however, furnished
by the *Morning Chronicle*, there is a passage to be
found, which seems to have been the foundation of the
dictum. Describing Mr. Probert's position, it adds,
" he always maintained an appearance of respectability
and kept a gig," which implies a connection between

respectability and the vehicle. It is hard to part from tho dramatic dialogue, and the naive reply of the intelligent witness.

Gill's Hill cottage became a perfect show, and thousands came down to look at it, paying a shilling for admission. There was an auction presently of the furniture, and the auctioneer, to enhance prices, would invite attention to the fact, that the sofa was the " identical " one on which Hunt " lay down " on the night of the murder. It was described as " a green couch with cotton cover, squab, and bolster, and stained with blood." It fetched 3*l.* 10*s.* A particular interest attached to Probert's " brown gig," which fetched 19*l.*

Before the trial came on the managers of the Surrey Theatre announced that " in order to convey a more impressive sense of sad reality, and the more effectively to produce the emotions for which it was intended," they were going to produce a piece called

" THE GAMBLERS,"

which they would " embellish with facsimilies (*sic*) of the scenes now so much the object of general interest, on an extensive scale, *peculiar to the limits of the stage.*" Here too was the succession of the scenery as required by the author, including " correct views taken on the spot," by Messrs. Tomkins, Walker, &c., " who have been expressly engaged for this piece."

" Probert's cottage and garden, Gill's Hill Lane, and

Gap, 'The Bald-faced Stag' on the Edgeware Road, where will be introduced

THE IDENTICAL HORSE AND GIG!"

In consequence of this, attraction it was no surprise to learn that "the free list must be suspended during the present week."

Unluckily, not the free list only but the piece itself had to be " suspended," for the friends of the accused, considering the performance an indecent proceeding and likely to prejudice them at the trial, moved for a criminal information against the "enterprising" managers, who thought it advisable to take the piece out of the bills "in the full tide of success," it being suggested to them that "it was likely not only to wound domestic feelings, but to prejudice the public against certain unfortunate individuals." Thus the managers, in defiance of "their own notions of the subject, had resolved to withdraw it until such time as the incidents shall no longer *coincide* with the appalling occurrences of the day."

To make all complete, and let the mysterious power of the gig assert itself to the very end, after Thurtell had been duly "finished" by the hangman, his remains were to be handed over to the surgeons "for the benefit of science," as in the case of Mrs. Gamp's husband. After an interval some persons arrived, and placed the body in a sack, as he had placed Weare's. It was then put into a gig which it was noted was exactly of the pattern of the original gig, and driven away to Bartholomew's.

Among other odd incidents and accidents of the case were these : Thurtell's father, a respectable citizen of Norwich, was elected mayor about the time of the trial. There was a fellow of Caius College, Cambridge, bearing the same name, who, it was understood, was his brother. Hunt's brother, a popular Garden singer, made his *début* in Dublin, as Captain Macheath, on the day the trial began ; and, strange to say, was received in the most cordial and sympathetic fashion, though the relationship was well known.

Amateurs of what is called the " Catnach" literature, know that the grandest *coups* of this enterprising person were made in connection with this case. His broadsheets, containing details of the murder, last dying speech, &c., were sold in thousands. When public interest was fairly exhausted, he sent out other sheets headed " *We-are* alive again ! " During the trial Mr. Chitty seems to have anticipated Counsellor Phillips in importing his own personal convictions into the case. In taking a legal objection, he said, " It was his solemn opinion before God ! " " Oh ! oh ! " interrupted Mr. Justice Park, and when he came to give his judgment, added the rebuke, " I must hope that in future counsel will not appeal to the Deity for the sincerity of their opinions, for such an appeal gives a sort of sanction, like an oath, to their opinion."

When Thurtell was ascending the scaffold, he begged the sheriff to let him know the result of "the mill" between Spring and Langham. When he was told that Spring was the victor, " God bless him," he exclaimed, " he is an old friend of mine."

We have quoted the " Catnach " ballad that was sung about the streets, one verse of which used to be repeated with enjoyment by Sir Walter Scott :—

> They cut his throat from ear to ear,
> His brains they battered in,
> His name was Mr. William Weare,
> And he lived in Lyon's Inn.

But there are other versicles almost as good, and which are worth preserving :—

> Confined he was in Hertford gaol,
> A jury did him try ;
> And worthy Mr. Justice Park
> Condemned him for to die.

> Now Mr. Andrews he did strive,
> And Mr. Chitty too,
> To save the wicked wretch alive,
> But no, it would not do.

It was said, however, that these lines had not the genuine " Catnach " inspiration, and were the work of Theodore Hook or Mr. John Wilson Croker.

In proof of the extraordinary interest excited by this remarkable case, it may be mentioned, that a reporter of a superior cast, who was writing with Elia and

L 2

others for the *London Magazine*, went specially down to Hertford, and furnished a very striking account to his journal. This was a person of tact and observation, and his description goes far beyond the trivial " photographic " details usually furnished in such cases, and which are presumed by their abundance of details to bring the incidents vividly before the reader. In this account a regular drama seems to unfold itself before us.

The extraordinary fantastic and even weird-like character of everything in the case has been remarked. Among other singularities, it was noted that solitary as the spot was, and desperate as was the murder, the actors and witnesses all " fell into clusters." The murderers were in a cluster : the farmer that heard the pistol, had his wife, child, and nurse with him : there were two labourers at work in the lane on the morning after : there was a merry party in the cottage : there were clusters of publicans and ostlers, witnesses of the gang's progress in their blood journey ; and the gigs and pistols, even the very knives ran in pairs. It seemed as though the victim, Weare, was to be the only solitary thing of that fatal night. Again, all through the night before the trial, Hertford presented a strange scene of confusion. There was a noise of men sitting up and walking the streets : chaises were clattering in. The innkeepers were up all night. Everywhere, as it was described, a ceaseless buzz was heard, and endless iteration of the words "Thurtell," "Probert," "Hunt," &c.

There was delay before the prisoners appeared, owing to some hesitation as to removing their irons, which was thought a dangerous step. Hunt appeared dressed in black with a white neckerchief, and the "carefully arranged disorder of his hair" was remarked. He appeared to be a poorish creature, weak and womanly in the expression of his features. "Beside him stood the murderer, complete in frame, face, eye, and daring. The contrast was singularly striking, indeed fatal, by the opinion which it created of Thurtell. He was· dressed in a plum-coloured frock-coat, with a drab waistcoat and white breeches. The lower part of his face appeared to hang like a load to the head, and to make it drop like the mastiff's jowl. The upper lip was long and large, his nose was rather small, and his eyes, too, were small and buried deep under his protruding forehead, so indeed as to defy you to detect their colour. The forehead extremely strong, bony, and knotted." Nor was there a farcical element absent. As when the cook, Woodroofe, was asked by the counsel "if the supper was postponed," she answered, "*No, it was pork.*"

When Probert was called the most intense excitement prevailed. Hunt stood up and was much agitated; Thurtell eyed him sternly and composedly. Probert's face was marked with deceit in every lineament. The

eyes are like those of a vicious horse, and the lips thick
and sensual. His forehead recedes villainously in
amongst a bush of black grizzly hair, and his ears project out of the like cover. His head and legs are too
small for his body, and altogether he is an awkward,
dastardly, and wretched-looking animal. He gave his
evidence in a brazen style.

The closing incident, when Thurtell made his
wonderful display, was truly dramatic. "The slow,
solid, and appalling tones," said a listener, "in which
he wrung out the last words can never be imagined; he
had worked himself up into a great actor. He clung
to every separate word as though every syllable had
the power to buoy up his sinking life. The final word,
GOD, was thrown up with an almost gigantic energy,
and he stood after its utterance, with his arms extended and his face protruded, as if the spell of the
sound were yet on him, and as though he dared not
move lest he should disturb the echoing appeal. Yet
this had all been learnt by heart, and the month before
he had rehearsed it to Pierce Egan, being assured that
with his gentlemanly dress and manner it would carry
him through."

While the miserable Hunt was completely prostrated
by the sentence, Thurtell—as the directions for his
own dissection were being given by the judge—
"actually consumed the pinch of snuff which had, up
to that moment, been pausing in his fingers."

GILL'S HILL COTTAGE.

CHAPTER VIII.

THE CATO STREET PLOT.

THOSE who are familiar with the social history of the first quarter of the century, must often smile as they read or hear of the forebodings of those who now bewail the increase of radical violence, and the spread of revolutionary opinion. The contrast with the genuine discontent, and insurrectionary fury of those days is extraordinary. Then there were conspiracies of a dangerous kind, fearful plots for risings and massacres, conflicts often between soldiers and armed men, personal insults to the royal family ; hootings, and discharges of stones at their carriage, with other significant exhibitions of fury. We are told of loaves of bread being found smeared with blood at the gate of the Regent's Palace, with the legend,

> . . . . . *Bread,*
> *Or the Regent's Head !*

The government of Lord Sidmouth became conspicuous for its vigorous mode of dealing with the disorders, and the whole train of spies, informers, &c.,

were in full activity. On their testimony abundant convictions were obtained, and it was not surprising that the government was held in much odium for using such foul agencies. Castles, who figured in the case we are now following, was lashed in these bitter verses of Charles Lamb :—

THE THREE GRAVES.

Close by the ever-burning brimstone beds,
Where Bedloe, Oates, and Judas hide their heads,
I saw great Satan, like a sexton stand,
With his intolerable spade in hand,
Digging three graves. Of coffin-shape they were,
For those who coffinless must enter there
With unblest rites. The shrouds were of but cloth,
Which Clotho weaveth in her blackest wrath ;
The dismal tinct oppressed the eye that dwelt
Upon it long, like darkness to be felt.
The pillows to these baleful beds were toads,
Large, living, livid, melancholy toads,
Whose softness shocked. Worms of all monstrous size
Crawl'd round ; and one, uncoil'd, which never dies.
A doleful bell, malleating despair,
Was always ringing in the heavy air ;
And all about the detestable pit
Strange headless ghosts, and quarter'd forms did flit ;
Rivers of blood from dripping traitors spilt,
By treachery slung from poverty to guilt.
I asked the fiend for whom these rites were meant ?
" Those graves," quoth he, " when life's brief oil is spent,
When the dark night comes and they're sinking bedwards,
I mean for Castles, Oliver and Edwards."

Truly an awful denunciation.

This wretch Castles had become concerned with Dr.

Watson, and others, in a conspiracy formed in 1816, of a very bloody kind. It was nothing short of seizing on the government, setting fire to the principal buildings, sabring the soldiers, &c. These men were in earnest and laid their plans in the most elaborate way. Some of the devices seemed of a childish kind—among others, a cohort of a hundred young women was to be sent on in front with the object of attracting or distracting the soldiery. Pikes were manufactured according to a pattern, and designs for a diabolical engine—a low cart, with a number of scythes sticking out from the wheels—and which was to be driven in among the cavalry soldiers—were prepared. Attempts were made at a propaganda among the dock-labourers and others, but without success. This Castles was the chief agent in these manœuvres, and, when all was ripe, communicated with the Government. His attempt, however, to implicate " Orator " Hunt, fatally damaged the case, and all the accused, among whom was Thistlewood, were acquitted.

Thistlewood's history was an eventful one. His father was a respectable land-steward in Lincolnshire, who obtained a " pair of colours " for him in the army. After serving in the West Indies he threw up his commission and led a wandering life, and as an adventurer found his way to America, and thence to France, where he arrived just after the fall of

Robespierre. He then joined the French army, and became known as a competent officer and good swordsman. But he had also imbibed all the more ferocious principles of the revolution. On the peace he returned to England, where a tide of ill-luck seemed to pursue him, and drive him downwards. His first wife had a fortune of 10,000*l.*, but it proved that she had only a life-interest in the same, and she died within a year. He sold for 10,000*l.* some property which he possessed to a person at Durham, but who became bankrupt before paying over the money. Thus disappointed, and having many grievances against the Government, and becoming addicted to gaming, he gradually sank into abject poverty, and presently began to conspire. His violence, indeed, it seemed that nothing but a violent death could check. He actually sent a challenge to Lord Sidmouth on account of some language spoken of him, for which act he was punished by imprisonment. In 1820 we find him connected with persons of a lower and more ruffianly class, of which the principals were Ings, a butcher, Davidson, a man of colour, and many more. Dismissing any idea so Utopian as a general rising in the metropolis, they devised a more practical but uniquely horrible plan, perhaps the most atrocious scheme that ever disgraced criminal annals in England, from the bloodthirsty spirit in which it was conceived, and from the truculent, thoroughgoing fashion in which the ruffians set themselves to execute it. They determined to murder all the ministers in one batch, as it were, seizing on an opportunity when they should be assembled together, and went deliberately to work to arrange their plans.

Lord Sidmouth and the other ministers recollected afterwards that on getting out of their carriages when going to dinner-parties, they had often noticed, in the dark, figures watching them—the conspirators thus trying to make themselves familiar with their appearance. Thistlewood succeeded in enrolling over twenty desperadoes—who were ready for any bloody work, and had resolution enough to carry it out in any way.

A short way up the Edgeware Road we turn into a mean street, still known by the odd name of Cato Street. It was then a lonely, far-off district, and was appropriately close to Tyburn. In this lonely street was a disused stable, with a loft over it, and the neighbours had lately noticed men arriving with sacks, and ascending to the loft by a steep ladder. One of the spies, Edwards, who had joined the conspirators for the purposes of his trade, regularly conveyed news of their proceedings to ministers. Wednesday night, the 23rd of February, he reported, was fixed upon for the execution of the hideous plan. On that night it had been announced that a "Cabinet dinner" was to be given at Lord Harrowby's house, in Grosvenor Square. One of the gang was to knock at the door, with a parcel just about the moment when the ministers were sitting down to the dinner-table. As soon as the door was opened the others were to rush in, bind or kill the servants, and then burst into the dining-room and massacre the Cabinet. To one man was alloted the special task of cutting off Lords Castlereagh's and Sidmouth's heads, and of bringing them off in a bag brought for the purpose. The ministers determined that the dinner should go on as ordered, though they were not prepared to face the risk of assembling at the house. So cautious were they that even the servants were not let into the secret, but continued their preparations for the banquet. Such was the savage and brutal element conspicuous in all plans of these "friends of liberty," and it was no doubt suggested by the French Revolution.

The courage displayed in dealing with these villains was extraordinary. It was determined to secure them on the evening which they had fixed upon. Mr. Birnie, the magistrate, himself directed the party, which consisted of a strong force of officers, including Ruthven, Wright, and others of known resolution. They were to be supported by a body of foot-guards; but, unluckily, these were not ready at the time, and the police proceeded without them. It was said later that this was owing to some jealousy on the part of the

force, who purposely started earlier. All day long
Ruthven and others were watching the stable from a
public-house opposite. Notwithstanding, the plan had
all but miscarried owing to the attack being delayed
till past seven o'clock, the hour fixed for the dinner,
when the non-arrival of the guests had already excited
the suspicions of the gang.

The moment having arrived, the police surrounded
the place. They met a sentry at the foot of the
ladder, who was at once secured; and then Ruthven
ascended, followed by Ellis, Smithers, and others of
the patrole. On bursting open the door they found
the whole gang, nearly thirty in number, in the act
of hastily arming themselves before setting out, the
room being filled with swords, cutlasses and other
weapons.

On bursting in, Ruthven called out that he was a
police officer, and bade all surrender. Thistlewood was
next the door, a sword in his hand, and when Smithers
advanced on him ran him through the body. The
unfortunate officer fell into the arms of his companion,
exclaiming, " O God, I am— ;" but died before he
could finish the sentence. Ruthven tried to discharge
his pistol at Thistlewood, but it missed fire. West-
cott, another officer, was hit in the arm by a shot from
Thistlewood. Wright was stabbed in the side by
another of the gang, while Brookes was shot in the
shoulder by Ings, the butcher. The lights had been

put out, so this bloody conflict was carried on in the dark.

The Guards, who had at last arrived at the critical moment, now rushed in, and found the room filled with smoke. Captain FitzClarence,[1] who led the party, had

---

[1] Many years later, Lord Adolphus FitzClarence, brother of the officer concerned in the Cato Street adventures, was on shore at the Cape. but was unexpectedly summoned back to his ship, the *Pallas* frigate.

After driving some miles, as Lord William Lennox tells us, he came to a turnpike, and the usual payment was demanded. In the hurry of departure the gallant blue-jacket had forgotten to take his purse with him ; and upon beginning to explain who he was, he had the gate closed in his face. "I am a Captain in the Navy, and command the *Pallas* frigate."

" That won't do," responded the other. " It's no use ; if you haven't got any money, you must return and get it, for without that you can't pass here." So saying, he locked the gate and entered his small hut.

FitzClarence now found himself in what the Americans term " an awful fix."

" Look you, my man," said he, " you will see by this button that I belong to the Navy, and I pledge you my word that the toll and a trifle for yourself shall be sent by me, or given to you on my return."

"'We've had so many tricks played," responded the other, " and my orders are so peremptory, that I dare not disobey them."

" Is there anybody near here I could appeal to ?" continued the Captain. " If so, just send and say that Captain FitzClarence of the *Pallas* frigate—"

" FitzClarence ! " interrupted the man, " are you Captain Fitz-Clarence ? I know that name well."

" I am—"

" Jump in—I'll advance the money out of my own pocket, that's not against orders."

Adolphus was completely taken aback, and looked steadfastly at the man, trying to remember if ever he had seen him before.

a narrow escape, as one of the ruffians was about to discharge a pistol at him, when his sergeant, rushing forward, received the shot in his arm. A terrible scene of disorder followed.

Unluckily, the bulk of the party succeeded in escaping, but nine were captured. Arms and ammunition for at least 100 men were found and conveyed to Bow Street.

The following morning the officers discovered the hiding-place of Thistlewood at No. 8, White Street, Moorfields. Lavender headed this party, and first surrounding the house, they broke into an upper room, where he was discovered in bed with his clothes on, and some ball-cartridges in his pocket. Others were speedily captured, and in Ing's room were found 1000 ball-cartridges.

At the trial the prisoners all made inflammatory speeches, Thistlewood appealing to the example of

"Look here," said the gate-keeper. "I now see a likeness between you and that officer who captured us in Cato Street. He was kind and gentle to us, and treated us very differently from those Bow Street Officers."

"He is my brother."

"That's enough, send the money back at your convenience. My offence has been forgiven, and I am now doing all in my power to show my gratitude to the government who appointed me to this post."

FitzClarence shook the man by the hand, re-entered his vehicle, joined his ship, arranged the business for which he had been summoned, and returned to Cape Town. I need hardly add that the money advanced was returned with interest—in the shape of a handsome present.

Brutus, and inveighing against the informer Edwards. As may be imagined, all were found guilty and sentenced to be executed on the following Monday.

Some visitors who obtained leave to visit the condemned were greatly struck with Thistlewood's calmness. " The governor approached the prisoner, and asked him some question which we did not hear, as, not wishing to obtrude ourselves upon such an awful occasion, and being only desirous of seeing Thistlewood, we remained near the door.

" ' Won't the gentlemen come forward ? ' said the prisoner, in the calmest manner imaginable, and conversed with his visitors in a careless, indifferent fashion."

The scene at the execution was most extraordinary from the behaviour of the criminals. It is said that Thistlewood made that strange, significant remark, " Now I am going to find out this great secret."

The chaplain had offered his ministrations, which were rejected with contempt by Thistlewood. Ings, the butcher, seemed to be in a sort of delirium as they ascended the gallows, shouting, " Come, my old cock ! it will soon be over." He sucked an orange, laughed, and sang,—

" O give me death or liberty ! "

He then yelled and danced, and sent his remembrance to King George IV., to the disgust of his companions.

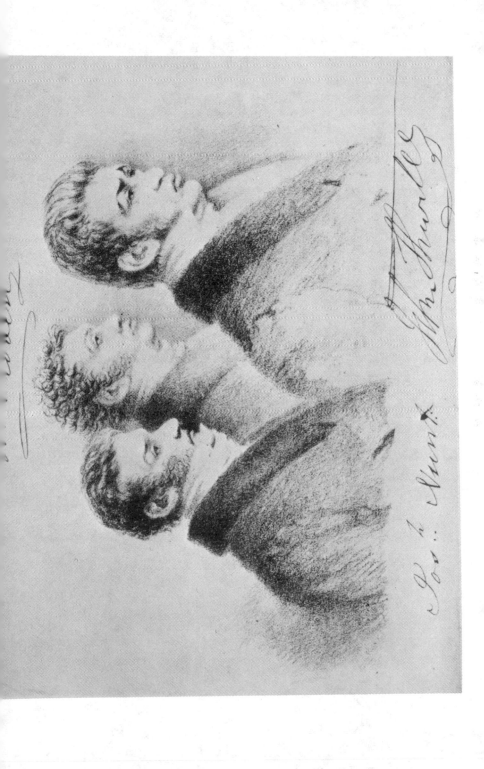

The crowd were sympathetic, and voices were heard to cry, " God bless you, Mr. Thistlewood."

After the hanging came a barbarous exhibition. A masked figure came on the scaffold, and proceeded, according to the sentence, to cut off their heads—an operation performed so scientifically that it was assumed he was a surgeon. Such was the episode, painful and shocking in all its details from the beginning to the end.

Mr. Raikes, the diarist and " man about town," who took care to see whatever was worth seeing, long after related to the Duke of Wellington at Walmer, the incidents of the execution which he witnessed. They were of a rather exceptional kind.

" A friend proposed to Alvanley and myself to go with him to the sheriff's room in Newgate. It was the first execution I ever saw, and shall be the last. It was a fine morning, and the crowd in the Old Bailey was perhaps, greater than ever was assembled on such an occasion; all the house-tops were covered with spectators; and when we first looked out of the window of the sheriff's room, there was nothing to be seen but the scaffold, surrounded by an immense ocean of human heads, all gazing upon that one single object. At length the procession issued out from the debtor's door, and the six culprits came on, one after the other, and were successively tied up to the gibbet. Thistlewood came first, looking as pale

as death, but without moving a muscle of his features
or attempting to utter a word, except that when the
rope had been adjusted round the neck of him who
was next him, he said, in a low tone to him, ' We shall
soon know the grand secret.' Ings, the butcher,
appeared in a great state of excitement, almost as if
under the influence of liquor ; he gave several huzzas,
and shouted out to the crowd, ' Liberty for ever ! '
twice or thrice, but it was evidently a feint to try to
interest the bystanders. The last in this sad rank
was a dirty-looking black man, who alone seemed to
be impressed with a sense of his awful situation ; his
lips were in continual motion, and he was evidently
occupied in silent prayer. At this moment, one of
the gentlemen of the press, who had posted himself
in the small enclosure, close to the foot of the scaffold, looked up to Thistlewood with a paper and
pencil in his hand, and said, ' Mr. Thistlewood, if you
have anything to say, I shall be happy to take it
down, and communicate it to the public.' The other
made him no answer, but gave him a look. As they
were about to be launched into eternity, a well-dressed
man on the roof of one of the opposite houses, got up
from his seat, and looking at Thistlewood exclaimed
in a very loud but agitated voice, ' God bless you !
God Almighty bless you ! ' Thistlewood slowly
turned his head to the quarter whence the voice came,
without moving his body, and as slowly reverted to

his former position, always with the same fixed, impassible countenance. The caps were then pulled down, the drop fell, and after some struggles they all ceased to live. The law prescribed that their heads should be severed from their bodies, and held up to public view as the heads of traitors. The executioner had neglected to bring any instrument for the purpose, and we in the sheriff's room were horrified at seeing one of the assistants enter, and take from a cupboard a large carving-knife, which was to be used instead of a more regular instrument. When we were able to leave the prison, which was not for some time, on account of the immense crowd, I drove to Seymour Place, and found —— at breakfast, and gave him an account of the scene; when I ended by mentioning the apparent devotion of the black man, he observed, ' He was quite right ; you should never give away a chance.' "

The duke listened with much interest to this narrative, said it was very curious, and the observation of the friend a singular trait of character.

Nearly twenty years before Thistlewood's conspiracy, another man, quite as desperate, had contrived a plot for the assassination of the king, which was happily frustrated. This was Colonel Despard, one of those disappointed men, like Bellingham, who had brooded over grievances, fancied or real, until he had worked himself into an insane frenzy of revenge. The incidents of the case are familiar; but the way in which the plot was discovered is curious. This is told in a letter of Queen Caroline's—which is given in Mr. Harcourt's unpublished collection of letters from the Royal family to his ancestor, Lord Harcourt :—

" 20 Nov., 1802.

" .... We have indeed reason, my dearest Lady Harcourt, to thank God for the fresh proof of his goodness in this horrible & abominable Conspiracy being found out. The K. has never named it to anybody ; but every body else talks of it..... The affair was discovered thus. A man was guilty of Felony; & in searching for that man, they entered a house, where they found Col. D—— & 29 other men. The moment the Bow Street runner appeared, one of the men dropped a *list;* which, thank God, was taken, as well as all their papers. This atrocious deed was to have taken place on next Tuesday, when it is intended my Father should go to the House; & when they had dispatched Him, the intention was to enter the Queen's House, & make *mince meat* of us all. To attack the Tower, arm themselves ; & then march to the Bank, open the Prisons, & turn all into anarchy and confusion."

CHAPTER IX.

THE QUEEN'S FUNERAL IN 1821.

ORDERLY as the current of life has always run in London—its people being of sober and decorous habits—the great city has still witnessed some very strange and exciting incidents in its streets. These have varied in their character, and within the last month the engagements between the police and the organized crowds for the possession of Trafalgar Square offered many dramatic episodes. The London mob, however, to exhibit any genuine or characteristic manifestation, must have its sympathies and prejudices thoroughly roused and inflamed. The unhappy story of Queen Caroline—the unworthy object of so much devotion and popularity—was on the whole creditable to the instinct of the crowd who espoused her cause because they considered her to be a helpless woman oppressed by a king, ministers, and the great and powerful. They held by her with much constancy through all her persecution, and when she died, chose the occasion of her funeral for a striking display of their passions and sympathies.

When this event occurred, which was on August 7th, 1821, the king was away, being saluted with the frantic shouts of his Irish subjects. But though her dissolution brought him release from the annoyance and anxieties of many years, it was felt that the obsequies were likely to be the occasion of a display which was certain to lead to disorders and confusion. Her decease took place at Hammersmith, at Brandenburg house, which had been the residence of an eccentric being, who also had passed through many troubles, and whose character was in some points not unlike the Queen's—viz., Lady Craven, the English Margravine of Anspach. Her last moments were associated with much that was pathetic, and it was said that the foreign princess was crushed and broken by the repulse she had met with on the day of the coronation. Mr. Brougham expressed a hope that she felt herself easier and better. She answered, " Oh, no, my dear Mr. Brougham, I know I shall die, and I do not at all regret it." In the course of the evening she said, " I do not know whether I shall suffer bodily pain in dying, but I can assure you I shall quit this world without regret; I have no reason to be attached to life." She added, that in this world, whether in England or abroad, the rancour of her persecutors would always beset her, and it was only in another world she could look for peace and justice. She expressed the deepest regret that she was so little able to reward those faithful servants who had stood by her in her difficul-

ties, but hoped that Government would not let them
want.   " England," she said, " has certainly been to
me a land of sorrow and persecution, but I know how
to love those faithful English who have always
sympathized with my sorrow, and have done all in
their power to defeat the malice of my persecutors."
Her enemies had been for years plotting and conspir-
ing to destroy her.   " At last," said she, " they *have
destroyed me*, but I forgive them.   I die in peace with
all mankind."

On Sunday, the 6th, she asked that Mr. Busch should
come and measure her for her coffin; the servants
made excuses; she told them he must make the shell
of cedar wood.   All through she behaved with astound-
ing firmness and calmness.   Observing by her bed-
side Dr. Holland—afterwards the well-known Sir
Henry Holland—who, during her illness, had often
expressed a hope of her recovery, she said with a smile
and accent of the greatest sweetness, " Well, my dear
doctor, what do you think now ? "   A few hours before
her death she observed, " The doctors do not understand my malady ; it is here " (laying her hand upon
her heart), " but I will be silent; my lips will never
make it known."

At half-past eleven o'clock on the 7th, this bulletin
was issued :—

" Her Majesty departed this life at twenty-five minutes past
ten o'clock.

" M. BAILLIE, H. AINSLIE, W. G. MATON,
P. WARREN, H. HOLLAND."

By her will the body was directed to be conveyed to Brunswick, and as Harwich was the port at which it was embarked, the Government was conscious that the passage through London offered an opportunity for a display of devotion and attachment which would be disagreeable to his Majesty. In our time the happiest mode of treating such an awkward incident is toleration and sufferance. But ministers determined to "put it down with a strong hand." The most stringent orders were issued that the procession should *not* pass through London, and in spite of the protests of executors and others, the Government took complete control of all the arrangements, ordered soldiers to be in readiness, and even appointed their own undertakers. The Lord Mayor and Corporation, however, made preparations to receive the funeral in the city, and all her friends and followers were determined that she *should* be taken through the city, and it was generally felt or feared that there would be a serious struggle.

August 15th was fixed as the day of the solemnity, and on both sides elaborate preparations were made. At the last moment the ministers announced their decision that the procession, coming from Hammersmith, should turn off at Kensington, going up Church Street till it reached Tyburn and the New Road, and should then be directed by Islington and Romford, thus avoiding Piccadilly, the Strand, and the city itself.

When this programme became known it was determined the gentlemen who proposed to attend the procession on horseback should meet at Hyde Park
Corner at six on Tuesday morning. Persons were to
be stationed at every outlet by which it was possible
for the remains to be carried ; and, should the procession not pass by Hyde Park Corner, the intelligence
was to be communicated with as much speed as
possible, all which looked ominous enough. On the
other side the Bow Street magistrates were in readiness—the Life Guards and other troops were to
attend, and it was determined to force through, if
necessary, the arrangement determined upon.

At six o'clock precisely, a squadron of the Oxford
Blues, under the command of Captain Bouverie, arrived
from their barracks, Regent's Park (which they left at
a quarter before five o'clock), at Brandenburg House,
and rode up the avenue from the lodge, and formed
into a line in front of the house. The helmets of the
officers were partially covered with black crape. The
gates of Brandenburg House were kept by one of the
officers of Bow Street, who admitted only those whose
names were on a list.

Mr. Bailey, the Government undertaker, now gave
orders for every person to be in readiness to depart,
and directed the Lord Chamberlain's officers to deliver
up the body to the persons in waiting. The disorderly
struggle now began with the following scene :—

First the well-known Dr. Lushington came forward and protested:—

"Sir George Nayler and Mr. Bailey," he said; "you know what has been the expressed wish of her late Majesty's executors, and also the disgraceful conduct that has been persisted in by his Majesty's Government (in such direct opposition to the known will of her late Majesty) in forcing into the funeral procession a great body of soldiers. I enter my solemn protest against the removal of her Majesty's body, in right of the legal power which is vested in me by her late Majesty, as executor. Proper arrangements for the funeral, and the long journey, and voyage by sea have not been made; there has not been time for it, and I command that the body be not removed till the arrangements suitable to the rank and dignity of the deceased are made."

Mr. Bailey: I have orders from Government to remove the body, which is now in custody of the Lord Chamberlain; I must do my duty, the body must be removed.

Dr. Lushington: Touch the body at your peril. You have no power to act contrary to the will of her Majesty's executors; and they do their duty by protesting against such an usurpation.

Mr. Bailey: You do not mean to use violence, and prevent by force the removal of the body, I trust, Dr. Lushington?

Dr. Lushington : I shall use no violence myself.

Mr. Bailey : Nor recognize it in others ?

Dr. Lushington : I shall neither assist in, nor recommend violence; nor shall I join the procession in my official character of executor, but merely go as a private individual, to show my respect for her Majesty.

Mr. Bailey : Very well, sir; I shall discharge my duty firmly, and I trust properly.

At the door Mr. Wilde, afterwards Lord Chancellor, also assailed the undertaker "in warm language,"— protesting against the service. Bailey reasonably complained, "that every impediment was thrown in his way by those who ought to assist him." The other declared that he would not go to the procession in the route mentioned by Mr. Bailey, nor should the body be taken, except by force ; and, when the body stopped at the first stage, he would have the body removed according to his own will and that of her late Majesty, without squadrons of soldiers. Mr. Bailey said that his orders were imperative, and that nothing should prevent him doing his duty. He would take upon himself the peril of removing the body.

In which menacing state of things the procession set out. It was a very imposing one, innumerable mourning coaches, soldiers, heralds, &c. All the road from Hammersmith was lined with spectators. But the rain was pouring down. All went well and decently until Kensington was reached, when there was a halt at the foot of Church Street next the church. Up to this moment the route had been kept a profound secret, and the public generally believed that the diversion from the main road would not take place until Hyde Park Corner was reached, when the procession would be turned into Park Lane. But at Kensington a strong body of constables were seen drawn across the High Road, and were diverting the leading carriages up Church Street. Instantly shouts were raised of " Shame! shame! *Through the city! Through the city!* " As these remonstrances were not attended to, the mob proceeded to enforce its wishes. A scuffle followed which brought the procession to a stand-still. A communication was made to the superior powers lower down in the procession; and while this was taking place, the people assembled in Church Street set to work with an alacrity and success that were truly surprising, to render ineffectual an attempt to pass that way, by blocking up and cutting up the street. Waggons, carts, &c., were brought and placed across the streets; the linch-pins were taken out, and some of the wheels were taken off, and all the horses were removed. Higher up the stones were removed, trenches were dug in the roadway; even the water-pipes were opened. Crow-bars and pokers were at work, and the workmen were cheered with cans of porter, and with the applause of the multitude. A stoppage of as impassable a

Printed by F. Major, 4 Greenland Place Cromer St.   Price 1/. plain - 2/. colored

(N.º 2.)

CATO STREET CONSPIRACY.

INTERIOR VIEW of the **HAY-LOFT** where Thistlewood & the Conspirators assembled to assassinate His Majesty's Ministers on the night of Wednesday the 23.ʳᵈ of Feb.ʳ 1820.

. Carpenters Bench on which the candles, Daggers, Guns, Pistols, & Grenades were placed, previous to delivery.

. Ladder by which the Police Officers ascended, - very narrow.

. The exact Spot where Smithers the Police Officer (one of the Patrole) was killed.

D. Two Apertures from the Hay Loft to the Hay-rack, thro' which it is supposed many of the Conspirators escaped in the Dark.

. Window looking to Cato Street.

. Door of the Hay Loft as seen from the Street firmly closed.

. Shutter used for the window.

. Entrance to the small room, into which Thistlewood retreated, & where he stabbed Smithers.

. A small Room, not used for any particular purpose.

K. Rail upon which the Conspirators mounted to escape by the back window.

. Drawer with marks of blood.

M. Top of a large Chest.   (Size of the Room 16 ft. by 12 ft.)

nature was thus created in less than half an hour, as ever was raised by a retreating army to check the pursuit of an enemy.

In this crisis a soldier was forwarded to town with a despatch to Lord Liverpool for orders. As Mr. Bailey, the conductor of the procession, would not take upon himself the responsibility of moving in any other direction than that laid down in the written directions, the whole cavalcade halted until new instructions arrived.

Meanwhile numerous crowds had assembled at Hyde Park, anxiously looking out for the arrival of the procession. They were distracted with uncertainty, for there nothing could be ascertained of the route intended. Cries were raised, " Let our lives be lost before we let her pass this way." A voice exclaimed, " Sir Robert Baker, remember you have not read the Riot Act." A soldier from the roadside of the gate rode up to cut down those hanging on to the gate, when one of the committee-men rode up between them and interposed. The cry was now, " Horsemen ! horsemen ! stand in the gate." Several persons now got up to the gate, and though the soldiers were not three yards from it, several large stones were thrown at the military, one of which struck a soldier on the breast; and the cry of " murder " still continuing, Sir Robert Baker said, " Open the gate, and we will go on," The gate was opened, Sir Robert Baker came out, and headed the procession, and it proceeded on towards Hyde Park Corner, the people crying out, "The City! the City! Nothing but the City! Fly to Hyde Park Corner; block up, block up; every man in the breach." The people now began to fly towards Hyde Park Corner, when they reached the gates they were closed, and the military were stationed close to the gates inside the park. The gates were soon opened sufficiently for them to come out one by one; they were then closed again, and the military rode through the crowd to Park Lane, with their horse-pistols in their hands.

When the procession reached Hyde Park Corner, a troop of Life Guards was drawn up; at whose appearance much dissatisfaction was expressed by the people. A thousand voices exclaimed, "Why are the soldiers here?" and the hissings and hootings accompanied and followed them along the road. The soldiery bore those attacks at first with apparent good-humour. The Life Guards, who had before signalized themselves in the same neighbourhood, were not now so gentle, and struck with the flat of their swords some of those persons who reproached them. They attempted to force, *vi et armis*, a passage up Park Lane; but the dense mass of people, and the coaches, carts, and cars, which in a very few minutes were thrown across the road, rendered their efforts wholly abortive. Here there was a delay for a few minutes; until at length the officer of the guard having consulted with some

Printed by E. Mosss, 4 Greenland Place Cromer St.

(N.º 1.)

VIEW OF CATO STREET.

DESCRIPTION OF THE PLATE.

A. Front view of the Stable in Cato Street occupied by the Conspirators on the night of Wednesday, the 23.rd of Feby. 1820, taken from the Blacksmith's Shop opposite, the entrance to which is by the Gateway from John St.

B. The Stable Door.

C.C. The Coach house Doors.

D. The window of the small room into which Thistlewood retreated.

E.F. The door & window belonging to the Hayloft. — The words "Cato Street" are seen on the adjoining House. The Horse & Groom Public House, where the Inquest on the dead body of Smithers the Police Officer was held on Friday, Feby. 25.th may be seen on the right hand side of the Gateway leading from Cato Street to John Street.

persons near him, the procession was ordered to turn, and it entered the park at the corner gate, and proceeded towards Cumberland Gate. The Life Guards were drawn up six on each side of the gate. The appearance of this fresh supply of military force occasioned the most boisterous uproar. Some of the Guards, displeased with the abuse they received, struck the people; but the people, though unharmed, did not refrain from their maledictions. The scene at this moment was most awful—the carnage of Manchester rapidly shot across the memory of the people.

Park Lane, the then contemplated route, had been stopped up almost as effectually as Church Lane at Kensington. The procession was thereby again brought to a complete stand-still, one that was rendered the more painful and alarming, owing to the increased numbers of the populace, as well as of the horse soldiers. Several hundreds of Horse Guards and of Blues lined the streets. At last all this suspense was relieved, and the head of the procession was seen slowly approaching the corner. But as soon as the procession arrived at Hyde Park Gate, by Kensington Barracks, Sir Robert Baker, who was the Bow Street Magistrate, entered it, with the view of heading the procession. The joy ceased, and loud cries were heard of " Shame! shame! she shall not go through the park! let us die first." Some one crying out, " Every man in the breach," meaning the single gate that was then thrown open; the soldiers behaved roughly and threatened "to chop off their hands if they did not let go the gate." Sir R. Baker knew not what to do; officers of the Guards said they must obey their orders—they were positive—they were peremptory. The most dreadful consequences now were to be apprehended—pistols, as well as swords, were drawn, the Guards displaying the most determined demeanour.

Mr. Hurcombe, the common councilman, at this fearful moment, rode up to Sir R. Baker, " For heaven's sake! Sir Robert," he said, " let the procession proceed through the City! You see the people will not be satisfied without such a course be pursued. There is every reason to apprehend that in such case blood will be spilled—lives will be lost. Therefore, reflect well, and let the procession proceed through the City."

Sir R. Baker : I know not what to do ; the orders are positive—peremptory : I cannot change them.

Mr. Hurcombe : You see that the lives of your fellow-citizens are placed in jeopardy—you see what is the state of the public mind. Should lives be lost, will not you be answerable ? Then take on yourself the responsibility.

Sir R. Baker : I will.

Mr. Bailey now intimated a desire that the cavalcade should again attempt to pass up Park Lane into Oxford Street; but it was found impracticable. The head of the procession was then moved down the line of

Piccadilly, and had proceeded nearly as far as Lord Coventry's house, when it was met by a fresh reinforcement of horse soldiers, by whom its further progress in that direction was stopped. After some hesitation, the whole made a retrograde movement towards Hyde Park Corner. Upon this the mob gave a loud and deep shout, and mud and missiles flew at the soldiery from all directions. A party of dragoons were immediately sent round to Park Lane, with strict orders to remove the carts ; in which service, we regret to say, many of them, as well as the crowd, were badly wounded, the former with stones, the latter with the swords of the soldiery. One dragoon had his eye severely cut with a stone; and he would no doubt have killed the man with his sabre, had it not been for the humane interference of Sir R. Baker. The line of waggons, however, was so very compact, that it was found impossible to remove them, and this circumstance being communicated to the magistrate, whose strict orders were, that it should take no other route than that prescribed by the officers of his Majesty's Government, it was, after considerable stoppage, agreed to open Hyde Park Gate, and orders were given to admit the whole cavalcade, and to exclude the crowd, which was at length effected, after considerable resistance and pelting on the part of the latter.

" At about twelve o'clock the procession entered the park, and during its passage through it a scene of confusion and outrage ensued of which the annals of this or any other country can, it is hoped, present few parallels. Vast numbers of persons on foot and on horseback passed with great speed along Park Lane, and in all directions towards Cumberland Gate at the end of Oxford Street. Their object was suspected by the Guards to be to reach that gate before them, with a view of meeting the procession and again forcing it to turn back. To prevent this the Guards galloped through the park at full speed, in order to gain Cumberland Gate before them. Simultaneously with this movement of the Guards and the multitude attendant on the royal funeral, the procession itself moved at a very quick pace through the park. Suddenly, however, it halted, and it was understood that the people had closed the gates.

" It now became necessary, in consequence of the peremptory orders issued to the Guards, to force a way for the procession through whatever impediments might present themselves, for them to disperse the multitude at Cumberland Gate, and clear a passage. The people were equally bent on turning the procession, and forcing it into the route of the city. Here a contest arose, and here blood was shed. Some stones and mud were thrown at the military, and a magistrate being present, the soldiers were sanctioned in firing their pistols and carbines at an unarmed crowd. Screams of terror were heard in every direction, and

numbers were seen flying across the park in dismay.
The number of shots fired was not less than forty or
fifty.   This disastrous event, which was the cause of
several lives being lost, somewhat sobered the opposition, and the procession was enabled to go its way
through Oxford Street.[1]   Hyde Park would have been
the scene of a tragedy as dreadful as that acted
at Manchester, had not the large open space towards Bayswater afforded ample opportunities for
escape from the murderous weapons of the soldiery.
The Guards were galloping about in all directions. So
completely did the soldiery appear at this period to
have lost the good temper and forbearance they previously evinced, that they fired several shots in the
direction in which the procession was then moving.
Some gentlemen who occupied a coach next to that of
Alderman Wood, narrowly escaped with their lives. A
ball passed through one of the panels of the coach, and
came out at the other side, but most providentially
without any injury to those within it."

The procession now crossed the end of Oxford Street;
and, leaving Tyburn Turnpike on the left, passed down
the Edgeware Road towards Paddington.   Almost immediately upon the cessation of the firing, the latter part
of the procession, which during the continuance of the
unfortunate affray between the military and the people

[1] The Life Guards were long known by the name of " the Piccadilly
butchers," and whenever they appeared were assailed by the mob.

had remained in the park, proceeded rapidly forward, and joined the rest of the funeral train in the Edgeware Road.

The conductors of the procession might now hope that their difficulties were removed and hurried on. But they did not reckon on the indomitable character of the mob with which they were confronted.

It was about half-past one when the head of the procession had advanced to the end of the new Paddington Road, and was about to cross the top of Tottenham Court Road, for the purpose of continuing the route to the City Road. Here, however, a sudden and insurmountable obstacle presented itself : the people, who at Cumberland Gate had been checked in their endeavours to turn the procession out of the by-paths chosen by the Government into the open public street, now made a second and more successful attempt to effect the object of having the Queen carried through the metropolis.

" A common feeling ran from one to another with all the simultaneous rapidity of an electric shock. In an instant every waggon, cart, coach, and vehicle, of whatever description, was seized, or rather spontaneously seemed to go and form itself into parts of a dense deep mass, extending the whole width of the road, and almost a hundred yards in depth. The leader of the procession looked at the impenetrable mass with dismay, and turned down into Tottenham Court Road, making another fruitless effort to deviate into a lone

and by-way; but the skill and dexterity of the multitude again anticipated and defeated them.   Francis
Street, Tottenham Court Road, down which the leader
of the procession attempted to pass, was in an instant
blocked up with carriages of all descriptions, which
seemed to rush to a common centre as if by instinct.
The procession was thus compelled to move on in a
straight line towards St. Giles's, every street which
leads out of Tottenham Court Road towards the New
Road being rendered inaccessible by the instantaneous
blockade of the multitude.

" At the bottom of Oxford Street those who acted in
opposition to the wishes of the people intended to turn
the procession back into some of the by-streets, by
means of a regiment of foot soldiers; but the military
were too late, either by passive obstruction or by firing.
The procession now moved onwards till it reached the
top of Drury Lane; and here the main passage down
Holborn being completely blocked up, it was compelled
to take the direction towards the Strand.   Nay, so
anxious and so determined were the people not to be
defeated, that it having occurred to them that another
attempt might be made to regain the irregular path,
by turning out of Drury Lane into Great Queen Street,
and thus returning to Holborn, they effectually blocked
up the avenue of Queen Street, and forced the procession to descend into the Strand.   It may here be
proper to remark, that the Oxford Blues, who were on

duty at the time the Life Guards fired on the people, did not participate in the outrage. They were, of course, during the whole day, favourites of the people, and were repeatedly cheered.[2]

[2] This popularity of the Blues seems to have been a good deal owing to the moderation and good temper of the officers, notably of Lord William Lennox, who gives an account of this scene :—

" One of the most unpleasant duties that I ever was called upon to undertake, was the command of a troop or squadron of my regiment during the riots which took place in London, from the time Queen Caroline first landed in England, up to the day of her funeral. It constantly happened that we were called out to clear some street in which thousands of mischievous persons had assembled, and although we knew that among the mob were men of desperate characters, bent upon stabbing or laming the troop horses, cutting our reins, and trampling down any dismounted man, we were also aware that innocent men, women, and children, from idle curiosity, formed part of the throng, all of whom would suffer if an order to fire upon or charge the mob was given.

" So hateful were the military forces, especially the Life Guards, who went by the name of the ' Piccadilly Butchers,' that pamphlets were printed and circulated, suggesting that iron balls with sharpened spikes should be scattered about the streets so as to maim the horses, and that every man should carry a knife so as to stab, or at all events cut the reins and thus render them unmanageable. To prevent the latter cowardly practice being carried into execution, the officers had a chain rein covered with leather. While the Life Guards were denounced by the mob, pelted, and insulted on every occasion, the Blues were made much of, and attempts were made to get them to fraternize with the lawless rabble.

" At that period a squadron was always kept in the barracks ready to turn out at a moment's notice, and one day, when at dinner in the Regent's Park, I was ordered at once to proceed to Charlotte Street, Portland Place, to disperse a mob assembled there, who were breaking

When the cavalcade arrived at the bottom of Newcastle Street, a body of infantry was drawn in a semi-
circular line across the street from the New Church to
prevent the people from passing.　Upon reaching
Temple Bar, the procession halted for a short time ;
and part of the body of Life Guards which had hither-
to accompanied the cavalcade, here separated from it
and returned to the west-end of the town.

Thus after this persevering struggle the crowd had
their way.　The shade of the " murdered queen " must

windows and extinguishing the lamps.　A magistrate was in attendance to read the Riot Act, and the affair began to get so serious, stones
and brick-bats being hurled at my men, that it was found necessary to
put a stop to it.

" ' I shall read the Riot Act,' said the timid magistrate ; ' all I hope
is, when you proceed to clear the street, should resistance be made,
that you will order your men to fire over the heads of the mob, and
pray be very careful not to have them trampled upon.'

" ' I hope,' I replied, getting rather impatient at the treatment my
men were receiving, ' that I shall do my duty in as humane a manner as
possible, but if we are to be kept much longer a passive mark for the
mob to attack, I can hardly answer for my men keeping their temper.'

" The Riot Act was read, and again was I appealed to by the really
kind-hearted but mistaken magistrate.

" ' Pray be careful,' said he.

" ' Your duty is over,' I replied, amidst a volley of stones, ' and
mine begins.'　So giving the word ' draw swords,' I hastily exclaimed,
' Spare all men not mischievously engaged, and above all women and
children ; but cut down any one attempting to unhorse you, or stab
your horse, or caught in the act of throwing a missile.'

" Following this exhortation by an order to trot, the mob scampered
away, and in less time than I can narrate it the street was cleared."

have been gratified at the triumph. The ovation was tremendous. The Lord Mayor and Corporation were taken by surprise and rushed to meet it, and the immense procession was taken through the very heart of the city.

Among the friends and sympathizers in the procession, was found a distinguished man, Sir Robert Willson and his son. Such was the frantic partisanship of the time, that this gentleman, who was a distinguished officer, took part with a crowd who were engaged in conflict with his Majesty's regiments —or, at least, did not dissociate himself from it. This scandal—and it is rare that we find political partisanship so overpower *esprit de corps*—could not be passed over, and without loss of time the offending officer was summarily dismissed from the army, not to be restored until many years had elapsed. The magistrate also, Sir R. Baker, who had shown, as it was thought, such weakness, was compelled to retire.

After this inauspicious start the luckless cortège posted on its way, travelling through the night till it reached Chelmsford. After only two or three hours' delay the party started, once more, but halted for a night at Colchester. A few faithful friends and servants attended the remains through all the inconveniencies of the route.

The executors now thought that a fitting opportunity had arrived for carrying out the instructions of their deceased royal mistress, and during the night had a plate affixed to the coffin with this inscription :—

HERE LIES
CAROLINE OF BRUNSWICK,
THE INJURED QUEEN
OF ENGLAND.

But the persons in charge of the funeral promptly interposed, and, in spite of the most vehement remonstrances of the executors, summarily removed the plate. There had nearly been the scandal of a scuffle between the contending parties over the body in a church.

On the Thursday Harwich was reached, and on the Monday following the remains were landed at Stade. Not till the following Friday did the weary pilgrimage cease, when Brunswick was at last entered, and the remains of the unhappy lady were left to rest.

CHAPTER X.

THE RESURRECTION MEN.

ABOUT the beginning of the present century the sudden revelation of the lawless and revolting proceedings of those familiars of the surgeons known as "Resurrectionists" startled the kingdom, and the later villainies of Burke and Hare, which added murder to the original crime, followed. Few are aware that at this time this was a regularly organized system, with highly-paid gangs, headed by *entrepreneurs* more or less skilled and daring, and who made their calling a regular profession. Much obloquy naturally attached to these spoilers of the graveyard; but just as it has become the fashion to "whitewash"—as it is called—certain notorious historical characters, reversing established judgments, so it is actually possible to do some justice by these professors, and prove that the real delinquents were the persons who fostered, employed, paid, and urged them on to their odious task.

One of the most amiable and accomplished men of

his profession was the late Sir Astley Cooper, and his life, written by his son, shows us the steady, laborious course of a high-minded man, working his way to eminence through all sorts of difficulties. No one was so just, kind, and forbearing, or so tolerant of others ; and none could have made his way by means more legitimate. He rose strictly by force of character and talent. It is pleasant to read of his touching affection as a son, and of his happy domestic virtues. He had a jealous instinct for the honour of his profession and of all that concerned it, and a passionate devotion to its advancement. It was, however, this zeal or passion that led him into partnership with the scum who ministered to the scientific necessities of the profession, and which, but for the lax administration of the police at the time, would have been brought within the grasp of the law.

Mr. Cooper lived in St. Mary Axe, having succeeded to the residence of the famous surgeon Cline. At the back portion of his house he fitted up a dissecting-room, and hither, as we learn with some astonishment, came all the leading Resurrectionists with their booty, obtained, we are assured, with the full knowledge of this eminent man, in the most unlawful way.

" Mr. Cooper," says his nephew, " was altogether unconscious that, as the enactments relating to dissection at that time stood, he was not only benefitting by an infringement of the laws on the part of the body-snatcher, but was himself, as the receiver after the disinterment, actually liable to be tried for misdemeanour, with a risk of incurring severe penalties. He therefore made no secret of the nature of his occupations in this apartment; contenting himself merely by painting the windows so that persons outside might not observe him while engaged in his investigations, a moderate degree of circumspection being used by the Resurrectionists who brought the subjects to him, with a proper caution being exerted on his own part, to prevent any offence to public feeling.

" On one occasion, however, the presence of mind and activity of Mr. Cooper alone prevented, in all probability, a disturbance ensuing. In the winter session of the year 1801, in consequence of certain disagreements between the hospital porters and the Resurrectionists, who were in the habit of supplying the Anatomical School, the latter were prevented taking the subjects into the dissecting-room. They therefore adopted the plan, of course with Mr. Cooper's sanction, of depositing them at night in the courtyard before his house in St. Mary Axe, from whence they were removed to the hospital in a coach, under the superintendence of a man of the name of Butler, who at that time had the dissecting-rooms at St. Thomas's under his care.

" One night, a Resurrectionist of the name of Harnett

had deposited three hampers within the gates of Mr. Cooper's house, and Butler, having received information of the fact, as usual, came with a coach to remove them. The hampers being safely packed in the vehicle, Butler got inside with them, and ordered the man to drive to St. Thomas's Hospital. All went on very well till they got into Gracechurch Street, opposite to an inn called ' The Coach and Gate,' when the coach suddenly stopped. Butler, at once suspecting discovery, without showing himself, listened; and heard the coachman calling out to some one that 'he had got a load inside, that he didn't much like the looks of, and he didn't know whether he wasn't getting himself into trouble.' This was enough for Butler, who, opening one of the doors, slipped out unseen by either of the parties, and, leaving his charge in the coach, ran back to St. Mary Axe to give an account of what had occurred."

At midnight Mr. Cooper was roused up by the hackney coachman who had brought his freight, and was attended by the watchman, who insisted on inquiring into the business. He was with difficulty got rid of, but announced his intention of laying the whole matter before the Lord Mayor in the morning. It shows how comfortably embarrassments of this sort could be disposed of, when we learn that the surgeon himself was with the Lord Mayor betimes " while at breakfast," and at once related to him, as his nephew naïvely tells us, " the facts of the whole transaction ; and the conversation which ensued ended by an assurance from his lordship that Mr. Cooper should not be molested any further. Curiously enough, on descending the steps of the Mansion House, my uncle met the watchman about to give in his report of the occurrence. The constable, having seen him only when in bed, did not recognize him ; Mr. Cooper, however, remembered him at once, but passed on without notice."

The defence made by the surgeons was that it was impossible to obtain " subjects " in any other way : the patients in hospitals, naturally objecting, in Dickens's humorous phrase, " to have their remains disposed of for the benefit of science." Thus physics, anatomy, and surgery would be compelled to stand still. The schools were crowded with pupils, and there was then a sort of eagerness for entering the profession ; but it was impossible to teach without " demonstrations." An eminent professor at the Theatre of Anatomy, Blenheim Street, so late as 1823, assailed this sad state of things, in a letter to his friend Cooper. There is an amusing disregard of all other considerations, save the important one of their common science :—

" My dear Sir Astley,—In answer to your application, relative to the best means of procuring subjects for the anatomical schools, I beg leave to notice that, from *the very disorganized state of the system at pre-*

sent pursued by the resurrection-men, little is to be expected from their services. To enumerate some of their practices :—First. A most infamous plan has lately been practised by several resurrection-men, of breaking open the doors of out-houses and dead-houses, where the bodies of suicides are deposited, previous to a coroner's inquest being held, and thus committing a felony to procure them. Secondly. They are in the habit of destroying the tombs, vaults, and expensive coffins of the more wealthy part of the community, to obtain their prey. Thirdly. Violent quarrels almost always ensue, when two opposing parties meet in a cemetery, which, by rendering all liable to detection, tends much to increase the alarm that the public experience from their depredations ; and, lastly, from the number of searches by warrants, &c., that almost daily take place in our premises (for, to speak individually, I have had several subjects seized by police officers, three within the last month, *for which I had paid large sums*), it is to be presumed, that after receiving the money from an anatomist for a body, an information is subsequently laid against him by one of the party; whilst another, pretending to be a relative, claims the subject, or re-stealing it, afterwards sells the same again at a different anatomical theatre.

" The exactions, villainy, and insolence of many of the long-established resurrection-men are such, that

I have for some time past ceased to employ them ; in consequence, my school has a very precarious and scanty supply; and that only from strangers and novices not able to cope with those desperadoes, *who have had an entrée,* by means of grave-diggers, into the various burial-grounds in and near the metropolis, for a very considerable period.

"Here allow me to call to your recollection the following fact, of Mr. Smith, one of your pupils, who subsequently attended a summer course of my lectures. This gentleman being engaged alone in dissecting in the Borough, a resurrection-man entered the apartment, and immediately proceeded to cut up the subject with which he was then occupied, threatening at the same time to assassinate Mr. S. should he offer the least resistance. *I might further remark that I almost owe my existence to the proximity of a police-office;* for on more than one occasion, in consequence of commotions raised by these ruffians, my whole premises would have been laid waste, were it not for the prompt and friendly interference of the magistrates in the vicinity, particularly of Sir Robert Baker."

The way, indeed, in which these professors were often "done," as it is called, is illustrated by a trick played on the same professor. One night he was knocked up by a man, who informed him he had got a subject for him. Mr. Brookes himself rose to receive it, according to his custom, and desired the man to bring it in, paid him a portion of the money, for which he was particularly anxious, and desired him to call the next day for the remainder. He then with a kick rolled the parcel down six or seven steps which led to his dissecting-room, and turned away. As he was ascending the stairs to his bedroom, Mr. Brookes was surprised to hear what seemed to him to be complaints issuing from the package, which he had just so unceremoniously dismissed into the passage leading to the dissecting-room, and found that a live man had been placed in the sack. The man, alarmed, at once, in a tone of supplication, begged him to let him go, saying he had been put into the sack when he was drunk, and that it was a trick which had been played upon him. Mr. Brookes, who did not believe a word of the fellow's story, but felt convinced that it was a preconcerted scheme of the Resurrectionist to rob him of as much money as he could get from him, opened the door, and at once kicked the subject into the street.

There were a few " leading " men in the business, with whom the surgeons were in communication, and the art, ingenuity, and courage displayed by these fellows might have raised them, in a more respectable profession. An Irishman named Murphy, with Crouch, and a couple more, "worked" for Mr. Cooper. But they had to be remunerated on a very costly scale. At the beginning of " the season " they would come to make their arrangements with the schools, and as they had a sort of monopoly, they could almost fix their own terms. At the commencement of a new session at the hospitals, Crouch or Murphy would be seen flitting about the dissecting-room, bowing complacently to the lecturers, and either by a proffered smile inviting confidence, or perhaps merely by silence leading the anatomical teacher to believe that his school was to be the chosen scene of his traffic during the coming winter. Each of these parties was shy in commencing conversation. Some such kind of dialogue as the following usually occurred :—" Well, Mr. ——, what does Sir —— mean to stand this season ? " " Oh ! I don't know, Murphy—whatever's fair. What will you take this morning ? " " Nothing, I thank you, Mr. ——, but I don't mean to work this season without I get ten guineas a subject." " Oh, indeed ! well, we don't mean to give more than eight." " Then you may go and tell Sir ——," would be the rejoinder, " that he may raise his own subjects; for not one will he get from us ; "—and the negotiations would be broken off for the present. In the interim, perhaps, some new men would be employed, but it generally happened that their efforts were crushed in the commencement, they being either detected by police through means of information from the old Resurrectionists, bribed off, or in some other manner hindered from the prosecution of their endeavours. This having failed, Murphy would come back again, and say, "Come, you can't get on without us—give us fifty pounds down, and nine guineas a body, and we will work for your school, and no other." This arrangement was often acceded to. As was to be expected, these rascals, though promising an exclusive supply, entered into contracts with as many schools as would entertain their proposals. This shows how sordid was the motive that induced the professors to make these agreements, viz. to secure as large a number of paying pupils as possible.

Sometimes these surgeons, objecting to be victimized in this fashion, determined to deal directly with the sextons and other persons employed by relatives to watch the graves ; and the Resurrectionists, with much cunning, would offer to assist them in their immoral attempts at corruption. The unsuspecting surgeon would be brought to the house of the sexton under circumstances of guilty secrecy, when some such scene as this would follow. At length, with the utmost hesitation and diffidence, Murphy, at the request of his companion, would break the ice, and then gradually explain the object of their visit. The grave-digger listened seemingly with the most profound consideration. At last, he sternly though quietly said : "And this is really what you have come to me about ? " Mr. S—— assented. " You are sure of it ? " he continued, in the same measured tone of cool surprise, while at the same time, stooping down, he deliberately drew from under the bed a huge horse-pistol, the muzzle of which he caused to stare directly in Mr. S——'s face. Mr. S. instinctively drew back ; but before he could make any remark, was assailed with a volley of oaths and abuse, so fearfully violent, and such threatenings of vengeance if he dared to approach the ground under his care,—the pistol all the time, which the fellow swore was loaded, shaking in his hand, exactly opposite to the trembling visitor's head,—that perhaps Mr. S—— had never before experienced a degree of relief from terror and alarm to be compared with that which he felt when he again found himself with Murphy among the crowd of people on Holborn Hill.

The following morning, Murphy was again at the hospital. The surgeon said he was certain such extreme violence must be peculiar to that individual, and asked him if he knew of no other man more likely to suit their purpose. Murphy was prepared, and mentioned another of his allies, the superintendent of a chapel in St. George's in the East.

Mr. S—— was soon joined by a demure, respectable looking person, and Murphy having introduced them to each other, fell back behind. They had not been many minutes together, when a repetition of the scene of the preceding evening occurred, modified only by the different positions of the parties. Murphy, sidling up to the doctor, as if in a state of alarm, hurried him

away : followed, however, for some distance by the
sexton, expressing the greatest anxiety to meet with a
watchman, and regretting only that he had not got
the "rascals safe in his own premises."

It may be imagined that the history of these men
exhibited a curious record of low adventure. As we
have stated, Murphy, before alluded to, Crouch,
Butler, Harnett, Hollis, and Vaughan were the leading
spirits. These, indeed, were the only *regular* Resurrectionists ; the others of the body being composed
of Spitalfields weavers, or thieves, who found the disguise of this occupation convenient for carrying on
their own peculiar avocations.

Butler is described as a short, stout, good-tempered
man, with a laughing eye, and Sancho Panza sort of
expression. He was much addicted to gin. When
drunk, he was a great boaster, and inclined to be
violent ; but was easily cooled down by goodhumoured
treatment.

He was originally a porter in the dissecting-room
at St. Thomas's ; afterwards followed his father's
business of an articulator, and dealer in bones ; and
subsequently dealt much in teeth. He went to Liverpool, and under an assumed name practised for some
time with considerable prosperity as a dentist. His
dissolute habits, however, soon prevailed, and prevented the continued success of a business which
might otherwise have secured his independence. He

became involved in debt, and was obliged to fly from his creditors. Some years previous to this period, the Edinburgh mail had been stopped and robbed by persons, none of whom, I believe, were at the time apprehended. Butler had not left Liverpool very long, after his failure in that city, before he was taken up, for trying to pass a five-pound note, the number of which, by proving it to be one of those stolen on that occasion, and a train of other circumstances, led to the detection of his connection with the robbery of the mail. He was tried, and received sentence of death.

From some circumstance, his execution was delayed considerably beyond the usual period, and Butler, who had accumulated a great quantity of information on various matters, and was in other respects an entertaining companion, contrived to attract the favourable attention of the governor of the gaol. Having complained to him of the want of occupation his position entailed upon him, the governor, who had learned that he had been in business as an articulator, procured for him the carcase of a horse. The bones of this animal were prepared in the usual way, and Butler, to whose cell they were afterwards removed, proceeded to articulate them so as to form the skeleton.

The Austrian Archdukes, John and Lewis, were at the time in this kingdom, and, among other places, paid a visit to Edinburgh ; and on visiting the gaol, found Butler at work in his cell, articulating the bones of this horse. Their Imperial Highnesses were much struck by the circumstance, and having learned from the governor that he was under sentence of death in consequence of robbing the mail coach, interested themselves in his favour, and sued to the Prince Regent for his pardon. This was, after much difficulty, granted, on condition that he left the country immediately, and did not attempt on any account to return. He accordingly took his departure, and was never heard of again.

Crouch, or Ben Crouch, as he was called, was the son of a carpenter who worked at Guy's Hospital. He was a tall, powerful, athletic man, with coarse features, marked with the small-pox ; and was well-known as a prize-fighter. He used to dress in very good clothes, and wore a profusion of large gold rings, and a heap of seals dangling from his fob.

He was always rude and offensive in his manners, exceedingly artful, very rarely drunk, but, when so, most abusive and domineering. In his prosperous days, he was the councillor, director, comptroller, and treasurer of the whole party, and in dividing the spoils, took especial care to cheat every one. He continued actively engaged in the business till about 1817, when he gradually withdrew from it, and occupied himself principally in obtaining and disposing of teeth.

He went abroad several times, and followed this occupation both in the Peninsula and France, in conjunction with another Resurrectionist, with whom he was always on the most intimate terms, of the name of Jack Harnett.

Upon these occasions, they used to obtain licences as suttlers, in order that they might be considered legitimate camp-followers. In addition to their object of procuring teeth, they had other designs of even a more revolting nature. This was to follow closely the troops into the field of action, and to rob the killed as soon as prudence would allow them to employ themselves in their diabolical transactions. The epaulettes from the shoulders of the officers, and the bullion from their regimentals, offered a considerable source of gain on these occasions, and I have been informed by those who were made acquainted by the very men with the facts, that they not unfrequently found trinkets of value, and even considerable sums of money in the pockets of the slain.

They generally obtained the teeth on the night succeeding the battle, only drawing them from those soldiers whose youth and health rendered them peculiarly fitted for the purposes for which they were to be employed.

" At one time during their Peninsular expedition, these companions became separated by accident, and entirely lost sight of one another for three weeks ;

each considering that the other had fallen a victim to his occupation. The circumstances under which they again met are worthy of relation. Crouch heard of a château which had been deserted, and immediately made up his mind to plunder it of its valuables. No sooner was it dark than he entered the deserted house. While groping his way he suddenly stopped to listen to what he believed to be an approaching footstep. The deadly silence was only interrupted by the suppressed breathing of the two guilty depredators ; but, remarkable as the fact may appear, this was sound enough to inform one of them who was his companion, for Crouch recognized the peculiar breathing of his lost friend Harnett, and in total darkness challenged him by name. The recognition was mutual, a light was quickly struck, they related briefly their adventures since their separation, regaled themselves upon the ample supplies the house afforded, packed up portable valuables for which they afterwards obtained 400*l.*, and on the following morning left the pillaged mansion to prosecute their usual occupation.

" From the produce of these adventures, Crouch was enabled to build a large hotel at Margate, and this speculation at first seemed likely to answer his expectations. By some chance, however, the nature of his previous occupation in life was discovered, and such was the effect of this disclosure, that his house was avoided, and he was obliged to part with it, at a very heavy loss. During the time he kept this establishment, he paid occasional visits to the continent to collect teeth, in company with his friend Harnett. However, from the number of Jews and others who gradually entered into this traffic, the profits were much diminished, and Crouch became very poor, and on one occasion, being in emergency, he surreptitiously obtained possession of property belonging to Harnett, who was at that time in France, and applied it to his own purposes. Harnett immediately came over to England, followed Crouch, who had gone into Scotland, and having found him gave him into custody. He was tried and sentenced to imprisonment for a twelvemonth. He afterwards came to London, where he lived awhile in great poverty, and was one morning found dead in the tap-room of a public-house near Tower Hill."

Jack Harnett, above alluded to, was a rather stout, red-haired, ill-looking fellow; uncouth in his address and manner of speaking, fond of watch garniture, and always the firm and steady friend of Crouch, until the incident just related. Those two always held together whenever disputes occurred in the party. In the latter part of his career he accumulated a considerable sum of money in the manner already described, and not being a speculator like his companion, died comparatively rich, leaving nearly 6000*l.* to his family.

A characteristic touch was associated with the end of this desperado. When he was dying of consumption in one of the hospitals, he sent for one of his old employers, and with the greatest anxiety solemnly extorted from him a promise that his body was to be spared the indignity of dissection!

Harnett, on his return from Spain, had placed the proceeds of the tour in a large chest which he valued at 700*l.*, and with which he landed at the Tower. This precious cargo he forgot in a hackney coach, through the carelessness of his daughter, and the coachman, thinking that he had a prize of value, was not a little disappointed when he found out the nature of what he had stolen, but he succeeded in disposing of a good deal of the booty to the dentists of the metropolis.

Murphy was known as " the King of the Resurrectionists," but the whole class, as may be imagined, offered a combination of all that was infamous, and it is astonishing that physicians and surgeons of honour and respectability should have contaminated themselves by any dealings with them. The professional gentlemen not only profited by their labours, but assisted them in their difficulties, and shielded them from legal prosecution, and assisted them when in the grasp of the law. Yet the objects of this patronage were as eager to defraud those who protected them as they were to betray their fellows, and they were perpetually denouncing each other to the officers of the law. Nearly all combined other offences, such as horse-stealing, highway robbery, &c., with their regular profession, and were often transported or hung. One of the fraternity, named Millard, who had "worked" for Sir Astley Cooper, on being sentenced to imprisonment for robbing a grave, became infuriated against his patron because he did not obtain a free pardon for him, and swore he would have his life. On his dying in prison his wife published a curious pamphlet detailing his grievances, "An account of the circumstances attending the imprisonment and death of the late William Millard," in which a bitter attack was directed on Sir Astley Cooper, who was vilified for not obtaining the man's release, and settling a pension on his widow. With more show of reason it assailed the London hospitals, who were the real culprits and ran none of the risks which their instruments did.

Sir Astley Cooper's nephew gives some extraordinary instances of the manner in which the surgeons assisted their "friends" in difficulty. "When the regular Resurrectionists 'got into trouble,' especially if they were active and useful men, and there was nothing very flagrant in the case, the surgeons often advanced large sums of money to keep them out of gaol, or to supply their necessities during imprisonment. Sir Astley Cooper has expended hundreds of pounds for this purpose; nor did the expense rest here, for during

the confinement of the husbands, the support of their
wives and families was a further tax upon him. The
first three items in the following bill, which is copied
from an account in my possession, will give some idea
of the usual rate of these payments :—

1828.		£	s.	d.
Jan. 29.	Paid Mr. ——, to pay Mr. ——, half the expenses for bailing Vaughan from Yarmouth, and going down	14	7	0
May 6.	Paid Vaughan's wife	0	6	0
„ 29.	Paid Vaughan for 26 weeks' confinement, at 10s. per week	13	0	0
	Four subjects, two male and two female (Murphy), at twelve guineas each . .	50	8	0
June 18.	Paid Murphy, Wildes, and Naples, finishing money	6	6	0

" When I was first appointed to the anatomical
chair at Guy's Hospital," says the same writer,
" Murphy had been placed in confinement on account of some disturbances he had been committing
in the churchyard at Yarmouth ; a professional friend
of mine went down to liberate him, and the amount of
his expenditure on this occasion was 160*l.* Another
friend of mine, an anatomical teacher, incurred an expense of 50*l.*, being the amount of a weekly allowance,
continued for two years, to one of the Resurrectionists
who was confined in prison."

Though eager to secure what belonged to their
rivals, the great hospitals showed, or what seemed so,

a praiseworthy desire to protect their own burial-grounds, and employed highly-paid watchmen to keep guard all night long. But this tender solicitude, it proved, was with a view to secure " the subjects " for themselves. It operated in this way :—

"They wished that the burial-ground connected with the institution should be maintained strictly inviolate, in order that such hospital patients as were conscious of approaching dissolution, might know that in that ground their bodies would remain undisturbed ; a conviction which, strange to say, often produced on their minds a state of resigned feeling. From the influence produced by this regulation, many patients requested that their bodies might be ' examined ' after death, because they thus secured a right of being buried at the expense of the hospital, a confidence which was never permitted to be abused."

For the especial protection of this ground a well-known and confidential Resurrectionist was handsomely paid to take up his nightly station in a watch-box on the premises during the dissecting season. For some months his presence effected the desired object ; for he resisted every attempt made to bribe him or elude his observation. At last, however, upon the occasion of a body being buried there, of peculiar professional interest, one of the surgeons of the very institution, sent some men to obtain it, having offered an unusually large reward, as an inducement for them to exert all their ingenuity on the occasion. They accordingly tried all the ordinary methods for acquiring possession of the prize, but were invariably baffled, until one evening, when they diverted the attention of the watchman as to their object, in making him drunk, and then succeeded in carrying off the prize.

Some of these adventures had a sort of farcical air, and were at least creditable to the ingenuity of their practitioners.

" An intimate friend of a Resurrectionist named Patrick was employed in the service of a gentleman, whose residence was at a short distance from London. One day this man called, in company with a fellow-servant, on Patrick, and informed him that his master was dead, and that he thought something in the way of business might be done with the body, as it was lying in a back parlour, the windows of which opened on to a large lawn. Patrick made several inquiries, and ascertained that the funeral was to take place on the following Sunday.

" And accordingly on the night of Saturday he entered at the back of the premises, and, being admitted to the parlour by the servant, commenced his operations. Unassisted by any light, he drew out all the screws, took off the lid, and, having formed an estimate, as accurate as the circumstances would allow, of the weight of the body, removed it into a box which he had brought with him for the purpose of containing it. He next placed in the coffin a quantity of earth, which the servant had procured from the garden, corresponding to the weight of the corpse. The lid was then replaced, carefully screwed down, the pall thrown over it, and the box containing the body passed out of the window to Patrick. For this 'subject' Patrick received fifteen guineas. Being anxious to observe that all went off without interruption, he attended the funeral, which took place in a church adjoining the house."

Another of these fellows, in walking near a hospital, saw a person stagger and fall heavily on the ground. He impulsively ran to him with a view of offering assistance, but he had hardly reached him when the man ceased to live. The body-snatcher no sooner perceived this, than a new train of thoughts entered his mind. No one could have bewailed the loss of an attached relative with more sincerity than he affected to do, while soliciting the passers-by to assist him in conveying his cousin to the hospital, though he feared it was too late to offer any reasonable hope of his recovery. Having deposited him in the care of the house surgeon, to whom the body-snatcher was not known, he was told in as gentle a manner as kindly feeling could dictate, that the person was quite dead ; upon which information the afflicted relative soon afterwards left. The following day, a coroner's inquest having sat upon the body, he came for it and took it away in a shell and disposed of it to another hospital "for the benefit of science."

A favourite plan was to ascertain in the various poor-houses, infirmaries, and hospitals, within the Metropolis, the names and connections of those who had lately died in such institutions. On these occasions, if they found the bodies of any who seemed destitute of relations or friends, or at any rate, whose connections had exhibited very little concern about them, they would call on the proper officers, and assuming an appearance of distress, assert some close relationship with the deceased, and claim the body for the purpose of burial. The demand was not very unfrequently complied with, especially at the work-houses,—the officers at these establishments being neither anxious to investigate the rights insisted on by the applicants.

" The resurrection-men were occasionally despatched by surgeons on expeditions into the country to obtain possession of the bodies of those who had been subjected to some important operation, and of which a *post mortem* examination was of the greatest interest to science. Scarcely any distance from London was considered as an insuperable difficulty in the attaining of this object, and as certainly as the Resurrectionist undertook the task, so certain was he of completing it. This was usually an expensive undertaking, but still it did not restrain the most zealous in their profession from occasionally engaging these men in this employment. Sir Astley Cooper, *as may be surmised from a consideration of his character*, was not backward in availing himself of these opportunities. I have known him send one of these men considerably more than a hundred miles to obtain a subject for the purpose of examining the effect of an operation performed years previously, actuated by the desire of acquiring a knowledge of any new facts which the inspection might afford." [1]

This almost fanatical longing to prosecute the study of science was pushed to an incredible extent, and seems to have ended in a complete blunting of all feelings of propriety and respect for the rights of others. It will hardly be credited that a physician, who had been attending some interesting but perplexing case in the country, would be found coveting the patient after his decease, in order that he might satisfy his medical speculations.

---

[1] The following is a bill on account of one of these expeditions :—
" 1820, June 1st.—Paid Hollis and Vaughan for getting a Subject from ——, in the county of ——, a man that Sir Astley Cooper performed an operation upon twenty-four years ago.

Coach for two there and back . . .	£3 12	0
Guards and Coachmen	0 6	0
Expenses for two days	1 14	6
Carriage of Subject, and porter . . .	0 12	6
Subject	7 7	0
	£13 12	0

" A surgeon residing at or near the neighbourhood from which this subject was obtained, had watched the case there for years, and, on the death taking place, immediately wrote to Sir Astley. Sir Astley, on learning this event, sent for the person from whom I obtained the above account, and desired him to make an arrangement with the above-named men to obtain the subject, his concluding remark being, ' *cost what it may.*' "

Cost what it may ! So enthusiastic was this eminent surgeon, and so powerful his influence with these men, that there was no limit to the gratification of his wishes. " I heard him," says his son, " when wishing to expose to a certain person the power of these men, and his influence over them, offer to procure, within three days, the body of *a dignified official personage*, who had been buried in a place apparently of impenetrable security. I have every reason to believe, that had he chosen, he could have effected this object." Sir Astley Cooper, indeed, stated as much before a Committee of the House of Commons :—" The law does not prevent our obtaining the body of an individual if we think proper ; for there is no person, let his situation in life be what it may, whom, if I were disposed to dissect, I could not obtain." And in reply to another question, he said, " The law only enhances the price, and does not prevent the exhumation : nobody is secured by the law ; it only adds to the price of the subject."

There was an irresistible temptation for the sexton of a burying-ground to join in or connive at this spoliation. He was beset by the robbers with tempting bribes—or threats—and if he once yielded he was in the power of the confederates. One of the most noted of the fraternity had a curious history. He had been originally in the navy and the king's service. He was for some time on board the *Excellent*, and served in that vessel in the engagement off Cape St. Vincent. He returned to England after this battle, and having soon disposed of this prize-money, went on board a vessel cruising about the Channel. Becoming tired of this employment he ran away, and came to London, where he soon afterwards obtained the situation of a grave-digger to the Spa-fields burial-ground. Here he was entrapped into connection with the Resurrectionists by a Scotchman of the name of White. This man invented a most ingenious plan for combining the two callings. He first buried, then " snatched " the subject. He was obliged to be extremely cautious, for at one end of the ground was a house, in which resided two of the proprietors, while his own residence was immediately opposite. After a funeral had taken place, and the mourners left the ground, before commencing to fill up the grave, N—— used to remove the body out of the coffin, and place it in a sack, which he had ready for the purpose. He then threw in sufficient mould to cover this, and afterwards gradually filled up the grave, taking care to draw the sack nearer and nearer to the surface as he proceeded, until it was covered only by a thin layer of loose earth, which formed the surface of the mound. At night he dragged it up out of this hiding-place, by means of the mouth of the sack, which he always left in such a position that it could be readily reached by him. This system was continued for two or three years, when one evening as White was carrying a subject along the streets, packed up as usual in a nut-basket, he was stopped by some Bow Street patrols, who insisted on examining his parcel. The subject was exposed, but White contrived to make his escape ; an examination, however, was made of the various burial-places, to ascertain, if possible, the parties concerned in the transaction, and, among others, that of Spa-fields. After several graves had boon opened, the vacant coffin was discovered, and N——was sentenced to two years' imprisonment in the House of Correction, or the "Bastille," as it was familiarly called by the Exhumators. From this place N—— contrived to escape, in company with a fellow-prisoner, by making an opening through a skylight in the roof, and afterwards scaling the outer walls of the prison, by means of a rope which they had formed out of the oakum, the picking of which was their ordinary day's employment. N—— was afterwards retaken, in consequence of information given against him by his enemy Crouch ; and it was only through the mediation of Sir Astley Cooper with the Secretary of State, that he escaped the punishment due to this aggravation of his original offence. He was more frequently imprisoned, perhaps, than any other Resurrectionist, and on each occasion in consequence of information given by Crouch, or some of his party.

As the Resurrectionists grew more violent and daring the public feeling began to be roused, an agitation sprang up, more vigilance was shown, and the service became one of corresponding danger. It was no unfrequent occurrence for them to be severely beaten, or perhaps fired at or captured by the guards, who were greatly increased in numbers, and in many cases both honest and vigilant, and thus every man employed in the business became liable to be shot, or at any rate to suffer a loss of liberty, often for a lengthened period of time. They were not so often wounded, however, as might have been expected. " A man, in whose veracity I had confidence," says Mr. Cooper, " told me he had been fired at five times, on each occasion without any injury whatever. Murphy, in scaling the wall at Bethnal Green churchyard, had once a very narrow escape, for a heavy charge from a blunderbuss fired by one of the watchmen, entered and shattered a brick scarcely an inch from his loin ; he was wounded by two or three of the shot."

Sometimes they found the coffin filled with quick-

lime, or buried so deeply as in certain soils to admit a
foot of water above it. Occasionally, too, they met
with cast-iron coffins in place of the usual wooden
receptacles. The latter contrivance was considered
as an insuperable obstacle to the Resurrectionists
effecting their object, and indeed had they come
generally into use, would have proved so, for although
the lids could be readily broken into pieces by a
sledge hammer, the noise which necessarily attended
the operation was a sufficient preventive to its being
carried into effect. The imperishable nature, however, of the material of which they were made, itself
offered the objection to their employment, for in a
few years every churchyard in London would have
been thus rendered useless as a further receptacle for
the dead.

As a further security the walls around the burial-
places were now sometimes raised six or eight feet
above their usual height, and several tiers of bricks
left loose upon the summit, and broken glass or iron
spikes placed there, in order to offer further obstacle
to their being scaled. Added to these means of defence, parties of men were now and then set to watch
the Resurrectionists into the inclosures, and while they
were busily employed, would suddenly rush upon them,
and attacking them, while unprepared, either capture
them or beat them unmercifully.

Spring-guns were often set in various directions in

the churchyards, but these never answered the purpose intended by them. If a Resurrectionist proposed to work where these instruments of danger were used, and when he was not intimate with the grave-digger or watchman, he sent women in the course of the day into the ground, generally at a time when there was a funeral to note the position of the pegs to which the wires were to be attached. Having obtained this information, the first object of the party at night would be to feel for one of these, and having found it, they carefully followed the wire, till they came up to the gun, which was then raised from the surface of the grave mound (its usual position), and deposited safely at its foot.

An extraordinary episode is curious as illustrating not merely the rancorous vendettas that raged between the gangs, but some odd features of social manners ; such as the two old ladies who kept a private burying-ground as a source of income. Two of the men, Murphy and another, had been " fortunate enough," says Mr. Cooper, " to get a plentiful supply from a private burial-place near Holywell Mount, the property of two old women, whose premises indeed formed the entrance to it. The exhumators had gained access by forming an acquaintance with a man of the name of Whackett, who had the sole superintendence of the ground, and officiated moreover as grave-digger. This man was in the habit of remaining on duty until

sunset; and used, upon his departure, to leave the
bolt of the gate undrawn, which although still locked,
offered no impediment to the entrance of his friends,
as he had supplied them with a key. Here Murphy
and Patrick used to pay their nocturnal visits, and
going over the ground looked for certain signs which
their accomplice always left to point out the situation,
of the particular bodies which he considered might be
removed with the least fear of detection. With these
facilities, they for some time carried on a most successful trade, and frequently brought away as many as six
bodies in one night. This prosperity excited the
astonishment and envy of their rivals in business as to
the source from whence they obtained their supply;
and some of them determined to adopt means either
to participate in their harvest, or to discover and
destroy the source from whence they reaped such
benefits.

" Two of the exhumators, named Holliss and Vaughan,
at last got scent of the scene of action, and as soon as
they had discovered it, determined to make Whackett
admit them ' to a share of the job,' or threaten to
expose the whole transaction. The next day, accordingly, they tried to deceive him by saying, that
although he was not aware of it, they were sharers
with Murphy in the profits derived from his ground.
Whackett obstinately resisted every attempt. Notwithstanding this opposition, they persisted in their

importunity, and at last enraged Whackett so much,
that he ran across the street to a public-house which
was full of labourers, and pointing through the
windows to the two men, called out, ' Those fellows
are body-snatchers, and are come here for the
purpose of bribing me to let them raise from my
ground.' This was enough : the whole party rushed
out of the house, impressed with a common determination to inflict instant punishment upon these objects
of their abhorrence.· Vaughan and Hollis saw them
approach, and guessing their intention, ran off,
and outstripping them by their speed, altogether
escaped.

"The spirit of retaliation urged the enraged and
disappointed Vaughan and Holliss to seek revenge, and
they went directly to a police· office where a magistrate
was at the moment sitting, and, in the midst of a
crowded court, informed him, in a loud tone, that if
he sent officers to Holywell Mount burial-ground, they
would find every grave despoiled of its dead; the
grave-digger, Whackett, having sold them to the body-
snatchers. The people present simultaneously caught
an impulsive feeling of indignation, and hastened
towards the spot. As they went along, their numbers
increased, and having arrived at the burial-ground,
they broke open the gates, and commenced digging
up the graves. Whackett's escape was prevented, and
he was made to witness the extent of his own depredations, until the mob, becoming more and more enraged

as the empty coffins were severally exposed, suddenly seized him, threw him into one of the deepest excavations, and began shovelling the earth over him. My informant told me he would certainly have been buried alive, had it not been for the activity of some of the constables, who had followed the people from the office. The excitement was so great that the mob went to Whackett's house, where they destroyed every article of his furniture, seized his wife and children, whom they dragged through a stagnant pool in the neighbourhood, and then proceeded to break the windows in the house of the two old women who were the owners of the property, although they were perfectly innocent, even of any connivance with the parties implicated in the transaction."

As may be imagined the Bow Street office had its share in detecting and prosecuting these villainies, and one of the most active officers, Ellis, who had been placed at the head of the Plymouth Police, availed himself of his town experience to frustrate the schemes of a gang who had arrived. One Vaughan, a skilled and successful Resurrectionist, had taken a house conveniently close to a churchyard, and had brought down two of his friends to assist him in the operations. It was suspected that they had come for smuggling purposes, and the *ci-devant* Bow Street Runner entered *con amore* into the business. "Disguising himself, he went on the following day to the dwelling of the suspected individuals, and, after sauntering about some time, recognized Vaughan as a London body-snatcher, without being himself observed by any of the party. Ascertaining that two funerals were to take place the next day, he resolved to watch their movements, and habiting as a countryman, in a smock-frock, with other appropriate disguise, he attended at the burial as a mourner for one of the deceased. He was not surprised to see the whole of the suspected set, women as well as men, joining in the crowd which followed at the heels of the procession. No sooner were the bodies committed to the grave, than Ellis went back to Plymouth; but being now fully convinced of the intentions of the party, he returned to the churchyard at nightfall, bringing with him three men. So determined was he to get every proof of the guilt of Vaughan and his party, that he apprised the relatives of the deceased of his suspicions. Thus prepared, Ellis and his party secreted themselves in the churchyard, and about ten o'clock saw the exhumators commence their work, and soon afterwards deposit the bodies in their place of dwelling.

" In about an hour, after watching the house, Ellis rapped at the door. Vaughan himself obeyed the summons, and immediately recognizing Ellis, who had thrown aside his disguise, hurriedly asked him what had brought him there so late at night. On learning his errand, he begged of him, with apparent indifference, to search the house. A signal was immediately given by Ellis, his assistants came up, entered the house with him, and the bodies were found secreted in a back kitchen. The relatives of the exhumed bodies were sent for, and at once identified them, and the whole party of Resurrectionists, before daylight, was safely lodged in the gaol at Plymouth.

"This outrage was rendered felonious, instead of being a mere misdemeanour, by the circumstance of their having taken some of the clothes in which the bodies had been buried. They were sentenced to seven years' transportation."

It is not generally known that one of our greatest humourists was subjected to this indignity. After dying in a lonely, deserted fashion in a Bond Street lodging, his dissolution being witnessed by a footman who had accidentally called, the Rev. Mr. Sterne, the delightful " Yorick," was interred in the Paddington burial-ground, where his monument, set up by strangers, can still be seen. Two days after the body was taken up or " snatched," and sent down to Cambridge, having been " disposed of for the benefit of science," to Mr. Collignon, M.B., Professor of Anatomy in that University. He invited some amateurs to witness his " demonstration," and one gentleman, who was acquainted with the departed Shandean, was greatly shocked at recognizing his departed friend.

CHAPTER XI.

WHEN Mr. Dickens, then a young man full of bright promise, was taken over Newgate, some fifty years ago, what chiefly struck him were two horrible casts of murderers' heads, whose aspect, he said, warranted summary execution at any time. There were seen in the horrible row, Bishop and Williams—names that at one period excited a thrill. A few will recall, personally or by tradition, the "Murder of the Italian Boy," as it was called, and the extraordinary excitement it occasioned. The reason was that it touched all the sources of popular sympathy and terror. There was the hideous type of the murderers which excited repulsion; the even more odious object of the deed, which was to sell the body of the hapless victim for dissection; whilst the hideous fashion in which the deed was carried out belonged to the vilest type of melodrama.

In the year 1831 the public had not recovered from the effect of the discoveries connected with the Burke and Hare atrocities, and there was an uneasy feeling abroad that the system was still being pursued, though undetected. There were many instances of mysterious disappearance assumed to be associated with the hideous traffic. The surgeons, however, in their ardour for science, pursued their old course, purchasing what was brought to them, and thus holding out irresistible inducement to the ruffians who lived by the traffic.

On November 5th, Mr. Partridge, the professor of anatomy at King's, was personally informed by the porter of the hospital that a subject had been offered for sale, about which there were circumstances of suspicion. It had been brought by two villainous-looking fellows, Bishop and May, who, however, were the regular providers of such things to the institution. A dispute arose about the price —whether it should be nine or ten guineas, but it was agreed that the subject "should come in "—that being the technical phrase—at nine guineas. In the afternoon it was brought in a hamper. When the body was inspected, it was remarked that it had the look of not having been buried. There was a cut on the forehead, though this appears to have been the result of an accident after the death. This Mr. Partridge, many years later, attracted notice from his expedition to Italy to extract the ball from Garibaldi's wound, and in which task the famous Nelaton was more successful. Having made a regular examination, and found all the evidence of violence, he sent out for change of a 50*l*. note, as an excuse for detaining the men. The police arrived promptly, and conveyed them to Bow Strcet. This was destined to be the' first important inquiry of the newly-formed " force," and the eyes of the kingdom were upon them. It was noticed that the prisoners were in a state of drunkenness. May declared that he had nothing to do with it, that " the subject was that gentleman's," pointing to Bishop. Two other men, who had assisted in carrying the hamper—Williams and Shields—were also charged.

It was presently discovered that the victim was a poor Italian boy, named Carlo Ferrari, who carried about white mice, which he had trained to revolve a circular cage—a once familiar form of street entertainment. The coroner's jury found a verdict against persons unknown, but intimated that grave suspicion attached to the prisoners.

A visit was made to the house where they lived, which was No. 3, Nova Scotia Gardens, in Bethnal Green, then a sort of suburb. Mr. Minshul, the Bow Street magistrate, undertook the whole investigation of the case, and it was through his exertions that the affair was successfully investigated and the evidence collected. The house was a semi-detached one with a curious roof that sloped from the front wall to the back. It had a garden behind, in which was a well. This well involved as hideous a mystery as did the one in Miss Braddon's novel. The first thing done was to search the place thoroughly, when clothes stained with blood were found. At successive searches, the gardens were pricked all over with iron rods, and then regularly dug up to a depth of some feet. Here clothes that would fit a boy were found concealed, all torn and stained with blood. The house next door belonged to Williams; so that both residences were in possession of the fraternity. On searching the next house, a woman's clothes were found buried, with evidence that a regular system of murder had been pursued. As all these discoveries took place, the popular excitement became frantic: mobs gathered, and were with difficulty prevented from wrecking the house; thousands of persons were allowed to view the premises on payment of a small fee; and, as the police pursued their diggings, enormous crowds looked on; the inquiry meantime proceeding at Bow Street, until November 25th, when the three prisoners were committed for trial. Before this took place, it was already ascertained that some of the clothes had belonged to a woman named Pigburn, who had mysteriously disappeared, and who, it was ascertained, had been decoyed away and murdered for sale to the surgeons.

The trial took place on December 2nd, 1831. The three prisoners were charged with the murder of the boy Ferrari, but there seems to have been some uncertainty as to the identity of the body; so a second count was added, charging the murder of a person unknown. Mr. Adolphus was for the prosecution. The case was clearly proved. The details produced general horror, and the wretches were found guilty and sentenced, when, as was to be expected, they displayed the most abject terror. It was remarked, however, that May alone showed some firmness, and, when they were being removed, was heard to exclaim : " *I am a murdered man !*"

The day being fixed for this execution, and the condemned sermon having been preached to them, two of them made confessions. Of Bishop's, the following is a portion :—

" *I, John Bishop,* do hereby declare and confess that the boy supposed to be an Italian boy was a Lincolnshire boy. I and Williams took him to my house about half-past ten o'clock on Thursday night, the 3rd of November, from the ' Bell,' in Smithfield. He walked home with us. Williams promised to give him some work. Williams went with him from the ' Bell ' to the Old Bailey watering-house, whilst I went to the ' Fortune of War.' Williams came from the Old Bailey watering-house to the ' Fortune of War ' for me, leaving the boy standing at the corner of the court by the watering-house in the Old Bailey. I went directly with Williams to the boy, and we then walked all three to the Nova Scotia Gardens, taking a pint of stout at a public-house near Holywell Lane, Shoreditch, on our way, of which we gave the boy a part. We only stayed just to drink it, and walked on to my house, where we arrived about eleven o'clock. My wife and children and Mrs. Williams were not gone to bed, so we put him in the closet and told him to wait there for us. Williams went in, and told them to go to bed, and I remained in the garden. Williams came out directly, and we both walked out of the garden a little way, to give time to the family getting to bed. We returned in about ten minutes or a quarter of an hour, and listened outside the window to ascertain whether the family were gone to bed. All was quiet; and we then went to the boy in the closet, and took him into the house. We lighted a candle, and gave the boy some bread and cheese; and after he had eaten, we gave him a cupful of rum, with about half a small phial of laudanum in it. I had bought the rum the same evening in Smithfield, and the laudanum also in small quantities at different shops. There was no water or other liquid put into the cup with the rum and laudanum. The boy drank the contents of the cup directly in two draughts, and afterwards a little beer. In about ten minutes he fell asleep in the chair on which he sat, and I removed him from the chair to the floor, and laid him on his side. We then went out and left him there. We then had a quartern of gin and a pint of beer at the 'Feathers,' near Shoreditch Church, and then went home again, having been away from the boy about twenty minutes. We found him asleep as we had left him. We took him directly, asleep and insensible, into the garden, and tied a cord to his feet to enable us to pull him up by. I then took him in my arms, and let him slide from them headlong into the well in the garden; whilst Williams held the cord to prevent the body going altogether too low in the well. He was nearly wholly in the water, his feet being just above the surface. Williams fastened the other end of the cord round the paling, to prevent the body getting beyond our reach. The boy struggled a little in the water with his arms and legs, and the water bubbled a minute. We waited till these symptoms were past, and then went indoors, and I think we went out and walked down Shoreditch to occupy the time; but in three-quarters of an hour we returned and took him out of the well, by pulling him by the cord attached to his feet. We undressed him in the paved yard, rolled his clothes up, and buried them where they were found by the witness who produced them. We carried the boy into the washhouse, laid him on the floor, and covered him with a bag. We left him there, and went and had some coffee in Old Street Road, and then (a little before two in the morning of Friday) went back to my house. We immediately doubled the body up, and put it into a box, which we corded so that nobody might open it to see what it was, and then went again and had some more coffee at the same place in the Old Street Road, where we stayed a little time, and then went home to bed— both in the same house and in our own beds, as usual. We slept till about ten o'clock on Friday morning, when we got up, took breakfast together with the family, and went both of us to the 'Fortune of War,' in Smithfield. We had something to eat and drink there; and after we had something to eat May came in."

He then gives an account of the other murders, notably of the unfortunate woman they had decoyed into this den :—

"*I also confess*, that I and Williams were concerned in the murder of a female, whom I believe to have been since discovered to be Frances Pigburn, on or about the 9th of October last. I and Williams saw her sitting, about eleven or twelve at night, on the step of a door in Shoreditch, near the church. She had a child, four or five years old, with her on her lap. I asked why she was sitting there. She said she had no home to go to, for her landlord had turned her out into the street. I told her she might go home with us, and sit by the fire all night. She said she would go with us, and walked with us to my house in Nova Scotia Gardens, carrying her child with her. When we got there we found the family in bed, and we took the woman in, and lighted a fire, by which we all sat down together. I went out for beer, and we all partook of bread and beer and rum (I had brought the rum from Smithfield in my pocket). The woman and her child lay down on some dirty linen on the floor, and I and Williams went to bed. About six in the morning I and Williams told her to go away and to meet us at the 'London Apprentice,' in Old Street Road, at one o'clock; this was before our families were up. She met us again at one o'clock at the 'London Apprentice.' She had no child with her. We gave her some halfpence and beer, and desired her to meet us again at ten o'clock at night at the same place. After this we bought rum and laudanum at different places, and at ten o'clock we met the woman again at the 'London Apprentice,' without her child. We drank about three pints of beer, and stayed about an hour. We should have stayed there longer, but an old man came in who knew the woman, and she said she did not like him to see her there with anybody. We therefore all went out. It rained hard, and we took shelter under a doorway in the Hackney Road for about half an hour. We then walked to Nova Scotia Gardens, and I led her to No. 2, an empty house adjoining my house. We had no light. Williams stepped out into the garden with the rum and the laudanum, which I handed to him. He there mixed them together in a half-pint bottle, and came into the house to me and the woman, and we gave her the bottle to drink. She drank the whole in two or three draughts. There was a quartern of rum and

about half a phial of laudanum. She sat down on the
step between the two rooms of the house. She went
off to sleep in about ten minutes. She was falling
back ; I caught her to save her fall, and laid her back
on the floor. Then Williams and I went to a public-
house, got something to drink, and in about half an
hour came back to the woman. We took her cloak off,
tied a cord to her feet, carried her to the well in the
garden, and thrust her into it headlong. She struggled
very little afterwards, and the water bubbled a little at
the top. We fastened the cord to the palings to prevent her going down beyond our reach, and took a
walk to Shoreditch and back in about half an hour.
We left the woman in the well this length of time, that
the rum and laudanum might run out of her mouth.
On our return we took her out of the well, cut her
clothes off, put them down the closet of the empty
house, carried the body into the washhouse of my own
house, where we doubled it up, and put it in a hair-
box, which we corded, and left it there. We did not
go to bed, but went to Shields' house in Eagle Street,
Red Lion Square, and called him up between four and
five in the morning. We then went with Shields to a
public-house near the Sessions House, Clerkenwell, and
had some gin ; from thence to my house, and stayed a
little to wait the change of the police. I told Shields
he was to carry the trunk to the London Hospital.
He asked if there was a woman in the house, who

could walk alongside of him, so that people might not take any notice. Williams called his wife up, and asked her to walk with Shields, and to carry a hat-box, which he gave her. There was nothing in it, but it was tied up as if there were. We then put the box with the body on Shields' head, and went to the hospital, Shields and Mrs. Williams walking on one side of the street, and I and Williams on the other. At St. Thomas's Hospital I saw Mr. South's footman, and sent him upstairs to Mr. South, to ask if he wanted a subject. The servant brought me word that his master wanted one, but could not give an answer till the next day, as he had not time to look at it. During this interview, Shields, Williams and his wife were waiting at a public-house. I then went to Mr. Appleton at Mr. Grainger's, and agreed to sell it to him for eight guineas; and afterwards I fetched it from St. Thomas's Hospital and took it to Mr. Appleton's, who paid me five pounds then and the rest on the following Monday. After receiving the five pounds I went to Shields and Williams and his wife at the public-house, when I paid Shields 10s. for his trouble, and we all went to the 'Flower Pot,' at Bishopsgate, where we had something to drink, and then went home. I never saw the child after the first time before mentioned. She said she had left the child with the person she had taken her things to, before her landlord took her goods. The woman murdered did not tell us her

name ; she said her age was thirty-five, and that her
husband, before he died, was a cabinetmaker. She
was thin, rather tall, and very much marked with the
smallpox.

" *I also confess* the murder of a boy, who told us his
name was Cunningham. It was a fortnight after the
woman. I and Williams found him sleeping, about
eleven and twelve o'clock at night on Friday, the 21st
October, as I think, under the pig hoards at Pig
Market, Smithfield. Williams woke him, and asked
him to come along with him, and the boy walked with
Williams and me to my house in Nova Scotia Gardens.
We took him into my house, and gave him some warm
beer sweetened with sugar, with rum and laudanum in
it. He drank two or three cupsful, and then fell
asleep in a little chair belonging to one of my children.
We then laid him on the floor and went out and got
something to drink, and then returned, carried the boy
to the well, and threw him in it in the same way as
we served the other boy and the woman. He died
instantly in the well, and we left him there to give
time for the mixture to run out of his body. We then
took the body from the well, tore off the clothes and
buried them in the garden. The body we carried into
the washhouse, and put it into the same box, and left it
there till that same evening, when we got a porter to
carry it to St. Bartholomew's Hospital, where I sold it
to Mr. Smith for eight guineas. This boy lived in

Kent Street with his mother, but said he had not been
home for a twelvemonth or more. He was about ten
or eleven years old."

It will be seen that all exculpated May, and this,
though not conclusive, had weight with the authorities.
A curious dramatic scene occurred when the final
decision was conveyed to the criminals. Dr. Cotton,
the chaplain, and Mr. Wontner came to the three
convicts, and instead of announcing what they had to
tell, the clergyman produced a paper which he began
to read with all formality. The unhappy men were
kept in suspense, and the agonies of May and " the
anxious attention " of the others were naturally extraordinary. " His agitation was dreadful," and
when the reader came to the words " that the execution of the sentence upon John May shall be respited
during his Majesty's most gracious pleasure," he fell
to the ground as " if struck by lightning." So severe
was the fit that those present thought he could never
recover, so that it was naively believed " the warrant
of mercy had proved his death-blow." When he
came to himself his tumults of joy were extraordinary, " and he poured forth his gratitude to God and
to the persons who had exerted themselves for him."
He added that when the reverend gentleman began
to read his communication he thought it was his
death-warrant, and that on hearing he was to be
spared " he thought his heart had burst in his bosom."

All hope being now gone for the others, attempts were made to prepare them for death which were not received in a very encouraging way. Williams on being pressed to listen to some religious reading, said roughly, " I had religious talk enough during the day; I will have none of it to-night." He, however, addressed this precious piece of counsel to his fellows:—

" If you will be kind enough to let my brother prisoners know the awful death I shall have suffered when you receive this, it will, through your expostulations, prevent them from increasing their crimes when they may be liberated, and tell them *bad company and drinking and blasphemy is the foundation of all evil.* Give my brotherly love to them, and tell them never to deviate from the paths of religion, *and have a firm belief in their blessed Saviour.*"

Descriptions given of executions, though having a sort of hideous interest, can never be found acceptable, and the curtain may well be allowed to fall at the close of the trial. What occurred on the occasion of these two wretches being " finished " by the law is so dramatic, and has been told in so exciting a fashion, that it will certainly be found of interest— not less remarkable as a survival of the old barbarous days, are the singular proceedings that followed it, which seem now well-nigh incredible.

Bishop's demeanour was that of abject terror;

he seemed to relapse into his former stupor; his eye was bent on the ground, and he moved mechanically up to the officer, who stood ready to tie his hands, the wrists being closely pressed, when he stretched forth his arms. When that part of the preparation was concluded, he turned round and allowed his arms to be pinioned. This done, he took his seat at a side bench, without uttering a word. One of the under-sheriffs took a seat at his side, and in a low tone asked him if he had anything to confess. His answer was, " No, sir, I have told all." Williams was next introduced, and came into the room with the same short, hasty step which was noticed at the time of his sentence. Since then, however, his whole appearance had undergone the most terrible alteration. That cunning and flippant air which was noticed in him on his trial had left him. His look, as he entered the press-room on Monday, was one of downright horror—every limb trembled as he approached the officer by whom he was to be pinioned, and his hands shook to that degree that one person was obliged to hold them up, while another bound them together. While submitting to this operation he frequently ejaculated, " Oh, I have deserved this, and more ! " One of the under-sheriffs asked him whether he had anything more on his mind, or wished to make any further disclosure. He replied, " Oh, no, sir, I have told all—I hope I am now at peace with God. What I have told is the truth ! "

" At a few minutes before eight the sheriffs, accompanied by their officers and the prisoners, proceeded towards the scaffold, the ordinary reciting part of the funeral service. Bishop moved on in the same gloomy and despondent manner, which we have noticed. His appearance underwent no change as he approached the foot of the scaffold. Williams became more and more agitated as he advanced. Just as he came to the room which led out to the drop, he expressed a wish to see the Rev. Mr. Russell once more. That gentleman came forward, and while Bishop was being led out seated himself near him. Mr. Russell said to him, ' Now, Williams, you have another moment intervening between you and death, and, as a dying man, I implore you, in God's name, to tell the truth ; have you told me the whole truth, Williams ?' ' All I have told you is true, Mr. Russell.' ' But, Williams, have you told me *all ?* " Williams gave him this singular answer : ' All I have told you is quite true.' "

This was the last remark he made, and in a few moments he ascended the scaffold.

The scene without the prison was no less exciting. There was an immense assembly on the spot. The crowd, as early as one o'clock in the morning, had amounted to several thousand persons, and continued rapidly increasing. By five o'clock nearly two-thirds of the Old Bailey were filled with a dense mass of people. The continued buzz among the multitude at this time, the glare of light from the torches that were used to enable the workmen to proceed with their labours, and the terrific struggles among the crowd, altogether presented a scene which those who witnessed it will not soon forget. When the fatal drop was stationed in its usual place, it was observed that three chains were suspended from it. As soon as Mr. Wontner, the governor, heard of it, he ordered an officer to remove one of them, in consequence of May having been respited. This was done, and although it was then dark, it was instantly communicated throughout the vast assemblage, and a general cry of " *May is respited,*" was uttered on all sides.

At daybreak there was not less than from thirty thousand to forty thousand persons assembled. In fact, from one end of the Old Bailey to the other was a dense mass, and the streets in the neighbourhood, although not a glance could be had of the platform or the proceedings, were, from an early hour, rendered impassable by the throng of persons hurrying towards the scene of execution. The assemblage was the largest that had ever been witnessed on an occasion of the kind since the execution of Holloway and Heggerty, upwards of twenty years before. Notwithstanding the precautions taken to prevent accidents, several occurred at the end of Giltspur Street, immediately opposite the " Compter," where a very heavy barrier had been erected, and which gave way.

At eight o'clock the procession began to move from the press-room, the appearance of the executioner and his assistant on the scaffold indicated that the last ceremony was at hand. A general cry of " Hats off ! " took place, and the immense multitude uncovered. Bishop was first conducted to the scaffold, and his appearance was the signal for the most tremendous groans, yells, and hootings from all parts of the crowd. The wretched man came forward apparently unmoved by the dreadful reception he experienced. The executioner proceeded at once to the performance of his duty, and having put the rope round his neck, and fixed it to the chain, placed him under the fatal beam. A terrific cheer from the crowd proclaimed their satisfaction at the completion of the preparation for his exit to the other world ; but still, though placed on the brink of eternity, and about to be launched into it amidst the execrations of his fellow-creatures, the miserable criminal betrayed scarce a symptom of fear. The same listless, sullen manner that had marked his conduct throughout, appeared to be preserved by him to the last moment. Not a muscle appeared to be moved, not a limb to shake, though he remained during the awful interval of two minutes that elapsed before Williams was brought forward, exposed to the indignant hootings of the multitude.

Williams next ascended the scaffold, on reaching which he bowed to the crowd, who returned his salutation by the most dreadful yells and groans. He appeared to labour under extreme anguish, and his demeanour formed a complete contrast to that of his guilty associate. While the cap was being put over his eyes, and the rope adjusted by the executioner, his whole frame was convulsed by a universal tremor. The Rev. Mr. Cotton having engaged him in prayer— in which Williams appeared to join fervently, wringing his hands and ejaculating aloud—gave the signal for the falling of the drop, when they were launched into eternity. Bishop appeared to die almost instantaneously, but Williams struggled several minutes. The moment the drop fell, the crowd, which had been yelling all the time, *set up a shout of exultation* that was prolonged for several minutes !

The bodies having been suspended for the usual time were cut down at nine o'clock. That operation was performed by the executioner, amidst the shouts and jeers of the crowd, which still continued very great. An extraordinary and barbarous incident succeeded.

Immediately after, a small cart drove up to the platform, and the bodies of the two culprits were placed in it, covered by two sacks. The cart then moved on at a slow pace, followed by the sheriffs and City Marshal and a large body of constables, along Giltspur Street to the house of Mr. Stone, 33, Hosier Lane. The vast crowd yelling and making other dis-

MAY WILLIAMS

cordant noises as they proceeded. On reaching Mr.
Stone's it was with difficulty the bodies could be removed from the cart, the crowd appearing anxious to
get possession of them. The bodies were placed on a
table, and in the presence of the Sheriffs (in conformity
with their duty) an incision was made in their chests,
after which they withdrew. The bodies were removed
that night, Bishop's to the King's College, Williams' to
the Theatre of Anatomy in Windmill Street, Haymarket, to be dissected. They were publicly exhibited
at both places on Tuesday and Wednesday, when
immense crowds of persons were admitted to see their
remains.

The skeletons of the two criminals still adorn the
museums of the schools in which their bodies were
dissected. To complete the extraordinary inversion of
all laws, human and divine, exhibited in this case, it
was found later that the convict Bishop had been
married to his own step-mother!

Notwithstanding the minuteness of the confessions,
the full truth had not been told. Even when ascending
the scaffold Williams could not resist some evasion
in the form of his replies. It was the general
opinion that they were responsible for many more
unconfessed murders. This, it has been remarked, is
one of the invariable incidents of such confessions—
the explanation of which is that the murderer cannot bring himself to forfeit all chance of a reprieve.

A common form of evasion is to declare they have been condemned on false evidence, meaning—which may be true—that the act did not take place in the exact way detailed at the trial. The recent case of Lipski, where the murderer was actually writing his confession when a reprieve arrived (on which he tore it up), might be a warning to others to withhold confession to the last moment, after the cynical opinion of Mr. Raikes' friend "never to throw away a chance."

It may be noted in this place that one of the best testimonies to the truth of Lavater's doctrines might be found in the repulsive hideousness of many notorious malefactors, whose faces seem to indicate the foulness of their hearts. If, as old Macklin once remarked, "God writes a legible hand" their villainy was unquestionable. It is scarcely fair, however, to the murderer, to accept the evidence of these dreadful "casts taken after death," for allowance must be made for the violence of the process by which the patient was despatched; and we could fancy an apologist for this class of the community—it might have been De Quincy —making protest against thus unfairly condemning this unhappy section of society. On the other hand, there are some heads—such as that of Dr. Dodd, now before me—executed for far less heinous offences—which do not at all exhibit these odious traits.

Some of the persons who have been brought up at

Bow Street, have presented awful types of this
hideousness of crime.   If the portrait is to be trusted,
a woman, named Gibbs, charged in June, 1799, with
extorting money from innocent persons, seems to have
exceeded all precedent, and to have abused the privilege of criminals to be hideous.   An unfortunate man
named Jeremiah Beck had been her victim.   She had
waylaid him in Kensington Gardens, and succeeded
in extorting from his fears various small sums.   By
an unlucky chance she had attempted the same system
with no less a person than Dr. Ford, the Ordinary of
Newgate, who, when she came under his professional
charge, "had an opportunity of exhibiting his generosity
of soul."   The Press were generally struck with this
abnormal hideousness, describing her with much hearti-
ness as "an ill-favoured, disgusting figure," and there
was some humorous surprise at a person under such
disabilities selecting a department for which some
small share of good looks were necessary to give even
a plausible air to the accusation.

CHAPTER XII.

SIR J. DEAN PAUL AND CO.

IN most police cases, as they are called, there is a sameness, and even vulgarity which arises from the display of the "seamy-side" presented in all its repulsive force. But there is occasionally found a dramatic spirit which elevates the episode to a higher level, owing either to the appearance of persons whose position in life, or whose private life, it might be supposed, had set them above the temptations of those who have become victims of circumstances, or some cruel and unfortunate combination. Here we have the elements of surprise and expectation to pique or excite curiosity. For such incidents the ingenious novelist, such as the late Mr. Charles Reade, warily looks, and notes and turns to his profit. Few cases have so answered these conditions as the one we are about to enter upon.

In the year 1855 there were few persons in London whose name was mentioned with greater respect and sympathy than that of Sir John Dean Paul, well-known as one of the "good-people," connected with that

D EXECUTION

illiams, & John Bishop,
FOR THE
der of an Italian Boy.

Who were Executed this Morning at the Old Bailey.

Confession of Bishop & Williams!

Printed at BIRT's wholesale a. ' retail Long and Ballad Warehouse, No. 39, Great St. Andrew-Street, Seven, Dials, London.
Country Orders punctually attended to.

Handbills, Cards, &c. Printed on the shortest notice, and cheaper than any House in London.
One trial will prove the fact

JOHN BISHOP, aged 34, THOMAS WILLIAMS, aged 30 and JAMES MAY, aged 26. were indicted for the Wilful Murder of Carlo Ferriau, otherwise Charles Ferrier, & when placed at the bar, they seemed but little moved by the awful situation in which they were placed. A number of witnesses were examined, and from their evidence, the following particulars transpired :—On Saturday the 5th of November, the above three men took the body of a boy to the King's College, in the Strand, for the purpose of disposing of it for dissection, and for which they asked twelve guineas ; but one of the surgeons on examining it found a fracture on the back part of the head, which made him imagine that the boy had been murdered, and mentioning his suspicions to another of the profession, they kept bargaining with the men, while a messenger was dispatched to the Police Station, in Covent Garden, and procured the assistance of several constables, who, after a great resistance secured the prisoners, and conveyed them to Bow-street, where they underwent an examination, but no person being enabled to identify the body, they were remanded for another hearing. On the Sunday, the body was proved to be that of a poor Italian Boy, who travelled about London, with some white mice and a living tortoise, and the body having been opened by the surgeons, they stated that the poor fellow had been murdered. It was proved that Bishop & Williams resided in a cottage called Nova Scotia Gardens, Bethnal-green, and that the poor Italian boy, whose death is the subject of the present examination, was noticed within 20 yards of their house, with his, mice and tortoise, and has never been seen since ; a hackney coach was also observed to drive up to the corner of Nova Scotia Gardens, and three men, Bishop, May and Williams jump out of it, and proceed to Bishop's house, and soon returned with a sack, containing something heavy, which May had on his back, and Bishop holding it up behind. After it was put in they drove off, supposed for some hospital, on purpose to dispose of the body. Since the prisoners had been in custody, the premises of Bishop and Williams were strictly examined, and in the privy were found several large pieces of human flesh, and the entire scalp of a female with portions of the hair attached to it. The garden behind Bishop's house was carefully searched by digging, and two jackets, two pair of trowsers, two waistcoats, and two shirts were found buried in the earth. The privy of the next house was also searched, & a bundle discovered, which on inspection was found to contain an entire suit of female apparel.

On the conclusion of the evidence, the Judge summed up & the Jury returned a verdict of GUILTY against Bishop, May, and Williams.

The prisoners each put in a written defence, declaring themselves innocent of the Murder of the boy, but acknowledged themselves as resurrectionists for many years. The Recorder then in an impressive manner, passed the awful sentence of death upon them, exhorting them to prepare for the change they would soon undergo, he then sentenced them to be executed on Monday morning, and their bodies delivered over for dissection, and to be anatomised The prisoners heard the sentence unmoved, and when they were ordered to be taken from the bar, May raised his voice, and in a firm voice said, " I am a murdered man, and that man (pointing to Bishop) knows it.

Confession of Bishop and Williams.

On Bishop's return to prison after his trial, he seemed quite aware of his approaching dissolution, and on Saturday morning, being attended by the Rev. Mr. Williams, of Hendon, he made a confession of the Murders of which he had been guilty. He admitted that he had been concerned in the commission of FIVE Murders—that of the Italian boy ; of Frances Pigburn, the woman whose clothes were found in the privy ; of a drover boy, who had come to Smithfield with cattle from Lincolnshire ; a young child, and also a poor negro man. He entered into a minute description, most horrible in its details, of the mode by which he had perpetrated the inhuman murders Their method of destroying victims was by giving them laudanum to render them insensible, and then by throwing them headforemost into the well in Bishop's garden.—Williams also made a confession, and stated that the body which was swore to as the Italian boy, was that of a drover boy in Smithfield, about 15 years of age, whom he enticed to their house in Nova Scotia Gardens, when they gave him some rum, and he became stupified. They then took him into that garden, under the pretence of conducting him to the privy, and on their way threw him down, and pushing his head into the water, held him until he was suffocated.

Both men declared that May was not necessary to any of the Murders, and in consequence several gentlemen waited upon the Judge who tried them, and had four hours conference with him ; no respite was granted, and on Saturday evening a warrant was sent to Newgate ordering the execution of the three.

This morning before day-break every place that could command a view of the place of execution was crowded to excess, and when the Murderers ascended the drop, the yells & groans of the populace were deafening, and continued without intermission till the drop fell.—Their bodies will be given to the King's College for dissection.

YE tender hearts that love to share	His teeth they to a Dentist sold,
Another's grief or joy,	On wicked lucre bent,
How will ye bleed to hear the tale,	And with his folly in a sack,
Of the poor Italian Boy!	Straight to King's College went ;
White mice within his box confin'd	But May, then that saw the cruel deed,
He slung across his breast;	Has stopp'd their vile career,
And friendless, for his daily bread,	And sacred Justice for the crime,
Through London streets he prest.	Has doomed a death of fear !
To Bethnal Green he bent his way,	And on a public scaffold now,
As hapless fate design'd,	Unpitied and forlorn, [here
Nor thought when never doing harm	These wretched culprits they have
A Murderer's how to find !	The mark of public scorn !
Bishop, with Williams, basely there	And like their victims shall the knives
Their hearts to pity steel'd,	Of Surgeons strip each vein
Did to the horrid Burking plan	Tho' unlike them they will not feel,
Their cruel natures yield !	The murderers dying pain.

immense denomination, "the Religious Societies,"
and one of the heads of a snug, old-fashioned banking
company, "Strahan's." For any good or charitable
work Sir John Dean Paul's name was always sought
and found on some substantial cheque. At meetings
of the true Exeter Hall flavour, "opened with prayer,"
he was to be seen in person. This sort of reputation
is as good as "Capital" itself, and it speaks well for
public feeling in this country that whereas in France
such a character is looked on with suspicion, perhaps
from the recollection of Tartuffe, in England the combination of religion and villainy on a great scale, is
thought too odious and almost incredible to be
accepted.

One morning, June 23rd, 1855, the town was
astonished to learn that the sound old-fashioned bank
"Strahan's" had failed, and that the pious Sir John
and his partners had been brought to Bow Street,
where they were charged with fraud and swindling.
Many now will recall the astonishment and incredulity
with which this news was received. After a few
hearings, a strange story of swindling, of the most
coarse and vulgar type, was revealed, and the three
partners, Strahan, Bates, and the "Saint" Sir John,
were found to have been carrying on a system that
differed in no respect from the worst of the ordinary
"street charges" dealt with at the office.

Strahan's Bank was an old established one, in favor

with simple country customers. It was originally
"Snow, Paul, and Co.," but about the year 1838 a Mr.
Bates and Strahan came into the business. A
Prebendary of Rochester, Dr. Griffiths, had been one
of their oldest customers, and had banked there for
thirty years. At one time he took a fancy to make a
large purchase of Dutch bonds, which were procured
for him to the value of nearly 30,000*l.* At the bank
he had a private box, of which the partners had one
key, and he another, the bonds were carefully secured,
and, as he fancied, good easy man ! in safe keeping.
Every half-year the interest was received and duly
posted to his account.

Towards the end of the year 1854 it was remarked
with some surprise that the good Sir John was making
many visits to other banks, discount-houses, &c., for
the purpose of turning securities into money. Of
the other partners, Bates was an old man, and did
not take much share in the business, while Strahan
lived " in style " at a handsome place in the country,
and was reputed to be very wealthy. Sir John had a
mansion near Reigate. It was suspected that the
bank was in a crisis. Sir John at the time addressed
a letter to Gurney's Bank which ran : " My dear
friend, you will greatly oblige me by raising as much
money as these securities will cover, *pending the purchase of an estate.* You know for what purpose, and
also my reasons for not wishing my name to appear.'

The securities sent were a parcel of Dutch bonds, representing some 26,000*l.* in normal value, and on these the banker wished to raise 30,000*l.* " for the purchase of an estate." The Gurneys agreed to undertake the transaction, and offered to procure 27,000*l.*, which was done. Other operations of the same kind were undertaken, and securities representing about 113,000*l.* in all were thus disposed of. Nothing would do, however, the bank was tottering to its fall, and presently had to close its doors. The city articles were mildly severe on the directors, and their general imprudence ; it was said, too, that the bank had been kept open some days longer than it should have been, for they had continued paying out till there was scarcely anything left. One lucky man thus succeeded in getting a large deposit which he would otherwise have lost. Bankruptcy proceedings in the usual way were begun, and among the Exeter Hall folk there was much pity for the good man who had been thus afflicted.

But the poor Prebendary at Rochester grew uneasy as to his " ducats," and hurried to London to visit his strong box. He was told they were gone. With some difficulty he got admission to Strahan at his private residence. This gentleman, in a plausible fashion, frankly told him all that had happened—that they had been obliged to use his bonds—and assured him that he was doing himself great injury by taking any harsh or violent measures ; for the Prebendary had applied for a warrant for the arrest of the defaulters. Strahan, in the same plausible strain, assured him that had he gone to the bank in a reasonable spirit he would have been met in the same way ; for " directions had been given that notes of hand should be prepared for him. Time was all they wanted," &c. One is inclined to smile at these absurd pleas. But the height of farce was when the poor swindled Prebendary was told, " This is the first dishonest act of my life. *I never before defrauded any man of sixpence.*" A delightful speech, worthy of Tartuffe himself, and having a rich flavour of comedy. For the boast that he disdained to rob any man of " sixpence," addressed to a victim whom he had just defrauded of nigh 30,000*l*., is exquisite from its true Pharisaical flavour. The Prebendary was not to be " got over," and the warrants were issued. There was some little difficulty or hesitation in securing the culprits. On Tuesday, June 19th, Strahan was arrested when visiting a friend at Bryanston Square. Bates was also secured; while the officers went down to Sir John's place at Reigate, where they found him. As it was very late they consented to let him remain the night, under careful guard. At breakfast in the morning they conversed together on the case, when Sir John feelingly remarked that Strahan was to be pitied. " A year or so ago he was worth 180,000*l*., now he was not worth so many pence. He had nine children, and a beautiful residence at Dorking "—all which was very sad indeed.

But on their setting out for London some curious incidents occurred. Beguiled, no doubt, by their host's feeling reflections on the instability of human things, time so glided away, that they barely " caught the train." As the officers were getting tickets it began to move, when in an easy, natural way, Sir John stepped quickly in. The officers attempted to follow, but—such was the value of a gentleman's character in a rural district!—were pulled back by the porter, who positively refused to let them enter. They threatened him at his peril to stop them, but he said the orders of the Company were positive, and quoted the old familiar rule : " *none shall enter or leave a carriage when the train was in motion.*" This frustrating the officers of the Law, *by* Law, was another pleasant touch of comedy, and the mortified officers had to see their prey carried away from them to London. They rushed to the station-master to signal to stop the train. Not he—nothing of the kind. It was against the rules ! He agreed, however, to send a telegraph message, requiring the officials at London Bridge to stop the fugitive.

Another train came up presently, and the unlucky officers got in, to arrive in town only a few minutes after the other. But there was no Sir John in custody. The official there did not know him by sight.

How were they to stop him? It must have been an anxious moment for Sir John as he tendered his ticket, but he walked away quickly, and was lost in the crowd. It seems he went to Peele's coffee-house, where the officers, who had soon got on his track, were able to follow him. They arrived only a few minutes after he had gone. However, on that night, about eight o'clock, the banker walked into Bow Street Police-Office, and gave himself up. It was thought that he might have escaped, but the chances were too much against him, and his friends counselled him to surrender. He said : " My name is Sir John Dean Paul, and I have come to give myself up." He then explained how he was carried off by the train, but gave no reason why he did not wait for his captors at London Bridge.

The three bankers duly appeared at Bow Street, and were committed for' trial. Heavy bail was required, and found for two to the amount of 10,000*l*. each. Their trial did not come on until October 26th, a long interval, during which they must have suffered agonies of protracted suspense. Defence was, of course, hopeless, but the three culprits never anticipated the severe sentence which the judge passed on them—fourteen years' penal servitude ! The shock was noted in their faces. But every one thought it was richly merited. A striking incident followed. The defrauded and plundered Prebendary was seen to weep bitterly as he heard the sentence !

The bankers were conveyed to their prison to endure their punishment.   Time went by imperceptibly. The term, shortened according to the rule, was exhausted, and in due course the "good" banker was again seen flitting about London, and no doubt found worthy people to believe in him again.

CHAPTER XIII.

THE WATERLOO BRIDGE MYSTERY.

THE strange eventful panorama of adventure and crime which we have been witnessing, would be incomplete without the regular undiscovered " mystery." Nothing is so satisfactory and gratifying to the public as a genuine protracted mystery. Encouraged by hopes of discovery, or completely baffled for the time ; police officers, newspaper men, and ingenious speculators, all work together, and pursue the common track. Every one, during the process, is entertained, and excited. But these incidents are rare. It seems incredible now, how much these feelings were roused by the trivial matter now about to be recorded, and which for many weeks absorbed general attention. This was the celebrated WATERLOO BRIDGE MYSTERY.

On the 9th of October, 1857, a great sensation was created throughout the country in consequence of the finding of a carpet-bag upon one of the stone ledges of one of the abutments of Waterloo Bridge.

The discovery was made about half-past five in the morning, by a youth, named James Barber, who, in company with another man, was rowing up the

Thames. At first sight they imagined that the bag contained the proceeds of some great robbery that had been committed, and that it probably held a prize, but on opening, to their great horror, they discovered that it contained portions of the mutilated remains of a person evidently murdered, and deposited therein, together with a portion of wearing apparel, saturated with gore.

The men at once conveyed the remains to the Adelphi Arches, where they called the police, who took them to Bow Street Police-Station. The inspector immediately ordered a minute examination to be made, and an inquiry instituted.

General horror was excited and speculations were rampant. An inquest was held, when one of the men in the boat, a youth named Barber, reported how he had found the bag. He had noticed that there was a cord fastened to it, and a portion of the end of the cord was in the water. The bag was lying on the third abutment of Waterloo Bridge, and was lying on its side. This was about six o'clock on Friday morning. He and the man who was with him in the boat, got hold of the cord and dragged it into the boat. As soon as they got it in they broke the bag open by bursting the lock, and emptied its contents into the barge. When they saw that there was nothing but a lot of bones and flesh and clothes, they gathered them up again and put them into the bag.

A surgeon deposed that he had examined the contents of the bag. " It contained a quantity of bones and clothes, the same which the jury have seen. I fitted the bones together, and found that they must all have belonged to the same person. They formed a complete skeleton, with the exception of the cervical, seven of the dorsal vertebræ, some portions of the ribs, with the hands and feet, and a portion of the lower third of the lesser fibula, or some small bone of the leg. All the principal bones were sawn into two or more portions, and all of them had pieces of muscle or tendon attached to them, as if they had been cut off in a haggling manner. On four places only was the skin left adhering to the bone—a piece of considerable size being on the back of each wrist, and on the right tubercle of the left tibia. Those portions of the skin left were partly covered thinly with short, black hair, showing that the individual had been a vigorous adult. Between the third and fourth ribs was a cut in the flesh of rather smaller size than the cuts in the shirt and under flannel waistcoat. The reason of wounds in the flesh being smaller is because when the instrument is withdrawn flesh contracts again directly."

Asked whether he could state positively whether those injuries were inflicted during life, he said :—

" I can. Around the stab a good deal of blood was extravasated into the tissue, showing that the injury must have been inflicted during the life of the individual. That would not be the case unless the person was alive. The second and third ribs immediately under that I have mentioned, being missing, accounts for no other marks to correspond with the others on the shirt being found. The bones were clean sawn, except in one or two places, where great roughness seems to have been used. The saw must have been a fine one, and from some of the false cuts that have been made in some places, I should imagine it was a very narrow one. Several bones of the upper half of the back-bone are missing. I found the bones of such large make, that, taking the fact in connection with the portion of skin with short dark hair upon it, I should say it was a male. I have measured the bones of the deceased with those of my own, and I think that at least he must have been five feet eight inches in height. There were some dark hairs from whiskers. I think that the body was not cut to pieces till the rigidity of death had set in some time, because in fitting together the portions of the right leg I found the right knee-joint and hip-joint firmly fixed, so that the thigh must have stiffened at right angles with the rest of the body. The right arm had also stiffened with the fore-arm under, and pointing towards the body."

Asked, was he satisfied that the wound he saw in the chest was given during lifetime?

"I am certain of it, as the blood has infiltrated the

tissues extensively; I should not be surprised from the appearance of the remains if it was found that they had been boiled, or partially boiled. I imagine that that may have been the case from the rigidity of the tendons. I have not the least doubt that the body was never used for anatomical examinations. It is not possible that such could have been the case. A medical man must have wanted a body either for the muscles, nerves, arteries, or bones. The muscles, nerves, and arteries I can most positively assert have not been dissected, and the bones have been destroyed."

The toll-keeper of Waterloo Bridge, who used to see a good deal of dramatic life in the course of his business, next came on the scene. He was on duty at half-past eleven. "I remember seeing a person dressed as a woman come up from the Strand side. She was alone, at least I did not notice any one with her. She had a carpet-bag with her. The carpet-bag now produced I believe to be the same. She laid a halfpenny on the iron plate, and took the bag with her longways. In trying to get it through with her she turned the stile twice. I said to her, 'Why did you not ask for some one to help to lift your bag up for you? see what you have done, you have caused me, by turning the stile twice, to lose a halfpenny toll.' She said something in reply in a gruff tone of voice, and I stooped down and took the bag by the handles, and put my hand under the bottom, and so lifted it up on to the iron plate of the stile. I am certain from that that it had leathern handles, with bottom and sides. I particularly noticed the bag, as there was a strong gas-light from the lamp, and on the side I noticed that there was a bright flower in the pattern. On the bag now produced is a flower which I believe to be the same that I noticed. I am not certain that I should know the woman again, but I think I should if I saw her. Her hair seemed as though it had been thickly powdered and plastered down on to her forehead. I particularly remarked that she seemed agitated, as if she was in a hurry, and I thought she was hurrying to go by the train from Waterloo, which starts at 11.45. She spoke rather gruffly, it was certainly in a masculine tone of voice. Her height might have been about 5 ft. 3 in. She was a short woman and rather stout. I have no recollection of ever seeing her come off the bridge again."

It seems astonishing that men in such a position, with thousands passing by, should be able to retain a distinct idea of any individual or their behaviour; but experience shows that railway porters and others, in the habit of dealing with vast passing crowds, gradually acquire a sort of professional instinct, and unconsciously note and retain any peculiarity that differs from the uniform course.

Later a " general dealer," called Ball, recollected
that he had passed over the bridge close upon midnight, and this is what he saw: " I live at 10, Grove
Place, Waterloo Road, and am a general dealer. On
Thursday night, the 8th of October, I was going along
Waterloo Bridge, from the Strand side, between eleven
and twelve o'clock. As soon as I had passed the
turnstile I turned back to beg a light of Evrington.
When I got there, I saw a short party dressed in
female attire, and about 5 ft. 3 in. in height, passing
through the turnstile. I heard Evrington say to her,
' If you can't lift the bag yourself, why can't you ask
some one else?' I then saw Evrington lift the bag
over. It was a carpet-bag, but I did not notice the
colour of it, or whether it had leather sides. The
person in question also had a parcel. When Evrington
handed the bag over to her, she took it from him, and
I then caught sight of her full face. She had a sallow
complexion, with rather sunken eyes, and a mark on
the left cheek, near the nose, which I took to be a
mole. The hair was a kind of white, but it did not
look a natural colour. I saw her features distinctly,
but did not take any notice of her dress. She proceeded along the bridge about half way, and then I
overtook her, and passed her. After I had passed her,
I saw a rather tallish man on the opposite side of the
bridge, and near the Surrey end of it, walking easily
towards the Strand. He was about the first recess on

the Surrey side. I did not take any particular notice of him, and could not identify him if I saw him."

Dr. Alfred Taylor, a well-known authority on what is called "medical jurisprudence," went minutely into the whole case, and his report is most interesting, as showing the wonderful fashion in which science can work, even when supplied with slender materials. It suggests Professor Owen's power of reconstructing a whole animal from a single bone or joint. After stating that it was clear that the remains were those of a man, he thus ingeniously argues from the position of the remains.

"The left arm was fixed in such a direction as to be widely separated from the left side of body, instead of lying parallel to it, and on this side the forearm was firmly bent on the arm at an angle of 45 deg. On the right side, viewing the direction of the bones, as fixed by the portions left in the joints, the forearm was bent on the upper arm at an angle of 80 deg. On examining the joints it was found there was no ossification or other disease to account for this firmly-fixed condition of the upper or lower limbs on the right side, and the upper limbs on the left side.

"So I infer from this examination that the limbs had not been relaxed since they had undergone the rigidity of death, that the body had been cut and sawn while in this rigid state; and that the mode in which it was subsequently treated, tended to preserve the fixed condition of the joints, as a result of cada-veric rigidity in a constrained posture.

" The cutting and sawing of these remains took place after death. The cutting has been effected roughly with a knife, while the sawing has been performed in the shafts with a fine saw.

" In one portion of the left side of the chest, com-prising the second, third, and fourth ribs, with one half of the chest bone attached, there is an aperture in the flesh presenting the appearance of a stab. It is situated in front, between the third and fourth rib near their junction with the chest bone.

" Assuming that this wound has been inflicted during life, it would have penetrated the heart and produced rapid if not immediate death. The muscles of the chest through which this stab had passed were for some space around of a dark red colour, evidently produced by blood which had been effused as the result of this wound.

" This appearance is unlike that produced by a cut or a stab in a cold dead body in which circulation has ceased. The edges of the wound are averted, and this fact, together with the infiltration of the muscles with blood, which even *the soaking in liquid for a week had not removed,* lead me to the conclusion that this wound was inflicted on the deceased either during life or within a few minutes of death—i.e., while the body was warm, and the blood was liquid.

" The joints had been sawn through, evidently with great trouble, at points where a scalpel, even in the hands of a young anatomist, would have speedily effected a separation of limbs. The acromion process of the right scapular, or bladebone, had been sawn through in order to remove the shoulder.

" In short, the clearest examination, coupled with the knowledge derived from a period of seven years spent in the study of anatomy by dissections, lead me to the conclusion that these remains have not been employed for any anatomical purposes whatever, and that they have been boiled in water.

" This would carry the probable time of death to the last week in September or to the first week in October. The period may have been shorter than this—that is, that death may have taken place more recently; but considering that the weather during that time was mild, humid, and favourable to putre-faction, I do not think it was longer."

" Had death occurred at a more remote period I should have expected to find some visible changes indicative of putrefaction in the interior of the right hipjoint, and on the deep-seated portions of flesh around the joint."

Conclusions.

" The conclusions which I draw from this examina-tion are :—

1. " That the remains are those of a person of the'

male sex, of adult age, and in stature of at least five feet nine inches."

2. "That they present no physiological or pathological peculiarities; also that the limbs had not been relaxed since they had undergone the rigidity of death; that the body had been cut and sawn while in this rigid state, and that the mode in which it was subsequently treated tended to preserve the fixed condition of the joints, as the result of cadaveric rigidity in a constrained posture.

3. " That the cuttings and sawings of the remains took place after death, and that the cutting was roughly done with a knife, while the sawing has been roughly performed in the shafts with a fine saw; that in all probability the deceased died from the stab in the chest, which penetrated the heart.

4. "That the body has not been used for dissection for the purposes of anatomy, but that on the contrary, from the period at which the rigidity of death took place, the remains have been rendered perfectly useless for any purpose whatever; that all those parts which are useful to anatomists have been destroyed by a person or persons quite ignorant of the anatomical relation of parts. They have been cut and sawn before the rigidity of death had ceased—i.e., in from eighteen or twenty-four hours after death, and in this state have been partially boiled and subsequently salted. The body of the deceased has not been laid out or attended to like that of a person dying from

natural causes, and which body might be lawfully used for anatomical purposes.

5. " That the person of whose body these remains are a part may have been dead for a period of three weeks prior to the date on which they were examined by me—namely, the 21st of October.

" The examination of the articles of clothing leads me to the conclusion that the body of the person who wore them must have been subjected to great violence. The stab, penetrating from behind the double collar of the over-coat, must have been inflicted with great force, as it extends from the collar to the under-coat and waistcoat.

" The clothes, however, have been exposed and washed since they were stained with blood, and this creates a difficulty in forming an opinion. But the cutting and tearing of the right sleeves of the over-coat, under-coat, and shirt are consistent with the assumption that the body had become rigid after death in a disordered position, and that the clothes were torn from it. This position is indicated in the remains, especially on the right side, by the fixed or bent condition of the hip and elbow-joints."

Nothing, however, was ever discovered, and it remains a mystery to this hour. In spite of this deliberate opinion of the experts, the " Wise Men " hold that it was a practical joke of some medical students, which seems likely enough:

The toll-keeper of Waterloo Bridge, standing by his

little hutch, night and day, witnessed, as I said, many curious and half-dramatic scenes. Twenty years ago a regular stereotyped heading in the papers was " Suicide from Waterloo bridge," and it will be recollected how constantly recurred some sad tragedy of some young woman flinging herself from the centre parapet. It is curious to find that, since the tolls have been abolished, this mode of suicide, which was as much in favour as casting oneself from the Duke of York's Monument—has fallen out of fashion.[1]

Mr. Dickens, in one of his pleasant journeys through London, did not forget the Waterloo Bridge toll-keeper and the dramatic opportunities of his situation. One night, escorted by his favorite police, he paid him a visit.

Our author ensconced himself in the toll-house and had a long and interesting talk with the toll-man on all the incidents he observed in his professional life. First, on the " suicides," which now appear to have " gone out " with the tolls.

" ' This is where it is,' said Waterloo. 'If people jump off straight forwards from the middle of the

[1] It was at last found necessary to enclose the gallery of that monument with a hideous cage, which really destroyed the whole symmetry of the upper portion. The present writer may take credit for the disappearance of this eyesore, having suggested to Mr. Plunket, the present Chief Commissioner of Works, that as no one now ascended to see the view, or for other purposes, it might be restored with safety to its original state. This was promptly done.

parapet of the bays of the bridge, they are seldom
killed by drowning, but are smashed, poor things;
that's what they are; they dash themselves upon the
buttress of the bridge. But, you jump off,' said
Waterloo to me, putting his forefinger in a button-hole
of my great-coat; 'you jump off from the side of the
bay, and you'll tumble true into the stream under the
arch. What you have got to do is to mind how you
jump in! There was poor Tom Steele from Dublin.
Didn't dive! Bless you didn't dive at all! Fell down
so flat into the water, that he broke his breast-bone,
and lived two days!'

" I asked Waterloo if there were a favourite side of
his bridge for this dreadful purpose. He reflected, and
thought,—yes there was; he should say the Surrey side.

" He considered it astonishing how quick people
were! Why, there was a cab came up one boxing-
night, with a young woman in it, who looked, according to Waterloo's opinion of her, a little the worse
for liquor; very handsome she was too—very handsome.
She stopped the cab at the gate, and said she'd pay
the cabman then : which she did, though there was a
little hankering about the fare, because at first she
didn't seem quite to know where she wanted to be
drove to. However, she paid the man, and the toll
too, and looking Waterloo in the face (he thought she
knew him, don't you see!) said, ' I'll finish it somehow!' Well, the cab went off, leaving Waterloo a

little doubtful in his mind, and while it was going on at full speed the young woman jumped out, never fell, hardly staggered, ran along the bridge pavement a little way, passing several people, and jumped over from the second opening.' At the inquest it was giv' in evidence that she had been quarrelling at the 'Hero of Waterloo,' and it was brought in jealousy. (One of the results of Waterloo's experience was, that there was a deal of jealousy about.) 'Sometimes people haven't got a halfpenny. If they are really tired and poor we give 'em one and let 'em through. Other people will leave things—pocket-handkerchiefs mostly. I have taken cravats and gloves, pocket-knives, tooth-picks, studs, shirt-pins, rings (generally from young gents, early in the morning), but handkerchiefs is the general thing.'

" 'Regular customers ?' said Waterloo. 'Lord, yes ! We have regular customers. One, such a worn-out used-up old file as you can scarcely picter, comes from the Surrey side as regular as ten o'clock at night comes ; and goes over, *I* think, to some flash house on the Middlesex side. He comes back, he does, as reg'lar as the clock strikes three in the morning, and then can hardly drag one of his old legs after the other. He always turns down the water-stairs, comes up again, and then goes on down the Waterloo road. He always does the same thing, and never varies a minute. Does it every night—even Sundays.' "

CHAPTER XIV.

MANY will recall the sudden shock which the news of Orsini's diabolical attempt to assassinate the French ruler at the Opera House, gave to all who were looking on at the theatrical and rather tawdry glories of the Second Empire. In mediæval chronicles we read of the reckless poisonings, conspiracies, &c., which impart such a dramatic colour to history, with a sort of wondering curiosity, as though they belonged to barbaric times, and were now finally swept away. Yet our generation has witnessed elaborately planned conspiracies that exceed anything conceived in the darkest and most violent eras—explosions, destruction of the innocent to secure that of the obnoxious—burnings, stabbings, poisonings, on a scale that throws previous attempts in the shade. But nothing has ever exceeded the Orsini attempt, or the Clerkenwell atrocity in this country.

On the night of January 14th, 1858, it was known that the Emperor would visit the Opera House, the old, somewhat dilapidated institution in the Rue Le

Pelletier. This opportunity was seized on by a gang of Italians, who had arrived specially for the purpose, to arrange a plot for his destruction. As it proved, he had the narrowest of narrow escapes. Orsini, Gomez, Rudio, and Pierri repaired to the place, each provided with a bomb, about the size of a soda-water bottle, and charged with an explosive substance. Each of these grenades, which were of iron, had a number of projectory nipples, so contrived, that on whatever side they fell, an explosion was sure to take place. On the morning fixed the four assassins had held a council in the Rue Montmartre, and at half-past six finally met at Orsini's lodgings in the Rue Monthabor.

The Emperor and his party were expected to arrive in State between eight and nine o'clock, and a crowd of some hundreds gathered to see him. Owing to certain suspicious circumstances, a police-officer was attracted to Pierri, who was found hovering about the private entrance to the Emperor's box, and arrested him. Being searched at the station one of these alarming bombs, charged with fulminating mercury, was found upon him, with a revolver and a dagger.

But now the Imperial carriages arrived in all show and state, and of a sudden a terrible explosion followed. Three of the bombs had been thrown at or under the carriage. One of the horses was instantly blown to pieces, and over 500 wounds were inflicted on the helpless crowd, whose shrieks of horror and suffering filled the air.[1] Orsini himself was struck by a fragment, and, by a strange fatality, was tracked by the blood which streamed from his wound. The others were speedily arrested at their lodgings, and on Rudio 260*l.* was found in gold.

It was natural that this horrible attempt, with its attendant display of indifference as to the lives of innocent persons, should have roused universal indignation. The consequences, however, had nearly been somewhat serious for this country, for it came out in the investigation that the whole had been plotted in London by a number of Italians and Frenchmen, who went backwards and forwards to Paris to lay their plans, always returning for shelter to their lair in London. The bitter and angry feeling was excited in France. The "French colonels" vapoured loudly, offering the Emperor to go and seek the conspirators in their dens. As is well known, Lord Palmerston showed a complaisance in meeting the complaints and menacing pressure of the French ministers, that seemed strongly inconsistent with his old and much vaunted *Civis Romanus* declaration.

A Dr. Bernard, a native of France, who had been

---

[1] The escape of the Emperor and Empress was a narrow one. His hat was perforated by some projectile, the aide-de-camp who sat beside him was wounded in the neck, and two footmen were seriously hurt.

a surgeon in the navy, had been driven from his native country, and had found shelter in England, where he had been living for some five years. There he had become intimate with many refugee Italians, among whom were the conspirators who had taken part in the attempt, namely, Orsini, Pierri, Gomez, and Rudio, with an Englishman named Allsop, who had escaped. The Englishman, in October, 1857, had gone to Birmingham, and employed one Taylor there to manufacture six "instruments," as his counsel called them, but which were, in fact, hand grenades. Bernard was living in Park Street, Bayswater, Orsini in Kentish Town. Shortly after the bombs were made, Bernard was found to have ordered a quantity of nitric acid and alcohol, which it seems are used to manufacture explosive substances, such as "fulminate of mercury," and the bombs might now be assumed to be complete, and furnished for their deadly purpose. Next Orsini was found to have visited Brussels. Bernard visited a Swiss cafe-keeper, and employed him to bring over the "machines" to Orsini, he himself following shortly afterwards. When Orsini set out for Paris, he brought a letter from Bernard, introducing him, under the assumed name of Allsop, to a gun-maker. Pierri later appeared at Brussels, and, on presenting a letter from Bernard, he received from the cafe-keeper a portion of one of the machines. Orsini was furnished with a

large sum of money—435*l.*—which he exchanged for
notes at the Bank of England, and one of the notes
for 20*l.* Bernard was found to have changed at a
money-office. With this cash Bernard went to the
house of Rudio, another of the conspirators, who was
in a state of destitution, and who immediately afterwards repaired to Paris, furnished with a false pass-
port, procured for him by Bernard. These were awkward facts, and seemed to prove, in the strongest
way, the prisoner's complicity in the conspiracy.

Mr. Edwin James, a great legal personality of the
day, was Bernard's counsel, and found it an easy
task to contrive a defence. It was ready to his hand
in the excited state of public feeling, and the text was
a plausible one. What, England, that has always
sheltered the oppressed, was she now to be the minion
of the despotic Governments?

Was she now to yield up the poor persecuted refugee to the threats of the foreigners? The prosecution
could never have been sustained but for pressure from
without. "His friend the Attorney-General had
omitted to explain how it was that now, for the first
time in the annals of English jurisprudence, this case
had been brought before a jury. His friend had not
explained how it was that at the bidding of those
who were not content with the blood of Pierri and
Orsini, they were asked to stain an English scaffold
with the blood of the prisoner." At Bow Street they

had begun by trying to make out the charge of conspiracy, but that had failed them. The act they found too weak for the purpose, so they tried to mend their hand by the odious Conspiracy Bill. When this also failed them they had to fall back on the charge of murder, which he contended had not been made out. He then passed to the facts, and maintained it was essential to prove that the grenades handed to Orsini were those which had passed through Dr. Bernard's hands. He admitted that Bernard was joined with Orsini in an insurrectionary movement; but denied that it had been shown that he was concerned in this particular conspiracy.

He alluded next to what seemed always a strong point, viz., the letter of Walter S. Landor, who had offered a substantial sum to any man who would rid the country of the tyrant. There was a sort of toleration extended to this tempestuous, erratic being, as though he were not quite responsible, or that his words did not bear any serious meaning. An awkward bit of evidence was the finding of a letter of Allsop's in Bernard's possession. " If I were in California now, I would at once offer double the amount offered by Landor, to the man who would rid the world of that most wretched caitiff. *He must be killed,* and with him the systems, which he seems necessary to keep up." That such a letter should have been addressed to Bernard by one of the admitted conspirators was

certainly strong presumption of guilt. Mr. James, however, disposed of it in an airy fashion, saying that all
public men must have letters as extraordinary addressed
to them, the mere receipt of which should not compromise them. But his real defence was the rather
" clap-trap " one of " Old England " being not merely
the home of the free, but the shelter of the oppressed,
and Old England would never allow herself to be
made the tool and executive of the oppressor! The
jury took this view, and amid shouts of applause,
which Dr. Bernard led, waving his hat over his head,
the prisoner was acquitted. In the midst of these
transports he was astonished to find himself placed at
the Bar on a fresh charge, and there was something
almost ludicrous in his air of discomfiture; but this
was merely a formality for disposing of the other
accusations which the Crown did not mean to urge.

CHAPTER XV.

Towards the end of the year 1865 there had been a
sort of outbreak of the negroes in Jamaica, who, inflamed by Baptist ministers and others, rose and committed some acts of violence. A small body of about
a score of volunteers, having resisted them, was cut to
pieces, and the custos of Morant Bay was murdered.
The governor of the island, Mr. Eyre, took energetic
measures to put down the insurrection, and promptly
arrested a minister named Gordon, who was believed
to be the chief instigator of the insurrection. He was
tried by court-martial and executed. Great excitement was caused in England by this high proceeding,
which had the effect of crushing the disorder. It
was urged that Gordon was innocent and had been
arrested at Kingston where martial law had not been
proclaimed. This feeling of sympathy was gradually
worked up into a sort of fanatical passion. Every one
took sides, society was divided, religious feelings and
passions were roused. The ministers found themselves obliged to suspend the governor, and send out

a commission to inquire into the case. Meanwhile private persons and societies set on foot what seemed a persecution of the luckless governor. Indictments were laid against subordinates, which, however, grand juries and judges rejected.

Nearly three years afterwards, and two days after the presumed Clerkenwell conspirators were committed for trial, Sir Thomas Henry was disturbed by the appearance of Sir Robert Collier before him, instructed to make an application " on behalf of Mr. John Stuart Mill and Mr. P. A. Taylor, of the Jamaica Committee," that a warrant should be granted to arrest Mr. John Eyre, for the murder of Gordon. He named the several Acts of Parliament, declared that a " great crime " was believed to have been committed, and called on the magistrate to comply with his application. The magistrate declared that the highest authority in the country had laid down the law to a grand jury who had thrown out the bill. During the twenty-eight years he had held his office he had never heard of a magistrate granting a warrant on a charge which a grand jury had declared to be unfounded. Holding this view he declined to grant one.

Nothing daunted, the committee set to work and brought their case to the court of Queen's Bench, where on May 8th they obtained an order directing Mr. Vaughan, the Bow Street magistrate, to hear the case and commit him for trial if necessary. Accordingly on the 20th there was another field-day at the office, and Mr. Vaughan was induced to commit the governor for trial. The unfortunate man gave vent to his feelings, declaring that now for two years and a half he had been the victim of a ceaseless, rancorous persecution, and added this prophecy " he was convinced that those who had combined against him would not influence or be accepted by the higher tribunal to whom he now appealed."

The " persecution," however, went on for some time longer, in spite of the vehement advocacy of Carlyle and others; but gradually, public opinion seemed to come round to his side; and in 1872, the Government felt itself justified in defraying the expenses he had been put to, and which were said to have amounted to nearly 10,000*l.*

CHAPTER XVI.

THE BARON DE VIDIL.

IN the month of June, 1861, a considerable sensation was caused by the news of an attempt by a French baron, who was well known about St. James's, to murder his own son. The incidents of this attempt were truly extraordinary, dramatic, and unaccountable. The name of the assailant was Baron de Vidil, who belonged to good clubs, and was known as a warm adherent of the Orleans family.

The country between Teddington and Twickenham was in 1861 much more open and secluded than it is now, nor had the so-called "Jerry Builder" as yet invaded the district. On the evening of the 28th of June, a little after seven o'clock, a woman and a man who were walking down one of the lanes close to Orleans House, were startled by a young man, a Frenchman he seemed, running towards them in a sort of panic. His face was bloody, and when he reached them, he flung himself to the ground, "crouching down between them," so it was described, exclaiming, "O, mother, protect me!" Next a riderless horse made its appearance—thus there were two —which was closely followed by another apparition. An older gentleman rode up, and with real or affected astonishment asked, " What was the matter," adding that the young man's horse had shied and flung him against the wall of the lane. Having made this statement, he rushed through the hedge, being much torn by some tenter-hooks, and disappeared. The young man was carried to the " Swan " Inn, and a surgeon was sent for, Mr. Clark, who found two severe wounds, one in the forehead, as from a blow, while at the back of his head there was another. The elder gentleman who had followed, was now recognized as the Baron de Vidil, for he was well known at Orleans House, and to the doctor he repeated the story of his son having been thrown against the wall. Mr. Clark had been struck by the terror shown by the son at every movement of the father and at the idea of being left alone with him. His suspicions were aroused by the two wounds, which were not consistent with the story. The son presently contrived to whisper to the doctor that he must get his father away, and an assistant was then placed in charge of him. In the morning the party went up to London, when the young man was taken to his uncle, to whom he revealed the fact that his father had made a murderous attack upon him in the lane. It was thought

right that a warrant should be asked for at Bow
Street, and the painful spectacle was to follow of a
father being arrested at the instance of his son.

It appeared that this Baron de Vidil was the son
of a wealthy glove-maker, who had been ennobled by
Louis Philippe. The son had come to England, where
he had married a lady worth 30,000*l.*, on which he
had withdrawn from business. He had become an
attaché at the French Embassy, and became well
known in society. His manners were pleasant, and
he was now about fifty-five. The wife was dead, and
there was only this son, Alfred, who was to inherit
his mother's fortune, after his father's lifetime, which
in case of the son's dying without "appointing," as
it was called, or making a will, became the father's
absolutely. This had an awkward air. The father,
Baron de Vidil, did not appear to answer to the
charge, and, it was found, had fled to France. An
application for his extradition was made to the French
Government, but it was believed that, through some
looseness in the clauses, the treaty did not apply to
his case. Acting, however, on advice, the Baron
thought it better to return, and arrived in London,
accompanied by two of the French police.

When he appeared at Bow Street an extraordinary
scene took place. The young man when he entered
the witness-box refused to testify against his father,
in spite of much pressure and admonition from the

magistrate, and the case was adjourned to give time for reflection. When the case was resumed another curious scene took place.

Mr. Pollock stated that in consequence of the continued refusal of the young man to give evidence, he was instructed to retire from the prosecution, and to leave the matter entirely in Mr. Corrie's hands. Mr. Sleigh, amid some expressions of disapprobation, suggested that "the ends of justice would be entirely answered by the defendant being called upon to enter into sureties to keep the peace towards his son, M. de Vidil." The young man was then put into the witness-box, and, in answer to the magistrate, expressed his determination not to give evidence. The magistrate addressing him in a kindly manner, said, " Since you were here the other day you have had an opportunity of reflecting upon what I said to you, and also conferring with your friends and legal advisers. Am I to understand that you still refuse to give your evidence, fully and truthfully, in this case ? "

" Yes, sir," replied he, " I do refuse."

Mr. Corrie then stated his intention to adjourn the case until the following Monday, so that the Government might consider the question of the expediency, or otherwise, of prosecuting the Baron on their own responsibility. He intimated that he should express an opinion to the Secretary of State favourable to his interference in the matter. However, next day an intimation was forwarded by Government to the magistrates of Bow Street to the effect that the case of Baron de Vidil must be dealt with in the ordinary way, and that it was not their intention to put themselves forward as prosecutors.

On Monday the Baron was finally examined and committed for trial. The son was in attendance, and sat opposite the witness-box. The prisoner, as before, kept his face covered by his hands throughout the inquiry.

There was nothing new in the evidence as to the committal of the assault. Mr. Parker, an uncle of M. de Vidil, produced a letter written to him by the Baron on the day after the assault. In this letter he said :—" I am very anxious this morning about Alfred, who has left his lodgings at 40, Duke Street, without letting me know where he has gone. I am the more anxious that he met yesterday with an accident in riding, the horse having hit him on the forehead in rearing. I sat with him till twelve last night, and told him I would call early in the morning. I beg you will be so kind as to inform me whether you have heard from Alfred. With best regards to Mrs. Parker and children, believe me, &c.

The prisoner's son was then sworn. He said, " My name is Alfred John de Vidil. I am the son of the prisoner. I still decline to give any evidence against my father." Mr. Corrie asked, " You persist in that resolution ? " To which witness replied, " Yes, I do," and then sat down.

Mr. Sleigh addressed the magistrate for the prisoner, saying, " If you are resolved to commit the prisoner for trial I shall not waste the time of the Court by addressing you, but shall prefer to reserve our defence. I hope I may take it for granted, however, that you will admit the prisoner to good substantial bail. Happily, in this country, every man is held innocent until a conviction is recorded against him, and as there can be no other object here than to ensure the attendance of the prisoner, I trust you will now consider that we are entitled to this concession. You have heard from the officers that the Baron came to England of his own free will to meet this charge. There was no power in the world to compel his production here, for the treaty did not meet his case ; and yet he requested that he might be brought to London in order that the inquiry might be fully gone into."

Mr. Corrie said he must pursue the course usually taken in cases of this description, according to the rule laid down by the judges. " We must consider the nature of the punishment to which the prisoner is liable in the event of his being convicted of the crime of which he stands accused, and then ask the question, ' Is he likely to forfeit any sum of money rather than expose himself to the risk of such punishment ? ' Looking at the question in this point of view, I think it is my duty to decline accepting bail.

I feel the less hesitation in coming to this decision because there is an immediate appeal from my judgment if you like to avail yourself of it. There is a judge in town to whom you can apply, and who can reverse my decision within twenty-four hours, if he is disposed to entertain your application."

The prisoner was then committed to Newgate for trial. Application for the release of the baron on bail was made to the Lord Chief Justice: it was refused.

In due course a regular prosecution followed. It was felt that, in the default of the most important witness, there was no chance, not of a conviction merely, but of even going through the ordinary forms of a trial. But by a strange chance, a labouring man, who, since the assault, had been lying seriously ill, was heard of—who, it was rumoured, had been close to the lane and had witnessed the whole incident. When he was restored to health, he came forward, and deposed to what he had seen, completely confirming the young man's story of a murderous assault. The Baron de Vidil was accordingly convicted, and sentenced to a term of imprisonment with hard labour. The young man still refused to depose against his father. He made a mysterious announcement, however, which caused some speculation. He declared that his father had threatened to make some serious charge, and that if this was persisted in, his lips would be unsealed, and that he would reveal all. Nothing, however, resulted in either direction. Still refusing to give his testimony, the law proceeded to deal with him in its practical automatic way—without too much severity, yet at the same time firmly enforcing its practice. He too was sentenced to a term of imprisonment for " contempt of court."

CHAPTER XVII.

THIS case seems to recall the days of Captain Kidd, or the Buccaneers ; and as the eight swarthy, truculent-looking pirates stood ranged in the dock to stand their trial for murdering their English captain so lately as the year 1864, the spectators turned away with horror. Even the name of the craft, *The Flowery Land*, had a romantic sound, and was suited for a story-teller of the sea like Mr. Clark Russell.

On the 28th of July, 1863, *The Flowery Land* sailed from London for Singapore, with a general cargo of wine and other goods. The captain was one John Smith ; the first and second mates were Karswell and Taffir. There were two Chinamen, a Norwegian, and the rest were Spaniards, Italians, Greek. A few spoke English none understood, but it must have been on the whole a suspicious and dangerous miscellany for an English captain to go to sea with.

During the voyage the motley crew showed signs of indiscipline, and ropes' ends and confinement had to be used freely. One Carlos was so bad that he was brought up and strapped to the bulwarks, but Captain Smith, who was good-natured and humane, seeing that he was ill, came himself and sent him below. They were always grumbling at the food and the duties they had to perform. Sometimes they quarrelled among themselves, as did the two men Blanco and Carlos, when the mates roughly separated them, giving Carlos a blow. Their ferocious spirits were all the while registering such affronts, and nursing their revenge. On the night of the 10th of September, the second mate had come down from his first watch at midnight, and was relieved by the first mate, and went to sleep. He was awoke at four o'clock in the morning by a noise of hammering on the deck. He jumped up and tried to ascend the steps, but was stopped by the prostrate figure of a man whom the others were beating about the head with handspikes or bars. A blow promptly sent him below. He called to the captain and receiving no answer, rushed to look for him, and found him lying in a pool of blood quite dead. The bloodthirsty wretches had mutinied, and were murdering their officers. Presently all the noise ceased —and the band, who consisted of Lyons, Blanco, Duramo, Santos, Carlos, Vartos, Narcolino, and Lopez, came into the cabin and gathered round the second mate. He asked, did they want to kill him. They said no, but he must navigate the vessel to Buenos

Ayres. He next saw them about to throw the captain's body overboard, but the faithful officer interposed, and begged to be allowed to sew it up decently in canvas, which was permitted. They next rummaged all the captain's boxes, dividing the money among themselves. The cargo was then rifled and champagne bottles were seen lying about the deck.

The ship being put under the direction of the second mate Taffir, he was regarded with much suspicion, as though he were likely to betray them, and when he spoke a strange vessel, there was a great noise among the Manilla men, who spoke in Spanish, fancying he had been telling tales. His life, indeed, was constantly in peril. Once he saw one of the ruffians stick a knife through the arm of the steward. At last, on October 2nd, after an awful period of suspense, they sighted land, when the boats were got out and filled with provisions and champagne. The steward was thrown overboard, and the ship scuttled. They had their story ready prepared—shipwrecked mariners, an American vessel which had foundered at sea, laden with guano for Bordeaux, and they had been in the boats five days and nights. The captain had got into another boat, but they had lost him. On landing the second mate told his story, and on inquiry five of the men were executed.

Another of these mutinies at sea, accompanied by

violence and murder, took place more recently, and once more recalls the piratical atrocities of the Buccaneers of the Spanish Main. This was the mutiny on Board the *Lennie*, the result of that extraordinary mixture of sailors of all nations in a single vessel.

The *Lennie* was a Canadian vessel, loading at Antwerp for New Orleans. The captain was a Canadian named Hatfield, the first mate an Irishman called Wortley, while MacDonald, an Englishman, was second mate, the steward, Von Hoydonck, was a German, and eleven hands, Greeks, Italians, &c., were engaged to fill up the motley crew. Among others there were Lettes, Renken, Cannesso, *alias* Green, Peter Petersohn, Angelos, otherwise Demetrius, or Andres, or Little George; Moros or little Johnny, Carcares, otherwise Kalair, or more familiarly " Joe the Cook;" Kaida or George Thomas, or "Lips;" Leosis, *alias* Lewis; Caludis, *alias* Meletos or "Big Harry." Such was the miscellany which the luckless captain had to control. A few of this extraordinary gathering spoke a sort of English, but it was difficult to get the orders understood,

The vessel sailed on October 23, but there soon arose difficulties between the captain and his men. " It was a teetotal ship," said the steward, " and we had no spirits at all on board. We had sixteen on board all told. My orders from the captain were to give the men plenty of everything they wanted, and we went on very well for a few days. He was a very nice man, who seldom went on deck ; he used to read by the cabin fire. For the seven days we were at sea, before four a.m. and ten p.m., every day was quiet, but I cannot answer for other times when I had turned in. On the morning of the 31st October I was in my berth about four a.m., and I was awoke by a noise on the poop. I then said to the second steward, who slept in the berth below me, ' There is a row ; turn out, and see what time it is.' He went to the fore-cabin and looked at the time, and said to me, ' It is twenty minutes past four.' We then went together to make some coffee, and took six steps up to the deck, but the companion doors were shut, and the boy told me they would not let him up. I tried to get up then, but the prisoners Caludis and Leosis were standing there, and Caludis said the best thing I could do was to stop down below. They were standing against the door watching, so that no one should come out of the cabin. Before this I heard the order ' ship about.' The braces got foul. All hands would be wanted for putting the ship about. The captain said ' This is always the case,' referring to the braces— ' you are no sailors, you are a lot of soldiers.' Then I heard the captain halloo, as if his throat was cut, he cried, ' Oh, oh ! ' I heard four or five kicks on the deck. He was killed right over the top of my head ;

that was how I heard so well. The next I heard five shots fired, and all hands went forward after the reports. The shots were very shortly after one another. About twenty minutes after I heard a second rush on deck, all over the main deck as if they were after the second mate. Then, about 5.30 or 5.35 a.m., all hands came down into the cabin, the whole eleven of the prisoners. Before then I went to the captain's cabin through the skylight as soon as I heard the row, but found no one in it or the mate's cabin. I found in the captain's bunk two loaded revolvers. After the row I went to the pantry and put the revolvers amongst a lot of dry apples used for the men. Then I went to the skylight and tried to get out. Charley Renken was standing at the wheel, and sang out, 'There is the steward coming out of the skylight!' I put my head in then, and shut the skylight inside, and remained till all hands came down. George Green said, 'Well, steward, we have finished now!' I and another sailor, who was on deck, witnessed the details of this foul murder. The captain gave the order, 'About ship,' in English, and the ship was put about. The captain was swearing because they could not 'pull well' the braces. The captain said, using the foulest language, 'Pull those braces well,' in English. He said no more. Big Harry put his knife in the captain's stomach. He drew his knife out of its sheath, and stabbed the captain close to the cabin door; I was within two feet of him at the time. Big Harry said something at the time in Greek. The captain was looking on the weather side. The captain when he was stabbed went right round the poop. French Peter on the other side of the poop stopped the captain and stabbed him with a knife in the front of the head. I could not see the knife; it was dark then. Then Big Harry caught hold of the captain and heaved him down on the deck; and pulled off his boots and cap, and threw them down on the deck. There was blood all over the deck and the captain. He was a long time alive; his face was covered with blood. I saw the second mate coming from the weather side of the house on the main deck crying, and put his hands on the boatswain's neck, and said, 'Boatswain, save my life.' The second mate before that went and tried to put the captain in the cabin, and then Big Harry put a knife through the second mate twice. After that he ran forward. I saw him coming from the weather side of the house when he spoke to the boatswain, and asked him to save his life. The boatswain shoved him away, and then Big Harry stabbed him again several times in the back of the neck. The second mate fell on the deck on the lee side, close to the fore-braces. They then pulled off his boots and cap, and braced the fore-yards sharp up. 'Lips' was at the wheel when the captain gave the order to put the ship about. 'Lips' then went on the fore-rigging. The first mate had then gone to the middle of the fore-yard. 'Lips' had a revolver in his hand, and he fired at the chief mate from the middle of the fore-rigging. He fired four times. After each shot the mate said, 'Oh, oh!' I did not see if he was hit, but the prisoner aimed at the chief mate. The chief mate lowered himself down on to the deck by the four buntlines. Joe the Cook was standing close to him when he got down, and he stabbed the mate through, I should think he put the knife through him twenty times all over." *Joe the Cook here smiled and passed a remark to Nicholas, who stood next to him, as if it was rather an amusing reminiscence.* " The chief mate then fell down on the deck and I saw the blood all over French Peter and Big Harry, who had then come forward, and French Peter put his foot on the mate's stomach, and cut his head half off. Big Harry and the whole five were standing close." *The five implicated men here laughed and passed remarks.* "They then got ten fathoms of mooring-chain, made it fast round the mate's legs, and pitched him overboard. All his clothes were on except his cap, which some one took off. All five helped to heave the body and the chain overboard. The mooring-chain was got from the top of the anchor-chain. Joe the Cook then made fast the cat-block to the second mate's legs. All the five were together. The second mate was then dead. He was lifted up by the five together, and heaved overboard on the port side, at the waist, or middle of the ship.

DANIEL GOOD,

The supposed Murderer of Jane Jones

From a sketch taken at Bow Street, Thursday, April 21st 1842.

After the second mate was thrown overboard, we all went into the cabin."

After sailing for some days they began to grow suspicious of the steward, on whose superior knowledge they had to depend for the guidance of the ship. " On the 5th, we went out to sea again. Green said, ' You have nothing to do with the case, but you may choose to sell all my countrymen.' I said, ' No, I shall not sell your countrymen, but it is no use going to sea to carry all the sails away.' I said, ' I will go to sea again to please you, but you are no friend of mine, or you would stick to me as you are an officer in this ship.' He said, ' If I did, they would kill me.' We went out to sea for three days, and then Peter Petersohn, after we got clear of the land, took charge of the ship. When out of sight of land French Peter said, ' I will do the same with you as I have done with the others.' He spoke in French. I answered, ' I was prepared to die as much as he, that they might do as they liked with the ship, and I would do no more.' He said at first, ' You go down below, we don't want any more of you,' and then Petersohn took charge of the ship for two days. Then French Peter came to me in the cabin, and said, ' We want to see the land ; what course are we to steer ? ' I said, ' Let the man who is in charge of the ship tell you ; don't come and bother me,' then Big Harry came down and said, ' Steward, you take charge of the ship again ; that fellow can't navigate, I know.' I said, 'Yes, on condition you leave me alone, obey my orders and I will see you right.' All hands came down to the cabin, and I told them I would only take charge on condition that none of them interfered with me. Then Big Harry said, 'The first man who interferes with the steward in the navigation of the ship we will cut his ears off.' I took charge of the ship then, and took her into Isle de Re. It was then about eleven o'clock, blowing a gale from the westward, and I shortened sail, and took her back to Isle de Re the next day, and I said, 'We have been working hard for seven days, and have made no way yet, and the best thing is to let go the anchor.' I told the boatswain to get the anchor ready. We got in about 8.30. Big Harry asked me what place it was. I told him it was Cadiz, and they did not know better, and thought they would get to Gibraltar the next day, when a fair wind came. I told the boatswain to get fifteen fathoms of chain over the windlass. Before anchoring, French Peter, who saw it was not Cadiz, said, 'We won't stop here, we will go out to sea again.' But wind and current being too strong against us, Petersohn, who again took charge, and put about, could not beat out. Then French Peter said to me, 'See you put the anchor right, and as soon as we get a fair wind we go to sea.' I said, 'All right.' That was about half an hour before we anchored, between eight

and nine p.m.   That night we threw two dozen bottles
overboard, containing a message in French and English,
for assistance.   We anchored that night, and I let
out sixty fathoms, though only in eight fathoms, to
give them plenty of time and trouble to get the anchor
up again.   On the morning of the 8th, at four a.m., I
hoisted a signal to show the ship was in distress, and
it remained up till eight a.m., when Big Harry asked
what it was up for.   I told him it was to let the shore
know we were windbound.   He went forward and
asked Renken and Petersohn if they knew the
flags.   They came out and looked at the flags,
and turned and said that they were for the police.
Then French Peter came and asked me what the flags
were for, and I told him the same.   He said, " Never
mind windbound,' and he hauled the flags down,
and was walking on the poop, and Joe the Cook came
to me and said, ' Steward, don't fret.'   I said, ' No,
I won't fret.'   He said, ' We won't do you nothing ;
we have done enough ; we killed three, we don't want
to kill any more.   They want to put away the boy,
because they are afraid he will split on them when
they get ashore, but I won't agree to that, for I like
him.'   I said, ' The first man that comes aft to do
anything to him, it will be life and life, for our life is
as sweet as any of yours.'   He then went forward,
and four men—Big Harry, French Peter, Joe, and
Leosis—came and said, ' Steward, now look out that

the boy when he comes ashore, don't say anything.'
I said, ' Don't you trouble ; I will look out for him.'
French Peter pulled down the signal himself. On
the 8th, in the morning all hands went forward,
and they unshackled the chain at seventy-five
fathoms, to slip if a fair wind came, without getting
the anchor. A pilot-boat then spoke us on the 8th.
French Peter told me to go below before the
boat got alongside. When the pilot came alongside
at Isle de Re I was ordered down below by French
Peter. I was down half an hour. French Peter told
the pilot that they were waiting for a wind, and that
their chronometers had run down. The pilot was
alongside twenty minutes, and asked what ship it was.
I told them it was a Republic, that there was no police,
and that they had better go ashore. I promised them
not to do anything for two weeks. I said I would
stop aboard. They came down into the cabin,
searched everything and took what they wanted.
They said they had no money, and I told them
I had none. They searched one another; they would
not trust one another. I told them that I thought
Lips had got the money. He was stripped of his
clothes. The others were only felt over. I am not
aware that any money was found. Some of the men
kissed me before they left. French Peter, Joe the
Cook, and Big Harry kissed me before they left.
Johnny Moore did not leave the vessel. He could

not. The boat which left was full. I heard Peter
Petersohn and some others talking on the deck. They
said the others had gone, and they would go ashoro
too."

In due course Justice overtook these wretches; they
were brought to England, tried, and executed.

CHAPTER XVIII.

MULLER.

Of all the days of excitement which Bow Street has seen, few could approach that Saturday in 1864, when the railway stations at Camden Town and Euston, from top to bottom, were crammed with eager sight-seers. The reader will readily guess who was thus waited for: one, who had been captured after an anxious expectancy and an almost providential combination of chances—the notorious Franz Muller, the German, who had murdered the poor old city gentleman, in the North London Railway carriage, on the evening of July 9, 1864, the deed being done within three minutes and a half—the time spent between two stations. There were incidents of savagery and merciless brutality, that seemed to call out from the hideous wounds—" *No mercy for him.*" In that short space this wretched being had fought and conquered the old man after a desperate struggle, and then flung him out on the permanent way—leaping out himself with his miserable booty—only a watch —no cash after all !

Now of all the difficult things, the tracing a murderer

—whose victim has been thus casually met with—
seems one of the most hopeless. But the English
police really distinguished itself on this occasion.
A little before ten o'clock that night, as the train from
Fenchurch Street arrived at Hackney, a gentleman,
who was about to enter a carriage, called the guard's
attention to its condition. The cushions were saturated, there was a pool of blood upon the floor, and on
the brass work of the window were distinct impressions
of bloody fingers. Almost at the same time, an engine-
driver returning from Hackney Wick saw a dark object
lying in the way, and getting down with his mate
found it was the body of a gentleman who still lived.
He was carried to a house, and it was found that his
skull was fractured and battered fearfully. He lingered on till midnight, when he expired. From letters
found in his pocket, it was discovered that this was
Mr. Briggs, an old and faithful servant and chief
clerk in the bank of Messrs. Robartes, of Lombard
Street. He had left his bank at three, had dined with
his niece at Peckham, and had been seen into an
omnibus in the Old Kent Road, which would take him
to the city, when he would return home comfortably.
On examining his pockets, a sum of four pounds ten
was found in gold and silver, while a portion of his
gold guard hung from his button, showing that he had
been robbed of his watch. Further, a hat—which was
not Mr. Briggs' hat—had been left in the carriage.

Many will recall the horror, indignation and pity caused by this barbarous murder : it touched the whole sympathy of the city—and there seemed to be this element in the case, that the murderer had committed the crime to little purpose, and had been disappointed in his hopes of profit.

As soon as the dreadful incidents were published in the papers, the hat and the watch furnished their mute but convincing testimony. A silversmith in Cheapside, bearing the significant name of Death, recalled that a man had exchanged a watch-chain with him, and it was found to be Mr. Briggs'. A cabman named Matthews then appeared, who described a young German from Cologne, named Muller, who had lodged at his house, but had disappeared since the murder. This man had been engaged to Matthews' sister, but the match had been broken off. With an extraordinary infatuation he had on his departure presented her with a little card-board box which was marked with the Cheapside silversmith's name, DEATH. The hat, too, was recognized as Muller's, for, by a strange chance, there had been much discussion between the pair, on the subject of hats; Muller admiring one of a particular cut and pattern on his friend's head, who was persuaded to order him one like it, for which he was never paid. To his late *fiancée* he had given his photograph, which was recognized by Death as that of the person who had brought him the chain.

While these things were being put together, there
was a small sailing-vessel belonging to Messrs. Grim-
sell, that was on the point of sailing to New York.
She was called the *Victoria*—and Muller came down
to the London Docks, and paying 4*l.* for his passage,
embarked. He had told one of his friends that he was
to obtain a situation in the colonies worth 150*l.* a year.
The *Victoria* sailed about July 15th, and some six weeks
after was seen off the harbour of New York, when on
August 24, a boat put off from the shore and boarded
her. Two men had a short conversation with the
captain, who called Muller to the after part of the
ship. One of the men, who was Inspector Tanner, of
the London police force, seized him by the arm. He
asked what was the matter, when the other, who was
a New York police-officer said, " *You are charged with
the murder of Mr. Briggs.*" Thus justice had secured
her prey. It had soon been ascertained in London
that a man answering Muller's description had sailed
in the *Victoria*, and Tanner, and Sergeant Clarke,
with Death, the silversmith, and Matthews, the cabman,
had embarked in the *City of Manchester*. They had to
wait some weeks in New York—every day looking out
anxiously for the arrival of the sailing-ship.

After the customary formalities he was handed over
to the English officers. One of the most exciting
days Liverpool has witnessed was September 17,
when the *Etna* arrived, having the officers and their
prisoner on board. From Liverpool he travelled in

the custody of Inspector Tanner and Sergeant Clarke, and reached the Euston Square terminus at about a quarter to three in the afternoon. " Both at the Camden Station and at Euston, hundreds of people had assembled long before the train containing the prisoner was due. The uncertainty had the effect of lessening the pressure at one particular point, which was great enough as it was, and strong precautionary measures were taken at both places by the police and by the officials of the company to maintain order. Some hundreds of people had congregated on the Camden ticket-platform, and a telegram preceding the arrival of the train having been received there that Muller was in the last compartment of the last second-class carriage, a rush was made towards the lower part of the platform as the train, which was a very long one, appeared in sight. On its stopping the carriage containing the prisoner was besieged by the crowd. While the tickets were being collected the most eager curiosity was shown by the crowd to catch a glimpse of the prisoner, who sat between Tanner and Clarke, with his face to the engine, and great excitement prevailed. The tickets having been collected, the train moved on, many of the people as it did so giving vent to their feelings by hooting and groaning. On its arrival at the Euston Station the excitement was still more intense, and the exertions of a strong body of police were required to keep order. The train was drawn up so that the carriage containing Muller was

immediately opposite a side outlet into Seymour Street.
There the Bow Street police-van stood, with its door
towards the platform, ready to receive him ; and the
moment he stepped upon the platform, which he did in
a light, jaunty manner, he was assailed with groans.
The officers Tanner and Clarke, having each hold of
an arm of the prisoner, hurried him across the platform, and, amid a scene of tumult, entered the prison-
van, which was then driven off, amid many mani-
festations of popular indignation. He was taken by
way of Hampstead Road, Tottenham Court Road, and
St. Giles's to Bow Street. There the same intense
curiosity was shown to catch a glimpse of him.
As the van passed along Bow Street, it was guarded
by constables on foot and followed by an excited mob.
The moment it stopped in front of the police-station a
fearful rush was made towards it. Some minutes
elapsed before a passage to the entrance to the station
could be made and kept; but at length the door was
opened, and Muller alighted, amid a storm of groans
and hisses, with a light step and almost flippant air.
He did not seem in the least disconcerted by the hooting with which he was assailed by the mob, and to
them his appearance was evidently disappointing.
Slim, pale, short, with light sandy hair, and anything
but attractive features, dressed in thin, shabby clothes,
and wearing a battered white straw hat, he had a very
ordinary appearance.

" In the inspector's room the usual examination took

place, and the property found on him was described in general terms, and under this heading the only words entered on the sheet were ' A hat and a watch.' When Mr. Durkin read the charge over to him, his head drooped a little, and there was an appearance of exhaustion about him as he was being conducted from the inspector's room, but on gaining the yard outside he brightened up again and walked rapidly to his cell."

In due course he was tried and convicted. The German community in London took up his case with more than national ardour. On the very eve of the execution the King of Prussia telegraphed to her Majesty, asking that her prerogative of mercy might be exercised. It was felt, however, that public feeling would not allow of this being granted, and the request was refused. The 14th of November was the day of execution, which took place publicly at Newgate, under the old system. All night long the streets were blocked up with people waiting to see the painful exhibition, and it was said that 12*l.* was the price paid for a "room with a good view." The criminal showed much indifference, not to say courage, in his extremity, and, it was noted, raised his eyes with a sort of curiosity to the beam from which he was presently to be suspended. It was impossible, however, to feel sympathy for him; one had only to recall the scene in the railway carriage when he was battering out the brains of an old man, and then flinging him out on the railway, to be cut in pieces by the next passing train. On the first glimpse, a storm of yells broke from the expectant crowd. An extraordinary incident attended his last moments. Dr. Cappel, a German clergyman, who attended him, had been unwearied in his attempts to extract a confession. The cap was drawn over his face when this strange, momentous conversation occurred :

Dr. Cappel: Muller, in a few moments you will be before God. I ask you again, and for the last time, are you guilty or not?

Muller: Not guilty.

Dr. Cappel: You are not guilty?

Muller: God knows what I have done.

Dr. Cappel: God knows what you have done? Does He also know that you have committed this crime?

Muller: Yes, I have done it!

At this moment the clergyman's face was bent over close to the shrouded head of the criminal, and the sound of the last words—" done it,"—was overpowered in the crash of the falling trap. The next second his body was swinging in the air.

CHAPTER XIX.

THE year 1867 was to be remarkable for what was known as the Fenian scare. A few bold and desperate men had come from America, and had been diligently "enrolling" vast numbers of the Irish resident in England. Arms and money were brought into the country, and various *soi-disant* generals and colonels, whose commissions were conferred by the gang, imparted a theatrical colouring to the schemes. It seems clear that the rank and file followed reluctantly, and were intimidated; their support was but half-hearted; for all the violent acts which marked the year were the work of a few daring men, who succeeded in imparting general terror. The names of " General Halpin," " General Burke," " Colonel Healey," and " Captain McCafferty " became familiar.

What distinguished these Fenian attempts from other revolutionary acts was their hideous barbarity. Nothing could be baser or meaner than the murder at Manchester of a police sergeant (once described by Mr.

Gladstone as " a casualty ") ; and not less astonishing is it that the perpetrators should have since been held up as " martyrs." Another Fenian, known as " Captain Clancy," hotly pursued by two policemen, fired three times with his revolver at one, narrowly missing him. When finally captured he declared complacently, " Well, it was a good battle, and a fair duel well fought." In speeches like this all heroism seems to be extinguished, for the policemen were unarmed.

The complete success of the Manchester rescue —for the prisoners " Colonel Kelly " and " Captain Deasy " were never re-captured—disturbed the public mind a good deal. In most of the counties meetings for self-protection were held, and special constables sworn in. In London, too, there was much disquiet, as it was known to the police that the Fenian captains were plotting something. On November 20th two men were arrested by the police in Woburn Square, after a sort of scuffle and attempted rescue. Their names were Burke and Casey, and it proved that they were high and important personages in the Fenian ranks. They were brought up on many occasions at Bow Street. No doubt, encouraged by the success of the Manchester rescue, plots were laid to intercept the prison-van on its way to Bow Street ; while other schemes were contrived, with the great Clerkenwell disaster, by a small party of desperadoes, who seemed to have been intoxicated by the power placed in their hands, and the supplies of money which were freely sent to them from the " States." This idea, that supplies of money signify actual power and support, has often deluded the demagogue to his own destruction. Nothing so cajoles the dupe as the display of gold by his leaders. The two prisoners who were confined at Clerkenwell were allowed to see their friends, and it was declared that the bold suggestion to blow down the wall of the yard, while the prisoners were at exercise, was made by one of them. There were some half a dozen conspirators of a more feeble class—the two Desmonds, Mullany and Mullady, English, and some others, residing in the decayed streets around Golden Square.[1] They seemed to have little power to originate anything striking, and, accordingly, after a short delay, two more vigorous conspirators—one Barrett, and a " Captain " Murphy—came specially from Glasgow. Strange men and women were now observed to be hanging about the prison, puzzling the neighbours, who suspected them to be detectives. One of the conspirators, who revealed the plot, described how he frequently saw Barrett, and that their talk was all upon Burke, and how the

---

[1] It was felt to be important that prisoners of such distinction should be rescued, and the precedent of the Manchester attack was encouraging. But these men either lacked daring or ingenuity ; and, indeed, the situation offered extraordinary difficulties. They were, in most cases, forced to act, owing to the terrorism of their associates.

release was to be contrived. " But nothing was done
for a time until a letter was received from some party.
I was asked to purchase some green copperas,
which was used to bring out some invisible ink, and
the letter was then read by Captain Murphy. The
letter contained a drawing or plan of the House of
Detention. The letter stated that a sewer ran under
part of the wall, which was very weak at the place, and
that a barrel of gunpowder must be obtained, and *it
would blow the wall to hell* "—such was the favourite expression. "It must be also done about four o'clock, and
they must get money to buy the powder a little at a
time ; and," added the worthy conspirator, " if they did
not do it they *ought to be shot.*" They had a full
meeting about ten o'clock at night on December 11th.
About a dozen, including Captain Murphy, who was
lucky enough to disappear later, assembled. Strange to
say the money necessary was difficult to make up ; but
the powder had been gradually brought together, enough,
in small portions, to fill a barrel. In this strange
council it was resolved to make the attempt on the
following day.

At this council Barrett was flourishing a revolver,
which went off and severely wounded one of the
party, named Ryan. Captain Murphy then loaded
another pistol, and presented it to one of the conspirators. It was settled that all should attend near
the prison on the following day. The " Captain "

undertook the job—a ball was to be thrown over the wall to give the signal. But the Captain failed in the operation, and the fuse did not light. Barrett was very indignant, and undertook it himself on the following day, making the favourite declaration that " he would blow the place to hell."

In this case, as in most others, the inevitable informer makes his appearance. Only the day before the explosion Mr. Pownall, the chairman of the magistrates, received a secret communication, warning him that an attempt would be made. Accordingly the governor, instead of allowing the prisoners to exercise in the ground at the usual hour—between three and four—changed it to ten in the morning. The police were also informed, and some extra men were sent to keep watch in the streets surrounding the prison. Many significant incidents were noted. A man came to one of the houses commanding the prison, and begged to be allowed to go up to the top that he might have a glimpse of some relative who was confined there. He was refused. A woman named Anne Justice was seen hanging about the prison all the day, and talking with men. One of the warders, looking up from within, noticed a window filled with men who were eagerly gazing down into the prison yard. Finally, as the hour drew on, it was noticed that Burke became much excited, and went often to the window of his cell.

One of the informers thus graphically described a

scene when Desmond was setting out to execute the hellish plot. " He kissed my wife, and bade her good-bye, saying he was going to take a jump. She told him not to be so foolish. He then leant over the door and whistled to me, and whispered, ' *the thing must be done.*' I asked him what he meant. ' They're going to blow up the prison,' was the answer. I asked when ? and he said, ' The thing must be done. We have found out from Anne Justice, by going in with Casey's dinner, the time at which they exercise in the yard, and the trick must be done between half-past three and four o'clock.' He then bade me good-bye and said, ' Jemmy, when I am blasted into eternity, pray for me; or, if I get off and am arrested, the next place will be Mill-bank.' "

On the momentous day, between three and four o'clock, some children were playing in Corporation Row outside the prison wall. People were passing and repassing; others were at their windows. A boy of thirteen, named Abbott, was standing at his door and noticed a man wheeling a small cart, containing a barrel, which he drew up close to the prison wall. He left the cart for a few moments and presently returned with what seemed fuses or squibs in his hand. The savage, ignorant brutality of what followed is un-matched in any country. Some children were playing about, and interested in his proceedings—to them he gave the squib he did not want. One of the older boys was smoking, and from him he obtained a match. Then without a word this ruffian ran off, the others waiting to see the result.

But a policeman had noted something of these proceedings, and his suspicions were roused. When the man ran off he pursued; but just as he passed the cart a terrible explosion took place, convulsing the neighbourhood; while nearly the whole wall crumbled down in ruins, revealing the prison-yard. The officer was hurled to the ground, but with characteristic resolution he recovered himself, and leaped up.

Two men were rushing away, and the woman before alluded to, were caught by a policeman, who bravely held the men, one by each hand, until assistance came up. Six men were finally captured. The Desmonds, English, Mullany, Allen, O'Keefe, and the woman Ann Justice were brought up to Bow Street before Sir Thomas Henry. As the authorities were now dealing with desperadoes, the novel spectacle was seen of policemen armed to the teeth with revolvers and cutlasses, for fear of a rescue. There were several remands. Strange to say the woman Justice, on the night of her arrest, made a desperate attempt upon her life, and was with difficulty saved.

One of the informers met English, another of the conspirators, late that evening. He came to the door, saying, "For God's sake, Jemmy, give me as much as you can, for we want to send them off."

The other asked, "For what?" "What, haven't you heard?" was the reply; "the House of Detention is blown bang up." Then, as he said, he gave him two shillings, and could spare him no more, as business was slack. Next morning he heard him reading from the placard of a newspaper, and saying aloud the word "diabolical," when he added, "We'll burn the whole of London yet, and that will be a sight more diabolical."

The damage done was appalling, an immense piece of the wall was blown out nearly to the ground, some houses near were levelled, and windows were shattered far and near. But more disastrous was the effect on the innocent persons of the neighbourhood. Upwards of forty were injured more or less severely; one was killed on the spot, three more died shortly afterwards; little children playing close to the prison were shockingly mutilated, even infants in arms were shockingly injured. Yet this reckless, brutal business, an eminent statesman, the same who spoke of the Manchester murder as "a casualty," was now found to describe as an important political event, valuable as "having drawn attention" to the Irish Church.[2]

[2] As much obloquy pursued him for this statement, which was turned to great profit by the Irish agitators, who declared that such violence was the only way of obtaining consideration for their wrongs, Mr. Gladstone furnished a justification of himself. He now likened the effect of the explosion to the sound of "the chapel bell" on some

It was known, however, that they had not found the man who had fired the barrel. Many of the persons who were near the spot declared they would recognize him. After many inquiries, and diligent investigation, the authorities turned their eyes to Glasgow, where they discovered that the whole plot had been hatched. A description of him was sent to that city, but he had disappeared, after having left his work. A strange accident discovered him. During the night of January 14th, a policeman heard the sound of firearms in the street, and hurried to the spot where he found two men. On being questioned they put him off with "chaff," saying it was some boys discharging a squib. They then offered a drink, but the officer was not to be got rid of, and insisted on taking them to the station. On the road one of them ingeniously made a leap into the air, as if to stretch his limbs, and it was later found that he had thrown away a revolver. This sudden return and the likeness to the description sent down awakened grave suspicions. A telegram was despatched to London, which was answered by the arrival of Inspector

---

tranquil Sunday morning, when he was reading, "I trust," he added, "a *good* book." This blessed sound warns him that it is time to attend service. It is not the *cause* of his attending service, but it "draws his attention." This likening of the innocent chapel bell to the villainous explosion was in the worst taste, and did not improve the argument. Indeed, any deed of extra violence in Ireland is thus described as "ringing the chapel bell."

Williamson and four of his subordinates, who, convinced that he was the man they " wanted," carried him to London. It was indeed Barrett, and the man who had put the light to the fatal barrel, and when he arrived there were plenty to identify him. Mr. George Grossmith describes the rather alarming precautions taken at Bow Street Police-Office, the van being escorted by a large squadron of mounted police well-armed, soldiers also attending, who kept the streets clear. It seemed like an invested town. Nor were these precautions uncalled for; the ruffians, who showed as much stupidity as desperation, were going about with revolvers, which they produced on small provocation. As we have seen, a fellow was arrested in Bedford Square, who instantly discharged two shots from his revolver, and when thrown down attempted to fire again, but the ball jammed.

Whatever want of clearness there was in identifying Barrett was supplied by the informer Mullany, one of the accused, who gave fullest evidence against him. At the trial one of the usual *alibis* was manufactured in the Fenian circle—the plan of which was suggested by Barrett himself in a letter—in which he begged them to find out certain shoemakers to whom he had given orders on the very day of the explosion. They were to ask " if they *didn't* recollect his coming and his being angry at his boots not being ready," with other matters which were exactly recalled. This *alibi* was supported by a number of witnesses, mostly agreeing in their testimony, and was so ingeniously built up that the Chief Justice said, "It was the most remarkable instance he ever remembered." No doubt, as he suggested, the incidents of the boot-repairing had occurred—but not at that time. On this theory may be readily explained the ingenious fashion in which this *alibi* was supported. Nothing could be clearer than the evidence of Barrett's presence in London at the time, and so it appeared to the jury who found him " guilty."

When sentence was about to be pronounced, a curious and not undramatic scene was enacted. The prisoner was allowed to deliver an extraordinary, impassioned address, of a native dignity and pathos, that was scarcely in keeping with the crime for which he had been convicted. In fierce and bitter terms he denounced the witnesses and approvers who had appeared against him. "Never," he said, "did he feel the supreme degradation of his country till that day." He protested, but in guarded terms, his innocence. But he was going away to a land where justice would be done him, and those who had inflicted this wrong on him would have punishment meted out to them.

A deep impression was made on all who listened, and some had uneasy suspicions that such a calm and dignified demeanour could only be compatible with innocence. Yet one had only to turn back to the scene outside the prison, and contrast this sensitiveness as to his own life with the barbarous callousness to the fate of dozens of persons, young, old, and infants in arms, who were injured or killed by his act.

The execution was fixed for May 12th. There was much discussion as to the conviction, and many were impressed by the ingenious *alibi*. So earnestly pressed were these objections, that a respite of a week was granted; while commissioners were despatched to Glasgow to inquire into the *alibi*. This took up more time than was anticipated, and the respite was extended to another week. It was found, however, that the *alibi* did not gain by the examination; and the result was that, in the usual form, " the Secretary saw no grounds for interfering with the due course of law."

The execution took place on May 26th, and it was remarkable that this was the last public execution seen in England. Numerous crowds assembled round Newgate, and greeted the malefactor, as he appeared, with yells of execration; for the recollection of the brutal act which he had perpetrated, and the widespread destruction, had roused the mob. It was said he behaved with wonderful firmness, without any bravado; and his confessor declared that he showed genuine penitence, if not for the act, for his course of life.

CHAPTER XX.

THE alternations of tragedy and farce and even panto-
mime weekly exhibited at Bow Street Office, together
with the extraordinary variety of entertainment that
turned up, was perhaps never better illustrated than in
the decade of years that stretched from about 1870 to
1880. What could be more contrasted than the case of
Governor Eyre with Slade's, the slate writer; or of
Barrett, the villain of the Clerkenwell tragedy, with
that of the female personators?

On the morning of April 30th, 1870, the *habitués* of
the court were amused and astonished to see at the
bar two young men, arrayed, one in a cherry-coloured
silk dress and fair wig; the other in green silk, lace,
ribbons, and such female finery. They were two
young men named Boulton and Park; and the case,
which opened with this strange incident, was to draw
the town and excite an interest that grew from day to
day. It came out that the pair, who had a feminine
appearance, were in the habit of going about to
theatres and other places of amusement, such as the

Alhambra and the Burlington, dressed up as women—
painted and frizzed ; and it must be said, that whatever were the results they looked for from such visits,
their stay was of the briefest, for the guardians of
such places no sooner detected their presence, than
they ejected them summarily. A domiciliary visit being
made to their rooms, an enormous and costly female
wardrobe was discovered and seized; many dozens of
ladies' "pads," shawls, bonnets, hats, ornaments—
were found in profusion, and, it was said, to the value
of some hundred pounds. A now-forgotten phrase,
"going in drag," was, it seems, the term for this disgusting masquerading.[1] As in such theatrical cases,
the interest swelled in a geometrical ratio, and by
leaps and bounds. Crowds blocked up the street to
see the "Female Personators" arrive and depart in
the van. The court was invaded by celebrities from
the theatrical and literary world, together with many
members of the peerage, always curious in such cases.

As it was unfolded from day to day, an extraordinary picture of society, unsuspected by many, was
revealed. It appeared that there were a number of

[1] At this time Mr. Willing, the adventurous advertiser, about to start
a new journal called *London*, gave a grand dinner to the future con-
tributors ; and Mr. Sala, being in the chair, took occasion, I well
recollect, to rally his friend Arthur Sketchley on his favourite
creation of " Mrs. Brown," which he declared was a form of "going in
drag." With pleasant humour, too, he announced that the new journal
would appear on such a day, " *God willing.*"

persons who affected this effeminate mode of disguising themselves; and a ball was described, given by a patron—a university man, barely of age—at a respectable hotel in the Strand, when a large section of the company were gentlemen arrayed as ladies, and who gravely took part in the dances, round and otherwise.

So imperceptible are the changes constantly taking place in society, that we are apt to forget the curious contrast offered by what was in fashion fifteen or twenty years ago, and what odd humours then excited the public mind. How curious, for instance, was the excitement produced by a play called " Formosa," which called forth a vigorous controversy in the papers, and which, compared with some existing pieces, was a poor and shadowy attempt at portraying vice. So, too, with the raids on houses of entertainment in Panton Street and other localities, where bad champagne was drunk by noblemen and swells at prohibited hours. The public was then regularly shocked or scandalized by matter which now would cause a smile of wonder. On the other hand, things are, at least, more decorous. This instance of the " Female Personators," which in its development assumed an ugly and repulsive aspect, was but the outer eruption significant of a deeper social disease within. It will be remembered that at the time there were a number of young aristocrats " on town," whose low and vulgar extravagancies excited much attention and scandal. The name of one of these became connected with the present scandal; but before the law became seized of the case, he died.

After many hearings the young men were committed for trial, and the matter passed from Bow Street. At the trial the case broke down, and the two young men were acquitted.

CHAPTER XXI.

KURR AND BENSON.

WITHIN recent years there has hardly been a case which so curiously revealed the *haute école*, as it may be called, of criminal life, as the one which laid open the career of Kurr, Benson, and the police-inspectors. Modern practitioners have become rather clumsy and heavy of touch in this work; but in this episode we seem to be reading a chapter from Vidocq's memoirs; and, in spite of ourselves, are constrained to admire the ingenuity and clever intellectual arts by which those skilled swindlers carried out their designs. The ordinary race of thieves work in unintelligent fashion, and bring few intellectual resources to their calling; but we may suspect, or fear, that, if the higher qualities of patience, ingenious deception, and other mental powers, were duly applied, the resources of civilization and detection would be at a serious disadvantage. Nothing illustrates this so well as two modern instances—romances of crime—which occurred only a few years ago, the details of which have almost passed out of recollection. These are the wonderful plot contrived by Kurr and Benson, with the assistance of some police-inspectors—Meiklejohn, Palmer, and Druscovich ; the other case being the robbery of the Bank of England, carried out by Macdonnell and his confederates. Both of these schemes exhibited powers of elaborate contrivance and ingenuity which would have brought success to a better cause ; and both, it is to be remarked, were carried on by professors of foreign nationality, or who, at least, had graduated abroad.

The pair, Kurr and Benson, were extraordinary characters—of amazing energy, readiness of resource ; while Benson, in particular, possessed flexible gifts and a knowledge of character, and of the motives that work on character, in an exceptional degree. Kurr had been employed in a railway office ; but we soon find him seeking another and larger sphere of action, and acquiring the rudiments of roguery in a money-lending house. Here becoming familiar with the seamy side of the Turf, he began to see what an opening for money-making was offered in the *credulity* of a class of the community who can be attracted by disinterested offers to risk cash on races. In 1873 we find him at Edinburgh as " Gardiner & Co.," directing a society for what were called " discretionary investments." The day of such enterprises has long since gone by : the law has since been at work to check and destroy them : the public has learned distrust by severe experience. "Gardiner & Co." soon disappeared, and with it its director. Kurr would never have done much had not his fortune brought him in contact with an ally of superior tact and ability. This was Benson, whose father was a merchant of respectability in Paris, where the son had been educated. He was an accomplished linguist, and had acquired a French varnish and plausibility, together with a *finesse* and spirit of intrigue, which helped him to control or entangle the plain, trusting characters with whom he was to come in contact later. It is remarkable that almost every one of his enterprises were attended with brilliant success, and distinguished by ingenuity. Thus, during the late French War there appeared at Brussels, amongst the refugees, a fashionable Count de Montagu, son of a General de Montagu, who drove handsome equipages and attracted attention from the gay style in which he lived, being moreover an agreeable, insinuating, wealthy *viveur*. This versatile personage's career during this period was long remembered in that engaging city. Charitable subscriptions were then being collected in England for the relief of the distressed French, and a French gentleman of distinction presented himself to the Lord Mayor to solicit a share of the subscriptions for the population of Chateaudun, which had suffered much. He put their case so favourably, and with such winning grace, that he received a thousand pounds to distri-

bute among them. This proved to be the ingenious
Benson once more, who, however, was captured,
brought to London, tried, and sentenced to a year's
imprisonment in Newgate. Here he committed what
later must have appeared to him to have been a sad
bêtise and a blunder, for in his despair he set himself
on fire, and burnt himself so severely that he became
paralyzed and a cripple; though he afterwards recovered so far as to be able to walk with the aid of
crutches. Such a disability, however, added an additional difficulty to the carrying out his schemes—a
cripple being easy of identification; but this made him
develop his talents in other directions, where this impediment would not interfere.

Released, he sent out advertisements, offering literary assistance as a secretary or linguist, and by a
curious chance the notices fell under Kurr's eye.
This led to an acquaintance and partnership. Kurr
was at this moment planning some daringly ambitious
schemes. He felt that the United Kingdom was quite
too narrow a field for his operations, and that the
danger of working out betting frauds there was too
serious. The credulity and greed of the French, and
their taste for gambling, offered more favourable opportunities. Here was Benson—a half Frenchman
and linguist—ready to his hand, and the confederates
speedily concocted their scheme.

In the course of his various plans, Kurr had become

acquainted with one of the inspectors at Scotland Yard, a person named Meiklejohn, who was presently to be appointed chief detective officer at one of the chief stations in the North. The police were at the moment on the track of "Gardiner & Co.," one of Kurr's bogus schemes. Kurr being informed that Meiklejohn was in charge of the case, the two men soon became intimate; and about 1874 we find Kurr giving the officer sums of money—200*l.* on one occasion—to secure his protection. It was now that the brilliant and original idea—no doubt suggested by Benson—was developed, which was to obtain the general connivance, if not protection, of the leading detectives at the office; and it was obvious that if this could be contrived, the conspirators could pursue their work in perfect safety. So skilfully did they lay their plans, that they succeeded. They had plenty of funds, for no sooner had one bogus firm " blown up," than another was started; and " Archer & Co.," their latest association, had netted them a sum of over 10,000*l.* There was much art in this idea which could only be carried out by patience and many transactions; and thus, if they were in the power of the detectives, the detectives were in their power.

The inspectors they were to suborn were Meiklejohn, before named; Druscovich, who was engaged in foreign detective business; Palmer, and Clarke. All were under the direction of the better-known Inspector

Williamson, whom his subordinates considered somewhat old-fashioned and *passé*, or, at least, easy to
hoodwink. The whole presently became as interesting
as a romance, of course of the most seamy character.
The temptation was irresistible. The inspectors, in-
differently paid, found themselves brought into connection with these really opulent swindlers, who were
so brilliantly successful that they seemed to command
any sums of money; who were liberal too, and
clever, and in fact completely reversed the relation
between policeman and knave. The former had not
virtue enough to resist, and one by one fell an easy
prey to their tempters. The curious part was, as the
swindlers well knew, that each officer, as he suc-
cumbed, was the more eager to draw his fellows
into the conspiracy, for his own better protection. A
letter which Meiklejohn wrote to his friend in November, 1874, shows on what intimate terms the men
were, and how efficacious was the officers' protection :—

"DEAR BILL,—Rather important news from the
North. Tell H. S. and the young one to keep themselves quiet. In the event of a smell stronger than
now, they must be ready to scamper out of the way.
I should like to see you as early as possible. Bring
this note with you. In any circumstances, the brief is
out. If not, it will be so; so you must keep a
sharp look-out.—F."

This referred to the affair of "Archer & Co.," on whose track the police then were. For his kindly service in this respect, Meiklejohn received the handsome sum of 500*l.*, with which he was enabled to purchase a house in Lambeth.

Druscovich was now to be drawn in. His colleague mentioned that he was pressed for money, when Kurr, with much friendliness, offered him a sum of 60*l.*, which, after some hesitation, was accepted. Druscovich at this time was on the track of two confederates of Kurr's, Walker and Murray, who had been engaged in a "Society for Insurance against Losses on the Turf," the only "losses" not insured against being those of the dupes who sent them their money; and he had intercepted a letter from France containing cash.

We now turn to the sybarite invalid Benson, who had installed himself at Shanklin, Isle of Wight, in a handsome establishment, where he kept carriages and horses, and lived in good style under the name of Yonge. Cripple as he was, Mr. Yonge's gifts, as usual, left a deep impression on the neighbours. He made his way in society, composed and sung French songs with much taste and expression, and was generally acceptable. There are many who still can tell of the cordial receptions which the accomplished swindler met with; and on one occasion, when the Empress of Austria was appealed to for some charity or festivity, it was to the agreeable Mr. Yonge that a letter of effusive thanks was addressed on the part of her Majesty, recognizing his devotion. It is said, indeed, that the dramatic and powerful story of Miss Florence Warden, "The House on the Marsh," was suggested by this curious episode.

It was while he was down there that he learned that his confederate was in some danger ; and it occurred to him that it would be all important to gain over the chief inspector at Scotland Yard—one who was presumed to be honest, viz. Inspector Clarke. His operations in reference to this officer showed consummate tact and ability. Learning that he was engaged in hunting up one of their betting societies, he took the bold course of inviting him down to his house, holding out a hope that he could communicate some intelligence. After some hesitation, Clarke arrived, when Benson exhibited much art in his dealing with him, representing himself frankly as having been indiscreet, confessing that he knew the incriminated person, and had but a poor opinion of him. He then skilfully introduced the subject of a letter which Clarke had incautiously written to one of the parties, and which he now insinuated had been photographed for the purpose of ruining the inspector. Having thus sufficiently alarmed him, the host of Rosebank took another tone —affected to dread going into the witness-box, and in a friendly way pressed on his guest a note for 100*l.*,

to secure his aid in this respect. The inspector, however, put aside this handsome *douceur* without remark.
An arrangement, however, was made that they should
correspond, but it does not appear that with all his
exertions Benson succeeded in tampering with the
inspector; and the latter, though later put on trial,
was cleared of the charges.

With all these delights, however, Benson, or Yonge,
did not forget business.

The pair were now planning a bold, daring *coup*
which, extraordinary to relate, was carried through
with the utmost success, and was clearly owing to the
inspiration of Benson. The idea, we are told, was
first suggested *in a cab*, on the night of August 3rd,
1875. This brilliant notion was to change the whole
scene of action to French soil, and work on the fruit-
ful material of French greed and credulity. The plan
suggested was to scatter circulars broadcast among
the most gullible members of the community, of which
Benson's French experience could supply him with
knowledge. With the circulars were sent copies of a
single number of a French paper published in England,
and which in glowing terms set out all the advantages
of the system. This paper was " No. 1713," but the
truth was, it was the only number of the journal in
existence, and it had been printed specially at Edinburgh for the purpose. Other details of the plot were
arranged in the most elaborate way. Offices were
taken in various quarters, and members of this " long

firm " were allotted their parts. Thus, Kurr's brother
was ready to answer for " Mr. Montagu ;" one Ball
represented " Mr. Elliston ; " others were ready to
answer inquiries at Cleveland Row, Duke Street, &c.
Through the agency of the police-inspectors two local
postmasters were bought over, either to give notice
of or to intercept letters from France, presumed to
contain complaints. Thus, everything being duly
anticipated and prepared, they were ready to commence operations.

The confederates almost at once succeeded in
" hooking " a most desirable victim in the shape of a
Comtesse de Goncourt, who had some money to invest.
She was dazzled by the glowing programme set out in
Le Sport, the bogus newspaper sent to her. Here
was unfolded a wonderful story of the career of a Mr.
Hugh Montgomery, who had invented an extraordinary
and potent system of betting by which he had made
575,000*l.,* which sum, *Le Sport* added, he was now spend-
ing in works of charity. The bait took: the unhappy
lady was induced to send various large sums, in return
for which she received cheques drawn on " The Royal
Bank, London," another bogus institute, by one
" George Simpson." At first she was allowed to win
some money, and was gradually lured on to send sums
amounting to 10,000*l.* to a man called " T. Allerton,"
who ludicrously signed himself " *a sworn book-maker* "
—a happy and plausible description.

The letters addressed by these knaves to their dupe,

whom they managed with wonderful art, cannot be read without a smile. Cheques were despatched to large amounts on the mythical bank, which, it is to be presumed, were not to be presented till a certain time had elapsed. The success of these manœuvres was extraordinary. The confederacy calculated that they received in all about 14,000*l.* from a simple confiding French Lady. Not content with their booty, the sharpers persuaded her that, to effectually secure what she had won, "it was essential by the laws of England" that a further sum of 1200*l.* should be sent. This the foolish lady came to Paris to raise, but on consulting her man of business the fraud was discovered.

The defrauded Frenchmen applied at once to the police, who communicated with the officers in London. The Police had begun to stop the letters of the firm, containing, it was said, remittances to the amount of 8000*l.*, and had telegraphed to Dover to that effect. But Benson had contrived, by suborning some one there, to have the telegram intercepted, so that it did not reach the hands of Inspector Williamson. One day, however, Druscovich came to give the company a warning : " A big swindle had come in from Paris ;" the case had been put into his hands to follow up. The firm was not disturbed, for they knew that the officers must work in their interests. Then followed strange, mysterious meetings with Druscovich in that

deep archway which passes under the South Eastern
Railway at Charing Cross. The inspector was much
excited and agitated, for he knew the perilous,
" ticklish " position in which he stood—obliged as he
was to take action against his confederates, and yet
obliged by them to be slack in his movements. He
could not refrain from expressing his admiration of
some of the French letters from Benson that had come
into his hands. " You have got a clever fellow," he
said, " behind you. *Talk of Victor Hugo!* I never
read such French "—a compliment to " the address " of
the ingenious Benson. Still he would say desperately,
" I shall have to arrest *somebody;* what am I to do ?
However, I have told you, so look out for yourselves."
This, however, did not disturb them. They knew
well it was rather he who would have to look out for
himself. At last they were informed that a warrant
was actually out to take Kurr, and that its execution
was unavoidable.

A very exciting and agitating part of the drama
now begins. Confident as Kurr was that he would
be protected, he foresaw that the police might, after
all, be driven into taking action. The confederates
were also anxious about their booty, which was all in
Bank of England notes, whose numbers could, of
course, be traced. Here their ingenuity did not fail
them, and Benson was despatched down to Scotland,
to change the notes into Scotch ones. It seems at

that time it was not customary to take the numbers of Scotch notes. Meiklejohn had a friend at one of the banks near or at Alloa, and gave an introduction. This business was soon concluded, and Benson exchanged his valuable freight of 13,000*l.* for Clydesdale Bank notes. There was much friendliness between the bank manager, Mr. Monteith, and this important customer, who had besides deposited some 3000*l.* in this bank. A dinner was given to Monteith, but during the banquet an ominous telegram from the police-offices in London was put into Benson's hand. It ran :—" Important. If *Shanks* be with you, let him leave at once. D. (Druscovich) leaves to-night, and will be down in the morning." The confederates hastily made their apologies to their guests, and hurried away. Unluckily, they had to leave their 3000*l.* behind them. But the net was drawing round them. Druscovich duly arrived, found the birds flown. He made inquiries in a deliberate sort of way, and did what he could to help his friends.

Meanwhile, Benson came up by Derby, where he stopped to see Meiklejohn, who had just received 200*l.* from Kurr—notes which he changed at Leeds with a sort of reckless carelessness. His friend told him that this was foolish, when the other said that " the inspector at the place was his friend, and would keep all quiet." But it was now becoming impossible to check the course of pursuit. Druscovich's slackness

and general manner of proceeding was already causing
suspicion. Notice had been sent out to watch for
Clydesdale Bank notes, some of whose numbers were
known. Still the pair pursued their course uncon-
cernedly, being most eager to recover their deposited
money. It had been proposed to Druscovich, who
went down to arrest them, that he should arrange
matters with the manager. There were further interviews with Druscovich by night, who showed much
agitation, declaring that he was being watched by the
authorities. But at last word was sent that it was no
longer safe to stay, and Benson had to hurry suddenly
on board the Rotterdam steamer. At the New Bath
Hotel he gave the landlord one of his 100*l.* Clydesdale
notes to change, who presently returned with the
police, and he was carried off to prison.

Another confederate of these men now comes on
the scene. This was Froggatt, an attorney of a low
class—part of the seamy fringe of a police-court,
and who seems to have made a livelihood by giving
professional aid—large and small—to rogues of all
kinds. This man, who seems to have been more than
unscrupulous, was now consulted, and almost his first
act was the impudent one of sending a telegram in
the name of the London police to the effect that " these
were the wrong men, and that they were to let them
go!" This *ruse* had all but succeeded. He was then
furnished with money to go over and " square " the

Dutch judge, which, he said, it was notorious could be done for a few pounds! His efforts proved unavailing. A demand was then made for the extradition of Benson, and a strong party of police was sent to bring him over. Either by chance or intention, Druscovich was in charge of this force. It must have been a curious scene when he and his prisoner conversed in French in the cabin—the officer in a sort of despair declaring that he would have to go through with it all.

This virtually closed the career of the swindlers. Kurr, who was coolly attending the police-courts, and looking after other business, was actually negotiating with the De Goncourts for the restitution of some of the money; but it was now too late. He was arrested. Even when in the House of Detention these extraordinary men had elaborated a plot for their release, so ingenious and effective that it all but succeeded. They had succeeded in suborning some of the warders: and they had complete communication with each other. They used to carry on a correspondence by putting letters into the warders' boots. In due course they were tried and sentenced—Kurr to ten, and Benson to fifteen years' hard labour.

This, however, was not to be their last appearance on the stage, even though the prison doors had closed upon them. In September, 1877, to the astonishment of the public, the two men made their appearance at Bow Street in very dramatic fashion. In their prison they had taken thought of their condition, and perhaps the most exasperating of their reflections must have been the idea that those policemen, who deserved punishment as richly as themselves, should now be at large, and enjoying the fruits of their earnings with perfect impunity. Disclosures were made to the governor; the matter was legally investigated, with the result that the four officers were placed at the bar to confront the two convicts, who appeared in their prison dress. The officers, in due course, were brought to trial, when the whole of the curious incidents we have been following were unfolded. Clarke, as we have seen, was acquitted, to the satisfaction and applause of the audience. Meiklejohn, Palmer, Druscovich, and Froggatt the attorney, were sentenced to short periods of imprisonment with hard labour. All made despairing appeals to the judge, putting forward their wives and children as an excuse for lenient treatment.

Time rolled on, and the term that seemed lifelong at the beginning was exhausted. Last year, in 1887, the ingenious Benson was set free. But a person of such versatile talent was not likely to let it lie fallow long. After a short interval, rumours came from Switzerland of some skilfully devised fraud for raising, i.e. getting possession, of other people's money. An insinuating and accomplished stranger, speaking many languages, was named, and this proved to be

Mr. Harry Benson. In a very short space of time the swindler had contrived some fresh schemes that were quite worthy of his former exertions.

" Harry Benson," so ran the account, " who has been arrested in America, and has for some time been wanted in England, was in this country about a year ago, when he succeeded in eluding the vigilance of the police, who were then on his track. During his stay at Portsmouth Convict Prison, where he underwent the greater part of his fifteen years' penal servitude, Benson's father, who occupied an influential position, having offices in the Faubourg St. Honoré, Paris, died, and as soon as he was liberated Benson went there to ascertain whether any provision had been made for him, when he found that he had been cut off without the proverbial shilling. His brother, however, offered to find employment for him, but this Benson flatly rejected, and at once renewed his partnership with the Kurrs, who had kept up such a persistent correspondence with Benson after their imprisonment had expired, that the authorities determined to narrowly watch all three of them. The Kurrs accompanied Benson to Paris, whence after the nature of the will was discovered, they proceeded to America. There they turned their attention to starting companies, chiefly for working mines, and it is tolerably certain that in this way they made a great deal of money. Finding that the police were now making inquiries

about them, the party went to Belgium, where again
they exploited in companies. The Brussels police
were there assisted by the authorities of Scotland
Yard, and it was not long before Benson was arrested.
At his lodging the police found in letters that had not
been opened prior to the seizure 140*l.* in post-office
orders and cheques, and this money was at once returned to the senders. Benson was then sentenced
to two years and sixteen days' imprisonment. On
his release he returned to America, still closely
watched by the police, but it is alleged he succeeded
in several frauds, for which he is still ' wanted.' His
next adventure was at Geneva, where he passed himself off as an American banker, stopping at the best
hotels, presiding at the *table d'hôte,* and keeping his
horses and carriage. Here he was constantly receiving
telegrams from his confederates in America, telling
him that certain bonds were at a high price, and requesting his authority to sell. These telegrams he
carelessly allowed to lie about in the billiard-room,
smoking-room, and other apartments, where they
were read by others, and consequently enhanced the
reputation in which he was held. At this hotel he is
stated to have made the acquaintance of a retired
surgeon-general of the Indian army, and contracted
an engagement with the officer's daughter. He presented her with quantities of jewellery, and obtained
the father's consent to marriage. He discovered that

z 2

the officer was worth 7000*l.*, invested in the Indian 4 per Cents. At Benson's advice the doctor ordered his agent in London to sell out, and the money having been remitted to Geneva was placed in the hands of Benson, who gave in exchange certain scrip, which he pretended would double the officer's interest. The telegrams came now so frequently that Benson determined to return to America, and he left word as to the boat by which he would proceed, but his *fiancée*, having a desire to witness his departure, went to the boat and found he had gone by another route. It was then found that Mr. Churchwood—so Benson called himself— had gone to Bremen, booking there to America. He was arrested just as he was stepping on board. He was brought back to Geneva, but on refunding 5000*l.* of the money of the surgeon-general he was liberated. It was then found that the jewellery that he had presented to his *fiancée* was only brass and glass, while the scrip he had given in exchange for the 7000*l.* was worth only 32*l.* Soon after this Benson left Europe, completely baffling the police, who believed that he was in America, but since November they have been without any definite clue. They have therefore sent his photograph to every important centre in the world." [1]

---

[1] Since the above was written, Benson has added some extraordinary incidents to his strangely chequered career of adventure. Escaping to America, he passed to Mexico, where, by a brilliant *coup*, he con-

There is another case of the same *genre* as this other one we have been following, and which offers an extraordinary instance of misapplied ingenuity and cleverness. It belongs to the *haute école* of swindling, for here was found an extraordinary investment of patience. Large sums of money were laid out as it were at interest, so as to purchase an air of credit, with assumed habits of business, a part which could only have been sustained by skilled performers. This was the case of the bills forged on the Bank of England in 1873, for which an elaborate scheme was planned, and spread over many months. But for the most trifling of accidents it had succeeded, and the Bank would have lost by this great *coup* over 100,000*l*.! It must be said that the case does not legitimately fall within our province here, as it was dealt with at the Mansion House; but as it and the Kurr-Benson cases stand apart, and are the only two cases in modern times that show what Fielding would have called real "greatness," the story may not be thought out of place. After fifteen years the details are likely to have grown faint, and are forgotten by most persons.

trived to pass himself off as Mr. Abbey, Patti's *entrepreneur*, and succeeded in obtaining some 25,000 dollars, for tickets, &c. Being captured and brought to New York, and his appeal to the courts being rejected in the May of the present year, he decoyed his gaoler up a steep flight of stairs in his prison, and flinging himself over the bannisters, fractured his spine, and died shortly afterwards. He is said to have left memoirs of his singular life.

In Saville Row are found many professors of tailoring, including the eminent artist who has so long regulated the attire of the most eminent gentleman in the kingdom. In the month of April, 1872, a person of gentlemanly address and quiet manners came to order clothes at one of these establishments. He appeared to be an American, and, like most of his countrymen who come to England for pleasure, was a highly desirable customer. This gentleman, it proved, was at that time living in humble lodgings in Kingsland, with two or three friends, arch-swindlers, who had come to England to arrange some bold and ingenious schemes. He was well supplied with cash, and consulted his tailor how he was to place a large sum, about 1200*l.*, in safe keeping, as he was a stranger, and such was an embarrassment. Now this was an artful stroke, for an inferior intellect would have probably attempted what was the reverse of this proceeding, viz., some clumsy device to obtain money on the basis of the orders he had given. But after being thus fitted out by the tailor, he and his friends left their humble lodgings in Kingsland and departed in different directions. Austin Bidwell and Macdonnell repaired to the leading capitals of Germany, the others to France, &c. They went provided with letters of introduction, letters of credit from the leading banks and merchants in London, all of which were adroitly forged. So skilfully did they pursue their scheme that they returned to London without being detected, and with spoil amounting to no less than 8000*l*. In the next month they set off for Buenos Ayres, bearing with them a letter of introduction and letters of credit from the London and Westminster Bank. So favourably were these credentials received that they were enabled to carry off some 10,000*l*. booty.

The choice of "aliases" showed some skill, and was elaborate to a degree. But a genteel euphony is essential, and there is a sort of tact even in such trifles. Thus, Austin Biron Bidwell was "otherwise" Frederick Albert Warren, "otherwise" Charles Johnson Horton. His companions, however, did not venture on assuming other names. The chief conspirator was but twenty-seven, and the oldest of the party was only thirty-four. Austin Bidwell the contriver of the whole, was only five or six and twenty. Their history was a curious one. Two years before, Macdonnell, who had relations in Ireland, visited that country in company with his friend, Austin Bidwell. Their first operation was to convert a cheque on the Bank of Ireland for 3*l*. into one for 3000*l*. ! On this they obtained cash from a bank in Belfast.

In Burlington Gardens stands an imposing nobleman's mansion of the olden time, and of much pretension, and which is now used by the Bank of

England as its branch office. It was to be expected that the neighbouring tradesmen would make use of this establishment for the various transactions, and accordingly we are not surprised to find that the tailor's customer was introduced to Colonel Francis, at that time directing the bank. There was a subtlety in these introductory proceedings which certainly gave the fairest earnest of success.

Having walked with the tailor to the bank and deposited his money, the simple stranger innocently inquired of the manager if it were necessary when he had other funds to deposit, to bring his friend with him every time. The officials must have smiled as they assured him that the account was his own, and that he could pay in or withdraw as he pleased. Twelve hundred pounds was his first deposit, to which he presently added a thousand more. This was allowed to remain for some three months, when " Mr. Warren " asked the manager to sell some Portuguese stock for him, amounting to no less a sum than 8000*l*. At this interview, Warren or Bidwell, carelessly threw out that he was an American contractor who had come over to work the Pullman car business in this country, that they were to be built at Birmingham, where a factory would be started, and he hoped to have some ready for the exhibition then impending. There was no eagerness for money, and the bonds were left in charge of the bank, which was favourably impressed by

the character of "the new customer." But the confederates were not idle. In the interval they had been
preparing their plans, going over and making inquiries
in the various cities of Europe as to the great firms,
their mode of drawing bills, &c. Patience and no
precipitation were their watchwords. When two of
the party were ill the leading spirit wrote that they
must not suppose he would proceed at once. Far from
it, "the first consideration is your health, and if
necessary we will postpone business until Christmas:
if you require rest for ten days more, for Heaven's
sake take it. We have a good capital, and can readily
increase it on short notice." At Christmas their operations began.

The first point was to obtain genuine bills for discount, and great pains and labour were expended with
this view. One of the party went to Rotterdam and
purchased bills on the London banks. With much
ingenuity the forms of the various bills were copied,
engravers being employed on contrivances to prepare
the plates. The ground being thus got ready, it was
resolved after Christmas to deal their *coup*. Every risk
had been provided for. For instance, the bank which
was about to discount these bills would pay them in
notes, whose numbers would lead to detection. An
account was opened with another bank, the Continental, and by mixing up their operations in an ingenious
hocus, they would contrive to confuse the scent.

One single instance shows how cleverly the chief of the party could turn even an unexpected accident to profit. He had gone over to Paris, carrying with him a large sum of money—four or five thousand pounds—when an accident occurred on the Great Northern Railway, in which he was severely injured. To another this would have been a serious impediment, but the ingenious swindler turned it to profit. There was a flash of genius in this stroke. Bruised and battered, his head plastered over, he betook him to Messrs. Rothschild's bank, and begged of the manager to let him have one of his bills on London for 4500*l*. This was of course declined. To hold a Rothschild bill was a proof of commercial standing of the highest kind, and it was only the aristocracy of finance who were thus privileged. Thus rebuffed the applicant complained bitterly of his injuries, and said he would return. Baron Alphonse de Rothschild was a director of the railway, and as he happened to come into the office, Bidwell repeated his complaint; " See," he cried, " the way I have been knocked about on your line, and you won't do this for me ! " The baron relented, said he was sorry for him, and agreed to do what was desired. A few days later the swindler entered the Bank of England office, and throwing down the bill on the counter, said with a natural flourish, " Here, I suppose *that* paper is good enough for you ! " It was assumed that this bill had come over to him in due course of

business—a man who had such dealings was "sound."
The ground being thus prepared, about the middle of
January it was determined to strike. With a view to
avoid inconvenient questions or pursuit in case of
discoveries, the firm was obliged to go to the country,
to their Pullman car factory at Birmingham. From
Birmingham Bidwell now began to shower his forged
bills on the bank. His business had extended
enormously. The confiding manager by each day's
post received bills for two, three, and four thousand
pounds, which were discounted and their proceeds
placed to the credit of the firm. But there was no
suspicion. More than *one hundred thousand pounds*
were thus paid.

Not disturbed in the least by this influx of paper,
the bank continued to receive the bills, duly discount-
ing them. With each batch came plausible letters
from Bidwell, describing his business success, &c.
At this moment he and his partners were judiciously
dispersed to various quarters, ready on receipt of the
booty to fly. But unluckily two out of the numerous
bills attracted notice as being irregular. The acceptor's
name had been forgotten. Still there was not much
suspicion, it might be an accident. But an inquiry
was made; then all came out, and one of the most
daring and elaborate specimens of forgery was revealed.
We may fancy the terror of the bamboozled Colonel
Francis and the agonies he must have suffered as every

moment news was brought him of some new bill being
found spurious. The money was gone. As it had been
lodged by the confiding bank to their account, it had
been drawn out by cheque and thus transferred to the
Continental Bank. The swindlers on discovering that
their plan was "blown" upon, as it is called, fled,
some getting away beyond the seas; but rewards were
offered and all four were captured. One was discovered at an obscure Scotch country town, where a
policeman, seeing him walking in a garden, took it into
his head that there was something suspicious about him,
and laid hold of him. At the trial, two of the swindlers,
Macdonnell and George Bidwell, begged to be allowed to address the jury. The first said that so far
as he was concerned the evidence was conclusive, but
he wished to shield others who were innocent. He
with his friends had come to this country with the
purpose of carrying on business in a legitimate way,
but when they arrived and found the way bills were
negotiated—no inquiry being made as to the acceptor (which was the mode in America)—why
it became an absolute invitation, and the temptation
irresistible, "and the result of that discovery," added
the impudent fellow in a tone of pathos "is that I am
standing here!" He then put in a plea for Bidwell,
which he owned "cut the ground from under his own
feet." This was the accident on the French railway
which had given a tremendous shock to his friend, not

only physically but morally. It had opened his eyes to his sinful course, and from that moment he had withdrawn from the confederacy, and had become regenerate! The same effrontery was shown when a verdict of " Guilty " was brought in. Austin Bidwell, asking would it be any use to apply for a short postponement, and being told " None whatever," he folded his arms, and repeated melodramatically and with a sort of calm despair—"None whatever!" Then he proceeded to dwell on his mis-spent youth, perverted talents, lost opportunities, and apologized in feeling terms to the bank manager, hoping that time would soften any feelings he might have towards him. The judge in sentencing them, worthily described their scheme as " a fraud which for its audacity of conception, its magnitude, and the skill with which it was carried out, is completely unparalleled," and then proceeded to sentence them each to penal servitude for life. At the severity of this stroke the four men seemed to shrink away appalled.

Even at this stage they had not exhausted their resources of ingenuity. It was discovered that some of their relatives had arrived in town and that a bold plot had been contrived for their release, which had nearly succeeded. Three warders who were to be on duty on a certain night, had been bribed with a hundred pounds a-piece.

CHAPTER XXII.

DE TOURVILLE'S CASE.

THERE is a peculiar class of cases which excite infinitely greater interest and affect the public more keenly than others. This may be described as those belonging to "domestic melodrama," where, under much that is genteel and unobtrusive, some villainy lurks, or is suspected. This strikes far more than scenes of actual violence, which hold no mystery. Such was the character of this De Tourville case, followed with extraordinary interest both in England and on the Continent, and which occurred in the year 1876.

This De Tourville appears to have been a good-looking French adventurer, the son of a notary from Valenciennes, who had *exploited* his gifts among Englishwomen with some success. He had married twice in England, and both the ladies had good fortunes. The Rev. Mr. Glynn, who was a curate in Liverpool, once met him at a Scarborough hotel, when he uttered a very singular speech. He declared that " he knew of some infallible methods for disposing of a mother-in-law or a wife." For the first, you were to show her the mechanism of a revolver ; the weapon would probably go off, by accident. The wife was to be taken up some high mountain in Switzerland or the Tyrol, and there would be likely enough to miss her footing. These strange recipes naturally dwelt in the curate's mind, and he, of course, recalled them many years later, though at an awkward moment for De Tourville.

The second Mrs. De Tourville had a fortune of no less than 35,000*l.*, which she was not inclined to place at her husband's disposition. It was said, indeed, that all he was likely to receive in case of her death was a sum of 10,000*l.* The rest she intended for relatives. In July, 1876, we find them travelling in the Tyrol, exploring the beauties of the Stelvio Pass. They had hired a carriage in the Botzen district, which was to take them to Traigenhoe, and set out about nine in the morning. After driving until two o'clock, De Tourville sent away the carriage and set off with his wife walking. About half-past five he returned alone, carrying her parasol, which had lost its top, in his hand. All noticed his cool and indifferent air. The lady had met with an accident. She was admiring the view, insisted on going on to a dangerous declivity, when a stone had given way under her foot, and she had fallen. The carriage and some of the villagers returned to look for her. Strange to say he could not find the spot, but it was near, he said, to some "red stones." At last he pointed out the place, and they went down to look. But he waited in the carriage. They found the unfortunate lady at the bottom of the precipice among the stones, all covered with blood, her legs crushed, her forehead wounded, and what were articles of her dress—her hat, pocket-handkerchief—scattered about, and covered with blood. When they came up to tell him she was dead, he replied, "*Dead indeed!*" and offered them 200 florins to carry up her body, but it was against the law to touch it until some authority had seen it. When he returned, his story at the inn to the gendarmes—already suspicious—was that she was very "self-willed," would go forward in spite of warning, and had "high heels;" she slipped and fell, but not many feet. He tried to reach her but could not, and so came back for help. His story was changed when the gendarmes detained him. In his absence she had committed suicide. So plausibly did he put forward his account of the matter, and he furnished some evidence to prove that she was in terror of having to appear in some divorce case in London, that the simple-minded authorities of Botzen allowed him to depart.

But almost at once some evidence was sent over from England, which made the case highly suspicious. His mother-in-law, Mrs. Brigham, had met with her death in a singular way. He had been showing the mechanism of his revolver, when it went off, killing her on the spot. The Liverpool curate now recalled the extraordinary *modus operandi* which had been communicated to him at Scarborough, and had been so strangely carried out in both cases. Struck with this fulfilment he wrote to the authorities, and it was later proved by the hotel books that De Tourville had been there at the time he named. There was a story, too, of a fire in London, in which he and his son had been nearly burnt ; but it was explained on his behalf that he had rescued the child.

The Austrian authorities having investigated the matter, demanded his extradition. This was stoutly resisted by Mr. Newton at Bow Street, who insisted on hearing the whole case. De Tourville, however, was finally handed over to the Austrian courts, and the trial of this remarkable case began. It excited attention over the world, and the little town of Botzen, where it was held, was crowded with reporters from all the capitals. It began on June 18th, 1877, the preliminaries having thus occupied over six months in preparation. It continued for fourteen days, being interrupted to allow the jury to visit the spot of the supposed murder, when measurements and calculations of time and distance were made. On July 2nd a verdict was found that the prisoner, who delivered himself in a curious polyglot, passing from

Bedford Place, where, with the assistance of an agent, he displayed his mysteries—the chief of which was a direct communication with the unseen world. For the sum of a guinea he would put any visitor in relation with deceased friends, through the help of one "Allie," Slade's deceased wife. The communications were made on a slate. Many dupes came and went, the more credulous being much impressed and more than satisfied. A shrewd London professor, Mr. E. Ray Lankester, resenting what he thought was an imposture on science, with a friend, Mr. Donkin, determined to visit "the doctor" and if possible expose him.

When they arrived they were shown into an outer apartment where there were a few persons waiting. Here they were received by one Simmons, the doctor's aid-de-camp, whose duty it was to while away the time in easy conversation, thus, it was insinuated, drawing out facts or allusions which might be useful to the chief performer at his interviews. When their turn came the two visitors found themselves in presence of a fluent gentleman, seated with his back to the windows, and at a curiously-constructed table. There was first some general conversation, and the two friends seem to have acted their part very cleverly, simulating interest, credulity, and astonishment. Slade explained that the spirit which was ready to operate was that of "Allie." When all was ready the mani-

festations began, the doctor saying solemnly, " The
spirit is now present! " When a question was put
about a deceased friend, the doctor held a slate in a
mysterious way half under the table. They heard a
sort of scratching as from a pencil writing, but they
affected not to hear it ; and a written answer was thus
produced from " Allie," who acted as the intermediary
of one " Samuel Lankester." It proved that there
was a mistake in the Christian name, which was
" Edwin," and the doctor cheerfully had it substituted.
Then other operations were performed, such as raising
a chair a little way from the ground ; the table was
lifted, as they distinctly saw, by the agency of the
doctor's knee or leg. "I expressed," says Mr. Lankester,
" great admiration at all I saw." Then they experienced
some slight kicks and touches. He noted that when the
scratching on the slate was proceeding the doctor always
became afflicted with a sort of grating noise in his
throat—a curious sound intended to cover the other
sounds. During these operations the two visitors
became convinced of the imposture, it was carried out
so clumsily. Finding the moment arrived, they put
other questions as to the late Edwin. And as the
doctor took up his slate, it was violently snatched
from him—lo ! already written on it by the slate-
pencil were the words—

" I AM GLAD TO MEET YOU, EDWIN LANKESTER ! "
" You scoundrel and impostor ! " exclaimed the indig-

nant Lankester, the other calling him "a d——d rogue," or words to that effect. Slade was so dumb-founded that he was seen to turn ghastly pale, and sat there looking at them without being able to articulate a word. The two left him there, and came out into the other room, informing the expectant gulls of all that had occurred. The ready Simmons smiled. He said it would "only do them good." It had happened before, but *they had all come back again.* There was truth and a knowledge of human nature in this remark —as a fact, the exhibitions went on after this fiasco. Meanwhile other inquirers came to investigate, among them, Mr. R. Hutton, the editor of the *Spectator*, and Mr. Walter Pollock, of the *Saturday Review*. Mr. Hutton played the innocent inquirer with happy effect. On one occasion he brought with him a "locked slate," and pleaded earnestly that this satisfactory mode of testing the matter should be adopted, but Dr. Slade, *contra*, explained that really such devices were used only by prejudiced experimen-ters, who brought chemicals, &c.; so that she—the spirit Allie—had come to the resolution "never to have anything to do with such things." Mr. Hutton, with a touch of humour, pleaded that this resolution possibly did not commit the *other* spirits, "they might be so good as to do it for him." Slade goodnaturedly yielded so far as to consult "Allie" on the point, who answered firmly, "*Not one word,*" on which Mr. Hutton resignedly accepted the situation, saying "it was a disappointment."

During the progress of the case before Mr. Flowers, the entertainment, as we have said, assumed the most amusing, not to say farcical character. Mr. George Lewis conducted the prosecution, which was of a rather serious character in its issues, as the doctor was accused of having "with certain subtle means, craft, and devices, attempted to deceive and impose upon certain of her Majesty's subjects, to wit," Lankester, Sidgwick, Hutton, &c. In the court there was exhibited the actual table, which was curiously constructed, having a sort of concealed lever underneath, which was cunningly contrived, and would support or fix the slate, leaving the operator's hand free to write. But the fun became fast and furious when Mr. Maskelyne, of "Maskelyne and Cook," appeared in the box and proposed to perform feats of the same kind and quite as effectively. In vain the magistrate interposed to prevent the exhibition; the performer calmly went on, knowing that he had his audience with him. By the agency of chemicals he was enabled totally to obscure the writing on a slate for a few moments, but the characters re-appeared by-and-by, the operator being thus able to display a slate blank at first, &c. He explained the device of the "thimble pencil," which fitted on the top of a finger, and thus performed its office. There were, as in Mr.

Crummles' case, " cheers, tears, and laughter," roars indeed of the latter. Mr. Massey appeared as a sort of counsel, and identified himself with his client, at one period laying down his official garb to enter the witness-box. He had paid the doctor, he said, seven pounds, and was " satisfied with what he got for his money." On one occasion he had brought with him two slates bound together with cords, a pencil between them, and on loosing the cords, lo ! there was writing ! Other witnesses deposed to similar incidents, and expressed their faith in the doctor. So the case proceeded for many days and became what is called " the talk of the town," and there have been innumerable " talks of the town." At last, on November 30th, 1876, Mr. Flowers gave his decision, which was " that an offence had been committed against the Vagrancy Act, and that the professor must go to jail for three months with hard labour "—a sentence which was appealed against.

Such was this extraordinary scene, or series of scenes, and these frivolities for many days engrossed the attention of London.

CHAPTER XXIV.

§ *The Explosions.*

THE Bow Street Office has always offered curious contrasts, farce alternating with tragedy. It was now to witness a series of grim incidents, novel in their atrocity and imported from foreign countries. Londoners who had read with curiosity and horror of the desperate acts of the Nihilists, were now to find, to their consternation, that such villainies were being contrived in their midst.

The years 1883 and 1884 might be considered a period during which a new form of crime, newly introduced from America, was being systematically practised in this country. These may be called the great dynamite years. This shameful and barbarous mode of attack was organized by a succession of conspirators who came over provided with abundant funds, but who happily lacked the intrepid spirit necessary to secure success. By some lucky chances and a Providential interposition, all their attempts failed, little mischief was done, and what is a particular subject of congratulation, nearly all the conspirators were captured and brought to justice.

It is curious to find how the cowardice of the assailants prompted them, at the opening of the campaign, as they would have styled it, to make some feeble, half-hearted attempts—such was the depositing of some dynamite on the window-sill of the Government offices in Charles Street, Whitehall, and which exploded, blowing away a portion of the solid stone walls. This was in the month of March, 1883, and excited a good deal of alarm. After an interval of a few months, in the October of the same year, a more daring attempt was planned. The conspirators turned their thoughts to the underground railways of the Metropolis, which from the darkened and subterranean course offered favourable opportunities. There was something particularly base and cruel in their selection, as the victims were certain to be of the innocent class. In October of the same year a tremendous explosion took place on the Metropolitan line, by which a couple of carriages were shattered and nearly sixty persons were injured. The conspirators, it was assumed, had thrown their explosive from the window, but no clue to the perpetrators of the outrage could be obtained at the time.

Three months more passed over, and again was the public to be startled. On February 25th, when all the district about Victoria Station was taking its rest a terrific explosion took place, and those who rushed to see, found the wooden building which had for so many years done duty as offices for the Brighton Railway, a complete wreck—the roof blown away, the walls shattered, altogether a most melancholy picture of destruction. The explosion, it was found, had taken place in the luggage-room, and had been caused by one of those artful contrivances which had not long before figured as a dramatic element in one of the Drury Lane pieces, namely the clockwork detonator —set to go off at a particular moment. At other leading stations similar attempts had been made, but the machinery had happily failed to work. Here again no clue was obtained, though detectives had nearly been successful. It was found that two strangers with suspicious black portmanteaus of American make, had quitted an hotel in Great Portland Street the evening before. They departed in separate cabs and their portmanteaus corresponded with the description of them left at the stations. The next incident was the arrest in April, 1884, of a desperate character named Daley, at Birkenhead, on whom was found two phials of an explosive mixture, and no less than five clockwork machines. This man was known to be the most daring spirit of the dynamite gang, and is at the present moment suffering a long sentence of penal servitude for his offence.

Finally, in the December of the same year took

place the attempt on London Bridge, which happily miscarried. Three men had engaged a boat, and their plan was to place a charge of dynamite in one of the deep recesses left in the base of the piers. By an extraordinary chance these had been grated over not very long before. Thus foiled, the three men contrived to lower from the parapet of the bridge—close to the second arch from the Surrey side—a large packet of dynamite with a time-fuse attached. A tremendous explosion followed with much smoke, but as the dynamite had been unconfined little damage was done, though the wooden balks round the piers were started. Such were these preparatory experiments where the success was not encouraging. It would seem that new and more daring agents were despatched, who were required to run greater risks and do something more deadly and effective for their wage.

§ *The Gallaghers.*

Near to the bottom of Southampton Street, Strand, at the top of which is Garrick's old house—on the right, and within a door or two of Spooner's print-shop, is a narrow, dingy-looking house, which a few years ago was an obscure hotel, known as the "Beaufort." One night there arrived in a cab a man of American aspect, who brought with him a heavy trunk which was carried upstairs to his room. Not many hours later the police came and took him and his trunk away. The latter contained an extraordinary article—a pair of indiarubber fishing-boots, more than half filled with nitro-glycerine—a dangerous cargo, and we may be sure the police were cautious enough. To this hour one can never pass that mysterious-looking house without recalling the curious incident. The man thus arrested proved to be the inferior agent of a villainous gang which had come specially from America to carry out its schemes. His name was Norman, or Lynch. He had been living in New York, working to support his mother and sisters, when " a friend " (so-called) brought him off one night and had him enrolled in one of the innumerable secret societies of the city—the "Esperanza," " Michael Davitt," "Emerald," &c. There he had to take an oath to perform any duty laid upon him, and learned the passwords, &c. One day he received a summons from a Dr. Gallagher who lived at Brooklyn. He obeyed in a sort of helpless way, and was told by the doctor that he must go to London at once. He must "knock off" work that very day. The man urged that his mother and sister depended on him—no matter, they would be taken care of. There was here something of the mysterious force of the *Vehmgericht* in this provision, and this carelessness as to expense. Gallagher informed him further that he himself was embarking almost at the same time, and bade him, on his arrival, call on him at the Charing Cross Hotel.

The emissary embarked at once, and arrived in London, where he found Gallagher. He described a strange walk he had with his principal, in which they passed by the various public buildings. As they came to the House of Commons, Gallagher pointed out what a scene of destruction it would presently exhibit; another building " would go down also," &c.—a truly original way of " showing the Lions " to his friend.

After a few days had passed by, Norman was sent down to Birmingham to procure what was called " the material." Here there lived a man called Whitehead, who was engaged in manufacturing nitro-glycerine on a considerable scale. It is astonishing to find what an amount of folly or vanity existed among these conspirators, for the attempt to blow up the gas-works at Glasgow was only recent, and the police everywhere were on the watch. This carelessness or indifference no doubt came of the vanity of belonging to a society or " school," as it was termed, which was possessed of plenty of money, and some influence and power. Whitehead, however, pursued his operations and continued to fill " carboys " with the fatal mixture.

Gallagher now directed his visitor to go and purchase a suitable and convenient receptacle for the nitro-glycerine, and thus was procured the pair of indiarubber fishing-boots, in which was stored some sixty pounds or so of the compound. A Birmingham police sergeant, had, however, been carefully looking after Whitehead and his factory, and took an ingenious method to satisfy himself. In the disguise of a painter —carrying brushes, &c.—he called at the place, and while making inquiries, made excellent use of his eyes, noting particularly that the owner's fingers were stained as if with some acid. More than satisfied, he and some of his companions paid a visit in the middle of the night, entering by means of skeleton keys, and after a minute examination found enough to justify all their suspicions, with the result that Whitehead was arrested, tried, and convicted.

Norman (or Lynch) returned to London with his dangerous cargo, took a cab at Euston, and repaired, as we have seen, to the hotel in Southampton Street, where he was arrested the same night. Thus the whole plot " blew up." Dr. Gallagher, who was so quietly arranging his plans for " bringing down " London at his hotel, was promptly seized and conveyed to prison, with his brother Bernard and some others of the conspirators. It must have been a disagreeable moment for him, when brought to the bar, to find that his agent was not standing beside him; but his anxiety was soon relieved, for the bearer of the fishing-boots made his way into the witness-box and told the story that has just been related. This is, of course, the invariable procedure, and the last act of such conspiracies is the appearance of the informer. Trial followed in due course, and the whole party are at this moment working out a long sentence of penal servitude.

It is gratifying to think that in frustrating the many attempts at contriving explosions in London, the authorities have been so completely successful. The difficulties in such a contest are enormous, as the stroke has to be anticipated. At this moment there are over a score of these wretches in English jails, paying the penalty of their infamous and cruel plots.

§ *Burton and Cunningham.*

The explosion which had taken place on the Metropolitan line at Farringdon Street had been long forgotten, and it had been found impossible to trace the agents. But they were now, nearly a year later, to be discovered in a most singular way, through the aid of further villainies of the same kind. Not long after had followed the daring outrage in the crypt of Westminster Hall, memorable, too, for the courage and promptitude displayed by Constable Cole and his companion. A lady had noticed something smoking on the ground and emitting mephitic fumes. " I think," she said to the officer, " one of your mats is on fire! " But it proved to be a parcel of dynamite. Cole instantly seized it and carried it away, but he noted a strange sticky stuff exuding,—yellowish, ' like cheese," he said. It struck him that there was something "uncanny" about it, and he flung it away. Then followed the explosion, by which the two officers were seriously injured. These attempts, it was clear, were from the same hand or agency. But the conspirators, encouraged no doubt by this continued impunity, had now prepared a yet bolder *coup.*

On January 24th a most daring outrage was planned. It was a Saturday, which was a free day at the Tower, and a number of " half-holiday " folk were as usual wandering through the rooms, looking at the armour, &c., when a boy noticed something smoking on the ground, which he took to be a fusee which some one had thrown away. Of a sudden a tremendous explosion took place, a young woman was thrown down by the concussion, and the whole room filled with a dense, stifling smoke. A large hole was knocked in the floor, which was found to be on fire, and burnt for some twenty minutes. It spoke well for the discipline of the place, that within *four* minutes an order was given to close the gates, and not one of the visitors was able to leave the precincts. All were then interrogated, their names and addresses taken. These accounts proved to be satisfactory, except in the case of a single man—who gave a confused story of his address and occupation—which excited the suspicions of the police. It turned out that this was a man called Cunningham, or Dalton, or Gilbert, for he passed by all these names, and who had been living at Great Scarborough Street, near the Minories, without any apparent occupation—an "Irish-American," who had arrived in November last and had taken a lodging in Prescott Street, close to the Tower. He had brought with him a huge American trunk, which after a few days had been taken away by another man and an ordinary black box substituted. Without giving a reason, he had suddenly left his quarters, and moved to an adjoining street. Later on, when he was brought to Bow Street, and on his second appearance, another man was placed beside him. His name was Burton, and it turned out that it was he who had called for the trunk. By a curious fatality he had actually taken a room in a house where a policeman lodged, whose attention was speedily drawn to his proceedings. Notice was given to Scotland Yard, and a "plain-clothes" officer was specially appointed to watch him and his movements. It will thus be seen that it becomes rather difficult for the enterprising Irish-American who arrives in this country to escape attracting notice or to sink his individuality, even if he plunge into the obscure district of the Minories.

As it was, without evidence of any kind—the detective instinct or *flaire* at once pointed out these fellows as being in some way connected with the recent atrocities. It may be said at once, that by a wonderful bit of luck they were actually watching the very men—the authors and contrivers of another series of explosions. But no one could ever have expected that satisfactory proof, &c., would have accumulated, of the most convincing kind. It was found that the two men had arrived in England in the same month, and that they had made several journeys backwards and forwards. It is well known how difficult it is to recall a face seen in the train, in the street, or in a shop; or how puzzling it is, some weeks afterwards, to be asked to say " is *that* the person ? " Here, however, a perfect flood of identification was furnished. On the night of the explosions on the railway, one Myers, an auctioneer, recollected, as the train was crowded, that he tried to enter a break-van. But three men were in possession, and one was at the window, his head out, and leaning on the door : " You can't come in," said the fellow. " Why not ? " asked the other. " *Because you can't,*" was the impudent reply. On being shown one of the accused, he at once called out, " *That is the man !* " who had refused to let him enter. This was a curious retribution for unpoliteness, and the " cheeky " American Irishman little dreamed that when he was so complaisantly refusing the stranger, he was actually imprinting a vivid image of his own features on the man's memory. A porter at the station also recognized them as the men in the brake-van, others saw the pair crossing the railway, and it was all but clear that it was from the brake-van the dynamite had been dropped. A policeman also recalled them. A search was of course made at their lodgings, and, awkwardly enough, a detonating cap was found in Cunningham's box. Burton, too, was presently found to have been connected with one of the railway explosions, owing to a coat with curious buttons, which he was in the habit of wearing, and which was found in one of the portmanteaus deposited in the luggage depôt.

While this examination was going on at Bow Street, the police discovered that there was in existence a regular dynamite gang, whereof Burton was the actual director. Great precautions were taken against any desperate attempts at a rescue, and every day the " Black Maria " was escorted by a band of police armed to the teeth. There could, indeed, be no reasonable doubt that these ruffians had contrived all these explosions. Plans of London were found among their things, and also a " *Guide to the Tower.*"

They were duly committed for trial. That trial took place in May. Burton begged to be allowed to address the court, when he put forward a lame enough story that " he was entirely ignorant of any attempt against her Majesty, for whom they had all a great respect." But this plea did not avail, and they were convicted.

CHAPTER XXV.

THE NEW POLICE.

" WE are not by any means devout believers," wrote
Mr. Dickens in one of his interesting detective papers,
" in the old Bow Street Police. To say the truth, we
think there was a vast amount of humbug about those
worthies. Apart from many of them being men of
very indifferent character, and far too much in the
habit of consorting with thieves and the like, they
never lost a public occasion of jobbing and trading in
mystery and making the most of themselves. Con-
tinually puffed, besides, by incompetent magistrates,
anxious to conceal their own deficiencies, and hand-in-
glove with the penny-a-liners of that time, they became
a sort of superstition. Although as a preventive
police they were utterly inefficient, and as a Detective
police were very loose and uncertain in their operations, they remain, with some people, a superstition to
the present day. On the other, hand, the Detective force,
organized since the establishment of the existing police,
is so well chosen and trained, proceeds so systematically
and quietly, does its business in so workmanlike a

manner, and is always so calmly and steadily engaged in the service of the public, that the public really do not know enough of it to know a tithe of its usefulness." Our author then, in his own graphic style, proceeds to recount an evening at the *Household Words* Office, when the leading detectives assembled and related adventures drawn from their own recollections. Dickens was very partial to this well-trained body, and perhaps invested them with a good many of the gifts which he denied to the old functionaries; but it will be admitted, from the incidents we have been following, that, considering the difficulties in their way, and the rude condition of detective science, on the whole they did their work well and were successful enough in their calling. At the same time it must be admitted that, during the decade of years previous to the establishment of the new police, the Bow Street officers had become demoralized, and even untrustworthy, and the more prominent "Runners," from their dealings with the thieves, had become more or less corrupted, and used rather to shield than detect.

In the year 1832 the City of London, which in virtue of its privileges had always been responsible for the safety of its citizens, established "a day police force" of its own, which consisted of 100 men; and including superior officers, such as marshals and marshals' men, &c., it amounted to 120. The upper marshal received a yearly salary of 540*l.*, the under 450*l.* Each marshal's man had about 130*l.* a year, exclusive of fees for warrants and summonses.

In addition to the day police, the total number of watchmen and other persons employed in the City of London was, in 1833, of ordinary watchmen, 500; superintending watchmen, 65; patrolling watchmen, 91; and beadles, 54 : total, 710. The number of men on duty at twelve o'clock at night was 380. The total expense in 1832, was 9006*l.* The sums ordered to be raised and levied for the night-watch, was, in 1827, 34,700*l.*; in 1833, 42,077*l.* Though still under the management of the different wards, the night-watch had latterly been greatly improved by the substitution of able young men for the aged and often decrepid creatures who were too often appointed out of charity.

In addition to this regular force there was a body of " Ward constables," who were called out by the Lord Mayor in emergencies and which could muster nearly 400 men. This was a fair attempt at organization, though of a straggling kind. When the tremendous and engrossing question of emancipation had been disposed of, Mr. Peel addressed himself to the entire reform of the Police of the Metropolis. This was loudly called for. Crime was increasing out of all proportion to population. In the year 1828, out of a population of about a million and a quarter, the committals were 3560. " Moreover the mechanical improvements in the country so aided the perpetrators of crime, as to enable them to travel a great distance in a few hours." But the real cause, besides the immunity of offenders, was the multiplication of bodies that controlled such police as there was—so that there was no value in the protective or detective measures taken.[1]

In this state of things, on April 25th, 1829, Mr. Peel introduced his measure, abolishing the old system and establishing a new board, who would have the power to tax the parish and raise a regular force. There was a wonderful simplicity in the plan, which he declared was an experiment, and was to be tried at first in ten parishes only. The constitution of the force is familiar to all—its hierarchy of Commissioners, Inspectors, Serjeants, &c. Almost at once the machinery worked smoothly, and the system, in a short time, was extended all over the kingdom.

The new force was for some years highly unpopular. The first step had been the dismissal of all the old "runners," making a "clean sweep," as it is called, of these antiquated servants. Some were driven to the workhouse, others came before the magistrates and

[1] In the Hackney Parish, it was found that there were no less than eighteen different Watch Boards, or "trusts," all independent of each other; while in Lambeth there was no night-watch at all. Kennington—a wealthy and populous district, fifteen miles in extent—was protected by three constables and three head-boroughs; who were found to be "not very remarkable for their abstinence from liquor," and were moreover appointed by the Steward of the Manor. Most of the suburban districts, such as Wandsworth, Chiswick, did without police or watchmen, while in a town of such population and importance as Deptford there was no lighting, and only two constables!

iterated the hardships of their situation. This scemed a harsh proceeding, but in such cases it is found impossible to work an entirely new system with the old instruments. Unluckily, some of the new men had been selected carelessly, and a few " black sheep " had got in. The newspapers found satisfaction in reporting cases in which they figured with such headings as " *The New Police again*," " *Nice conduct of the Police.*"

The worthy Sir Richard Birnie, now old-fashioned enough after long service under the exploded system, did not regard the body with favour. When a policeman arrested a gentleman's footman for misconduct at Covent Garden Theatre, this dialogue took place :—

The footman : You threatened to take the coachman also, and have the carriage taken to the Green-yard."

Sir R. Birnie : " Of course ; and leave your master and his family to get home how they could—very pretty, indeed."

The officer stated, that in what he did he acted under the instructions of the Commissioners. Then said Sir Richard : " The fact is, the new policemen have such ridiculous instructions given to them by their superiors, who know nothing whatever of the duties of a police officer, that they are not half so much to blame on these occasions as their superiors."

Sir Richard must have been yet more gratified, when no less than ten discharged officers waited on him with their complaints. Upson, we are told, advanced and addressed him :—

" Sir R. Birnie, having been for a number of years connected with this establishment, and having, as I trust, on all occasions, conducted myself with the strictest propriety, it is with great pain that I now appear before you; but I could not quit the office without expressing to you, on behalf of myself and my brother officers who are with me, our most grateful thanks for the many kindnesses we have received from you and the other magistrates of this office."

Sir R. Birnie: " What, what ! are you discharged, Upson ? "

Upson: " Yes, Sir Richard, myself and nine others, without receiving a moment's notice, have this morning been discharged, and no fault has been alleged."

Sir R. Birnie: " You did not join the new Police, I suppose ? "

Upson: " We did not; we declined."

Sir R. Birnie: " I am surprised at your discharge ; I know that you have been a most vigilant and active officer, and that you have been repeatedly engaged on confidential public service."

Sir Richard was informed that Upson was engaged in the apprehension of Thurtell and Probert, and in many other cases where his ability and courage were put to the test.

Sir R. Birnie: " I know many instances of his active and praiseworthy conduct ; and I regret that I have no power to serve him."

Upson: " I have repeatedly received the thanks of the magistrates of this office, and of the magistrates of various counties for my exertions in bringing criminals to justice ; and I beg to say that I do not so much complain of the consequences that may ensue to me by being thrown out of a situation which I have so long held, as I do of the manner in which it has been done. I was actually going on duty when the discharge was put into my hands. I am sent about my business at a moment's notice."

Steggles, one of the officers, said that he and Upson belonged to the old patrol, whose district was in Surrey. The new police had not yet been appointed on that district, yet he and Upson had been discharged from the party to which they had belonged, and in their places persons quite inexperienced in police matters had been appointed.

Sir R. Birnie again stated that he could not help what had taken place, and he very much lamented their unfortunate situation.

These cases of hardship, however, were soon forgotten in the inestimable advantages derived from the services of the new force.

As we have seen during an entire century, magistrates, police, public, and prisoners, were content to accept the miserable and straitened "little ease" of the old Bow Street office with a resigned toleration. It is wonderful to think how the business was transacted under such conditions, but whether the case were of a pretentious, sensational kind, or of the smallest description, the accommodation seemed to fit itself to the occasion with a Procrustean facility. It was owing to Sir Thomas Henry's energetic and persistent exertions that the government was at last induced to take up the matter seriously. In due course of time the houses were bought, the ground cleared, and plans furnished by Mr. Taylor of the Board of Works. Nearly half an acre of ground was covered by the new buildings, which were laid out on the most spacious and roomy principles. There were two courts, each some forty feet long by thirty broad. There were separate approaches and stairs for the prisoners, and combined with the office was a barrack capable of housing 100 police. There was a great courtyard into which the prison van was driven, while a covered way led from the cells to the van, which was driven into the courtyard, the gates being closed behind it. Thus was the demoralizing spectacle of conveying the prisoners to the van in presence of an approving mob abolished for ever.

It was not until April 4th, 1881, as related in the first chapter of this work, that the doors of the old office were closed: while two days later, the spacious and imposing building opposite was opened for public business.[1]

[1] The last offender dealt with at the old office was a lad named Macarthy, charged with stealing firewood; and the first at the new office was an old woman, known as "Moll," charged with being drunk and disorderly.

THE END.

INDEXES

GENERAL INDEX.

~~~~~~~~~

INDEX OF
HEARINGS AND INCIDENTS.

~~~~~~~~

PATTERSON SMITH REPRINT SERIES IN
CRIMINOLOGY, LAW ENFORCEMENT, AND SOCIAL PROBLEMS

* new material added

PATTERSON SMITH REPRINT SERIES IN
CRIMINOLOGY, LAW ENFORCEMENT, AND SOCIAL PROBLEMS

* new material added   † new edition, revised or enlarged

PATTERSON SMITH REPRINT SERIES IN
CRIMINOLOGY, LAW ENFORCEMENT, AND SOCIAL PROBLEMS

* new material added   † new edition, revised or enlarged